Richard Ellis

DEEP ATLANTIC

Life, Death, and

Exploration in the Abyss

Alfred A. Knopf   New York   1996

THIS IS A BORZOI BOOK
PUBLISHED BY ALFRED A. KNOPF, INC.

http://www.randomhouse.com/

Library of Congress Cataloging-in-Publication Data

Ellis, Richard, [date]
   Deep Atlantic : life, death, and exploration in the abyss / by
Richard Ellis. — 1st ed.
     p.   cm.
   Includes bibliographical references and index.
   ISBN 0-679-43324-4
   1. Abyssal zone—Atlantic Ocean.   I. Title.
GC87.2.A86E45   1996
508.3163—dc20   95-46523
               CIP

Contents

Preface

The Atlantic! A vast sheet of water, whose superficial area covers twenty-five millions of square miles, the length of which is nine thousand miles, with a mean breadth of two thousand seven hundred. An ocean whose parallel winding shores embrace an immense circumference, watered by the largest rivers of the world, the St. Lawrence, the Mississippi, the Amazon, the Plata, the Orinoco, the Niger, the Senegal, the Elbe, the Loire and the Rhine, which carry water from the most civilised, as well as the most savage countries! Magnificent field of water, incessantly ploughed by vessels of every nation, sheltered by flags of every nation, and which terminates in those two terrible points so dreaded by mariners, Cape Horn and the Cape of Tempests!

JULES VERNE
Twenty Thousand Leagues Under the Sea

At the start, this book was supposed to be about an entire ocean. Never mind that this was an almost impossible task; I wanted to write everything about the Atlantic Ocean. I began with a flurry of enthusiasm, and wrote chapters about Atlantic discovery, commercial fishing, and the history of Atlantic oceanography. But I soon realized that there was no coherent way I could integrate these subjects with others, such as the beaches of Cape Cod, the sea birds of Scotland, the continental shelves, and a hundred other aspects of life in, on, and under the Atlantic. Moreover, it seemed that there was nothing that bound the chapters together thematically except the occasional inclusion of the words "Atlantic Ocean." The very size and scope of my subject temporarily defeated me, and I lost momentum. In an attempt to salvage something from the wreckage, I decided to address the question of Atlantic sea monsters. I knew that this would be a particularly relevant subject, since the creature that I consider the quintessential sea monster—the giant squid—made not only its first but many of its subsequent appearances in Atlantic waters. I began to research and write about the squid that washed ashore on various Newfoundland beaches in the 1870s, but after an energetic start, I was brought up short by the location of the next invasion of giant squid: New Zealand. And indeed, it was not a single specimen that washed ashore in the South Pacific, but a whole armada. How could I possibly reconcile this with my study of the Atlantic? I took the only route available to me, and wrote a book about sea monsters, with *Architeuthis* as the centerpiece.

When I had submitted the sea-monster manuscript, I came back to my diversely disconnected chapters on the Atlantic, which were waiting for me to find a way to bind them together. I wish I could remember the moment of epiphany when I realized that by entering the deeps I might be able to control the subjects, but it has faded from memory. Perhaps it was when I decided to address the subject of sea-floor spreading, or maybe it was the story of William Beebe's bathysphere that caught my eye and my imagination. In any event, I realized that I didn't have to find a way to integrate puffins and North Carolina's Outer Banks; I didn't have to create a connection between the tides of the Bay of Fundy, the breeding habits of the common eel, and Robert Fulton's first submarine. I saw no reason why I couldn't do those things—I would just need another fifty years. As Melville wrote of *Moby-Dick,* "This whole book is but a draught—nay, but the draught of a draught. Oh, Time, Strength, Cash and Patience!" I would write only about the deep Atlantic, arbitrarily abandoning the shallows and their inhabitants, as well as the birds, beachcombers, and fishing villages.

There are many aspects of this study that cannot be adequately explained without reference to another ocean. For example, the hydrothermal vent animals, which are now known to exist at various locations in the Atlantic, were first discovered in the Pacific, and it would be impossible to discuss them in purely Atlantic terms. Also, while the Mid-Atlantic Ridge has its own characteristics and idiosyncrasies, much of the work on sea-floor spreading, magnetic anomalies, and submarine canyons was done by scientists working in the Pacific, Indian, and Arctic Oceans, and again, to limit the discussion to the Atlantic would be to seriously shortchange the reader. Finally, many—perhaps even most—deep-sea fishes and invertebrates are characterized not by their horizontal distribution—for which read: geography—but rather by their vertical distribution—that is, the depth at which they can be found. Moreover, many species are so poorly known that their appearance in a particular location in no way precludes their appearance in another—we simply have not been able to look everywhere. Wherever possible, then, I have tried to restrict the discussions to Atlantic Ocean phenomena, but in the interest of accuracy, I have frequently referred to another body of water.

I have started this book twice, but finished it once. I hope it does not suffer from *oceanus interruptus.* As in all my oceanic wanderings, I am not a single-hander. On this voyage, I was ably assisted by Tim Berra of Ohio State University, who provided much useful information about William Beebe. Ted Pietsch of the University of Washington's School of Fisheries and Ocean Sciences kept me from getting lost in the complex (but bewitching) world of the deep-sea anglerfishes; David Pawson of the Smithsonian responded most generously to my plaintive requests for help in understanding the fascinating world of holothurians, those creatures that I wrongly believed boringly motored along in the sediments. Shelley Lauzon of Woods Hole Oceanographic Institution helped with the story of the submersible *Alvin* and other WHOI submersibles; Cindy Lee Van Dover (then at Woods Hole, now at the University of Alaska) read and corrected my discussion of *Rimicaris,* the rift shrimp she was the first to observe from *Alvin;* and Peter Rona of Rutgers provided the photograph. James Atz of the American Museum of Natural History led me through the bibliographical and taxonomic grottoes of deep-sea ichthyology, and provided incalculable assistance when he bravely agreed to read my entire discussion of the myriad fishes of the deeps. (All errors, natural and unnatural, are, of course, mine.) Oceanic cartographer Marie Tharp, who collaborated with Bruce Heezen on the mapping of the Atlantic, graciously agreed to read my discussion of deep Atlantic oceanography, and helped me to understand it and (I hope) explain it. Eugenie Clark of the University of Maryland has, often unknowingly, been an indispensable contributor to my efforts. She has not only allowed me to test out some of my theories on her classes, but has provided me with a wealth of ideas and materials that have contributed materially to my understanding of some of the more obscure aspects of deep-sea biology. (It was Genie who sent me a marvelous Japanese videotape of deep-sea animals that I had not known existed, and which enabled me to see what some of these creatures actually looked like.) Nina Root of the American Museum's library permitted me to explore the hidden canyons and treasures of the collection. Despite what I hope is its watery flavor, most of the research for this book was done in the dry comfort of the library on Central Park West.

My loyal editor, Ashbel Green, watched as the book changed course, came about, and finally plunged into the abyssal depths. Steadfast as always, through the vicissitudes of ocean voyaging above and below the surface, has been my friend and agent, Carl Brandt. None of this would have happened at all if it hadn't been for Stephanie, the person who understands, supports, and, *mirabile dictu,* even encourages my obsessions.

Part One

Exploration

Studying the Atlantic

The wonders of the sea are as marvelous as the glories of the heavens. Among the revelations which scientific research has lately made concerning the crust of our planet, none are more interesting to the student of nature, or more suggestive to the Christian philosopher, than those which relate to the bed of the ocean.

MATTHEW FONTAINE MAURY
The Physical Geography of the Sea (1858)

B y the sixteenth century, much of the geography of the Atlantic surface was known. After the Basques had led the way to the cod fishing grounds of Newfoundland and Labrador, the French followed in their wake, finding cod that schooled in unimaginable profusion. Basque whalers had visited Labrador, and their Dutch and British counterparts had explored the waters of the northern quadrant in their search for the bowhead whales that inhabited the cold waters of Spitsbergen, Jan Mayen Island, Greenland, and the archipelago that is now northeastern Canada. Within the next two centuries, Yankee whalers came to dominate the whale fishery, and by 1850, they had prowled the Atlantic from Newfoundland to the Bahamas for sperm whales. They employed the Gulf Stream's assistance in crossing to the North Atlantic, and "plum-puddinged" their way across to the Azores, Madeira, the Cape Verdes, and even the coast of western Africa.* It was not until the end of the nineteenth century that the whalers developed the heavy artillery to pursue the larger, more powerful blue and fin whales.

The fishermen, originally from England, France, Portugal, and Spain, were quickly followed by the colonists, who were even more familiar with the coasts and fishing grounds of North America. By 1800, America had become a

* In the whalers' parlance, a "plum-pudding" voyage was one that was restricted to relatively safe Atlantic waters, usually consisting of a four- or five-month excursion in the spring and summer, instead of the four or five years that a globe-circling whaling voyage might take.

nation, with most of its population clustered on the east coast. Philadelphia was America's largest city in 1790, with a population of about forty-two thousand. Although not a seaport, it was situated at the confluence of the Delaware and the Schuylkill Rivers, giving it a lead in shipping to the inland farm regions. It was surpassed in population within a few years by New York, which, of course, was a seaport. (The population of the entire country in 1790 was just over 5 million.)

We did not always know what was on the bottom of the ocean; nor did we know what the bottom of the ocean was made of. In most areas, we did not know where the bottom of the ocean actually was. One of the first men to try to find out was Constantine Phipps of the Royal Navy, who dropped a weighted line from HMS *Racehorse* in 1773. It went down for 4,098 feet (683 fathoms) before it touched the bottom of the North Atlantic between Norway and Iceland. When the French naturalist François Peron returned from a round-the-world journey in 1804, he reported—without any evidence to support such a conclusion—that the deeper the water got, the colder it became, and that the floor of the ocean was covered with eternal ice. Then, in 1818, John (later Sir John) Ross sailed for Baffin Bay in HMS *Isabella* with a grabbing device called the "Deep-sea Clamm" aboard. The "Clamm" was lowered 6,000 feet to the bottom of the Atlantic and hauled back up with a six-pound chunk of worm-filled mud, proving that "there was animal life in the bed of the ocean notwithstanding the darkness, stillness, and immense pressure produced by more than a mile of superincumbent water." But despite Ross's discovery, Edward Forbes would later gain wide recognition for his theory that life below 1,800 feet could not exist.

In the 1840s, various seafaring men had made soundings in the Atlantic and claimed that they could not touch bottom at 39,000 feet, then 46,000 feet, and finally, a Lieutenant Parker of the frigate *Congress* let out 50,000 feet of rope in the South Atlantic without finding the bottom. They were not, of course, over water that was ten miles deep, but rather, their sounding devices were inadequate to the task at hand, and were often carried by tides and currents that took the line and the weights far off the plumb. (The first accurate measurement of the deep ocean was made by Sir James Clark Ross (the nephew of Sir John), of HMS *Erebus* in 1840, when he measured a site in the Antarctic at 14,550 feet, a depth that has been confirmed by recent echo-sounding measurements.) The quest for information on the depth of the ocean—and myriad other questions pertaining to the biology, chemistry, geology, and physics of the sea—has acquired the name (and become the science of) oceanography. In the *Grand Dictionnaire universel* of 1878, the French introduced the term *oceanographie,* perhaps as a counter to the contemporaneous German *Thassographie*. But long before they had a name for it, there were scientists pursuing it.

Edward Forbes was born in 1815 on the Isle of Man. At the age of twelve, he is reported to have written an essay he titled "Manual of British Natural History in All Its Departments." While studying medicine at Edinburgh, he developed a passionate interest in mollusks, starfishes, and other animals of the littoral zone. He worked mostly with dredges in water less than 100 fathoms deep, but in 1841, while sailing aboard the naval vessel *Beacon* in the Mediterranean, he winched in a haul from 230 fathoms (then the record depth for a bottom haul) that inspired him to develop a theory of the eight bands of depth that could each be characterized by the presence of certain animals. He believed that the lower limit for living creatures was about 300 fathoms, and wrote, "As we descend deeper and deeper . . . the inhabitants [of the sea] become more and more modified, and fewer and fewer, indicating our approach to an abyss where life is extinguished or exhibits but a few sparks of its lingering presence." Forbes died at the early age of thirty-nine in 1854, and did not live to see the publication of his *Natural History of the European Seas,* in which he wrote, "It is in the exploration of this vast deep-sea region that the finest field for sub-marine discovery yet remains."

In his initial dredgings, Sir John Ross had discovered worms at 6,000 feet. Either they did not know of Ross's discovery or they chose to ignore it, but most scientists continued to argue that no life forms could exist in the dark, cold waters below 1,000 feet, where, they believed, the enormous weight of the water would crush any living thing. There were even popularly accepted ideas that water was compressed at great depths, causing sunken ships and other aquatic detritus to remain suspended above the floor of the ocean. François Peron held (and published) the theory that the bottom of the ocean was a frozen mass of ice, and since nothing could live in solid ice, the question of life in the depths was answered, Q.E.D. Others were convinced that the deep-ocean basins contained water that never moved. Without movement, there could be no renewal of food sources, and without food sources, there could be no life. Still others supposed that life in the abyss was quite different from that of the shallower regions, and that the deep sea harbored extinct creatures—"living fossils."* Such luminaries as Louis Agassiz thought that the

---

* In a limited sense, this turned out to be true. In 1864, Danish zoologist G. O. Sars dredged up a "sea-lily," an echinoderm that was thought to have died out in the Jurassic period; the coelacanth, a lobe-finned fish of a type believed to have been extinct for 70 million years, was discovered in 1938, from fishermen's hauls off South Africa; and in 1952, the Cambrian gastropod *Neopilina* was found to be alive and living in the mud of the North Pacific. The belemnites were fossil cephalopods thought to have died out some 50 million years ago, but living specimens of *Spirula spirula* were captured by the *Challenger* expedition and described by Thomas Henry Huxley.

depths of the ocean preserved environments that had expired on the land, and others suggested that the deeper seas were inhabited by the oldest animals, much the way the oldest rocks harbored the earliest fossils.

One of the first "official" U.S. government scientific expeditions was the Great United States Exploring Expedition of 1838–42. Under the command of forty-year-old Lt. Charles Wilkes, the six-ship squadron was originally commissioned to search for the hollow center of the earth, which a man named John Cleves Symmes had determined could be accessed from an entrance under the South Pole. However crackbrained this "holes in the poles" idea sounds now—we must remember that Jules Verne's *Voyage to the Center of the Earth* was published in France in 1864—on its face, it was enough to get President John Quincy Adams to encourage Congress to support the venture. (A more realistic, commercial objective was the search for new sealing and whaling grounds in the South Pacific, but Symmes's goofy plan was the nominal impetus for the expedition.) Symmes died in 1829, one year after Congress had authorized funds for the expedition (and nine years before the expedition actually set sail), and the job fell to Jeremiah N. Reynolds, who quickly recognized that the "holes in the poles" theory could be abandoned in favor of a more rational, scientific approach.*

The expedition, consisting of the flagship *Vincennes,* the *Porpoise, Peacock, Relief, Flying Fish,* and *Sea Gull,* departed from Hampton Roads, Virginia, on August 18, 1838. Most of their "exploring" would take them to the South Pacific and the Antarctic, well out of the range of this discussion, but the complement of scientists—known as the "scientifics"—gave the expedition an oceanographic importance far beyond its stated or subliminal warrants. The European nations had begun the tradition of scientific exploration, led by the redoubtable Capt. James Cook, who made three circumnavigations of the globe with botanists aboard, and James Fitzroy of the *Beagle,* who had as his naturalist Charles Darwin. The French had sponsored Dumont d'Urville, Bougainville, and La Pérouse, so the need to assert themselves in the quest for scientific stature and legitimacy was a significant factor in the U.S. expedition. On board were mineralogist James Dwight Dana, philologist Horatio Hale, naturalists Titian R. Peale and Charles Pickering, botanists William Brackenridge and William Rich, conchologist Joseph Couthouy, and artists Alfred Agate and Joseph Drayton.

On the outward leg of the voyage, the squadron put into Madeira for pro-

* Reynolds had earlier sailed aboard the whaler *Penguin,* and told of the ship's 1820 encounter with "Mocha Dick," a bull sperm whale that was "as white as wool," off the Chilean island of Mocha—hence the whale's name. It is likely that Melville knew of this story (it was published in *Knickerbocker* magazine in May 1839, eleven years before *Moby-Dick*), and therefore Jeremiah Reynolds's immortality is assured by his contribution to literature as well as to oceanography.

visions, passed the bulge of Africa, and stopped briefly at the Cape Verdes en route to Rio de Janeiro, where the botanists collected some fifty thousand specimens. Wilkes maintained the scientific nature of the voyage by seeing to it that hydrographic and meteorological data were collected regularly, and they traced the course of the Gulf Stream by taking the temperature of the water.* From Rio, they sailed south to round Cape Horn, passed Tierra del Fuego, and entered the South Pacific. Their legacy remains: the "scientifics" set the stage for all scientific expeditions to follow. The year the expedition returned, Matthew Fontaine Maury was put in charge of the government's Department of Charts and Instruments.

Born in 1806, Maury entered the Navy as a midshipman in 1825, and by 1830, having already circumnavigated the globe, he was promoted to lieutenant. He seemed on the way to a rewarding naval career, but a stagecoach accident lamed him in 1836, and he was declared unfit for active duty. In 1842, he was placed in charge of the Depot of Charts and Instruments, which eventually became the U.S. Naval Observatory and Hydrographic Office. Unable to find any charts that showed the winds and currents of the world's oceans (because there weren't any), Maury took it upon himself to scour the available records, primarily ships' logs, that made mention of these oceanic phenomena. For ten years, he accumulated data obtained from 265,298 days of observation—almost 727 years if sailed by a single seafarer. He coordinated this information and applied it to world charts, which he promised to supply to ships' captains if they would reciprocate by keeping the records he needed to perfect his project. (He also analyzed the logbooks kept by whaling masters, and he recorded not only the winds and currents but the location of the whales as well.) As he wrote in *The Physical Geography of the Sea,* "In a little while there were more than a thousand navigators engaged day and night, and in all parts of the ocean, in making and recording observations according to a uniform plan, and in furthering this attempt to increase our knowledge as to the winds and currents of the seas, and other phenomena that relate to its safe navigation and physical geography." At this time, he was primarily concerned with the length of time required for transoceanic voyages, and through his examination of the logbooks he was able to identify the most favorable winds and currents, substantially reducing the time required for most ocean voyages. (In 1848, one year after the publication of Maury's *North Atlantic Charts,* ships traveling from Baltimore to Rio, previously a fifty-five-day passage, could make the trip in thirty-six days.)

* In 1497, when John and Sebastian Cabot sailed up the eastern coast of North America in search of the Northwest Passage, they noted that the unaccountable warmth belowdecks fermented the beer in the hold and turned it sour. They thus became the first explorers to record their observations of what would later be known as the Gulf Stream.

Although successful, Maury quickly realized that his method of polling captains was too time-consuming and ineffective; he decided that the best way to study the sea was to sail on it. Accordingly, he petitioned Alexander Dallas Bache, the director of the U.S. Coast Survey (and a grandson of Benjamin Franklin) for a survey vessel, and was assigned the *Taney,* an unseaworthy 74-foot schooner that Maury proceeded to make even more unseaworthy by the addition of tons of wires, winches, and reels. Despite the precarious nature of his platform, Maury pursued his investigations throughout the Atlantic, from the Canaries to the Cape Verdes, taking bottom samples and testing the temperature of the Gulf Stream.*

Although his techniques were primitive by today's standards, and his understanding of fluid dynamics and geophysics inadequate to the task, Maury still published an extremely important work on oceanography in 1855. *The Physical Geography of the Sea* went through six editions in its first four years, and was translated into German, French, Italian, Norwegian, Dutch, and Spanish. There were chapters on navigation, winds, weather, currents, and also some of the sea's ephemera, such as sea dust and red fogs. Maury's charts were the best to be found—in most cases, they were the only ones in existence—but his contour maps of the ocean floor, made from soundings with weighted lines, proved to be less than useful. Also in 1855, in response to several disastrous collisions at sea in the ice-choked and fogbound North Atlantic, Maury worked out a plan for "steamer lanes," each 25 miles wide, where east- and westbound steamers would all travel in defined lanes to avoid collision. His plan was accepted—but not until 1898—and now, the "steamer lanes" are an integral part of North Atlantic ship traffic.

Samuel F. B. Morse invented the first operational telegraph in 1837, and sent the first intercity message ("What hath God wrought?") between Philadelphia and Baltimore in 1843, over a series of lines strung between poles. Almost immediately, the idea of a transoceanic telegraph cable seized the imaginations of various entrepreneurs and inventors, but first they had to figure out how to run an electrical wire underwater. Morse had tried an underwater cable in 1842 in New York Harbor, but the line was snagged by an anchoring ship, and even though messages had been sent for almost twenty-four hours, the project was declared a failure and abandoned. In 1845, a cable spanned the Hudson River, but the copper wires encased in an India rubber

---

* In his *Physical Geography of the Sea,* Maury wrote: "There is a river in the ocean. In the severest droughts it never fails, and in the mightiest floods it never overflows. Its banks and bottoms are of cold water, while its current is warm. The Gulf of Mexico is its fountain, and its mouth is in the Arctic Sea. It is the Gulf Stream. There is in the world no other such majestic flow of waters. Its current is more rapid than the Mississippi or the Amazon, and its volume more than a thousand times greater."

sheath proved to be susceptible to corrosion, so Werner Siemens developed a machine to apply gutta-percha insulation to cables, and in 1851, a telegraph cable crossed the English Channel from Dover to Calais. Cables were then laid across the North Sea and the Mediterranean, and by 1856, there was talk about an Ireland-Newfoundland cable that would span the 2,000 miles that represented the shortest route across the Atlantic.

Enter Cyrus Field, and, as his oceanographic adviser, Matthew Fontaine Maury. Field was a businessman and financier who was fascinated by the idea of a transatlantic cable, and, as of 1854, one of the founders of the New York, Newfoundland, and London Telegraph Company. A mere two years later, Field had raised £350,000, and the American Telegraph Company was born. When Field asked Maury what the sea floor was like between Newfoundland and Ireland, he was informed that "the bottom of the sea between the two places is a plateau which seems to have been placed there for the purpose of holding the wires of a submarine telegraph. . . ." In fact, Maury's "Telegraphic Plateau" did not exist at all; the proposed route spanned cliffs, canyons, valleys, and the jagged Mid-Atlantic Ridge, and the cable that they laid there failed within three months.*

To protect the cable underwater, a durable and pliant material was needed, and following Siemens, they tried gutta-percha, a rubbery material that comes from the bark and leaves of certain Malaysian trees. The first cable consisted of a seven-strand copper conductor, three layers of gutta-percha insulation, a further wrapping of tarred rope, and an outside armor of eighteen-strand twisted iron wire. In six months, British factories produced 335,000 miles of iron wire and 300,000 miles of hemp.

The first plan, implemented in 1857, was to have the American steam frigate *Niagara* carry half the cable to the mid-Atlantic, where she would meet the British man-of-war *Agamemnon,* sailing from Ireland. Somewhere in mid-Atlantic the cable would be spliced, and *Agamemnon* would sail off to New-foundland to complete the connection, unrolling her half of the cable as she went. *Niagara's* cable snapped at 5 miles out, then, after it was repaired, it broke again, and the ship had to return to Ireland, leaving 300 miles of useless cable on the ocean floor. They vowed to try again next year.

In June 1858, the same two ships met in the middle of the Atlantic, where they spliced their cables together and let them sink out of sight. As they headed back to their respective home ports, the cable snapped. They

---

* Its nonexistence did not faze the indomitable Jules Verne, who had the *Nautilus* sail over it at a depth of 1,400 fathoms off the coast of Newfoundland. Arronax spies the cable lying on the bottom (Conseil thought at first it was a giant sea-serpent), and delivers a learned discourse about the "bold promoter" Cyrus Field, and the laying of the cable. (It seems that Verne had sailed with Field, and interviewed him at some length before writing *Twenty Thousand Leagues.*)

spliced it together and sailed again, but this time they got all of 80 miles apart before it broke again. On the third try, *Niagara* made it easily to Newfoundland, but *Agamemnon* met with a nasty North Atlantic storm that threatened to swamp the overburdened vessel. A small boat was sent to bring the cable to shore at Newfoundland, and to the cacophonous sound of church bells and booming cannons, the transatlantic connection was completed. Queen Victoria sent President Buchanan a congratulatory message, and then the cable went dead.

Bad luck and poor design plagued the enterprise, and from 1858 to 1865, despite the enthusiasm (and capital) of Field, no messages crossed the Atlantic underwater. Because the Civil War occupied most engineers and naval personnel for the next few years, another effort was not made until 1865. It too failed. (In 1860, when a cable between Corsica and Sardinia at 7,200 feet in the Mediterranean was hauled up for repair, a deep-sea coral was found to be growing on it. Since corals are "sessile" animals—that is, they have to be anchored to a solid object—the coral had to have fastened itself to the cable at the bottom, again refuting Forbes's "azoic" theory.) The cables were made stronger and heavier (in addition to the gutta-percha insulation, they were further wrapped in jute, then bound together with a long coil of galvanized wire), but this made the spools so heavy that it is difficult to imagine their having been carried on a single ship.

Great Eastern to the rescue. In 1857, Isimbard Kingdom Brunel had designed a 4,000-berth passenger vessel, equipped with two 58-foot paddle wheels driven by 1,000-horsepower engines, and a 24-foot propeller turned by a 1,600-horsepower engine. At a length of 693 feet, and with a beam of 83 feet, she was five times larger than any ship in the world at the time. (Her length would not be exceeded until 1899, when the White Star liner *Oceanic* was launched.) She also had six masts capable of spreading 6,500 square yards of canvas. An attempt was made to launch her sideways, but she got stuck, and months would pass before she could be relaunched, and then only because of an extra-high tide. It was too costly to run her as a passenger vessel, so she was converted to a cable ship. This role became *Great Eastern*'s true destiny; because of her great size and capacious holds, she was the only ship afloat capable of carrying the thousands of tons of cable necessary to span the Atlantic. On July 12, 1865, the great ship picked up the cable hookup in Ireland and set sail for America. Although measurements are imprecise, it is estimated that the 2,700 miles of cable, coiled six stories high, weighed between 5,000 and 7,000 tons. In addition to thousands of tons of coiled cable, *Great Eastern* traveled with a veritable village aboard, consisting of 500 men, 20 pigs, 120 sheep, 20 oxen, a barnyard of chickens, and a single cow.

The *Great Eastern,* up to 1857 the largest ship ever built, was originally commissioned to carry passengers, but when this proved uneconomical, she was converted to a cable ship. In 1866, she laid the first transatlantic cable from Ireland to Newfoundland.

At about midway across the ocean, over two and a half miles of deep Atlantic, the cable snapped, but the crew had huge grappling hooks, and they dragged the bottom until they snagged the cable. They repaired it with specially designed shackles, but the shackles were not strong enough, and as they spooled the cable overboard, it separated again. After four more disappointing breaks, they gave up and sailed for home. Field raised another $2.5 million, improved the cable and the machinery, and on Friday the thirteenth of July 1866, *Great Eastern* sailed again.

This time, everything went smoothly, and the giant ship played out the cable steadily as she worked her way across the ocean. They sent messages

THE EIGHTH WONDER OF THE WORLD.
THE ATLANTIC CABLE.

"Heart's Content, July 27th 1866.
I hope that it will prove a blessing to England, and the United States,
and increase the intercourse between our Country & the Eastern Hemisphere."
Your faithfully
Cyrus W. Field.

PUBD BY KIMMEL & FORSTER,254-256 CANAL STRT.

Washinton, July 29th 1866.
To Cyrus W. Field, Heart's Content:
May the Cable under the sea tend to promote harmony between the Republic
of the West and the Governments of the Eastern Hemisphere.
Andrew Johnson.

When the transatlantic cable was completed in 1866, it was designated as "The Eighth Wonder of the World."

back to England reporting their progress. On July 27, 1866, *Great Eastern** brought the cable ashore at Heart's Content, Newfoundland, and the transatlantic telegraph was at last a reality.

In a few short years, the floor of the ocean had gone from an "azoic" region to one so rich that it came to be known as the source of all life. In the middle of the nineteenth century, the bottom of the ocean was thought to be composed of a primordial ooze that its "discoverer," the German biologist

---

* Controversy and mystery followed the ill-fated *Great Eastern* all the way to the wrecker's yard. A submerged rock had ripped an 86-foot-long gash in her hull off Montauk, Long Island, and when her hull plates were being riveted, workers reported a mysterious tapping. Legend held that a shipwright had been sealed in alive while the ship was being built, but the tapping was declared to be caused by underwater tackle, and the grisly tale was forgotten. Later (according to Alan Villiers in *Men, Ships, and the Sea*), when the great ship was broken up at Liverpool in 1889, "deep inside her double hull, so the story goes, wreckers found the bones of the riveter, who supposedly had jinxed her for all of her 31 years."

Ernst Haeckel,* thought to be a stage midway between the living and the non-living. Haeckel called this class of disorganized protoplasm *Monera,* and when Thomas Henry Huxley, examining mud samples dredged from the Irish Sea in 1868, found what he believed to be the skeleton of this organism, he renamed it *Bathybius haeckelii,* after its discoverer. Haeckel had discovered the *Urschleim*—"original slime"—in 1857, only two years before the publication of Darwin's *Origin of Species,* and some believed that it was one of the taproots of the evolutionary tree, one of the original life forms.

Upon examining some of this precipitated mud, Charles Wyville Thomson, who would later become the leader of the *Challenger* expedition (and spend a lot of time searching for this nonexistent material), wrote, "The mud was actually alive; it stuck together in lumps, as if there were white of egg mixed with it; and the glairy mass proved, under the microscope, to be a living sarcode. Prof. Huxley . . . calls it *Bathybius.*" William B. Carpenter, another organizer of the *Challenger* expedition, wrote, "It seems to be clearly indicated that there is a vast sheet of the lowest type of animal life, which probably extends over the whole of the warmer regions of the sea." J. Y. Buchanan, the chemist aboard the *Challenger,* realized that the primordial ooze that Huxley examined was actually bottom mud that had been sitting in alcohol for several years, and was simply a colloidal precipitate of calcium sulfate with radiolarian skeletons embedded in it; it was a chemical reaction, not a primordial life form. *Bathybius* disappeared forever into the abyssal oblivion reserved for "hopeful monsters," those scientific discoveries that their introducers are so anxious to find that they overlook the reality of the facts that might disprove the existence of their inventions.

Charles Wyville Thomson, along with William Carpenter, a medical doctor and physiologist, petitioned the Royal Society (of which Carpenter was vice president) "to give us the use of a vessel properly fitted with dredging equipment and all the necessary scientific apparatus," which they would use to study the conditions of the deep-sea floor. The Admiralty agreed to make available the survey ship *Lightning,* which departed for the North Sea on August 11, 1868. Beset by storms and bad weather, the *Lightning* nonetheless hauled in some interesting specimens, including a completely unexpected bright orange starfish (which was called *Brisinga coronata*) and several new species of sea urchins, sponges, and shellfish.

---

* Despite his misinterpretation of the *Urschleim,* Ernst Heinrich Haeckel (1834–1919) was one of the century's leading scientists, and one of the staunchest supporters of Charles Darwin's theories of evolution. He rejected the concept of an overall design for the family tree of all living things and, of course, dismissed the idea of an almighty creator as well. He hung his hat on a "fundamental biogenetic law" that he developed, wherein every living organism passes through stages reflecting its ancestry, the theory commonly summarized as "ontogeny recapitulates phylogeny." Like the *Urschleim,* however, Haeckel's recapitulation theory also proved to be unsound science.

Carpenter and Wyville Thomson were so gratified by the results of the *Lightning's* dredges that they requested (and were granted) the use of two more research vessels, the *Shearwater* and the *Porcupine,* for the summers of 1869, '70, and '71. Wyville Thomson's quest for new and exotic representatives of bathypelagic life forms was rewarded when a North Sea dredge hauled up a sea urchin the likes of which was believed only to have existed in the Devonian era. In *The Depths of the Sea* (1873), considered the first textbook of oceanography written in English, he wrote:

> We were somewhat surprised when it rolled out of the bag uninjured, and our surprise increased, and it was in my case mingled with a certain amount of nervousness, when it settled down quietly in the form of a little red cake and began to pant—a line of conduct to say the least of it, very unusual in its rigid, undemonstrative order. . . . I had to summon up some resolution before taking the weird little monster in my hand, and congratulating myself on the most interesting addition to my favorite family which had been made for many a day.

So to the voyage of the *Challenger,* the first major expedition dedicated to the exploration of the floor of the ocean. Under Capt. George Nares, the

HMS *Challenger,* the British oceanographic research vessel that sailed around the world from 1873 to 1876, covering more than 68,000 nautical miles and collecting over 13,000 plants and animals, many of which had never been seen before.

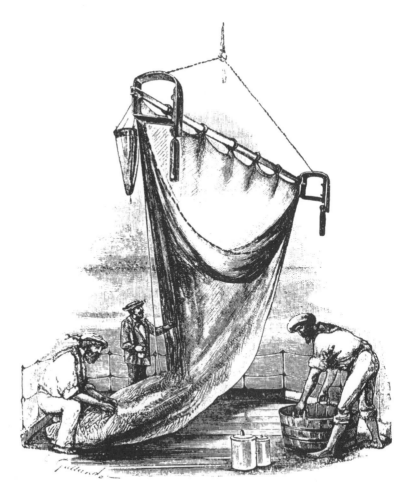

A plankton net being
hauled aboard
HMS *Challenger.*

2,300-ton, 226-foot auxiliary steam corvette sailed from Portsmouth on December 21, 1872, manned by a crew of 240 able-bodied seamen and six civilians. The scientific staff was led by Wyville Thomson, Edward Forbes's successor as professor of natural history at Edinburgh, and consisted of five other civilians: naturalists John Murray, H. N. Moseley, and Rudolf von Willemoes-Suhm; chemist John Buchanan; and the expedition's artist, J. J. Wild.

Originally commissioned as a warship, the *Challenger* was fitted out as a floating laboratory, with instruments for taking bottom samples and water temperatures; 144 miles of sounding rope (they had planned to use piano wire for the dredges, but on the first haul, the wire tangled so badly that one-inch hemp was substituted, and rope was used for the remainder of the voyage); 12.5 miles of sounding wire, sinkers, nets, dredges, a library, and "spirits of wine" for the preservation of specimens. All of this matériel, according to

Wyville Thomson, was to be used to investigate "the conditions of the Deep Sea throughout all the Great Oceanic Basins."

No hauls were made on the shakedown cruise of the *Challenger* from the Portsmouth to the Canaries, but twelve days out of the Canary port of Santa Cruz, the "Baillie sounding machine" was let over the side, and the first of the hundreds of dredges of the *Challenger*'s three-and-a-half-year expedition commenced. Hauling in the dredges took all day and most of the night, but finally, from the then astonishing depth of 3,150 fathoms (18,900 feet, or three and a half miles), 100 pounds of chocolate-colored clay was brought up on deck. There was not a sign of a living creature.

On future hauls, however, an astonishing plenitude of living things was brought aboard the research ship, including sea anemones, urchins, jellyfish, snails, sea slugs, squid, worms, barnacles, isopods, amphipods, and broken hunks of coral, proving conclusively that there was life at the ocean's greatest depths. (Because of the open nature of the nets, mid-water and even surface fishes were also trapped, as the hauls were pulled up. It would be only after the *Challenger*'s epochal voyage that a device for closing the nets was introduced, to ensure that the contents of a trawl came only from the bottom.) It was demonstrated that the sea floor was far from "azoic"; in fact, there proved to be a greater density of living animals on and in the bottom than in the water column above it. In the 1960s, Woods Hole biologists, using a self-closing deep-sea dredge, brought up more animals in a single haul than the *Challenger* had collected in three years.

The voyage of the *Challenger* was perceived by some—including some of the voyagers—as a logical venue for a continuation of the debate about Darwin's recently published theory of evolution. (The *Origin of Species* had been published in 1859.) Wyville Thomson did not believe, and he was hoping that his dredge hauls would demonstrate that the depths of the ocean harbored the planet's more primitive and unsuccessful life forms, those that had been bypassed by Darwin's "natural selection." Many of the day's foremost scientists—including T. H. Huxley and Louis Agassiz—supported the idea that the most ancient creatures would be found at the greatest depths, but the *Challenger*'s dredges produced only one anachronistic life form, a crab called *Willemoesia leptodactyla* (named for Willemoes-Suhm, one of the naturalists) that was similar to species that had become extinct 180 million years earlier.

One of the most remarkable events in the *Challenger*'s three-year collecting spree was the unexpected appearance of *Spirula,* a primitive cephalopod that was thought to have died out 50 million years earlier. The Cenozoic period saw the rise of the belemnites, squidlike creatures with a chambered, coiled shell inside the body, at least one of which (*Megateuthis*) reached a total length of nine feet, including tentacles. (Of the living cephalopods, only *Nau-*

Crewmen haul a shark aboard the *Challenger* as part of the pioneering research conducted during her three-year (1873–76), 68,000-mile voyage around the world's oceans.

tilus has a chambered, coiled shell, and it is on the outside. Squids and cuttlefishes have only an internal vestige of a shell, in the form of the pen, commonly known as "cuttlebone.") Although Huxley was the first scientist to describe *Spirula,* most of the work on living specimens was done by Johannes Schmidt, the Danish zoologist who found the breeding grounds of the eels in the Sargasso Sea. His nets, designed to catch tiny eel larvae, were also effective in capturing *Spirula,* which reaches a length of about three inches. The internal shell of *Spirula* is divided into twenty-five to thirty-seven gas-filled chambers and is found at the posterior end of the animal (the end away from the tentacles); its buoyancy causes the animal to orient in a tentacle-down position. In addition to the shell, *Spirula* is equipped with a beadlike light organ that glows with a steady yellowish-green light, making it visible from above. It lives at moderate depths—300 to 1,600 feet—but it sometimes descends to 3,000 feet. (Upon the death of its owner, the buoyant shell floats to the surface and often washes ashore, sometimes appearing in great quantities.)

During her thousand-day voyage, the *Challenger* crisscrossed the North Atlantic twice, rounded the Cape of Good Hope, sailed among—and crashed into—Antarctic icebergs (she was the first steam-powered ship to cross the Antarctic Circle), and visited Australia, New Zealand, New Guinea, Fiji, the Philippines, Japan, Hawaii, and Tierra del Fuego, altogether traversing some 68,000 nautical miles. It is impossible to isolate the expedition's Atlantic exploits, but since Wyville Thomson wrote "that to explore the conditions of the deep sea was the primary object of our mission," her stops at Lisbon, Gibraltar, Madeira, Tenerife, Halifax, and Bermuda are probably of much lesser importance than the creatures they observed and preserved, the measurements they made, and the samples they collected from the bottom. The expedition returned to England with over 13,000 plants and animals, 1,441 water samples, and hundreds of containers of sea-floor material. It would be another nineteen years before the results of the expedition were published, during which time Wyville Thomson died and John Murray was named head of the Challenger Commission. When the *Report* was finally published, 4,417 new

One of the more remarkable events in the three-year voyage of the *Challenger* was the appearance in the trawls of *Spirula,* a cephalopod that was thought (from fossil evidence) to have died out 50 million years earlier. It swims head down because it has a buoyant, gas-filled shell at the posterior end.

species had been identified, and 715 new genera.*

John Murray was born in Canada in 1841, but came to Scotland early to live with his maternal grandfather. As a twenty-seven-year-old ex–medical student without a degree, he managed to talk himself aboard an Arctic whaler

---

* The results of the expedition were chronicled in the official fifty-volume *Report on the Scientific Results of the Voyage of the H.M.S. Challenger During the Years 1873–76* (partially written, and totally underwritten, by Sir John Murray, who was one of the original naturalists), and also in the diaries of several of the scientists, officers, and seamen. In addition, any number of prominent scientists used the material and data collected on the voyage to publish various monographs on everything from the invertebrates that were collected, to meteorology, petrology, physics, and chemistry.

as a "surgeon" (an experience he shared with Arthur Conan Doyle, who sailed as ship's doctor on the Peterhead whaler *Hope* in 1880), and when he returned to Edinburgh, he was tapped by Wyville Thomson for a position as naturalist aboard the *Challenger*. Financially independent, Murray supported the work of Norwegian oceanographer Johan Hjort, which resulted in the 1910 cruise of the *Michael Sars* in the North Atlantic. The results of this expedition were published by the Bergen Museum, but Murray and Hjort collaborated on *The Depths of the Ocean* (1912), which was long considered the bible of oceanography. John Murray was knighted in 1898 for his contributions to the *Challenger* expedition, and died in 1914.

One of the benefactors of the *Challenger* expedition was Alexander Agassiz, son of the Swiss naturalist Louis Agassiz. Born in 1835 at Neuchâtel, Agassiz came to America in 1849 to join his father, who was teaching at Harvard. His early research was on echinoderms, but after publishing *Embryology of the Starfish* in 1865, he ventured west and became the superintendent of the Calumet and Hecla copper mines in northern Michigan. He retained that position until 1869, and was so successful that he was able to return to Cambridge with a considerable fortune, much of which he gave to Harvard. In 1874, he was named curator and then director of the Museum of Comparative Zoology. (As a measure of his interest in things oceanographic, he also contributed books and scientific apparatus to the newly formed Scripps Institute of Oceanography in California.) Agassiz was able to apply some of the experience and expertise he had gained in the technology of copper mining—such as the hoisting of heavy machinery and loads of ore—to his oceanographic studies when he accepted an invitation from the Coast Survey to lead two dredging cruises in the Atlantic aboard the steamer *Blake*.* In *The Education of Henry Adams,* the eponymous author wrote of Agassiz, "He was the best we ever produced, and the only one of our generation whom I would have liked to envy. . . . We did one first rate work when we produced him, and I do not know that, thus far, any other country has done better."

Unfortunately, the devices used aboard the *Blake* could do nothing to dispel Agassiz's belief in the azoic zone, but by then, other countries were sponsoring expeditions that used closing nets, and were thus able to demonstrate that life of one sort or another existed at every level of the ocean. In 1880, scientists aboard the British ship *Knight Errant* sampled the waters of the Faroe Channel (between Scotland and the Faroe Islands) and, like Wyville

---

* It was on the second of the *Blake*'s cruises that Agassiz dramatically (albeit unintentionally) demonstrated the power of the ocean's pressure. When one of his dredges produced chilled specimens, he decided to lower a bottle of champagne to the same depth. After an hour at 14,000 feet, the bottle came up suitably cold, but the cork had been driven into the bottle, allowing the wine to be replaced by vintage seawater.

Captain Nemo shows the engine room of the *Nautilus* to Professor Arronax.

Thomson, noticed that there were two masses of water that evidently did not mix. The *Knight Errant*'s researchers discovered—and named for Wyville Thomson—a submarine ridge that rose to within 200 fathoms of the surface. (The Wyville Thomson Ridge was a part of the great Mid-Atlantic Ridge that would not be identified and mapped until 1956.)

The French were not idle in the pursuit of knowledge of the sea floor, and the Marquis de Folin, a wealthy amateur, explored the water off Brittany and eventually published *Les Fonds de la Mer* (The Depths of the Sea). (Later, Prince Albert of Monaco would fund and participate in oceanographic research of his own devising, which involved an intensive study of the Gulf Stream, first from the platform of the *Hirondelle* and later aboard *Princesse Alice*, his personal research vessel.) It was also during this period of intense deep-ocean research that Jules Verne wrote *Twenty Thousand Leagues Under the Sea*. A great portion of the book takes place under the sea—although not 20,000 leagues under it (which would have been 60,000 miles), but rather over a *distance* of 20,000 leagues—and while Verne takes enormous liberties with science and the truth, it can be fairly stated that the book probably represents an approximation of how a nonscientist perceived the ocean's depths at that time.

After Professor Arronax, his servant Conseil, and the Canadian harpooner Ned Land have been captured and taken aboard the submarine *Nautilus*, we are given a cram course in unlikely oceanography by Verne, usually speaking through Captain Nemo, whose reverence for the sea is stated thus:

The sea is everything. It covers seven-tenths of the terrestrial globe. Its breath is pure and healthy. It is an immense desert, where man is never lonely, for he feels life stirring on all sides. The sea is the only embodiment of a supernatural and wonderful existence. It is nothing but love and emotion; it is the "Living Infinite," as one of your poets has said.

A thousand feet down and dressed in diving costumes, Captain Nemo and Professor Arronax set out for a nocturnal stroll on the ocean floor.* Since no one had yet walked on the bottom at depth, Verne was free to imagine the experience of doing so, and he becomes rhapsodic as he describes the wonders of an undersea promenade: "It was then ten in the morning; the rays of the sun struck the surface of the waves at rather an oblique angle, and at the touch of their light, decomposed by refraction as through a prism, flowers, rocks, plants, shells, and polypi were shaded at the edges of the seven solar colours. It was marvelous, a feast for the eyes, this complication of coloured tints, a perfect kaleidoscope of green, yellow, orange, violet, indigo, and blue, in one word, the whole palette of an enthusiastic colourist!" (Of course, none of this "kaleidoscope" is physically possible without artificial lighting, since the water absorbs most colors within the first 200 feet, leaving only blue and, shortly thereafter, black.)

While real-life oceanographers were struggling to drop nets and dredges to the bottom of the sea, Nemo's submarine easily descends to the astonishing depth of 16,000 yards (48,000 feet) in the Sargasso Sea.† After some hair-raising adventures with sperm whales, icebergs at the South Pole, and giant squid, our heroes end up in the Gulf Stream. According to W. J. Miller, who annotated *Twenty Thousand Leagues Under the Sea,* "Arronax is a disciple of Maury," so we are unlikely to experience the wild exaggerations that we encountered in other locations, but the submarine does find herself in a hurricane, and Verne writes, "Through the open windows of the saloon I saw large

---

* Verne's underwater breathing apparatus was modeled on the *aérophore* developed in 1865 by Benoît Rouquayrol and Auguste Denayrouze, which consisted of a canister filled with compressed air, released by a regulator valve, and with another valve that removed the exhaled air. "For my own use," declares Captain Nemo, "I have perfected the Rouquayrol-Denayrouze apparatus. In order to make it possible for a diver to withstand very great pressures, I have added a copper sphere to be placed over the head." In fact, such a sphere would have done nothing at all to protect the diver, and would have resulted in fatal hemorrhages. Moreover, the canisters developed by Rouquayrol and Denayrouze were not strong enough to contain the compressed air, and it would be another seventy-five years before two more Frenchmen, Emile Gagnan and Jacques-Yves Cousteau, would develop a fully functional "aqualung."

† Although Verne could not have known it in 1870, the greatest depth measured for the ocean is 35,840 feet, in the Mariana Trench in the western Pacific. The actual depth of the Sargasso Sea—depending on where the measurement is taken—is about 18,000 feet.

fish terrified, passing like phantoms in the water. Some were struck dead by lightning before my eyes." "Ah, the Gulf Stream!" he writes, "It deserves the name of the King of Tempests." They take refuge in the depths, where they discover only quiet, silence, and peace.

Finally, after a visit to the submarine telegraph cable that had been laid in 1863 (Verne is known to have interviewed Cyrus Field), the *Nautilus* is caught in a ferocious whirlpool off Norway, and just before the submarine is sucked into the "dreaded Maelstrom," the three wayfarers escape in a dinghy. Arronax is hit on the head and loses consciousness, and regains consciousness in a fisherman's hut on the Loffoden Islands.* The novel concludes: "And to the question asked by Ecclesiastes 3000 years ago, 'That which is far off and exceeding deep, who can find it out?' two men alone of all now living have the right to give an answer—Captain Nemo and myself. The End."

Of course, Jules Verne had every right to fabricate as much of his story as he wanted to, and the above discussion is in no way intended to ridicule a work that is so obviously fiction. But because so much of the underwater journey reflects the state of oceanographic (and ichthyological, geophysical, and chemical) knowledge of the time, it is worth more than a cursory examination.

To satisfy his oceanographic curiosity, Prince Albert I of Monaco collected those animals that might themselves have captured mid-water speedsters such as squid, and upon opening their stomachs, he found the elusive cephalopods. On the research vessel *Princesse Alice,* sailing through the Azores in 1895, Albert approached some Azorean whalers who had harpooned a 40-foot sperm whale, and observed that the dying whale was vomiting up large pieces of animal tissue. His crew collected the "precious regurgitations" and, upon analysis, recognized that they had the tentacles of a large squid. This technique so intrigued the prince that he promptly went into the whaling business, and commissioned two whaling boats to collect various cetaceans and report to him on the stomach contents. Albert's name is permanently associated with that of the squid *Lepidoteuthis grimaldii,* since *lepidos* means "scaled," and Grimaldi is the family name of the ruling princes of Monaco. With his personal fortune (indistinguishable from that of the principality he governed) being enriched daily by the casino at Monte Carlo, Albert expanded his oceanographic studies by building a museum in Monaco and subsidizing an institute of oceanography in Paris. The museum was dedicated

---

* The maelstrom itself, which really exists, is indeed a treacherous current off the Lofoten Islands of Norway, but it was exaggerated into a deadly whirlpool by Verne and also by Edgar Allan Poe in his short story "A Descent into the Maelström." Since Poe's story was published in 1845, it is possible that Verne's version was based in part on Poe's.

in 1903, and the Institut Océanographique de Paris was opened in 1911, but despite the Prince's enthusiasm (and Verne's popularity), oceanography did not exactly flourish in France.

All the various soundings and dredge hauls, along with the laying of the transatlantic telegraph cable, elicited a great curiosity about the actual shape of the sea bottom. There appeared to be a region in the middle of the North Atlantic that was considerably higher—several miles in some places—than the surrounding regions, which naturally gave rise to resuscitated rumors about the lost continent of Atlantis. Maury, who had based his 1854 map of the North Atlantic Ocean on some 180 soundings, called this rise (or ridge, or swell—nobody really knew what it was) "Telegraphic Plateau," but it soon became obvious that there was a single ridge that ran the entire length of the Atlantic, and from which had sprung Iceland and the Azores in the north, and Tristan da Cunha, Ascension Island, and Bouvet Island in the south.

Several years after his successful experiments aboard the *Blake*, Alexander Agassiz sailed on the steamer *Albatross*, the first ship ever built for scientific exploration of the oceans. Commissioned by Spencer F. Baird, the head of the U.S. Commission of Fish and Fisheries, she was an iron-hulled twin-screw steamer, 234 feet in overall length, and rigged as a barkentine with 7,500 square feet of auxiliary sail. *Albatross* was described as "a thoroughly seaworthy steamer capable of making extensive cruises and working with dredge and trawls in all depths to 3,000 fathoms." She was based at Woods Hole, a fishing village at the axilla of the flexed arm of Cape Cod, where Baird had decided to establish a permanent marine laboratory. By 1885, the laboratory and mess hall had been built, and the *Albatross*, the laboratory's flagship and research vessel, was at sea. In the summers, Agassiz cruised the western North Atlantic, from Cape Cod to Cape Hatteras, collecting shallow-water animals, studying the life cycle of various food fishes, and in general conducting a detailed ecological study of Atlantic waters. In 1886, she embarked on a mission to locate the mysterious "Hope Bank," a new fishing ground rumored to be off Sable Island near Nova Scotia. After several soundings, Capt. Zera L. Tanner reported that no such bank existed and was probably a ruse concocted by fishermen to keep their rivals away from the real fishing grounds.

In 1888, *Albatross* was transferred to San Francisco and, with Alexander Agassiz aboard, made several important voyages to Pacific locations. She visited the Galápagos Islands in 1891, and in 1907 conducted a two-and-a-half-year survey of the waters around the Philippines. She continued in service until 1924, when she was officially retired. In a 1925 article in *Natural History*, Charles H. Townsend wrote, "If ever the American people received the fullest possible value from a government ship, they received it from this one. The benefits to science, the fisheries, and commerce springing from her almost continuous investigations—the results of which have all been published and widely distributed throughout the world—are incalculable." Baird, the moving force behind the Woods Hole enterprise, died in 1886, but his friends and colleagues oversaw the building of the Marine Biological Laboratory (MBL) in 1888, a posthumous fulfillment of his fervent desire for a "summer university" at Woods Hole.

In 1934, newspapers reported the discovery of a "lost continent" in the Pacific after a Navy captain on a routine voyage from Hawaii to Japan had made a series of regular echo-soundings and discovered mountains, valleys, riverbeds, and other features usually associated with dry land. There was no "lost continent" there, of course, only the previously unsuspected existence of various seamounts that characterize the western Pacific. But the soundings—of which there were more on this one voyage than in all of the previous century—showed that SONAR (SOund NAvigation and Ranging) could be an extremely effective tool for investigating the ocean floor. (Sonar had actually been introduced shortly after the sinking of the *Titanic* in 1912 as a device for locating and avoiding icebergs.)

Underwater investigative devices, such as sonar (or asdic, as the British call it), proved to be particularly useful in detecting submarines. During World War I, a system was developed that enabled the British and French hydrophones and amplifiers to pick up the noise emitted by the engines of enemy submarines, and later, with the use of "active" sonar, where pulse sounds were transmitted and the rebounding echoes processed, they were able to detect a submarine even when its engines were shut down. Echo-sounding instruments, perfected during the wars, soon became the tools of oceanographers, used to plot the configuration of the ocean floor.

The Gulf Stream

As soon as the geography of the Atlantic Ocean was assumed to be known, people became interested in the other elements that affected maritime existence, such as weather, winds, currents, and tides. The Gulf Stream was first described by Ponce de León* around 1515, but its "discovery" is permanently associated with Benjamin Franklin, who learned of it from his Nantucket cousin, whaling captain Timothy Folger. Although Franklin drew a map of the Gulf Stream in 1770, it did not receive wide acceptance until 1786, when he published a paper in the *Transactions of the American Philosophical Society*. Franklin wrote:

> The stream is probably generated by the great accumulation of water on the eastern coast of America between the tropics, by the trade winds which constantly blow there. It is known that a large piece of water, ten miles broad and generally only three feet deep, has by a strong wind had its waters driven to one side and sustained so as to become six feet deep, while the windward side was laid dry. This may give some idea of the quantity heaped upon the American coast, and the reason in its running down in a strong current into the Bay of Mexico, and from thence issuing through the Gulf of Florida, and proceeding along the coast to the Banks of Newfoundland, where it turns off towards and runs down through the western islands. . . .
>
> The conclusion from these remarks is, that a vessel from Europe to North America may shorten her passage by avoiding to stem the stream, in which the thermometer may be very useful; and a vessel from America

---

* Juan Ponce de León was born in Spain in 1460, and sailed with Columbus on the second expedition in 1493. He later explored and settled Puerto Rico (the city of Ponce is named for him), and in 1513, while searching for the Fountain of Youth, he discovered and named Florida. (Its name comes from the Spanish *Pasqua Florida,* which means "Easter," because it was discovered during that season.) De León died in 1521, after a Seminole arrow pierced his neck during a landing at Charlotte Harbor.

to Europe may do the same by the same means of keeping in it. It may have often happened accidentally that voyages have been shortened by these circumstances. It is well to have command of them.

The South Equatorial Current, surging in a counterclockwise direction in the South Atlantic, debouches over the shoulder of South America and begins a northward journey that will take some of this water beyond Norway and over Finnmark toward the North Pole. Another arm of this current splits off and curls south again, becoming the Brazil Current and continuing the circle of the South Atlantic. Thus, a sizable portion of the South Equatorial Current plus the southern part of the North Equatorial Current converge into the Caribbean and the Gulf of Mexico, with no place else to go but the narrow channel between Florida and Cuba. Skirting the western boundary of the quiescent Sargasso Sea, these powerful forces combine to form the Gulf Stream, one of the most important ocean currents in the world.

The Stream—which is technically not a stream at all but a *gyre*—originates in the Caribbean, emerging through the Straits of Florida between the Keys and Cuba, where it is then joined by the confluent Antilles and North Equatorial currents. Off Cape Hatteras it veers to the east and continues on a northeast heading to Newfoundland, finally cooling and becoming the North Atlantic Drift. Despite its resemblance to a river (a popular book about it is called *The Ocean River*), the Gulf Stream is far larger and more complex than any land-based flow. It has constantly varying borders, and its shape and velocity are almost always in flux. It is much bigger than any river; at its point of maximum flow, off North Carolina, the volume of water is 70 million cubic meters per second, some thirty-five hundred times greater than that of the Mississippi River. At its narrowest portion, the Stream is some 50 miles wide, and moves at about 4 miles an hour.

Deeper blue and warmer than the ocean in which it flows, the Gulf Stream is also saltier. It is warmer on its eastern borders, but throughout, it may be as much as 20° F (11° C) warmer than the ocean that surrounds it. The Stream itself is not particularly productive in terms of fauna, supporting primarily migrating tuna and Atlantic salmon, and flying fish, but when it mixes with the colder waters of the Labrador Current, the turbulence and nutrients combine to produce the most productive commercial fishing grounds in the world, the Grand Banks. The meeting of the warmer waters of the Stream and the colder waters of the Labrador Current also produces the condensation that causes the consistent thick fogs of Newfoundland and Labrador. The Norway Current, a descendant of the Gulf Stream that flows past Ireland and Scotland, does the same job even farther north. The Gulf Stream also warms the land: the mild winters of England are also attributable to it, as well as those incredible areas of Devonshire and Scotland where palm trees and other tropical plants are grown.

In 1969, the mesoscaph (*meso* means "middle"; *scaph* means "boat"), *Ben Franklin* was launched on a historic voyage, thirty days underwater, following the Gulf Stream from Palm Beach, Florida, to a point south of Nova Scotia. Designed by Jacques Piccard (the pilot of the *Trieste* on her record dive to 35,800 feet in the Mariana Trench), *Ben Franklin* was 48 feet long, with twenty-nine viewing ports to permit maximum visibility for the crew of six. The portholes—among other things—differentiated the mesoscaph from conventional submarines, but at a dry weight of 130 tons, she was one of the largest and heaviest submersible vessels built for anything but warfare. Although she was equipped with motors for propulsion, *Ben Franklin* was designed to float submerged for the entire voyage.

On July 16, 1969 (the same day as the launching of *Apollo 11,* which put Neil Armstrong and Buzz Aldrin on the moon four days later), the vessel was launched in Florida. She drifted at depths ranging from 200 to 400 meters below the surface, making occasional scheduled dives to explore the bottom. At a depth of 252 meters (826 feet), three members of the crew watched as a small broadbill swordfish (perhaps six feet in total length) attacked the submersible, "dashing straight forward and striking the hull of the mesoscaph with the point of the sword, aiming perhaps at the porthole, but hitting only the steel of the hull. . . ."* Most of the other wildlife seen through the *Ben Franklin*'s ports were smaller and less aggressive. Piccard records (in his 1971 account of the voyage, *The Sun Beneath the Sea*) various planktonic species, including euphausiid shrimp, arrowworms, salpas, and copepods. He wonders "how biologists have managed to snatch so many secrets from the depths of the sea without either bathyscaph or mesoscaph."

About two-thirds of the way through the trip, on August 5, the mesoscaph was visited by a large school of tuna. They had been hoping for such an event, and took some extraordinary photographs of the fish. "To my knowledge," wrote Piccard, "no one had ever before observed a shoal of tuna from the depths." (They were later identified from the photographs as *Thunnus alalunga,* the albacore or longfin tuna.) On August 13, the thirtieth day of the voyage, the *Ben Franklin* received a telephone message from the Woods Hole research vessel *Atlantis II* asking if they have seen any sign of the deep-scattering layer (see pp. 260–64). The answer was negative. "The absence of the DSL," writes Piccard, "is a disappointment to me. . . . [N]ever has any oceanographic team been so favorably placed as to study this layer." Piccard et al. brought the mesoscaph to the surface on August 15, 1969, and were towed to Portland, Maine.

At the center of the North Atlantic gyre, like the eye of a hurricane, is an

The research submarine *Ben Franklin* under Jacques Piccard surfaces in New York Harbor in 1968, having spent thirty-one days underwater, exploring 1,400 miles of the Gulf Stream.

area of calm water, minimal winds, and no currents whatsoever. No more a sea than the Gulf Stream is a stream, the Sargasso Sea is one of the most unusual bodies of water in the world. It lacks terrestrial boundaries but is defined by various currents: the Gulf Stream forms its western and northern borders; the Canaries Current is at its eastern edge; and to the south, the North Equatorial Drift keeps this vast body of water more or less enclosed. The absence of land boundaries means that the limits of the Sargasso Sea are variable, but temperature differences have proven to be a more efficient measuring device, and it is now recognized as "a huge lens of warm water, separated from the colder layers below by a zone of sharply changing temperature" (Ryther 1956). The rotation of the Sargasso Sea causes water to pile up at the center, and it

* On July 6, 1967, at a depth of 610 meters (2,000 feet) off the coast of Georgia, *Alvin* had also been rammed by a swordfish, which was trapped by its sword in the sub's superstructure and brought to the surface, where it was eaten by Woods Hole scientists that evening. (See pp. 75–76 for an account of the ramming of the *Alvin*.)

is about two feet higher at the center than at the outer edges. Marked by temperature differences, it also has a lower limit of about 3,000 feet, which means that the shallow Sargasso lens sits on top of an ocean that may be 15,000 feet deep.

In his 1975 book, John Teal calls the Sargasso Sea "a vast desert within the Atlantic Ocean." Sailing ships were often becalmed in the center, surrounded by rafts of the thick algae known as sargassum weed, or gulfweed. The weed initially grows attached to the bottom in shallow Central American and Caribbean waters. Broken off by storms, it floats on currents to the open sea, where it collects in great rafts at the surface. It can grow and divide, but not reproduce. The free-floating weed is kept afloat by little, berry-like bladders known as pneumatocysts, and although the warm, saline waters are almost devoid of life, they do support a small but specialized fauna, such as the sargassum fish (*Histrio histrio*), a member of the frogfish family, which, with its mottled brownish coloration and weedlike growths, resembles the plants in which it lives, and is found nowhere else in the world.

Many other kinds of fishes live in the Sargasso Sea, which is a body of water roughly the size of the United States. But because this aquatic wasteland is plankton-poor, the inhabitants are spread out over so many thousands of cubic miles of water that it appears as if the fish fauna of the Sargasso is particularly sparse. The Sargasso is the breeding ground for the common eel (*Anguilla*), which then—for reasons not understood—disperses to either North America or Europe to mature. Along with the patches of sargasso weed, the surface is often marked by the translucent purple sail of the Portuguese man-of-war (*Physalia*), which is actually a colonial animal with specially dedicated cells for stinging and digestion. The "tentacles" are poisonous enough to kill small fishes and, incidentally, to deliver a nasty sting to a human swimmer. The Sargasso's surface is frequently broken by flying fish taking to the air, probably to escape from those species that prey on them: dolphinfish, tuna, sharks, swordfish. The predators are constantly in motion, since some of them—the tunas and the sharks—have no mechanism for pumping water over their gills and must keep swimming or die. There are also all sorts of invertebrates—squid, shrimp, crabs, amphipods, copepods, etc.—but they are not unique to the Sargasso.

The floor of the Sargasso, like that of most deep oceans, is a stable environment. As Teal has written, "Tomorrow will be the same as today, which was the same as yesterday, through many generations. Yesterday was, today is, and tomorrow will be dark, cold, salty, and well-oxygenated." Deepwater fish species, such as rattails, brotulids, and deep-sea cods, live here as well as in the world's other deep waters, and an occasional shark or ray cruises by. On the bottom itself, there are starfish, sea cucumbers, crinoids, sponges, crabs, and sea spiders. In his book *The Sargasso Sea*, John Teal describes a 1971 dive in the submersible *Alvin*:

> 100 meters down . . . Deep twilight outside. Nothing is visible except for the usual "snow." Nobody really knows what snow is but guess it is small animals, chitinous molts, phytoplankton, and bits of material on the way to the bottom. . . .
>
> 400 meters down . . . 11° C. There is quite a bit of bioluminescence from some big objects. What they are I can't tell. Can't even guess. A few euphausids were visible for a moment as we drifted down. It is slightly eerie to see these animals outlined by the glow of luminescence against dark water.
>
> 665 meters down . . . I see a medusa floating upside down with tentacles outspread. It must be about 5 cm across the bell and 15 cm across the whole animal. There is another ropelike animal, definitely a string of salps. Also some fairly large animals: crustacea, jellyfish, ctenophores. Many are upside down. Being upside down doesn't seem to make much difference at this depth, since animals don't have to relate to directional surface light.
>
> 1020 meters down . . . There's a fish now, sitting horizontally. I turned the outside light on and off. An explosion of light has erupted in a plume through the water. It could be some animal squirting out phosphorescent substance.
>
> 1740 meters down . . . Whango! Just hit the bottom and stirred up a great cloud of mud. . . . A heavy looking decapod is hanging just above the bottom. I see a red urchin with black spines and many leaf-like structures sitting on the bottom. . . . We seem to be in a plain of sandy mud. I can't see any rocks and I don't know how far the plain extends. . . . Now rattail fish and deep sea cods come into view. Also some small black fish. A few sea cucumbers lie on the left, rather light-colored and splotched. . . . Still no rocks, only mud. This is a definite contrast to a dive in Tongue of the Ocean in the Bahamas where boulders as big as a house precipitously overshadowed *Alvin* as we skirted sharp rises and canyons.

The Ocean Floor

The surface of the earth lies at two predominant elevations. One approximates present sea level and represents the interior lowlands, coastal plains, and continental shelves. The other lies approximately 4000 meters below sea level and represents the general level of the oceans' basins. The continents, steep-sided massive blocks surrounded by an enormous globe-encircling sea, have deep roots which project 30,000 or 40,000 meters into the earth's mantle while the ocean crust is but a thin 5000-meter-thick film frozen over the earth's massive mantle.

HEEZEN AND HOLLISTER
The Face of the Deep (1971)

O nce thought to be covered in a thick mat of living ooze—which was referred to as *Urschleim* ("original slime")—the ocean floor has been revealed to be a varied, ever-changing surface, more volatile by far than its terrestrial counterpart, constantly moving, rolling, erupting, ducking, growing, splitting, and even capriciously reversing its magnetic orientation. Now known to be comprised of various rocks and sediments, the sea floor appears to be the single most influential factor in the flux of the earth, affecting mountains, volcanoes, earthquakes, and even weather.

The skin of the planet is composed of eight large and several small "plates" that have shifted and slid over the fullness of time, carrying continents from one hemisphere to another, defining the places where men and animals may live, causing the rise and fall of mountains. Since most of the planet is underwater, it follows that most of this shifting takes place where no man will ever see it. Early theorists postulated "continental drift," a process whereby the one or two large landmasses broke up and drifted apart, but the more conservative element in the scientific community did not accept such a wild idea. The familiar jigsaw-puzzle fit of Africa and South America was cited as evidence of this idea, but the mechanism that drove these incalculably heavy and seemingly immovable objects was not readily forthcoming. If the continents had somehow separated, dredge samples should have brought up the same sort of granitic, sedimentary rocks that characterized the continents; instead, rocks like serpentine, peridotite, and gabbro were found on the Mid-Atlantic Ridge, along with basaltic lava, which strongly resembled the composition of the earth's mantle. Furthermore, the jagged nature of Ridge topography indicated a young feature, not an ancient rubble-heap.

Continental drift is now as much of a "fact" as any scientific theory can be. The evidence for this process is overwhelming, but since no one has ever seen it happen (and it certainly cannot be verified in the laboratory), it must remain, like evolution, "only a theory." The plates that make up the earth's crust are in constant motion, albeit at speeds—perhaps an inch a year—that make the term "glacial" seem fast. At the middle of the Atlantic Ocean, the raft that carries the North American plate away from the European plate separates in a great rift by means of earthquakes and the eruption of lava from the earth's mantle, forming new sea floor as it pushes the plates away from each other. (In 1992, K. C. Macdonald estimated that the amount of lava formed every year could pave the entire U.S. interstate freeway system with a layer of rock ten feet thick.) While much of the action on the sea floor remains hidden under miles of water, we can see indisputable surface evidence of the power of plate tectonics in Iceland, itself formed by volcanic action along the Mid-Atlantic Ridge. The most recent (and most visible) demonstration of this phenomenon is the Icelandic island of Surtsey, which erupted out of the ocean in a spectacular display of steam and incandescent lava in 1963.

Most of the peaks cresting the Ridge are underwater. They average 10,000 feet in height (measured from the ocean floor), and are usually at least a mile below the surface, except where some actually emerge above sea level as islands. The islands of the Ridge are the Azores, and Saint Paul's Rocks in the North Atlantic; and Ascension, Tristan da Cunha, and Bouvet Island south of the Equator. The highest point of the Ridge is Pico Island in the Azores, rising 7,750 feet above the surface of the sea, but 27,000 feet above the bottom.* The plateau that is Iceland lies on the Reykjanes Ridge, doglegged off the Mid-Atlantic Ridge by the Gibbs Fracture Zone but obviously an extension of the same fault system. The Ridge continues north of Iceland as the Nansen Cordillera.

In *Voyage to the Center of the Earth,* when Jules Verne has Professor Von Hardwigg and his nephew Harry descend through the mouth of an extinct Ice-

---

* Measured from its base, the highest mountain in the world is not Mount Everest, but Aconcagua in the Argentine Andes. From the floor of the ocean to the roof of the world, this mountain measures 22,834 feet above the surface of the Pacific, and another 25,000 feet to the floor of the Peru-Chile Trench, for a total rise of 47,834 feet—more than nine miles.

landic volcano, they discover that there are tunnels and pathways that enable them to wander in the interior of the hollow planet, which contains (among other things) the "Central Sea," a vast ocean inhabited by assorted dinosaurs. Harry stands transfixed on the shore of the underground ocean, which is lit by "a pale cold illuminating power . . . something in the nature of the aurora borealis," and says, "I cannot describe its awful grandeur; human language fails to convey an idea of its savage sublimity." Their subterranean travels take them out from under Iceland and under the Atlantic Ocean ("What mattered it," asks Harry, "whether the plains and mountains of Iceland were suspended over our devoted heads, or the mighty billows of the Atlantic Ocean?"), and finally, they are fortuitously ejected by a volcanic eruption. When they reach the surface, they cannot figure out where they are (Spitsbergen? Asia? The North Pole?), but they discover that they are "in the center of the Mediterranean, amidst the eastern archipelago of ancient memory," on the island of Stromboli. They had entered the earth by one volcano and come out by another. With this "final conclusion of a narrative which will probably be disbelieved even by people who are astonished at nothing," Verne ends his fantastic voyage, and demonstrates once again that he was never a man to let mere facts interfere with a good story.*

Even though Captain Symmes and Jules Verne professed a detailed knowledge of the earth's interior, our knowledge is still limited to scientific speculation rather than firsthand observations. There have been attempts to drill below the surface, but these have given us only an idea of the composition and age of the crust in various locations on land and under the sea. Our inability to dig 2,000 miles down—or even 20, for that matter—has not kept geophysicists from theorizing, and with more sophisticated tools being developed regularly, a clearer picture of our planet's interior is beginning to emerge. The primary device for determining the composition of the earth is the seismograph, a device that measures the movement of earthquake-generated shock waves through the various inner layers of the earth. Because these waves travel at different speeds through materials of different densities, laboratory tests using various substances have enabled us to identify the materials but not necessarily the state. We know, for example, that the outer core is iron, but we do not know if the tremendous pressure has rendered it a solid, or if it is in a molten state. We know only that it is very hot indeed. Recent develop-

---

* Jules Verne is known to have based his 1864 novel on a theory advanced by a man called John Cleves Symmes, who believed that the earth was hollow and could be entered through the "holes in the poles" (see p. 6). As he stares at the Central Sea, Harry ruminates on "the theory of the English captain who compared the earth to a vast hollow sphere in the interior of which the air is retained in a luminous state by means of atmospheric pressure, while two stars, Pluto and Proserpine, circled there in their mysterious orbits. After all, suppose the old fellow was right!"

ments in marine seismology include the introduction of computer-generated images of the earth's interior, something like a CAT scan (computerized axial tomography) that assembles composite X-ray images of the human body. The young science of seismic tomography can assemble the records of seismometers around the world and eventually produce a three-dimensional image of the inside of the earth.*

The plates, mountains, and valleys that comprise the surface of the earth are an expression of the internal structure and dynamics of the planet. The outermost layer is the crust, or lithosphere (from the Greek *lithos,* which means "stone"), incorporating the continents and the sea floor. The crust ranges from 6 to 25 miles in thickness, and is much thicker under the continents than it is under the sea floor. It rides atop the asthenosphere (from *asthenes,* meaning "weak" or "feeble"), an exceptionally plastic zone of fluid rock that extends some 200 miles down. The mantle is the next layer, nearly 2,000 miles thick and composed of a dense rock called peridotite, which consists mainly of the mineral olivine. (Peridotite is rarely found on the surface, but it sometimes occurs along the Mid-Ocean Ridge, neatly suggesting that mantle material has welled up and then solidified.) Almost everywhere but under the Mid-Ocean Ridge there is a sharp boundary between the crust and the mantle. This is known as the Mohorovičíc discontinuity ("Moho" for short), named for Andrija Mohorovičíc, the Yugoslavian seismologist who discovered that shock waves from earthquakes travel relatively slowly above the discontinuity, and faster below it, in the denser rocks of the mantle. Based on their readings of the relative densities of the materials that make up the inner layers of the earth, geophysicists have subdivided the mantle into an upper and a lower layer. The upper layer, known as the asthenosphere, is so hot that it is commonly thought to be in a molten state. It is this soft layer underneath the continents that allows them to float about so easily, like icebergs in water. Beneath the asthenosphere is the "lower mantle," where the pressure is so great that the rock (mostly perskovites and magnesiowüstite) is rigid and incompressible. At the center is the core, an almost unimaginably large ball of solid iron, which is hotter still than the mantle. It is now thought that every layer within the earth is actively convecting, a result of the continued escape of heat from the planet's interior.

The earth has been cooling since its inception, some 4.55 billion years ago. Since the heat passes from the interior to the surface by the fastest means possible (a direct result of the second law of thermodynamics, also known as the principle of entropy), and since rock is a very poor conductor, the heat is

---

* An abbreviated version of seismic tomography is used to "see" anomalous features buried in the earth. By generating artificial shock waves with a specialized shotgun, paleontologists can identify images of fossils below the surface without digging.

brought to the surface by heat-induced fluid motion: the convection within the mantle. On the surface, when the lithosphere cools over millions of years, it becomes heavier than the mantle beneath it, and the force of gravity pulls the plates downward.

Even before the *Challenger* set sail on her epoch-making, 68,000-mile oceanographic research voyage in 1872, Charles Wyville Thomson had discovered that masses of water between the Shetland and the Faroe islands were measured at the same temperature at the surface but were different at depth. He had encountered similar phenomena on previous cruises aboard the *Lightning* and the *Porcupine,* and surmised that something must be keeping them from mixing. "If our generalization be correct," he wrote, "a submarine ridge rising to within about 200 fathoms of the surface must extend across the mouth of the channel between the coast of Scotland and the Faroe Banks." This ridge, some 1,500 feet below the surface, has been named after Wyville Thomson, and extends from Iceland to the Faroes, from the Faroes to the Shetlands, then to Scotland, and into the main body of the North Atlantic, where it becomes the Mid-Atlantic Ridge, one of the most remarkable features on the face of the earth. (*Lightning, Porcupine,* and *Challenger* spent most of their time crossing the North Atlantic, and it was not until the German *Meteor* cruises of 1925–27 that the continuation of the Ridge into the South Atlantic was established.)

Around the middle of the nineteenth century, Matthew Fontaine Maury's primitive depth-sounding techniques showed a flat, elevated plain in the mid-Atlantic that he dubbed "Telegraphic Plateau" as a beneficence to those who would lay the transatlantic cables. Cyrus Field's engineers were anxious to learn about the topography of the ocean floor so the telegraph cable could be laid, but soundings taken by hemp and lead sinker were so time-consuming and inaccurate that the picture of the ocean floor that emerged was less than useful. (The unexpected ridges and valleys caused the failure of the cable within its first three months.) Scientists aboard the *Challenger* in 1873 also noted the presence of the Mid-Atlantic Ridge,* but their sounding techniques were not much better than Maury's and they came to the same conclusions: that it was a plateau in the middle of the ocean, only half as deep as the two troughs that flanked it.

It is obvious to anyone looking at a map of South America and Africa that

---

* As might be expected, discovery of a plateau in the mid-Atlantic encouraged those who believed that Atlantis was a drowned continent—or at least a drowned city. Never mind that Plato had located the lost city in the Atlantic Ocean just off the Pillars of Hercules (Straits of Gibraltar); never mind that no signs of any sort of historic civilization were associated with the Ridge; and never mind that there was no evidence that the Ridge—or any part of it—had ever been above the surface. The mere discovery of something that was not flat sea bottom brought out the Atlanteans, and many of them are still trying to show that the Ridge is really the Lost Continent.

there is a remarkable congruence of the east coast of the former and the west coast of the latter, as if the two were parts of a gigantic jigsaw puzzle. Some early geologists believed that the power of the ocean had carved out a great valley between the two continents; in 1908, Frank Bursley Taylor suggested that the moon had once been so close to the earth during the Cretaceous period that its gravitational pull had dragged the continents apart and their plowing through the ocean floor had thrown up the Himalayas and the Alps. Howard Baker presented the idea that Venus had come so close to the earth that it pulled a great chunk out, forming the moon and setting the continents in motion. Despite the astonishing fit of the coastlines, however, it was not easy to see how they might have come apart. Continents are not supposed to break in half and slide over the earth's surface like cookies on a greased tin. Weren't the continents rooted in the earth? How could something that weighed uncountable millions of tons slide around? It was a German explorer named Alfred Wegener who looked at the puzzle and saw the answer.

Born in 1880 in Berlin, Wegener had wondered for years about the congruity of the continents. He theorized that there had been a single landmass, which he called Pangaea, during the Carboniferous period, some 300 million years ago, and presented a paper in 1912 to the Frankfurt Geological Association suggesting that it was slowly breaking up. He was trained as a meteorologist, so Wegener's geological research was only a sideline, but the idea of drifting continents continued to intrigue him. He was invited to join a Danish meteorological expedition to Greenland, and then the War to End All Wars broke out. Wounded in Belgium, Wegener spent much of his recuperation developing his theory of continental drift. In the 1923 *Die Entstehung der Kontinente und Ozeane* (The Origin of Continents and Oceans), he wrote:

> He who examines the opposite coasts of the South Atlantic Ocean must be somewhat struck by the similarity of the shapes of the coastlines of Brazil and Africa. Not only does the great right-angled bend formed by the Brazilian coast at Cape San Roque find its exact counterpart in the reentrant angle of the African coastline near the Cameroons, but also, south of these two corresponding points, every projection on the Brazilian side corresponds to a similar shaped bay in the African.

He believed that the Mid-Atlantic Ridge, as well as Iceland and the Azores, was composed of material left over when the continents pulled apart. Mountains, he thought, were creases in the earth's crust caused by the pressure of the moving landmasses, and not, as had been previously believed, "wrinkles" formed by the planet's shrinking like a withered apple. The "shrinking" hypothesis (which had been supported by none other than Isaac Newton) was finally discarded when analysis of radioactive elements (uranium, thorium, and radioactive potassium) showed how much time had transpired since the rock formations had cooled and solidified. Since the core of the earth is still hot, the earth could not have cooled enough to produce those towering wrinkles. Furthermore, the Caledonian mountain system in Norway and Scotland has many features in common with the Appalachian system of North America, which indicated to Wegener that these features had once abutted. Summarizing the evidence, he wrote, "It is just as if we were to refit the torn pieces of a newspaper by matching their edges and then check whether the lines of print run smoothly across. If they do, there is nothing left but to conclude that the pieces were in fact joined in this way."

As obvious as continental drift was to Wegener, it was strongly opposed by most of his professional contemporaries, who were having a problem with the mechanism that was supposed to be moving the continents around. At the 1926 meeting of the American Association of Petroleum Geologists in New York, experts took the opportunity to deride Wegener and his wild theory. Charles Schuchert, a professor of historical geology at Yale, maintained that the continents did not really fit that well, and wrote, "It is evident that Wegener has taken extraordinary liberties with the earth's rigid crust, making it pliable so as to stretch the Americas from north to south about 1,500 miles." Bailey Willis of Stanford argued that drift would have created great faults and distortions that do not exist, and Wegener's book "leaves the impression that it had been written by an advocate rather than by an impartial observer." Alfred Wegener died in 1930, the apparent victim of a heart attack while on an expedition to take weather observations and measure the thickness of the ice in Greenland. "Thus ended the career of one of the most ardent advocates of continental drift," wrote Walter Sullivan, "a man who, had he lived to a ripe age, would finally have seen much of his theory vindicated." His countrymen thought so highly of him that they named the meteorological institute in Bremerhaven after him.

Wegener had postulated that Pangaea began to break up about 180 million years ago, but he was unable to identify the responsible agent. He thought that the continents had somehow barged around the ocean floor like ships plowing through pack ice, precipitating earthquakes before them and leaving the floor behind. In 1937, Alexander du Toit, a South African geologist (and a lifelong disciple of Wegener), suggested that rather than one continent, there had been two, which he named Gondwanaland and Laurasia. The eminent Cambridge geophysicist Harold Jeffreys was opposed to such heresies, on the grounds that the earth's crust and mantle were much too rigid for the continents to move around, but F. A. Vening Meinesz countered Jeffrey's argument by suggesting that the mechanism for movement came from thermal convection in the mantle.

Before Wegener, nobody could conceive that the crust of the earth moved in anything but a vertical manner; the cooling of the planet was thought to cause movement of the earth's crust. One view held that continents were somehow drowned like the "lost continent" of Atlantis, while another theory maintained that previously submerged regions had been uplifted and were now part of existing continents. Both of these ideas were anathema to those who believed that the relative positions of the land and the oceans appeared immutable; that the continents and the ocean basins were permanent features of the earth's crust. Indeed, it was not until the middle of the twentieth century, when sea-floor spreading was shown to be the agent that propels the earth's plates, that most geologists finally came to accept the idea of continental drift. (Those who so vehemently opposed the theory were correct in one respect: the continents do not drift; they move because they are part of the lithosphere, which does move.)

In 1925, 1926, and 1927, the German oceanographic research vessel *Meteor* produced the first detailed echo-sounding profiles of the Mid-Atlantic Ridge, revealing it as a rugged mountain range, but it would not be until continuously recording echo-sounders were developed during World War II that an accurate picture of the floor of the ocean would begin to emerge. Aboard the British research vessel *John Murray* in 1933, John D. H. Wiseman and Seymour Sewell had discovered a deep gully in the Indian Ocean, extending southeast from the island of Socotra in the Gulf of Aden. The two scientists discovered another ridge in the Arabian Sea, and noticed that these and other submarine ridges coincided with a pattern of earthquakes around the world. The plan to investigate the rift that split the Mid-Atlantic Ridge was interrupted by World War II, but at its conclusion—and with the improvement of echo-sounding equipment—it became clear that the earth was girdled by an almost continuous seismic zone.

In 1947, Maurice Ewing led a National Geographic Society–sponsored expedition aboard the research vessel *Atlantis I,* a 146-foot steel-hulled ketch equipped with a bottom trawl (for collecting living things), a rock dredge (for rocks), and a primitive underwater camera to record what no man had ever seen: the floor of the Atlantic, three miles below the surface. North of Bermuda, the scientists lowered coring devices to sample the bottom sediments, and discovered that the top layer was composed of globigerina ooze, a cream-colored, coarse-grained material rich in the tiny shells of the single-celled foraminifera. Eight inches below that, however, the material was white, like fine-grained chalk, containing foraminifera of the Eocene period. According to Ewing's 1948 *National Geographic* article, "This meant that an interval of 60 million years had gone by between the deposition of the chalk in the bottom of the core and the top eight inches of ooze. . . . So far as I know this is the first time that sediments older than a few thousand years have been re-covered from considerable depths in any ocean basin."

The *Atlantis I* arrived at its mid-ocean station, midway between America and West Africa, and set off explosive devices that would give them a reading on the bottom topography by continuously echo-sounding the bottom.* "Would the Ridge be a chaos of peaks," Ewing asked, "or would it follow some understandable pattern?" The "understandable pattern," of course, eventually turned out to be a deep valley flanked by rugged mountains, one of which "rises some 9,700 feet from the trench at its foot to its crown, or higher than the mighty Matterhorn. . . ." Their dredges hauled up igneous rock, "crystal-lized from a molten condition, like granite and many other rocks," as well as basalt, serpentine, and diabase, clear indications that the feature had been formed by volcanic action and earthquakes that had occurred in historic times. Even though their methods were slow and laborious, Ewing and his prede-cessors collected data that would reveal a world heretofore hidden from humans; the mapping of the floor of the ocean could now begin.

Ewing took *Atlantis I* back the next year, with eighteen men and equip-ment that consisted of various coring tubes and dredges, a deep-sea camera, and "2,000 toy balloons to be used as floats for the TNT charges we exploded for measuring the depth of bottom sediment." When the charge exploded, the sound waves traveled through the sediment and were reflected back from the solid bedrock. Because the sediments had been accumulating for countless ages, they expected the offshore measurements to show a thick blanket, but they were surprised to discover that the layers in the level basins that flank the Mid-Atlantic Ridge were only 100 feet thick. In 1949, Ewing could not know the reasons for this discrepancy, and he wrote, "Here is another of the many scien-tific riddles our expedition propounded."† They mapped the deep trenches of the Ridge and guessed that the "great faults . . . are the sources of the many submarine earthquakes that center there." (Toward the end of the cruise, Ewing had to return to Columbia University, and Bruce Heezen, then Ewing's graduate student, took over as chief scientist of the cruise.) In 1949, Maurice Ewing founded Columbia University's Lamont Geological Observatory, in a

---

* According to Bruce Heezen's recollections, the continuous echo-sounder aboard *Atlantis I* worked well enough in principle, but "the device had one disconcerting drawback; it depended entirely on the ship's irregular and intermittent electric power, which went off whenever someone opened the refrigerator. When that happened, no echo returned; instead, the sounder recorded measureless depths."

† In time, the riddle would be solved. As the Mid-Ocean Ridge pushes up through the ocean floor, it creates new, basaltic ocean floor, on which only a thin layer of sediment accumulates. As the newly formed ridge widens, it displaces the sediments toward the continents. Sediment washed into the sea from the continents is added to the layers shoved aside by the widening of the ridge, resulting in thicker sedimentation farthest from the ridge, thinner layers closest to it.

Hudson River mansion donated by the widow of banker Thomas W. Lamont.

In the early 1950s, the British geophysicist Sir Edward Bullard had employed a special probe to take the temperature of locations along the Mid-Atlantic Ridge, and discovered that the heat flow along the crest of the ridge was as much as eight times greater than on the surrounding ocean floor. He suggested that there was a crack in the earth's crust where new, hot material was welling up. Then Maurice Ewing, Bruce Heezen, and Marie Tharp proved him right.

Bruce Heezen died prematurely at the age of fifty-four in June 1977, as he was preparing for a dive on the Mid-Atlantic Ridge aboard the Navy's nuclear research submarine *NR-1*. He had studied geology at the University of Iowa, but upon hearing Maurice Ewing speak about the floor of the sea, he changed his focus from terrestrial to submarine geology and came east for the summer. His first assignment—extraordinary for an undergraduate—was to be chief scientist aboard the Navy vessel *Balanus,* using a new underwater camera to photograph the continental margins of the east coast. Upon graduation from the University of Iowa in 1948, he returned to New York to join Ewing as a graduate student. As Paul Fox wrote in his 1992 tribute to Bruce Heezen, "Marine geology was never to be the same."

In 1952, Marie Tharp, Heezen's research assistant at the Lamont Geological Observatory, began work on a map of the floor of the Atlantic using the echo-soundings that had begun to accumulate, mostly from the *Atlantis I* expeditions. Her preliminary efforts convinced her that there was indeed a rift valley bisecting the Mid-Atlantic Ridge, but it was only after many more soundings, plus land profiles, that Heezen and Tharp became convinced that it was real. Marie Tharp had plotted a V-shaped valley that ran the length of the ridge, and it appeared—to Heezen's consternation—to confirm continental drift. According to Tharp, when he saw that the valley ran down the center of the Mid-Atlantic Ridge, Heezen groaned and said, "It can't be—it looks just like continental drift." (In 1952, hardly anyone took the idea of continental drift seriously.) As early as 1954, with the publication of Beno Gutenberg and Charles Richter's *Seismicity of the Earth,* it was recognized that there was a belt of shallow earthquakes that followed the Ridge. (Charles Richter devised the eponymous scale that measures the magnitude of earthquakes.)

At the table adjoining Tharp's, Howard Foster,* a drafting assistant of

---

* In a letter to me dated April 5, 1995, Marie Tharp wrote, "Howard Foster was a graduate of the Boston School of Fine Arts. He was totally deaf. His parents were the live-in servants of a very wealthy man in Woods Hole, and this generous employer took it upon himself to send Howard to the School of Fine Arts. Howard plotted thousands of earthquakes on our maps. Having exhausted this project, he went on to plot sounding profiles of depth vs. time of the many *Vema* cruises. His profiles were so beautifully, neatly, and carefully drawn that they aided greatly in our bathymetric studies."

Heezen's, was plotting recorded earthquakes. In an article in *Scientific American*, Heezen wrote, "In 1953, Marie Tharp and I were making a detailed physiographic diagram of the floor of the Atlantic, based on a large number of echo-sounding profiles. As the preliminary sketch emerged, Tharp realized that she had drawn a deep canyon down the middle of the Mid-Atlantic Ridge. Detailed study of the profiles confirmed the existence of this gully. It was discovered, moreover, that the rift coincides with what Ewing and Heezen in 1956 called 'The Mid-Atlantic Ridge Seismic Belt.' " They wrote:

> The Atlantic belt of earthquake epicenters follows the crest of the Mid-Atlantic Ridge and its prolongations into the Arctic and Indian Oceans with a precision which becomes more apparent with the improvement of our knowledge of the topography and of epicenter locations. These are all shallow shocks. Their apparent departure from the narrow crests of the ridge seldom exceeds the probable error of location. The crest is 30 to 60 miles wide, very rough, and on a typical section shows several peaks at depths of about 800 to 1100 fathoms. There is usually a conspicuous median depression reaching depths of about 2300 fathoms. This is interpreted as an active rift zone which continues through the African rift valleys.

Seismographic data indicated a belt of earthquake epicenters along the bottom of the Atlantic, Indian, South Pacific, and Arctic oceans, and in 1956, Ewing and Heezen announced "that a continuous rifted ridge would be found to coincide with the mid-ocean epicenter belt and its branches throughout the world." In 1957, Heezen constructed a globe that showed the sedimentary basins and the Mid-Ocean Ridge, with the rift valley as a bright line encircling the globe. He took the globe to Princeton, where he showed it to Harry Hess, who said, "Young man, you have shaken the foundations of geology" (Sullivan 1974). Even though Ewing and Heezen had drawn the physiographic maps, they did not know what the rift actually looked like. (It probably didn't look much like the red-painted squiggle on Heezen's model.) At the First International Oceanographic Congress in New York in 1959, Tharp and Heezen saw a Cousteau film that was taken from a remote-controlled sled camera, and Tharp later wrote that it showed "great black cliffs of the rift valley, sprinkled with white glob ooze . . . convincing a few doubters at a critical time that our rift valley was really there." It was in that year that Heezen, Tharp, and Ewing published "The Floor of the Ocean: The North Atlantic," which was the first ever map of its kind and included everything then known about the Mid-Ocean Ridge.

Once the worldwide rift network had been identified, Heezen, Ewing, and Tharp confirmed that the Mid-Ocean Ridge is the largest single feature on the planet: a mountain range that is 45,000 miles long and characterized in the Atlantic by a central rift valley between roughly parallel mountain ranges. Heezen called it "the wound that never heals." The Ridge ranges in width from 300 to 1,000 miles and occupies approximately one-third of the Atlantic basin. In *The Floor of the Sea,* William Wertenbaker describes the Ridge:

> The Mid-Atlantic section of the Mid-Ocean Ridge rises nearly two miles above the adjacent plains. It fills the central third of the ocean basin. Lofty peaks at its crest soar ten thousand feet above the floor of the rift valley without intervening shoulders or steps. The mountains are harsh and un-weathered, draped only in a light sprinkle of sediment. While the Ridge gets steadily lower toward its flanks, the peaks there are just as sharp and ragged as the crest. It is like the inside of a shark's mouth. . . .

On either side of the ridge, the ocean floor is almost perfectly level. Over broad reaches, the abyssal plains will not vary in depth as much as a meter. In fact, they are the flattest regions on the face of the earth. Here the plain rises gradually—a rise of less than one part in one thousand—toward the land until it becomes a rise, a shelf, and then the continental slope before it finally emerges from the sea as a continental landmass.

During World War II, Harry Hess, a Princeton University geophysicist, commanded the USS *Cape Johnson,* an attack transport fitted with a device called a fathometer, an echo-sounder designed to draw continuous profiles of the sea floor that would enable troop-carrying ships to approach as close as possible to unknown coastlines. By studying the profiles, he became aware of a series of flat-topped submarine mountains he named "guyots," after the nineteenth-century Princeton geologist Arnold Guyot. He realized that these guyots were volcanic islands formed along an undersea ridge which at one time were above sea level (ordinary erosion would explain their peculiar flat tops) but had somehow submerged and drifted away from their original locations.

Like almost all of his contemporaries, Hess did not believe in continen-tal drift, so he had no way of explaining the wandering mountains. After much agonizing speculation, he concluded that the mid-ocean ridges are underlain by the hot, rising elements of convection cells* in the earth's mantle, and that the sea floor is being carried like a conveyor belt away from the ridge axes and thence under the marginal trenches of the continents. In 1962, he published a paper entitled "The History of Ocean Basins," which he referred to as "an essay in geopoetry," and introduced it with this disclaimer: "The birth of the

---

* Convection currents on a smaller scale move the hottest parts of a cup of coffee (or a bathtub) to the top, and then, as they cool, back toward the bottom. If a constantly generated heat source is included in the equation, a continuous cycle soon gets established, with the hotter ele-ments rising and the cooler descending.

oceans is a matter of conjecture, the subsequent history is obscure, and the present structure is just beginning to be understood."

The actual term "sea-floor spreading" originated with R. S. Dietz, who, simultaneously with Hess, proposed that the oceanic ridge and rift systems were created by rising currents of material spreading outward from the ocean floors. Then a University of Toronto physicist, J. Tuzo Wilson, suggested that the earth's surface is divided into several giant slabs called lithospheric plates, which interact at junctions that Heezen and Tharp had originally named "strike-slip faults," but that Wilson renamed "transform faults."* In her 1982 summary of the story of mapping the sea floor, Marie Tharp wrote, "However, for historical priority reasons and for the more pragmatic reason of putting names on a chart, these great shear faults are still called fracture zones."

W. Jason Morgan of Princeton extended the transform fault concept to the spherical surface of the earth and suggested that the lithosphere (which he referred to as the "tectosphere") is broken into numerous plates, which are moving either toward, away from, or sideways past each other. It now appeared that the Atlantic sea floor was spreading apart on both sides of a crack down the middle of the Mid-Atlantic Ridge, moving the North American plate away from the Eurasian and African plates and carrying the continents with them.

Ever since 1909, when Bernard Brunhes discovered that some ancient lava flows in France were imprinted with a magnetic polarity that was the opposite of older and younger rocks on either side, reverse magnetism was known but not understood. In 1929, Monotori Matuyama found many rocks in Japan that also showed reversed polarity, but he did no better than Brunhes in explaining what this discovery meant. The idea that the north pole becomes the south pole was so ridiculous that it was dismissed out of hand, even though the evidence for such occurrences was becoming more and more compelling. In a 1967 *Scientific American* article, Allan Cox, Richard Doell, and Brent Dalrymple of the U.S. Geological Survey wrote, "The idea that the earth's magnetic field reverses at first seemed so preposterous that one immediately suspects a violation of some basic law of physics, and most investigators working on reversals have sometimes wondered if the reversals are really compatible with the physical theory of magnetism."

The poles have switched position, roughly every million years for a thou-

---

* The three basic forces that control the movement of the earth's crust are tension, shear, and compression. "Tension" is expressed as a rift valley, first recognized on land as the Rift Valley of East Africa, which was seen to be a terrestrial continuation of the Mid-Oceanic Rift Valley. "Shear" is the sideways movement of sections of the rift valley, referred to as "fracture zones" or "strike-slip faults." When one plate of the lithosphere bashes into another, one of the plates is raised up, producing mountains, while the other subducts beneath it, creating a trench. The paradigmatic example of this "compression" can be seen where the Andes rise out of the Pacific on the west coast of South America.

sand million years, and the process appears to be speeding up. The field seems to remain one way for about a million years (a period known as an "epoch"), but it may be interrupted by switches called "events" that last for only tens of thousands of years. (The most recent period is known as the Brunhes epoch, named after the French scientist who first detected reversed magnetism in the rocks of the Massif Central. During the Matuyama epoch, the 1.8 million years that preceded the Brunhes, the earth's polarity was reversed.) Meticulous examination of paleomagnetic geological evidence showed that some 700,000 years ago, the north magnetic pole was in Antarctica, and according to William Wertenbaker's most helpful discussion, "it will eventually return there, creating navigational problems." (When the poles again reverse themselves, compass needles—if there are any—will point to magnetic south.) "Why it makes the excursion it does," continued Wertenbaker, "is thus far better known to itself than to magneticians, though it does leave plentiful signs of its passage."*

When lava cools, the ferrous particles align themselves with the earth's prevailing magnetic field, and therefore represent a "fossil" record of the field at that time. (Sediments can also be magnetized, but only one ten-thousandth as strongly as the basalt, which means that the magnetism of the underlying rock can be measured without significant interference.) First noticed in the 1950s by Lamont Observatory scientists who towed magnetometers behind research vessels, and then by a Scripps Institution survey of the Pacific off northern California, the ocean floor was striated with bands of magnetism of differing intensity, parallel to the mid-ocean ridges. What did these mean? Various geologists suggested various answers, but in 1963, Cambridge University's Frederick Vine and D. H. Matthews published an article in *Nature* in which they suggested that the oceans of the world were paved with parallel bands of rock, divided more or less equally between magnetic anomalies. They wrote: "If spreading of the ocean floor occurs, blocks of alternately normal and reversely magnetized material would drift away from the centre of the ridge and parallel to the crest of it." To Vine and J. Tuzo Wilson, who studied two sides of a ridge near Vancouver Island, this indicated that the bands of reversed polarity of new sea floor formed at the mid-ocean ridges, since it was seen that both sides of the ridge were striped symmetrically. This was a clear indication that the sea floor was spreading and pushing the continents around. Thus, we had a *proof* that the seismically active ridge was producing new sea-floor material that was moving away from the center, as if on matched conveyor belts.

---

* Now comes the theory that the magnetic flips can occur in *weeks,* rather than tens of thousands of years. In an article in *Nature* (April 20, 1995), Robert Coe, Michel Prévot, and Pierre Camps studied a lava flow at Steens Mountain in Oregon and concluded that the magnetic field shifted at the astonishing rate of six degrees a day over an eight-day period. The simplest explanation for this phenomenon is that the field was in the process of changing when the lava flow cooled.

As James Heirtzler wrote in his 1968 *Scientific American* article on sea-floor spreading, "The magnetic lineations in the ocean floor serve as 'footprints' of the continents, marking their consecutive positions before they reached their present positions."

Two Lamont graduate students, Walter Pitman and Ellen Herron, were participants in the 1965 cruise of the *Eltanin*, a research vessel taking magnetic surveys over the Juan de Fuca Ridge in the Pacific. Copies of two profiles (known as Eltanin-19) were accidentally laid face-to-face on top of each other, and Pitman realized that the bilateral symmetry was perfect—unequivocal proof of the Vine-Matthews hypothesis. By the 1966 meeting of the American Geophysical Union, virtually every geologist and geophysicist had been converted to the new faith. In *A Revolution in the Earth Sciences,* Oxford lecturer A. Hallam wrote:

> The year 1966 was undoubtedly one of breakthrough for the sea-floor spreading hypothesis. Before the year was out many Earth scientists began to take the idea of lateral mobility of continents seriously for the first time. Nowhere was the change in attitudes more dramatic than at the Lamont Observatory, which under the formidable directorship of Maurice Ewing had come to be without peer as an Earth sciences oceanographic institute. By all accounts the complete flip-over in beliefs of some of the leading personnel was as sudden and unequivocal as a magnetic reversal.*

The existence of magnetic anomalies was supported by the Scripps data collected off the west coast of North America (Raff 1961), and was further confirmed by Heirtzler, LePichon, and Baron in 1965, when they analyzed the results of airborne magnetic surveys flown over the Reykjanes Ridge, southwest of Iceland. "We found," wrote Heirtzler, "that the anomalies were linear and symmetrically distributed parallel to the axis of the ridge. This strongly supports the idea of sea-floor spreading from the ridge and the formation of magnetic anomalies, just as Vine and Matthews had suggested." The discovery that the earth's magnetic field reverses its polarity every million years or so firmly established sea-floor spreading as the phenomenon responsible for the changing surface of the earth.

Paleogeologists are no closer to explaining the flipping of the magnetic poles than they are to explaining the magnetic field in the first place, but as

---

* According to Marie Tharp, "Ewing held magnetics in very low esteem and saw no potential value in it. Nevertheless, he insisted that magnetic data from the towed fish be collected on every cruise. And so it was that a large collection of data grew, but no theories from the theoreticians or students to explain magnetic fields, anomalies, or pole-shifting. When a break-through first came in 1966, nearly twenty years later, there was abundant data available from *Atlantis I* and all of the *Vema* cruises."

usual, theories abound.* Considering the occurrence of tektite fields at scattered locations around the world, Bruce Heezen suggested that the flipping of the field may occur when the earth is struck by an alien body. Tektites, which have been found on the east coast of North America, in eastern Europe, in West Africa, and in Australia, are tiny glassy fragments that may represent splashes of rock thrown up in molten form from the catastrophic impact of a meteor or a comet. One such event took place some 700,000 years ago, coinciding with the beginning of the Brunhes epoch. Summing up his article on sea-floor spreading, Heirtzler wrote, "Every few months there are changes in the earth's rotational motion that effect sea-floor spreading and cause the earthquakes associated with it. If the change is large enough it may even reverse the earth's magnetic field."

Cox, Doell, and Dalrymple called the earth's magnetism "one of the best-described and least-understood of all planetary phenomena." Permanent magnets lose their magnetism when heated beyond a certain point (known as the Curie temperature), but this does not happen to the earth. While the central core of the earth is solid iron and nickel, the next 1,500 miles are molten metal. As the earth spins, the movement of the molten metal generates convection currents within this layer, which follow complicated paths because of the rotation of the earth. Since electrical conductors can generate magnetic fields, the entire planet acts as a permanent magnet with an electric field shaped roughly like that of a bar magnet with lines of force sprouting out of the planet near the South Pole and looping back toward the North Pole. (Mars has no core, and no field; neither does the moon.)

In 1952, Gordon Lill and Carl Alexis of the Office of Naval Research in Washington formed the American Miscellaneous Society (AMSOC) in an attempt to pigeonhole requests that came into ONR that could only be grouped under the heading of miscellaneous.† Requests considered too impractical for consideration elsewhere fell to AMSOC, and the suggestion that a hole ought to be drilled into the earth's mantle was submitted by oceanographers Harry Hess and Walter Munk. The first proposal was rejected by the National Science Foundation, but when AMSOC affiliated itself with the National Acad-

---

* The latest theory, which explains not only the earth's magnetism but also the flipping of the poles, was advanced in 1995 by Ronald E. Cohen of the Carnegie Institution of Washington. He suggested that the inner core of the earth was not merely solid metal but rather a single, giant crystal made of iron with its own magnetic field. A crystal core would also transmit seismic waves faster in one direction than another, explaining why the waves travel faster from north to south than they do from east to west. (Broad 1995b)

† The nature of the society at its inception can be divined from its five divisions: Etceterology, Phenomenology, Calamitology, Generalogy, and Triviology. It also became affiliated with the Committee for Cooperating with Visitors from Outer Space, and the Society for Informing Animals of Their Taxonomic Positions. The motto of the AMSOC was *Illegitimum non carborundum*—"Don't let the bastards grind you down."

emy of Sciences, the proposal breezed through. By 1957, the society had established a Committee on Deep Drilling, headed by Roger Revelle, the director of the Scripps Institute of Oceanography. Willard Bascom, a specialist in ocean engineering, was named staff director, and in a 1959 article in *Scientific American,* he coined the name "Project Mohole." (He wrote, "To obtain a sample of the mantle, we must drill a hole through the Moho. A Mohole.")

From land, the mantle lies under 20 to 25 miles of crustal covering, but under the ocean, the route can be much shorter—as little as 6 miles. (To a congressional subcommittee, Roger Revelle described the earth as "a golf ball that has a liquid core surrounded by a very elastic and quite heavy mantle that, in turn, is surrounded by a crust of slag, like the paint on the surface of the golf ball.") Among the locations considered for the Mohole drilling were the Puerto Rico Trench, where the Moho was only 4 miles below the sea floor, and the region of Clipperton Island, some 300 miles south of Cabo San Lucas, the southern tip of Baja California. In March 1961, the floating rig named *CUSS I* (for the sponsoring oil companies: Continental, Union, Shell, and Superior) set sail from San Diego, headed for the first test site, some 250 miles to the south. As described by the novelist (and sometime oceanographer) John Steinbeck, "CUSS I has the sleek race lines of an outhouse standing on a garbage scow."* Moored in water 2 miles deep, they drilled through the sea floor for about 600 feet through a layer of green clay and ooze, and brought up a small sample of basalt and hardened sediment.

That was the easy part. Having successfully sampled the bottom, Project Mohole now had to drill through another three miles of rock, and there was no rig in existence capable of such a feat. Revelle estimated that the continuation of the project—they had, so to speak, only scratched the surface—would require another ship, and another $20 to $25 million. AMSOC removed itself from the project and recommended that Project Mohole be entrusted to a "prime contractor." After asking for bids, the National Science Foundation chose the Houston engineering firm Brown & Root, who submitted an elaborate design for a 58,000-square-foot drilling platform with stabilizing columns resting on submarine hulls, which was to cost $40 million to build and $9 million per year to operate. In 1964, Daniel Greenberg published three articles in *Science* under the heading of "Mohole—the Project That Went Awry," calling

* Steinbeck shipped aboard *CUSS I* as supercargo, and in a *Life* magazine article (April 15, 1961), he wrote, "The drilling men are the cream of a very special profession already trained in offshore drilling in shallow water. Then we have engineers of a dozen kinds, oceanographers, geologists, paleontologists, petrologists, geophysicists, and seismologists. Our expedition should destroy the old and well loved error that doers and thinkers are different breeds—and about time too." Of the crew he wrote, "The men step like cats. There is nothing clumsy about them, as the steel sections of pipe rise and are screwed together and lowered, the drillers move with the timing and precision of a corps de ballet. They would throw me overboard if they knew I said this or thought it."

it "a running sore" and "a classic case of how not to run a big research program." Rumors of political payoffs surfaced, and the death of the project's major supporter, Representative Albert Thomas of Houston, meant that it was rudderless. By 1966, the estimated cost had escalated to $147 million, and Congress, who could see no military applications for drilling a hole in the bottom of the sea (except beating the Russians to it), killed the project.

While the Mohole project was winding down, interest in marine geology was not, and a contract was awarded to Scripps Institute of Oceanography for a Deep Sea Drilling Project (DSDP) to conduct scientific programs that were formulated by JOIDES, the Joint Oceanographic Institutions for Deep Earth Sampling. (The Joint Institutions were Lamont-Doherty, Woods Hole, Scripps, the University of Washington, and the University of Miami.) The ship chosen to carry out these programs was the *Glomar Challenger* (named for the original *Challenger* and Global Marine, the company that owned her), a 400-foot-long research vessel with a 200-foot derrick amidships, making her look for all the world like an oil well that has gone to sea. (Her appearance was far from coincidental; the technology for deep-sea drilling came directly from the oil industry.) Sophisticated position-keeping systems—some adapted from the ill-fated *CUSS I*—enabled scientists to remain over the drill holes for as much as a week at a time, regardless of ocean or weather conditions. *Glomar Challenger* operated steadily from 1968 until 1983, and during that fifteen-year period, according to Walter Sullivan, "contributed more to the history of the oceans than any expedition to date."

The wide-ranging *Glomar Challenger* is among the best-documented research vessels of all time. Journalist Peter Briggs sailed aboard the drill-ship for the second research leg (Hoboken to Dakar, October–November 1968), and got a whole book out of it (200,000,000 *Years Beneath the Sea,* 1971). Melvin Peterson and N. Terence Edgar also wrote about the ship's maiden voyage in the June 1969 issue of *Oceans* magazine. Walter Sullivan's *Continents in Motion* contains a history of the drill-ship's accomplishments up to 1974, and Kenneth Hsu, a well-known sedimentologist (and now professor of geology at the Swiss Federal Institute of Technology in Zurich), wrote two books about the ship: *Challenger at Sea: A Ship That Revolutionized Earth Science,* and *The Mediterranean Was a Desert: A Voyage of the Glomar Challenger.* Under co-chief scientists Lamar Worzel and Maurice Ewing, the first destination of the *Glomar Challenger* was the Sigsbee Abyssal Plain in the Gulf of Mexico, midway between Louisiana and the Yucatán Peninsula. Primarily for practice, the initial hole on the shakedown voyage was drilled 2,520 feet into the sediment 10,000 feet below the surface.

Much of the story of this research vessel does not directly affect our study of the deep Atlantic, but voyage number three (known as "Leg 3") was designated to test the theory of sea-floor spreading. Hsu was aboard for that cruise (December 1, 1968, to January 24, 1969), and he wrote:

> I did not believe in sea-floor spreading. I did not believe in the simple for-mula. I did not believe that sediment at the bottom of the hole would be 38 million years old; I was secretly hoping that it would be much, much older. Not only would we be able to look farther back in the history of the ocean; we also would disprove once and for all the ridiculous theory by the brash young graduate student from Chicago [Vine].

Cores were brought up from nine sites on the Ridge between Namibia and Brazil in the South Atlantic. While Hsu hoped it would not happen, the results of these drillings proved conclusively that the spreading concept was correct: the farther from the Ridge, the older the rocks. Conceding defeat, Hsu wrote, "The drilling campaign of Leg 3 was one of the greatest triumphs in geology. The theory of sea-floor spreading is right. The unbelievable as-sumption of a linear rate of sea-floor spreading is correct, at least for the last 70 million years." Sullivan became rapturous about the process:

> Today the active volcanoes that rise from the Mid-Atlantic Ridge are few and far between—those of Jan Mayen, Iceland, the Azores, and Tristan da Cunha—but, as the Atlantic was being born, this activity must have been on a formidable scale, with new volcanoes thrusting from the sea, dark-ening the skies, and exploding under cataclysmic steam pressure when rupture of their walls allowed the sea to pour in. . . .

At the same time that the *Glomar Challenger* was drilling holes in the sea floor, another line of inquiry was being pursued. Beginning with William Beebe's bathysphere in 1930, and followed by Cousteau's *Deepstar* and Woods Hole's *Alvin,* scientists were sending themselves into the depths to see for themselves what the bottom looked like and what lived there. The story of sub-mersible development and exploration is told elsewhere in this volume (see the following chapter), but every effort—from the bathysphere to *Alvin's* tri-umphs (among them the finding and retrieval of a lost H-bomb off Spain; the discovery of the previously unsuspected hydrothermal vent animals; the in-vestigation of the *Titanic*)—has added incrementally to our knowledge of the sea floor.

In the summer of 1994, a combined team of American, Japanese, and Eu-ropean scientists began their investigation of the TAG (Trans-Atlantic Geo-traverse), a huge mound located on the Mid-Atlantic Ridge, some 2,000 miles east of Miami. According to an article in *The New York Times* for August 9 (en-titled "Weird Mound Offers Clues to Mysteries of the Deep"), "Never before has a ship drilled into a deep, hot volcanic vent, and the prospect has put scientists in a state of high anticipation." The actual drilling will originate with the surface vessel *Joides Resolution,* a 471-foot-long vessel equipped with a drilling derrick that is twenty stories tall. At depths of up to two miles, the Japanese *Shinkai-6500* (currently the world's deepest-diving submersible) will be wiring the mound with sensor packages to measure the temperature and photograph the smoking chimneys. (One chimney that is 150 feet high has been nicknamed "Godzilla.") The instruments will be recovered in 1996 by trusty *Alvin.* In the *Times* article, marine geologist Peter Rona of Rutgers University is quoted as saying, "Although they're the most remote and inaccessible sites on earth, they have a major effect on the atmosphere. They're a major component in the dynamics of ocean environment and the climate."

Exploring the Deep

There have always been formidable obstacles to submarine exploration, not the least of which is the almost totally inhospitable nature of water. Man was obviously not designed to function in this medium, since he has lungs that breathe air, awkward arms and legs that are a poor substitute for fins or flippers, and a visual apparatus that functions so poorly in the aquatic environment as to be virtually useless underwater. Despite these handicaps, however, the urge to explore the depths of the sea has been almost irresistible. Of course, it has always been possible for a swimmer to hold his breath and dive toward the bottom, but given the inaptitude of the human body for aquatic pursuits, the best an unequipped diver could manage was about a three-minute stay.*

Enclosing the human body in some sort of container that is impervious to the pernicious action of water is the first step toward underwater exploration. Humans have to breathe, however, and dropping them below the surface in a closed container with windows might eliminate the problems of underwater vision and locomotion, but the problem of oxygen deprivation still remains. A device was required that would enable an aquanaut to breathe, see, and, to a lesser extent, move around. In addition to the fascination of exploring the underwater world, there were (and are) more prosaic reasons for men to remain submerged for protracted periods of time. Ships sink, often with valuable cargoes, and men have always sought ways to bring up either or both. The exigencies of naval warfare encouraged various inventors to attempt to plant bombs surreptitiously, or otherwise sink enemy warships without being noticed. These

---

* The record for a free dive—that is, without benefit of breathing apparatus—is held by Frenchman Jacques Mayol, who dived to a depth of 328 feet off the island of Elba in the Mediterranean in 1976. He descended down a line on a special weighted sled, and held his breath for three minutes and forty seconds. For comparison, the sperm whale, a mammal that has to dive to prodigious depths in pursuit of its food, can hold its breath for an hour and a half.

In this fifteenth-century woodcut, Alexander the Great is shown being lowered into the sea in what appears to be a glass-sided box, thus becoming history's first submarine explorer.

problems motivated people throughout the ages to invent a submersible, enclosed capsule, in which a man could accomplish his often nefarious deeds in the heretofore hidden and inaccessible world beneath the waves.

Alexander the Great is considered the father of submersible diving, primarily because of legends that tell of his descent in a "cage" (sometimes it is referred to as a "barrel") of glass. No further explanation of the Macedonian king's craft or exploits exists—the story first appeared in a thirteenth-century French manuscript—but salvage divers of sixteenth-century Italy are known to have descended in bells containing air reservoirs to explore sunken barges, and Leonardo da Vinci (1452–1519) toyed with the idea of a device for underwater exploration.* In 1578, an Englishman named William Bourne described

---

* Leonardo's device, known only from his sketchbooks, appeared to consist of a breathing tube that was kept at the surface by a float. A diver using such an arrangement only four feet below the surface would be unable to expand his lungs to overcome the external water pressure, and therefore could not draw air into the tube. Unlike water, air is compressible, and as water pressure increases around it, it occupies a progressively smaller space, whether or not the water is actually in contact with the air-holding vessel, be it a submarine or human lungs. As a submersible descends, the air pressure in the submersible and the pressure in the lungs of the occupants remains equal, and as long as enough fresh air is provided, the occupants of a submersible can continue to breathe.

a primitive submarine in his *Inventions and Devices* (subtitled "Very Necessary for Generalles, Captaines or Leaders of Men"), a vessel with a rigid wooden outer hull and a flexible inner hull that was made of leather. The double hull, of course, is still used in submarine design, as is his concept of submerging or surfacing the vessel by varying the amount of water it displaced. As far as we know, Bourne's invention was never implemented, but in 1620, a Dutch physician named Cornelis van Drebbel moved to London as tutor to the children of King James I. He delighted Londoners—the King among them—with his "submarine displays," which evidently consisted of rowers powering a greased leather boat downward until it was awash in the Thames. Van Drebbel, who dabbled in magic and perpetual motion, claimed to have discovered a "liquor" that could purify the air in his submarine, but he was so secretive about his inventions that the nature of his air purifier was never revealed.

John Wilkins, who was the bishop of Chester (and Oliver Cromwell's brother-in-law), published a little book in 1648 that he called *An Ark for Submarine Navigation; the Difficulties and Consequences of Such a Contrivance*. In his book (which evidently incorporates the first use of the word "submarine"), Wilkins cited submarines as *private* ("A man may thus go to any Coast of the World invisibly without being discovered or prevented in his journey"); "safe from the Uncertainty of Tides"; and free from "Pirates and Robbers which do so infest other voyages" and from "Ice and Great Frosts which do so endanger the Passage towards the Poles."

In 1653, a Frenchman named DeSon invented a wooden vessel that was reinforced with iron girders, and driven by an internal paddle wheel, but the clockwork engine was not nearly strong enough to move the 72-foot wooden craft and the project was abandoned. The German prince Charles of Hesse-

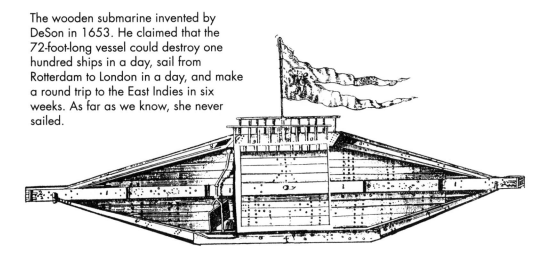

The wooden submarine invented by DeSon in 1653. He claimed that the 72-foot-long vessel could destroy one hundred ships in a day, sail from Rotterdam to London in a day, and make a round trip to the East Indies in six weeks. As far as we know, she never sailed.

Kassel commissioned the Frenchman Denis Papin to design a submarine for him, and in 1695, Papin first produced an iron-reinforced tin box, and then a wooden vessel that could deliver underwater explosives. When the Landgrave Charles went to war, Papin's submarine did not go with him. An English carpenter named John Day refitted the 50-ton sloop *Maria* as an underwater boat by installing seventy-five empty hogsheads amidships, and attached 30 tons of ballast that could be released from inside the cabin. His announced plan was to sink to 130 feet in the harbor at Plymouth in June 1774, remain below for twelve hours, then release the ballast and rise to the surface. The *Maria* sank to the bottom of the harbor easily enough, but neither Day nor his converted sloop were ever seen again. Day therefore has the dubious honor of being the first submarine fatality.

The next important phase of submarine design occurred across the Atlantic in 1775, when the American David Bushnell produced the remarkable *Turtle*. During the War of Independence, when British warships had blockaded the Atlantic coast, George Washington was seeking a way to break the blockade, and also, if possible, to disable the British warships. He commissioned Bushnell to solve the problem, and the Yale College undergraduate developed an ovoid vessel that floated upright on its long axis and was made of barrel staves and iron in the form of two tortoise shells, waterproofed with a thick coating of tar, and strengthened amidships by a baulk that also served as a seat for the pilot. (It actually looked more like an egg than a turtle.) An internal water tank that could be flooded and emptied by a foot pedal provided the means to raise and lower the little vessel in the water. Its propeller was powered by hand-turned screws, and the tight little boat could hold enough air to enable the pilot to remain below for about half an hour. Piloted by one Ezra Lee, the *Turtle* attempted to attach a bomb to HMS *Eagle,* the flagship of the British fleet blockading New York Harbor, but because the submarine's screw device could not pierce the copper-sheathed hull of the British warship, the attempt was a failure.

Bushnell's successor in submarine design was Robert Fulton, who went on to create the first successful steamboat. Because the memory of the War of Independence was still fresh, Fulton hated England, so he emigrated to France in 1797 and offered to design a submarine for the Directoire. The French Ministry of Marine thought his demands for payment for each English ship that was destroyed were excessive, and rejected his proposals. (The French also believed that submarines were comparable to fire ships, which were universally despised as weapons of war.) Under Napoleon, who came to power in 1800, the new Minister of Marine had no such reservations and awarded Fulton 10,000 francs to design and build a submarine. The result was the *Nautilus,* a trim little bullet of a boat that was constructed of copper sheet-

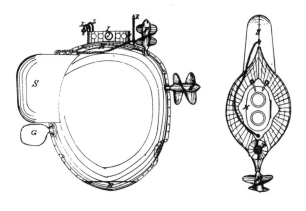

David Bushnell's *Turtle* was commissioned by George Washington in 1775 for use against British warships in the War of Independence. The egg-shaped vessel failed in its attempt to attach a bomb to HMS *Eagle*, the flagship of the British fleet.

ing over iron frames. She was equipped with a fan-shaped sail (to relieve the strain on her three-man crew, who powered the vessel by hand-operated screws), a conning tower for viewing, a depth-keeping hydroplane, and an explosive device that was trailed on a line. The *Nautilus* descended to a depth of 20 feet in the Seine (where the water was only 25 feet deep), and remained below for an hour, but the French reversed themselves again and decided that underwater sneak attacks were unethical, an opinion expressed by Admiral de Crès, who said the invention was "good only for Algerians and pirates."

Despite his professed hatred of England, Fulton succumbed to the blandishments of British agents and took his invention across the Channel in 1804, where he successfully demonstrated its capabilities to Prime Minister William Pitt. With Pitt's death in 1805, however, a change in the Admiralty revived the objections to Fulton's methods of warfare (Nelson had just demonstrated at Trafalgar how the British navy preferred to fight its battles), and even after Fulton had shown that his submarine could implant a charge and sink the 200-ton brig *Dorothea,* Admiral the Earl of St. Vincent said, "Pitt was the greatest fool that ever existed to encourage a mode of warfare which those who commanded the seas did not want, and which, if successful, would deprive them of it."

The German Wilhelm Bauer, a twenty-eight-year-old corporal in the Bavarian Light Horse artillery, designed the *Brandtaucher* ("fire-diver") in 1850, a porpoise-shaped affair made of sheet iron. Although not a shot was fired, the fear of an underwater attack caused Danish blockaders to retreat from the harbor at Kiel. (Bauer was almost killed during one of the *Brandtaucher*'s trials in the harbor at Kiel in 1851; the little submarine went out of control and plunged

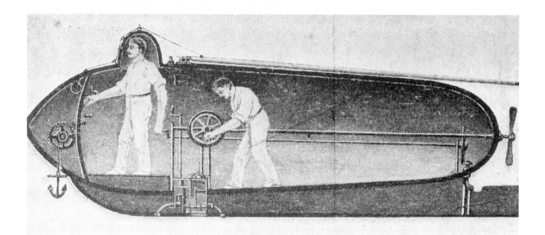

Drawing of Robert Fulton's submarine *Nautilus*, designed around 1800. In this cross section, the hand-cranked screws can be seen, as can the crank that raised the mast (lying flat along the top of the vessel), which was hoisted when the ship was at the surface.

Wilhelm Bauer's *Seeteufel* ("sea-devil"), a 52-foot-long, treadmill-powered submarine boat. In this cutaway view, we can see the little orchestra that is said to have played the Russian national anthem—underwater—at the 1856 coronation of Tsar Alexander II in Kronstadt Harbor.

nose first into the mud. With water pouring into the ruptured hull, he persuaded the two frightened crewmen to sit tight until the air pressure in the hull equaled the water pressure outside and he could open the hatches, enabling the men to swim to the surface.) Then he designed the *Plongeur-Marin* in 1851, and like Fulton before him, he tried to peddle his ideas to any government that would listen. He aroused interest in Austria and England, but his first real commission came from the Russians, for whom in 1855 he built the *Seeteufel* ("sea-devil"), a craft that was 52 feet long and 12 feet wide. She still relied upon the muscle power of treadmills, and although the submarine made an incredible 134 successful dives before being lost at sea, she never actually saw military service. The story—probably apocryphal—is told of the coronation of Tsar Alexander II in 1856, where the *Seeteufel,* with a little orchestra aboard, descended into Kronstadt Harbor in what is now Romania and played the Russian national anthem, the strains of which could be heard at the surface.

As James Dugan wrote in *Man Under the Sea,* "Submarines turned up in strange places and times." An example was the boat built in 1851 by a Chicago shoemaker named Lodner Phillips that was tested in Lake Michigan and remained submerged for ten hours. Phillips was killed when his submarine failed to surface during another test in Lake Erie, near Buffalo. In *The Illustrated History of the Submarine,* Edward Horton wrote:

> It will be apparent that so far the submarine, or submersible boat, had demonstrably failed to measure up to any of the claims made for it. It had neither assisted in underwater exploration nor become the scourge of surface warships. Whatever its potential (and as a mine-layer even the most primitive submarine has potential) it had proved hazardous only to its crews, and in large measure could be written off as the plaything of eccentrics.

It was during America's Civil War that the submarine achieved its potential as a device of war. Handicapped at the start by the lack of naval power to compete with the Union's, the Confederates pioneered the use of underwater attack vessels. An important contributor to the Confederacy's submarine intentions was Matthew Fontaine Maury, who was employed at the U.S. Naval Observatory at the outbreak of the war and had to choose between his employers in Washington and his loyalty to his native Virginia. He resigned his commission and reported for duty to the governor of Virginia, who assigned him to his advisory council. Maury diligently applied himself to the problems of underwater warfare, emphasizing floating mines. Of Maury's contributions, Alex Roland wrote, "It seems to be beyond doubt that he was the one man most responsible for introducing underwater warfare in the Confederacy."

The first official U.S. Navy attempt at a submarine was designed by Sko-

The *Intelligent Whale*, launched just as the Civil War was ending, never saw military service, and since 1865 has been docked outside the Department of the Navy in Washington.

vol Merriam, with the $15,000 financing to be supplied by private investors August Price and Cornelius Bristol. The result was the man-powered *Intelligent Whale*, which lacked a suitable weapons system and, as it turned out, suitable targets, since the *Whale* was launched just as the war was ending. The Navy continued testing the *Intelligent Whale* (later dubbed the "Intelligent Elephant"), but the 30-foot-long, ocarina-shaped vessel came to rest at the Naval Shipyard in Washington, where it remains to this day.

Submersible boats never quite made it into the Union navy's fleet, but the Confederacy managed to launch the first submarine to sink an enemy ship in warfare. Originally, submarines were seen primarily as a means to circumvent blockades, but the *Davids* (collectively—and optimistically—named because of their giant-killing potential) were equipped with spar torpedoes,*

---

* In the Oxford English Dictionary, a "torpedo" is defined as "a case charged with gunpowder designed to explode under water after a given interval so as to destroy any vessel in its immediate vicinity"—in other words, what we now refer to as a mine. (According to Drew Middleton [*Submarine*], "David Farragut was talking about mines, not torpedoes, when he uttered his celebrated 'Damn the torpedoes! Go ahead!'" at Mobile Bay.) It was not until the Whitehead torpedo of 1868 that the term was applied to a cigar-shaped, free-running device that enabled submarines to attack ships from a safe distance.

which protruded far enough in front of the bow to avoid—they hoped—mutual destruction. Because the *Davids* were steam-powered, they had to leave the hatch open to get air for the boiler, and a ship running awash with an open hatch at the surface is a poor design indeed; it is an invitation to a swamping. The first attack, on the Union ship *Ironsides* in Charleston Harbor in October 1863, was a failure (the *David* sank and the crew abandoned ship), but the following year, the Confederate navy introduced the *Hunley,* a modification on the *David* theme that was powered by an eight-man crankshaft and designed to run completely submerged. Unfortunately, the *Hunley* also had to keep her hatch open, which is a bad idea in a boat that has to be underwater.

During her trials, the *Hunley* sank four times, killing a total of twenty-three men. The *Hunley* was raised after the fourth sinking, and was immediately sent into battle in Charleston Harbor on February 17, 1864. ("The mystery of how the new crew was recruited," wrote Richard Compton-Hall, "is explained by the huge rewards, amounting to several hundred thousand dollars in today's money. . . .") Commanded by Lt. George Dixon of the Alabama Light Infantry, who steered the 40-foot-long vessel while standing up and look-

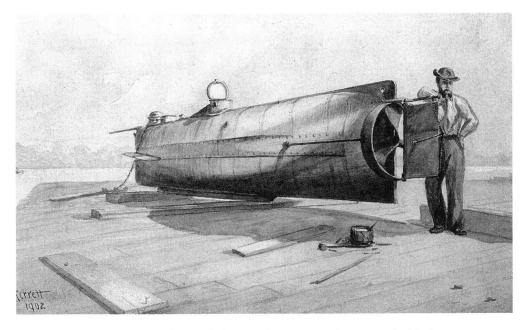

To its unfortunate occupants, the Confederate submarine *Hunley* was probably the most dangerous undersea vessel ever designed. During her trials, the *Hunley* sank four times, killing a total of twenty-three men, but she was raised and sent into battle at Charleston Harbor in 1864, where she blew herself up along with her target, the Union vessel *Housatonic.*

ing out the forward hatch, the *Hunley* was armed with a 143-pound gunpowder torpedo, mounted on a 30-foot projecting spar. With this "bomb-on-a-stick," she rammed the Union sloop *Housatonic,* but sank herself along with the target. Although something less than an unqualified success, this event marked the introduction of the submarine vessel to the catalog of war machines: for the first time, a surface vessel had been sunk by a submarine.

In Jules Verne's *Twenty Thousand Leagues Under the Sea,* the fictional *Nautilus** is powered by a "powerful agent, obedient, rapid, easy, which conforms to every use, and reigns supreme on board my vessel. . . . This agent is electricity." In 1870, the year *Twenty Thousand Leagues* was published in Paris, electricity was only a curiosity at carnivals. (Michael Faraday had discovered electromagnetic induction as early as 1831, and the forerunner of the dry battery was introduced in 1866, to be followed the next year by the first practical dynamos, but it would not be until 1878 that the way to the Paris Opéra would be lighted by "electric candles.") Captain Nemo extols the virtues of the *Nautilus* to Professor Arronax:

> No defects to be afraid of, for the double shell is as firm as iron; no sails for the wind to carry away; no boilers to burst; no fire to fear, for the vessel is made of iron, not of wood; no coal to run short, for electricity is the only mechanical agent; no collision to fear, for it alone swims in deep water; no tempest to brave, for when it dives below the water, it reaches absolute tranquility. There sir! That is the perfection of vessels!

Captain Nemo's *Nautilus* is fitted out with a dining room, a library, a drawing room, a kitchen (equipped with what is surely the first electric range), a berth room, and an engine room that is 65 feet long:

> The electricity produced is conducted aft, where it is worked by electro-magnets of great size, on a system of levers and cog wheels that transmit the movement to the axle of the screw. This one, the diameter of which is nineteen feet, and the thread twenty-three feet, performs about a hundred twenty revolutions in a second.

---

* Probably named for the chambered nautilus (*Nautilus pompilius*), the cephalopod with the gracefully curved, striped shell, but also dependent upon Robert Fulton's early submarine of the same name. Two gentlemen named Ash and Campbell launched a *Nautilus* in the Thames in 1888, but the 60-foot steel-hulled vessel sank to the bottom and was released from the mud only when the six passengers rocked the hull loose by running back and forth in unison. In 1931, the Australian explorer Sir George Hubert Wilkins was given an American submarine for a proposed voyage under the ice to the North Pole, which vessel was renamed *Nautilus.* The loss of a diving rudder prevented this *Nautilus* from cruising under the ice, but during World War II, yet another submarine received this distinguished name. And in 1955, the USS *Nautilus,* the world's first nuclear-powered submarine, was launched at New London, Connecticut, and in 1958 fulfilled Sir Hubert's dream: she became the first submarine to sail under the ice at the North Pole.

When Professor Arronax asks Nemo what sort of speed he can get from such an arrangement, the captain replies, "A speed of fifty miles an hour."

Most people are familiar with the exploits of the *Nautilus,* through either the book or the 1954 film made by Walt Disney Studios, starring Kirk Douglas as Ned Land, the Canadian harpooner, Paul Lukas as Professor Arronax of the Paris Museum, Peter Lorre as his servant Conseil, and James Mason as Captain Nemo. The submarine sails around the world several times; encounters all sorts of fishes, whales, sharks, manatees, and corals; battles a giant squid; sails through a subterranean tunnel that connects the Red Sea with the Mediterranean; explores the lost city of Atlantis; sails to the South Pole and thence to the Amazon; and finally, off the coast of Norway, the *Nautilus* is lost in the "dreaded Maelstrom." (Nemo goes down with his ship, but Arronax, Conseil, and Ned Land are cast ashore on one of the Lofoten Islands, there to await the next steamboat to France.)

Twenty Thousand Leagues Under the Sea is a marvelous tale; as Walter Miller points out, it is "typical of Verne's approach that he would choose a scientific subject at this stage in its development. Thus his immediate readers would live to see some of his prophecies borne out, while later generations would still be waiting for others to be realized." (The elongated cigar shape of the *Nautilus* contributed to early submarine design, even though it proved to be not nearly as efficient as the

Even though Jules Verne mentions a giant *squid,* the illustrator of the 1870 original edition of *Twenty Thousand Leagues Under the Sea* depicted a giant *octopus* hovering menacingly outside the porthole of the submarine *Nautilus.*

teardrop shape now employed in nuclear vessels.) It would indeed be some time before submarines were equipped with berths, let alone libraries.

German predation on British shipping at the outset of World War I is well known, and although it depended upon improvements and innovations in submarine design, it has little connection with the development of submersible vessels for underwater exploration. The story of submarines in World War II, including the Battle of the Atlantic, is of hardly any concern to us. Even the development of nuclear-powered subs that can sail around the world underwater has little bearing on this story, but there is one dramatic instance where the paths of submersibles and submarines converged: when the nuclear submarine *Thresher* was reported missing off New England in April 1963, the only vessel that could possibly search for her was the bathyscaph *Trieste*. At 8,400 feet below the surface, the remains of the submarine were found and photographed from the bathyscaph. The raising of the sunken submarine—or any part of it, for that matter—was considered, but the technological difficulties proved to be insurmountable, and the *Thresher* and the bodies of her 129-man crew were left on the bottom.

The paths of technology and experience garnered during the first century of submarine development pointed in divergent directions: one led to war and destruction, symbolized by the havoc wreaked by submarines during the two world wars, and then the maneuvering of Soviet and American nuclear missile subs in strategic chess games. (One of the major differences between combat submarines and research submersibles is the presence of windows or portholes in the latter.* Researchers want to see the flora, fauna, and topography around them; killer subs are blind. Submersibles often require the services of a surface support vessel, while submarines are completely self-sufficient.) The technology was also profitably employed in scientific pursuits, where the wonders of the undersea world were slowly revealed to investigators willing to climb into cramped, uncomfortable little submersibles, for the thrill of seeing what no man had ever seen before.

The amalgamation of submarine technology and submersible capabilities did not take place until 1969, when General Dynamics/Electric Boat Division built a 146-foot research submarine for the U.S. Navy. (For comparison,

---

* One curious exception to this rule was the submarine *Nautilus* that Sir Hubert Wilkins tried to take under the ice to the North Pole in 1931. Originally a U.S. Navy vessel, she was decommissioned and sold to Wilkins for one dollar, and (according to his biographer, Lowell Thomas) given "a complete overhaul and refitting." This refitting must have been quite extensive, because the sub seems to have gained something called "eyeports," through which the crew could see the "crystal blue water" and "the roughened flat undersurface of the floe." (The book itself is also curious, since it was called a "biography," and although written in the first person, it was not by Wilkins but by Lowell Thomas, who claims to tell "the story of Sir Hubert Wilkins' life and world of adventure as he told it to me over the thirty-odd years I knew him.")

USS *Triton,* the nuclear-powered submarine that circumnavigated the globe underwater in 1960, was 447.5 feet long.) Prosaically christened *NR-1* (for "nuclear research"), she was equipped with observation lights, portholes, sonar, and a nuclear power plant that enables her to remain submerged as long as the crew's food supplies hold out. Most of *NR-1*'s capabilities and accomplishments are classified, but in his chapter on the deep in the National Geographic Society's *Into the Unknown,* Philip Kopper tells us that "*NR-1* has searched for downed missiles and hydrothermal vents in its variety of missions." In a 1995 article in *The New York Times* ("Secret Sub to Scan Sea Floor for Roman Wrecks"), William Broad wrote, "The world's smallest and deepest-diving atom powered submarine . . . was launched in 1969 and performed a host of shadowy missions during the cold war, only a few of which the Navy will talk about." "Stranger than anything ever dreamed up by Jules Verne," wrote Broad, "the once-secret craft has wheels that let it roll along the sea floor as well as windows, lights, sensors, cameras and powerful manipulators for picking up lost objects. . . ."

The "secret sub" was newsworthy in February 1995, because a plan had been developed by Dr. Robert Ballard to use *NR-1* for exploration of "a graveyard of ships at the bottom of the Mediterranean Sea, along an ancient trade route between Rome and Carthage." Ballard intends to use "secret cold war technology in the service of classical archaeology" as he searches for the wrecks of Roman cargo ships, such as the one discovered on the Skerki Bank, some 60 miles north of Tunis. Associated with this wreck are iron anchors, amphorae, pottery lamps, a grindstone, and cooking pots, but the location of the wreck is as important as the artifacts, since it appears to be on a trade route between Rome and Carthage, and thus promises more evidence of life in ancient times.

Since Alexander the Great saw a creature that took three days to pass his submerged barrel, the idea of descending into the depths has fascinated mankind. Some of the problems—breathing, locomotion, stability—had been tentatively solved during the development of the submarine, but except in fiction, no one had yet equipped a submersible vessel with the necessary equipment that would enable its passengers to submerge for any length of time and observe what could be seen around them. Jules Verne took us twenty thousand leagues around the world underwater in 1870, and shortly before the turn of the century, the man who was responsible for *The Time Machine* and *The War of the Worlds* wrote a story that presaged the first descent in a bathysphere. Herbert George Wells (1866–1946), a former schoolmaster with a vivid and wonderful imagination, published a story he called "In the Abyss."

From shipboard in an unspecified location, a man called Elstead prepares to descend in a nine-foot-diameter steel sphere, equipped with "a couple of windows of enormously thick glass." With a complement of lead weights, the device is to be lowered overboard to sink five miles to the bottom, where Elstead proposes "to stay for half an hour, with the electric light on, looking about me." At the conclusion of his visit to the bottom, the sinkers will be cast off as a complicated clockwork mechanism releases a spring knife that cuts the rope so the sphere will shoot to the surface "like a soda-water bubble." (Elstead has calculated that at a rate of two feet per second, it would take three-quarters of a minute to reach the bottom, and the same amount of time to ascend.) Even in his wild imaginings, Wells could not make this Rube Goldberg contraption work, and instead of rocketing to the surface in a couple of minutes, the sphere does not reappear until dawn of the following day, when it is found bobbing at the surface with Elstead still alive.

He tells a story that would embarrass H. P. Lovecraft, never mind Jules Verne. Upon reaching bottom, Elstead was surrounded by "a heavy blackness—as black as black velvet," but soon saw "small, large-eyed or blind things, [some] having a curious resemblance to woodlice, some to lobsters." No one, especially Elstead, was prepared for what appeared next:

> It was a strange vertebrated animal. Its dark purple head was dimly suggestive of a chameleon, but it had such a high forehead and such a braincase as no reptile had ever displayed before; the vertical pitch of its face gave it a most extraordinary resemblance to a human being. Two large and protruding eyes projected from sockets in chameleon fashion, and it had a broad reptilian mouth with horny lips beneath its little nostrils. In the position of the ears were two huge gill-covers, and out of these floated a branching tree of coraline filaments, almost like the tree-like gills that very young sharks and rays possess.

Looking not unlike the 1954 "Creature from the Black Lagoon," this biped had a long tail and appendages "which grotesquely caricatured the human hand." Others of its kind assembled, and towed the sphere like a balloon to their city, where the "walls were of water-logged wood, twisted wire-rope, and iron spars, and copper, and the bones and skulls of dead men." The steel sphere was placed on an altar, where it was worshiped by the population of this drowned world, until the cord that still held it was somehow "cut through by rubbing against the edge of the altar," and Elstead shot to the surface, where he was rescued to tell his story. He seems to have had such a good time on his first descent into the abyss that he tried it again, but on his second trip he did not make it back to the surface. "It is hardly probable," concluded Wells, "that no further attempt will be made to verify his strange story of these hitherto unsuspected cities of the deep sea."

We do not know if William Beebe ever read H. G. Wells's story, but within thirty years of its publication, Beebe was being lowered toward the abyss in a steel sphere with thick windows. (We can safely assume that he was not looking for "unsuspected cities.") Designed and operated by Beebe and Otis Barton for the New York Zoological Society in 1930, the bathysphere was the first purely investigative submersible. It was made of cast steel that was 1¼ inches thick. Three inches less than 5 feet in diameter, it weighed 4,500 pounds and had three "windows," made of 3-inch-thick quartz, because, according to Beebe, "it is the strongest transparent substance known and it transmits all wavelengths of light." The bathysphere's passengers—there was room for only two—climbed in and out through a 14-inch door, which had to be lifted

William Beebe perched atop the bathysphere in which he descended to a then-record half mile down in the sea off Bermuda. Beebe was the first scientist to view many of the previously unknown creatures of the deep in their bathypelagic habitat.

on and off with a block and tackle and bolted shut with ten heavy bolts. The sphere was suspended from a braided steel cable that was ⅞ inch in diameter and 3,500 feet long. There was an additional electrical cable that carried the lights and telephone wires, and the air came from oxygen tanks fitted to the interior, with trays of "powdered chemicals" to absorb the moisture and carbon dioxide. The air in the capsule was kept circulating by hand-held, woven palm-frond fans.

Off Nonsuch Island in Bermuda, theirs was a simple descent; they climbed into the cramped, cold sphere, the hatch was bolted shut, and then the ball was lifted up by a crane and lowered into the ocean. As they descended, Beebe and Barton* watched the light change and carefully recorded each creature that passed before the quartz portholes. They saw many species of fishes and invertebrates that they expected to see, and many that they believed had never before been seen by the eyes of man. (Beebe also claimed to have observed several species of fishes that have not been seen or collected by anyone else since his singular adventure.) On one of the 1934 dives, the bathysphere reached a record 3,000 feet—actually more than the half mile of the title of Beebe's book—and Beebe recorded his impressions:

> Before we began to ascend, I had to stop making notes of my own, so numb were my fingers from the cold steel of the window sill, and to change from my cushion to the metal floor, was like shifting to a cake of ice. Of the blackness of the water I have already written too much. . . . Whenever I sink below the last rays of light, similes pour in upon me. . . . The only place comparable to these marvelous nether regions, must surely be naked space itself, out far beyond atmosphere, between the stars, where sunlight has no grip upon the dust and rubbish of planetary air, where the blackness of space, the shining planets, comets, suns, and stars, must really be closely akin to the world of life as it appears to the eyes of an awed human being, in the open ocean, one half mile down.

Beebe was not the only submarine explorer to compare the unplumbed depths of the sea to the unexplored heavens. In his 1961 book (*Seven Miles Down*), Auguste Piccard, the Swiss explorer who would go on to become the "father of the modern submersible," delineates his fascination with the depths:

> For centuries, the only ocean man knew was the sun-drenched wind-tossed surface. It was a two-dimensional element upon which he sailed his ships, on the fringes of which he built his cities. The world beneath the waves was a nether region, inhabited by monsters too fearful to contemplate. Nature had not seen fit to make the water as clear as the atmosphere. Man lived with the stars, but the deep sea was beyond his ken.

---

* Both Beebe and Barton wrote books on the subject of diving in the bathysphere. Beebe's is *Half Mile Down* (1934), and Barton's is *The World Beneath the Sea* (1953), but their bathysphere unexpectedly appears in Thomas Mann's *Dr. Faustus*, first published in 1947. In Mann's story, composer Adrian Leverkühn enters into a pact with the devil, where he offers to exchange his soul for twenty-eight years of musical success. Because he was seeking every sort of heightened experience, Leverkühn descends in "a bullet-shaped diving bell . . . equipped somewhat like a stratosphere balloon, and dropped from a crane into the sea." It is lowered to 765 meters (2,509 feet), and observes "predatory mouths opening and shutting; obscene jaws, telescope eyes; the paper nautilus; silver- and gold-fish with goggling eyes on top of their heads; heteropods and pteropods up to two or three yards long."

Earlier oceanographers, such as Edward Forbes, had dismissed the possibilities of life at great depths, referring to the regions below 300 fathoms as the "azoic," or lifeless, zone. But the collecting expeditions of Wyville Thomson's *Porcupine* and the *Challenger* in the latter half of the nineteenth century demonstrated that this was far from correct. The seabed was alive with invertebrate animals, some of which were discovered by the *Galathea*'s 1951 trawl to inhabit the deepest trenches in the world. In an article entitled "The Density of Animals on the Ocean Floor," Ragnar Spärck of the *Galathea* wrote:

> The result of our investigations in this field, therefore, is that on the ocean floor there are about 10 animals per square metre with a total weight of about one gram. This is an astonishingly large figure considering that at a depth of a few hundred metres in Northern European and Mediterranean waters there are only a few grams of animals per square metre. This surprising density right down to between 5,000 and 8,000 metres suggests that food conditions in the abyss are not so poor as we have been inclined to think, and this in turn leads us to suppose that abyssal water currents may be stronger than formerly believed.

Although he later traveled all over the world, exploring, diving, collecting, and filming, Otis Barton's true love was the bathysphere. He wrote: "Since coming home from the war, I had been living in a world bereft of meaning. . . . Only in the machine shop where parts of hydraulic presses moved about overhead, did I feel that I was touching reality." He designed and had built the "benthoscope," another 54-inch-diameter steel sphere with walls that were ½ inch thicker than those of the bathysphere. With this extra thickness, he wrote, "the benthoscope could dive to ten thousand feet whereas the bathysphere could in theory dive to only forty-five hundred feet before the water flattened it out." Whereas the bathysphere had cost Barton a total of $12,000 (he financed most of the expedition out of an inheritance), the 1948 version cost him $16,000. After several aborted tries in the Bahamas, Barton took the benthoscope to California, where he was lowered to a then-record 4,500 feet in the Santa Cruz Canyon. This 1948 dive stood as the record for manned submersibles until *Trieste* broke all the records.

Auguste Piccard's first attempt to send an unattached submersible vessel into the depths—and, most important, bring it back—occurred in 1948, off Dakar in West Africa. Based on the principle he had used to ascend into the atmosphere in a balloon filled with lighter-than-air hydrogen gas, Piccard had designed a submarine that carried as its buoyancy device a huge quantity of gasoline, which is lighter than water and, more important, is compressible with increased depth. The flotation tank was open to the sea, which meant that the gasoline always sat on top of the entering water, to provide buoyancy.

In addition to the gasoline-filled "blimp," *FNRS-2** consisted of a 10-ton steel sphere that served as the cockpit, two air tanks, and ballast hoppers filled with tons of magnetized iron pellets that would be demagnetized and dropped should there be a power failure, thus causing the vessel to "fall up" toward the surface. On November 3, 1948, from the Belgian cargo vessel *Scaldis,* the 15-ton, robot-operated *FNRS-2* was lowered over the side, and its tether slipped. (Watching from the deck of the French navy's oceanographic research vessel was the inventor of the aqualung, J.-Y. Cousteau, along with his colleagues Frédéric Dumas and Philippe Tailliez.) The unmanned submersible had descended to 4,554 feet and returned when an automatic timing device had unballasted it. The cabin withstood the pressure successfully, but the float was severely damaged upon surfacing in heavy swells, and more solid structures were designed for surface towing.

Auguste Piccard (right), photographed with Charles Kipfer after a balloon ride into the stratosphere that took them nearly ten miles up. The height of fashion in 1931 seemed to be a chapeau patterned after a balloon gondola. The young man with the droopy sock is Professor Piccard's son, Jacques, who would go on to set the depth record for a descent into the ocean.

Encouraged by their experiments with *FNRS-2,* Auguste and his son Jacques Piccard ranged the European capitals for funds, and finally amassed enough money to build *Trieste,* named for the Adriatic seaport where she was built. The 50-foot-long flotation hull was designed to hold 28,000 gallons of

* *FNRS* stands for Fonds National de la Recherche Scientifique, the Belgian "National Scientific Research Fund," which provided much of the financial assistance for the French endeavors. The original *FNRS* was the balloon in which Auguste Piccard ascended into the stratosphere, also built with Belgian financing.

gasoline, and suspended below it was the passenger compartment, a 10-ton, forged-steel chamber that was 7 feet in inside diameter. The portholes were 6-inch-thick truncated cones made of a newly developed, shatterproof plastic called Plexiglas. The bathyscaph descended by taking on water ballast into the forward and aft tanks and by valving off small quantities of gasoline. She could be moved forward or backward by the use of propellers located on top of the hull, but only in a very limited way. (James Dugan wrote that *Trieste* "functions as little more than an elevator, and is almost completely helpless in a situation calling for wide horizontal searching range.") In August 1953, off Castellammare in southern Italy, with Piccard *père et fils* aboard, *Trieste* made her first successful manned descent—26 feet down to the bottom of the harbor. There followed a succession of deeper dives in the Mediterranean from 1953 to 1956: 3,540 feet in the Bay of Naples; 10,300 feet in the Tyrrhenian Sea.

In 1958, Piccard sold the *Trieste* to the U.S. Office of Naval Research (ONR), but stayed on as a consultant. (Jacques was the primary pilot.) Previously, she had been based in Castellammare in Italy, but Piccard could not afford the upkeep and expenses on his own and needed government support. Robert Dietz, a geological oceanographer, was working for ONR at this time, and, with Piccard, realized the potential of the submersible for on-site observations of the deep ocean. In 1959, ONR transported *Trieste* to Guam for "Project Nekton," which Dietz named for the free-swimming animals of the sea, as contrasted with the plankton, which moves at the mercy of currents. They were going to send the submersible down 38,500 feet, to the bottom of the Challenger Deep* in the Mariana Trench; the dive to *la plus grande profondeur,* the deepest possible dive in the world.

The sphere that had been forged in Italy was not considered strong enough for such a dive, so a new one was manufactured by the Krupp steel works in Germany. New instrumentation was designed and built in Switzerland, and the revised electronics were supplied by the U.S. Navy. Record after record fell as the bathyscaph made practice dives: 18,150 feet; 24,000 feet; and finally, on January 23, 1960, with Lt. Don Walsh as copilot, Jacques Piccard and the *Trieste* landed on the bottom at 5,966 fathoms (35,800 feet). As Piccard described it:

> The bottom appeared light and clear, a waste of snuff-colored ooze. We were landing on a nice, flat bottom of firm diatomaceous ooze. Indifferent

* Although the greatest depth in the ocean probably ought to have been named for the greatest oceanographic expedition of all time, it was in fact named for a successor to the original *Challenger,* the British research vessel *Challenger II.* In 1949, at the southern end of the Mariana Trench, oceanographers recorded an echo that corresponded to a depth of 5,900 fathoms, almost 1,000 feet deeper than the previously known greatest depth in the Philippine Trench.

to the nearly 200,000 tons of pressure clamped on her metal sphere, the *Trieste* balanced herself delicately on the few pounds of guide rope that lay on the bottom, making token claim, in the name of science and humanity, to the ultimate depths in all our oceans—the Challenger Deep.

Immediately, Edward Forbes's smug declaration that no life could exist in the depths was resoundingly refuted once and for all, as a foot-long flatfish moved out of the way of the descending steel monster. At the very bottom of creation, in water that was seven miles deep, there was a fish, and, even more startling, a fish with *eyes*.*

Since that day in 1948, when he, Dumas, and Tailliez had watched the descent of Piccard's *FNRS-2,* Jacques Cousteau had campaigned for a submersible of his own. In 1954, he entered the sea in *FNRS-3,* a similar vessel sponsored by l'Office Français de Recherches Sous-Marines (OFRS). The little sub was launched from the *Elie Monnier,* the very ship from which he had watched Piccard's launch. At 4,000 feet they saw bright red squid ejecting clouds of luminous white ink; on the bottom they saw eight-foot-long sharks with bright green eyes. On February 17, 1954, Lt. Comdr. Georges Houot and Lt. Pierre Willm took *FNRS-3* to the record depth of 13,287 feet.

Depth records were not the goal of the Cousteaus; they needed a window into the sea to study the flora and fauna that intrigued them and their worldwide television audiences. So they built a "diving saucer" (the divers nicknamed her *"la soucoupe plongeante,"* but she was officially known as DS-2), a flattened sphere six and a half feet in diameter and five feet high, with two viewing windows. She descended by carrying a 55-pound iron weight, which was dropped when she reached operational depth, and to bring her to the surface, another similar weight was jettisoned. On the first test (off Cassis, on the southern coast of France), the tether snapped, and the diving saucer (luckily unmanned) sank to the bottom in 3,000 feet of water. OFRS had another shell ready, so the divers used the second one, leaving the first one

* It is unfortunate that *Trieste* was not equipped with an external camera. Shortly after *Trieste*'s historic dive, Torben Wolff of the Zoological Museum of Copenhagen published a note in *Nature* in which he disputed the identification of the fish. He suggested that despite the "eyes," it was not a fish at all, but probably a holothurian (sea cucumber), "perhaps related to the bathy-pelagic, cushion-shaped *Galatheathauria aspera,* which is almost a foot long and oval in outline." Even though he knew that "negative records are naturally of less value," he wrote that "no flatfish was collected in or close to any of the [other] trenches investigated," and that *Chascanopsetta lugubris* (the fish tentatively identified by Piccard) "was previously recorded only between depths of 220 and 977 m." (720 and 3,204 feet). In a *Newsweek* article published in July 1993 (on the subject of submersibles), writer Tony Emerson quoted ichthyologist Richard Rosenblatt of Scripps as saying, "Everyone agrees it was a sea cucumber."

The bathyscaph *Trieste,* holder of the world's record for deep-diving. On January 23, 1960, piloted by Jacques Piccard and U.S. Navy Lt. Don Walsh, she reached the deepest spot in the ocean, 35,800 feet in the Mariana Trench off the island of Guam. The record can only be equaled, never broken.

on the bottom. Unlike the previous submersibles, *DS-2* was equipped with jet nozzles that could move her in any direction—and even spin her on her horizontal axis—and she could be tilted up and down as well. The oxygen re-breathing system was good up to twenty-four hours. Harold Edgerton, the inventor of stroboscopic photography, had designed special depth cameras that were synchronized with a flash unit mounted outside the hull. Of one dive, Edgerton wrote in his log:

> Now we are slowly sinking, free of the cable. Above us, through the optical ports, we can see *Calypso* at anchor in the exceptionally clear water. Falco turns on the jets. We begin to move. Like an airplane we descend to where the reef drops off into deeper water. We are getting good clean oxygen. Being in the saucer is no different from being in an automobile, ex-

cept that we are more comfortable and loll on our mattresses like Romans at a banquet.

What a far cry from Beebe and Barton, cramped into their cold, damp bathysphere and hung from a ship on a tether like a great steel yo-yo. "The Diving Saucer," wrote Cousteau, "had proved herself. . . . Her hydraulic claw has brought back supermarket-basket loads of treasures. She has discovered dozens of species for science. Her mud and rock samples have confirmed and destroyed hypotheses on the formation and make-up of submarine canyons." As of the late 1950s, submersible observers were finding unusual species and surprising terrain, but aside from the occasional glimpse of a prettily colored fish, an unexpected cephalopod, or a spectacular coral formation, the divers were finding more or less what they expected. Deeper-diving submersibles were needed.

In 1962, Cousteau designed *Deepstar,* a three-man submersible that was a modification of the successful diving saucer, for Westinghouse's Undersea Division. Scallop-shaped like her predecessors, *Deepstar* regulated her depth by the adjustment of ballast, and using battery-powered propellers instead of the earlier water jets. It was from *Deepstar* that Eric Barham of the U.S. Naval Electronics Laboratory in San Diego resolved some of the mysteries of the deep-scattering layers, observing that the upper layer of a two-layer system was composed of lantern fishes; the lower of siphonophores. Concluding his 1966 article

Jacques Cousteau designed the diving saucer DS-2 ("*la soucoupe plongeante*"), a two-man vehicle that was much more maneuverable than the bathyscaphs. Shown here being lifted aboard the mother ship off the California coast, she was equipped with jet nozzles that could move her in any direction.

in *Science,* Barham wrote, "Investigations by deep submersibles in other water-mass regimes should provide additional information on the relative importance of these two types of scatterers and identify other causative organisms." (In another series of dives in the Atlantic, Barham found plenty of lantern fishes, but no siphonophores.)

Based on designs by Jacques Cousteau, and built by Westinghouse, a later version called *Deepstar-4000* (that being her maximum depth in feet) was launched in 1966. The 18-foot-long vehicle was self-propelled but, like all of its sister submersibles, had to be towed to the dive site. With a pilot and two passengers making up the ship's complement, *Deepstar-4000* was released from the surface and descended in a helical spiral at a rate of about 80 feet per minute. Oxygen was supplied from tanks, and lithium hydroxide "scrubbed" the air of carbon dioxide. Like its shallower-diving predecessor, *DS-4000* was equipped with a sophisticated camera system "making possible close-up photographs at great depths."* Pilot and photographer Ron Church (1971) used that system to record life on the floor of the Gulf of Mexico, including some of the earliest photographs of the tripod fish (discussed on pp. 247–50) and snipe eels (pp. 229–32).

Around 1966, J. Louis Reynolds of Reynolds Metals (later Reynolds Aluminum) commissioned *Aluminaut.* Built by Electric Boat of Groton, Connecticut, the 51-foot-long reinforced aluminum cylinder weighed 73 tons in air. Positive buoyancy was provided by the rigid, lightweight hull (the aluminum is less compressible than seawater, so the deeper *Aluminaut* went, the more buoyant she became), and negative buoyancy—the ability to descend—was provided by shot ballast. With a crew of three operators and three observers as well as a substantial array of equipment, she could perform many different chores, often simultaneously. Her great size and weight, however, meant that *Aluminaut* could not be lifted aboard conventional oceanographic vessels, and she had to be towed—often infuriatingly slowly—to her destinations. Originally designed to reach depths of 22,000 feet, she tested successfully only to 15,000, and in fact, the maximum depth she achieved was 6,250 feet. When *Aluminaut* proved incapable of diving to great depths, Woods Hole Oceanographic Institution let out bids for a more efficient deep-

---

* On one dive in the San Diego Trough, observers aboard *Deepstar-4000* saw (but did not photograph) a fish "30 or 40 feet long," which was described as having an eye "the size of a dinner plate" (Shenton 1972). Subsequent discussions with ichthyologist Carl Hubbs of Scripps suggested that it might have been a Greenland or sleeper shark (*Somniosus*), and indeed, when Isaacs and Schwartzlose (1975) used automatic cameras to record animals of the deep-sea floor off southern California, they found that "arctic sleeper sharks . . . must be quite common, since they have been photographed on nearly half of our missions off California down to 2,000 meters." (Sleeper sharks, however, reach a maximum known length of 23 feet, and their eyes are about the size of a silver dollar.)

The submersible *Alvin* at Woods Hole in June 1964, before being placed in service. Since that date, the little sub has found a lost H-bomb, dived in the Mid-Atlantic Rift Valley, visited the *Titanic,* and discovered a whole new ecosystem.

diving submersible. The competition was won by General Mills—the cereal manufacturer—but before construction was completed, Litton Industries purchased General Mills' electronics and manipulator division, and in 1964 delivered *Alvin.*

Named for its designer, Allyn Vine (1915–1994), an engineer at Woods Hole (but also related to the chipmunk song that was popular during the design phase), *Alvin* was built for about a million dollars. Although the 25-foot-long sub is more mobile than its predecessors, the people-capsule is essentially the same as the bathysphere: a metal sphere that encloses and protects the passengers, and can be separated from the frame in case of trouble. Like the submersibles that preceded her, *Alvin* depends on ballast—in this case, 200-pound blocks of steel—that can be jettisoned to allow the submersible to rise. There is one porthole in front for the pilot, two on the sides for the observers, and one that looks straight down. Passengers breathe oxygen from tanks, and canisters of lithium hydroxide absorb carbon dioxide, a system that provides two days' worth of livable atmosphere, even though most dives are supposed to last no more than eight hours. The original aluminum frame has been replaced by titanium, and her depth range has been increased from 6,000 to 14,764 feet.*

On January 17, 1966, the skies over the Spanish port of Palomares were illuminated by the fiery collision of an American B-52 bomber and its KC-135 refueling tanker. The wreckage of the two planes and their crews rained down on the fishing village, setting fires and destroying houses. The bomber was carrying four unarmed hydrogen bombs, three of which were recovered from the wreckage on land. The fourth landed in the Mediterranean. The U.S. government dispatched *Aluminaut* and *Alvin* to try to locate the missing bomb. (The Office of Naval Research owns *Alvin,* but WHOI has always operated it for the scientific and civilian community.) Rear Adm. William Guest, in charge of the task force, likened the search to "using a penlight to look for a .22 caliber bullet in a muddy, water-filled Grand Canyon."

After weeks of painstaking and fruitless searching, *Alvin's* pilots found the track that the bomb had plowed through the sediment, and followed the groove until they saw the not reassuringly named "Nuke 4" with a parachute wrapped around it. Five days later—after losing the bomb because it had rolled down a steep incline—*Alvin's* crew gingerly plucked the 'chute off the bomb with the grapnels, and with a Cable-controlled Underwater Research Vessel (CURV), they snagged the bomb. After seventy-five days, the bomb was safely aboard the USS *Mizar.* Secretary of the Navy Paul Nitze cabled Woods Hole:

> The result of your efforts to recover the missing unarmed nuclear weapon is a source of pride to all of us in the naval service. With competent professionalism the personnel of your task force conducted an intensive search unparalleled in history. . . . [W]ell done.

On July 6, 1967, at a depth of 610 meters (2,000 feet) 110 miles off the coast of Georgia, *Alvin* was rammed by a swordfish, which was trapped by its sword in the sub's superstructure. In an account published shortly after the in-

---

* In an article about the finding of the *Titanic* in 1985, Robert Ballard wrote, "My desire to search for the *Titanic* goes back many years, to about 1973, when the decision was made at Woods Hole to replace *Alvin's* original steel hull with a new one made of titanium alloy. Such a conversion would increase its diving range from 6,000 feet to its present operational range of more than 13,000 feet, making it possible to reach the *Titanic's* estimated depth." Ballard led the team that found the *Titanic* in 1985, but not from *Alvin.* The wreck was located by *Argo,* an unmanned, towed sled equipped with a television and side-scanning sonar. *Alvin* explored the wreck on a second Woods Hole expedition in 1986.

cident, geologist Rudy Zarudski reported that the pilot, Val Wilson, "had noticed a hummocky feature on the bottom about ten meters to starboard. Its color blended with the color of the mud. After we made our short hop ahead, the 'hummock' stirred up the sediment, identifying itself as a large swordfish." Swordfish are indeed known to hunt at great depths, but the "hummock" reference is more than a little puzzling. *Xiphias gladius* (its names are, respectively, Greek and Latin for "sword") is supposed to be a swift and powerful hunter, chasing down its prey and slashing at it with the sword blade. What was this fish doing lying on the bottom? On another occasion, in Florida waters, a blue marlin charged the sub, smashed two lights, and fell dead to the bottom.* (After these encounters, *Alvin*'s engineers tested the acrylic portholes by firing fish swords at them from an air gun, but the plastic held.)

The next event in *Alvin*'s exhilarating career occurred on October 16, 1968, and almost ended it permanently. During a routine dive off Cape Cod, the mooring cables snapped, and with the hatch open, the submersible filled up quickly and plunged to the bottom, some 5,000 feet below. (The three men aboard escaped before she sank.) *Alvin* sat on the bottom for almost a year, until *Aluminaut* located her sitting upright, dropped a T-bar in the hatch, and she was hauled to the surface, somewhat the worse for wear, but still serviceable. Retrieved from *Alvin*'s eleven-month sabbatical on the bottom was a plastic box containing the food from the aborted dive. The three bologna sandwiches and three apples looked fresh, and taste tests proved that although waterlogged, they were still perfectly edible. Subsequent controlled experiments by microbiologist Holger Jannasch showed that organic material protected (as the sandwiches were) from scavenging amphipods decayed very slowly. Jannasch wrote, "If . . . the true removal of pollutants is intended, then the slow rates of microbial degradation argue clearly against deep ocean disposal." The serendipitous retrieval of the sandwich box demonstrated that the deep sea is not a suitable environment for dumping solid organic wastes.

Deep-sea exploration in submersibles has not been without its tragedies. On June 17, 1973, the *Johnson Sea-Link,* a 23-foot-long, 9-ton vessel designed by Edwin Link, was diving in 360 feet of water off Key West, Florida, to check

---

* In 1940, E. W. Gudger, an ichthyologist and collector of zoological oddities, published a paper entitled "The Alleged Pugnacity of the Swordfish and the Spearfishes as Shown by Their Attacks on Vessels," in which he listed swordfish attacks on fishing boats, floating kegs, and even sharks. (Later, Norwegian cetologist Åge Jonsgard would cite instances of swordfish attacks on baleen whales.) Gudger attributes those attacks that were not prompted by the harpooning of the fish to missed thrusts at prey fishes, such as albacore or bonito, but this does not satisfactorily address the ramming and piercing of submersibles or whales, which would be difficult to mistake for mackerel.

out the artificial reef that had been created by the intentional scuttling of the *Fred T. Berry,* an obsolete destroyer. A surprise current swept the *Sea-Link* into the dangling cables of the sunken warship, and the small submersible was trapped. The occupants—one of whom was thirty-one-year-old Clayton Link, the son of the designer—were in two separate compartments, with no connecting passageway. Pilot "Jock" Menzies and scientist Robert Meek were in the forward bubble, and Link and Albert Stover were in the rear "lock-out" compartment that enabled divers to enter or leave the sub underwater. The forward compartment, made of acrylic, had partially insulated Meek and Menzies, but the aluminum lock-out compartment was uninsulated, and the temperature dropped precipitously. The reduction in ambient temperature meant that the CO_2-absorbing baralyme quickly began to lose its effectiveness. Menzies and Meek removed the baralyme from the "scrubber" and put it in an air-conditioning fan, providing themselves with cleaner air, but Link and Stover were running out.

The first vessel to respond to the call for help was the Navy submarine rescue vessel *Tringa,* but it took six hours for her to reach the site, and another six hours to get her into position over the trapped submersible. The same strong current that had caused the *Sea-Link* to become entangled continued to thwart rescue efforts, and a diving bell brought all the way from San Diego got itself hung up on the *Berry*'s floating rigging. Twenty-four hours after the "SUBMISS/SUBSINK" message had been broadcast, the oceanographic research vessel *A. B. Wood* arrived, equipped with sonar, a closed-circuit television, and a hook. With Jock Menzies on the radio to guide the grappling hook, the *Sea-Link* was finally raised, and while Meek and Menzies had survived, Stover and Link had not.

In testimony to the Coast Guard Board of Inquiry, Edwin Link wrote:

> The tragedy of this situation is that with an adequate undersea rescue system, this loss need never have occurred. . . . The Navy and the Coast Guard have recognized the problem for years, but with inadequate funds have not been able to develop such a system. It is inevitable that as man continues to invade the ocean depths, similar accidents are bound to occur in spite of every precaution. The sole remedy—rapid, effective submarine rescue systems, must be developed and kept in strategic locations. The technical knowledge of such a system has been available since the loss of the nuclear submarine *Thresher* ten years ago, but it has not been implemented.

In October of that same year, another tragedy was narrowly averted when the British two-man submersible *Pisces,* on a cable inspection mission in the

Irish Sea, sank in 1,300 feet of water. The Naval Undersea Center in San Diego sent the *CURV III* (an updated version of the device used to find the H-bomb off Palomares) to the scene, and after being trapped underwater for almost seventy-six hours, Roger Chapman and Robert Mallinson were hauled to the surface—alive. Exploration by submersible was exciting—and often dangerous—but the day was fast approaching when even this new technology would be rendered obsolete by remote-controlled television cameras.

"The study of the deep-sea benthos," wrote Frederick Grassle and colleagues in 1975, "has added greatly to our understanding. . . . Yet such investigations suffer because of the remoteness of the study area. Unlike our shallow-water colleagues, we do not have a framework based on the sort of common sense gained only through direct observation." Between 1967 and 1972, *Alvin* was used by biologists (Grassle et al. 1975) in a series of dives designed to investigate the megafauna ("operationally defined as organisms readily visible in photographs") of the Atlantic at depths between 500 and 1,800 meters. Photographs were taken with a pair of cameras (one color and one black and white), mounted on the front of the vehicle. Since the angle of the camera was a constant, they overlaid all photographs with a "Canadian grid," originally designed to delineate a study area in aerial photography. In their observations they were able to record that the predominant animals in the fauna were brittle stars, anemones, and urchins, but they also photographed various holothurians and fishes.

Since 1974, oceanographic research vessels had been investigating the Mid-Atlantic Ridge to learn what they could about the phenomenon known as sea-floor spreading. This movement of the crust of the ocean floor, which has resulted in the movement of the continents, is known as "continental drift," and also as "sea-floor expansion," "continental displacement," or "plate tectonics." The mechanism that moves the continents is not clearly understood, but it is accompanied by molten rock welling upward through the ever-widening rift valley of the world-spanning Mid-Ocean Ridge. When *Alvin* descended to 2,700 meters (8,856 feet) in February 1977, scientists aboard were treated to sights no human being had ever seen before.

Of course, they did not simply lower the submersible and hope for the best; the original bathymetric groundwork had been done by the research vessel *Knorr,* using narrow-beam echo-sounding to map the ocean's floor and locate the valley; then the remotely operated camera sled ANGUS (Acoustically Navigated Geological Underwater Survey) photographed some mighty unusual creatures, and only when the location of these mysterious animals was corroborated did the scientists go down in *Alvin* to have a look. Illuminated by *Alvin*'s lights were large white clams and white crabs that were living in water saturated with hydrogen sulfide. At another site (dubbed "the Garden of

Eden"), they saw the crabs and clams, a strange animal that looked like a dandelion gone to seed, and ten-foot-long worms with bright red plumes emerging from their elongated, tubelike white shells. All these creatures appeared to be thriving in an environment that was totally devoid of light—and therefore unable to employ a photosynthetic basis—and at a much higher temperature than the surrounding seawater. The heat vents spewed plumes of superheated water at temperatures of 350° C (650° F) but the animals lived alongside these vents, not in them.

The towed camera sled known as ANGUS was useful in early sea-floor exploration, but quite primitive in contemporary terms. Controlled from a surface ship, the two-ton sled was first used for Project FAMOUS (French-American Mid-Ocean Undersea Study) in 1974, and was subsequently involved in the discovery of hydrothermal vent animals in 1977. Onboard, still cameras recorded images at preprogrammed intervals as the vehicle was towed blindly over regions of suspected interest. (In the Galápagos Rift, ANGUS's cameras took a picture every ten seconds for fourteen hours, mostly of barren sea floor.) When the film ran out, the vehicle was winched aboard, and the pictures developed as the crew waited anxiously to see if anything of interest had been photographed, or if the camera had malfunctioned. In 1985, when *Argo* spotted the *Titanic*'s boiler, the crew on the surface ship *Knorr* saw the video images immediately.

In *Water Baby,* her celebratory history of *Alvin,* Victoria Kaharl quotes various scientists on the romance and importance of submersible exploration. For example, Tanya Atwater, a geophysicist from California, told Kaharl, "There's a profound thing that happens to every single person who gets in that sphere even if they don't get samples—they come back a changed scientist. Some jobs cannot be done except with *Alvin:* to explore in fine detail and get your eyeball and your gut calibrated." And Bill Ryan, a Lamont-Doherty geologist said, "We found as much variability in one dive in FAMOUS as we got in dredging the whole Atlantic." *Alvin* found the H-bomb off Spain; she led the flotilla of submersibles on Project FAMOUS; through her portholes scientists marveled at the first rift animals and black smokers; and she enabled human beings to see the *Titanic* for the first time in seventy-three years. Without what Kaharl called "that *pregnant guppy,* that *washing machine,* that *chewed off cigar with a helmet,*" we might still be dredging samples from the sea bottom and taking photographs of tube worms and vent clams. "How could anyone have known," asked Kaharl, "that it would so profoundly change the way we look at the world?" Indeed, *Alvin* has changed the way we look at the world, because it has changed the way we *can* look at the world.

In her 1996 book *The Octopus's Garden,* scientist and *Alvin* pilot Cindy Lee Van Dover described the little submersible:

She is an ungainly water creature, streamlined only at her aft end, where she terminates in a snub fiberglass tail cone and a stainless steel towing bridle. Forward, her Neanderthal brow juts out spiked with lights and cameras. A battered and burned work basket projects low down in front like a bumper. Manipulators, fed by red veins of hydraulic fluid, fold elbows-up beside her cheeks like legs of a praying mantis. Her sides bulge out like the flanks of a fattened pig. Perhaps we are fond of her just because she is so ugly and utilitarian.

Alvin is still functioning as the workhorse of the deep-diving vessels, approaching her three thousandth dive. (No other manned submersible comes even close to this figure.) Newer submersibles are now active in the depths, and as per Ballard's prediction, robotically controlled cameras enable scientists to probe the oceans' floor and even examine the deep flora and fauna with minimal risk. During 1988 salvage operations for the SS *Central America* about 300 miles off Cape Hatteras, the unmanned submersible *Nemo* filmed a large shark at a depth of 2,200 meters (7,436 feet). It was a Greenland shark (*Somniosus microcephalus*), estimated to be nearly 20 feet in length, and the depth is a record for any shark other than the Portuguese shark, *Centroscymnus coelolepis*.

Robert Ballard descended in *Alvin* to explore the Mid-Ocean Ridge, to examine hydrothermal rift animals, and even to look for the *Titanic*. (Paul Ryan wrote that Ballard "has probably spent more time on the bottom of the deep ocean than anyone alive.") But after many scientifically important voyages, he decided that the future of underwater exploration lay not in submersibles but rather in ROVs—remotely operated vehicles. In 1984, from his base at Woods Hole, Ballard gave an interview to the Cape Cod *Times* in which he was quoted as saying, "You'll never see much in *Alvin*; manned submersibles are doomed."

In Willard Bascom's 1988 book *The Crest of the Wave,* he expressed his dissatisfaction with small submarines for deep-sea exploration and investigation. He believed that submersibles were "too expensive and difficult to do useful work; they cannot stay below very long, or even see the bottom very well except with a television camera . . . and there are inherent risks in launching and recovering small submarines in rough weather." So Bascom, trained as a mining engineer (and the project manager of the ill-starred Mohole project from 1961 to 1963), designed his own system for the locating of sunken ships. Although a side-scanning sonar buoy towed close to the bottom might locate large objects, the movement of the tow precluded detailed examination, so Bascom figured that a better way of examining objects on the sea floor was by the use of a television camera on a long pipe, suspended below the ship like the drill pipe used in the Mohole (see pp. 47–48). The Alcoa Aluminum Company built the *Alcoa Seaprobe* to Bascom's specifications, and in an optimistic article in *Science,* published in 1971, he wrote:

The *Alcoa Seaprobe* . . . is capable of reaching down with its sensors, which are in a pod at the end of a pipe, and making a detailed examination of the bottom in water several thousand meters deep. It is equipped with sonar to systematically search the sea floor at a rate of about 1 square nautical mile every 6 hours. Men at the surface will be able to inspect objects on the bottom with television, dusting away sediment by means of jets and propellers. Photographs can be taken and objects of interest identified (and perhaps recovered) by means of grasping devices.

Although it tested successfully, he was "not able to obtain sufficient financial support to take it on a deep-water archaeological expedition. . . ."

In *The Crest of the Wave,* Bascom wrote that

while thinking about Jason's voyage around the Black Sea in 1200 B.C., the significance of the name "Black" struck me. The water of the upper 100 meters of the Black Sea is clear, full of fish and much like those of other great seas, but *its bottom is black because there is no oxygen there.* The blackness is caused by sulfide compounds; the deeper part of that sea is a *reducing* environment. There is no dissolved oxygen there and few animals can live without dissolved oxygen in the water, especially the marine borers that devour a wooden ship in the Mediterranean in a few decades. . . . It dawned on me that, if Jason's *Argo* or other ancient ships had sunk to the bottom of the Black Sea, they would survive forever.*

The Black Sea is an inland body of water, connected to the Sea of Marmara (and then the Aegean and the Mediterranean) by the Bosporus. It is far from the Atlantic, and since Bascom never actually plumbed these depths (the search for ancient wrecks in the Black Sea and the Mediterranean was the deepwater archaeological expedition for which the *Seaprobe* was built by Alcoa, and for which he was "not able to obtain sufficient financial support"), the idea of searching for sunken ships in an anaerobic environment does not concern us directly.[†] But others have pondered the lost ships of antiquity, and

---

* Bascom's 1988 recollections were originally published in "Deep-Water Archaeology," an article he wrote for *Science* in 1971, but which he had obviously been thinking about for some time. In 1962, he filed for and received patents for the search-and-recovery system described in the above-mentioned article.

[†] The search for ancient wrecks is an ongoing enterprise that, alas, has very little to do with the deep Atlantic. (When *Argo/Jason* was employed in the Mediterranean off Italy in 1989 to collect amphorae from the bottom at a depth of 750 meters, it was the first time that an antiquarian site had been probed by the mechanical arm of a robot.) There are certainly famous vessels that have sunk in the Atlantic, but the floor of our ocean is aerobically active, and wood does not last very long on the bottom. All the decking, stairways, and paneling on the *Titanic,* which sank in 1912, have already been consumed by wood borers.

they have even gone so far as to develop vessels—or, rather, equipment—to help them in their search.

Bascom may not have taken his brainchild to search for a sunken ship, but Ballard did. His first voyage in search of the *Titanic* in 1977 took place aboard the *Seaprobe*. "The ship and its rig represented a bold step forward in deep-sea technology," wrote Ballard (in *The Discovery of the Titanic*), "but it was far from ideal for my purposes. What I really needed was a system towed on a flexible cable that could be raised and lowered with relative ease, but the *Seaprobe* would have to do. It was the best thing then available." On this voyage, however, he experienced nothing but failure and disaster. They did not find the *Titanic* in 1977 (they would not find it for another eight years—and indeed, with a "system towed on a flexible cable"), and after lowering the *Seaprobe*'s pipe some 3,000 feet into the North Atlantic, the pipe broke and the entire length plunged to the ocean floor, completely aborting the mission.

At Woods Hole in the early 1970s, a group of engineers developed ANGUS, the towed camera sled that was used in 1974 for Project FAMOUS (see pp. 102–4), and later, Ballard's "Deep Submergence Laboratory" (DSL) worked on the *Argo/Jason* complex. ("Jason and the Argonauts searched for the Golden Fleece aboard the *Argo*," Ballard explained.) *Argo/Jason* was a remotely controlled deep-towed vehicle system that carried both sonar and television, combined with a tethered, self-propelled swimming robot that could be used for closer survey work. By 1982, *Argo* had been built by the U.S. Navy for use in undersea search programs, and *Jason Jr.* was constructed in 1986 and tested from *Alvin*—"the very vehicle it will someday replace," wrote Ballard. (In his 1987 book on the discovery of the *Titanic*, Ballard wrote, "I could now imagine the day when we would replace *Alvin* altogether with remote-controlled eyes of the deep.") Video cameras aboard *Argo* picked up the first signs of the *Titanic* in 1985; a view of one of the boilers resting on the bottom at 13,000 feet showed the topside viewers that they had found the final resting place of the great liner. After Ballard and his crew had photographed the wreck from the *Alvin*, they sent *Jason Jr.* down the *Titanic*'s grand staircase, for a view that would have been far too risky for a manned submersible.* For his 1994 expedition to the *Lusitania*, torpedoed in 1915 off the coast of Ireland (and now resting on the bottom in 295 feet of water), Ballard employed no submersibles whatsoever; his entire investigation was conducted with robotic television cameras.

---

* There were two "*Jasons*," and curiously, *Jason Jr.* preceded *Jason*. The prototype *Jason Jr.*— nicknamed "*JJ*"—was (according to Ballard's description in *Explorations*), "a sky blue cube of pressure-resistant syntactic epoxy foam surrounding two linked pairs of vertical and horizontal thruster motors and a glass-domed titanium vessel with a color television camera, 35mm still camera, and powerful strobe" that was operated from *Alvin*. *JJ* was lost in 1991, when a barge carrying it sank off the Galápagos Islands.

Manned submersible *Shinkai-6500,* the latest Japanese entry in the race to the depths. With a dazzling array of still and video camera equipment, this 30-foot-long vehicle can record scenes never before seen by human eyes.

In 1985, the French submersible *Nautile* joined the ranks of deep-diving submarines; others rated at over 20,000 feet include the U.S. Navy's *Sea Cliff,* which was given a titanium hull in 1984; the Finnish-built, Russian-operated *Mir-1* and *Mir-2* (launched in 1987); and the Japanese *Shinkai-6500,* which in 1989 dived in the Japan Trench to the record depth of 21,320 feet.* *Shinkai 6500*—which is "about the size of a small camper and looks something like a whale with a serious overbite"—in 1994 was participating in the exploration and mapping of the TAG (Trans-Atlantic Geotraverse) Field, part of the Mid-Atlantic Ridge, first described by Peter Rona in 1985, and discussed in detail in *Nature* (1986) by Rona, Klinkhammer, Nelsen, Trefry, and Elderfield. Located at 36° N (roughly midway between Florida and West Africa), this is the first hydrothermal field to be found on an oceanic ridge. Rona suggested that "other such ridges may exist along slow spreading oceanic ridges in the Atlantic Ocean," and indeed, this turned out to be the case. In 1993, *Alvin* made

---

* Although the record depth for a submersible descent is *Trieste*'s 1960 dive of 35,800 feet to the floor of the Mariana Trench, *Trieste* was tethered to a surface ship and lowered to the bottom. This record is for an *untethered* submersible, a vessel not attached in any way to a mother ship.

six dives on the "Lucky Strike" vent field at 37°17′ N, and encountered black smokers, along with a previously undescribed species of yellow mussels, shrimp, brachyuran crabs, and, for the first time at a vent site, sea urchins.

Dubbed "the Mother of all Vent Fields," the TAG Field has been known since 1972, when the NOAA research vessel *Discoverer* hauled up a black, crumbly, hundred-pound slab of almost pure manganese oxide. Peter Rona realized that such a slab had to have come from a mineral-rich vent, and with geochemist Geoff Thompson, he has been studying this extraordinary site for more than twenty years. From repeated dives in submersibles, they have surveyed a 15-square-mile zone that proved to be the largest, most varied vent site in the world. Ten sloping volcanic domes may mark the magma chambers that supply TAG's heat, and cracks and fissures spew forth plumes of black and white smoke. There are inactive zones named for *Alvin* and the Russian submersible *Mir*, and a sloping mound of strangely shaped chimneys known as "the Kremlin" for its resemblance to Moscow's onion-shaped domes. New crust spreads out from the axial valley at about two centimeters per year—the speed at which fingernails grow—which may account for TAG's abundance of features.

In 1989, geologists descended in the *Nautile* in the deep Atlantic just north of the Equator to sample the ocean floor. In a 1994 *Scientific American* article, Enrico Bonatti of Lamont-Doherty wrote: "We planned to descend to the seafloor—more than five kilometers down—in the submarine *Nautile* to explore the walls of the transform valley. We hoped to find an exposed, pristine section of mantle and crust." Bonatti collected samples of peridotite that revealed how the convective forces may shape the earth's mantle, and indeed may have caused the separation of Africa and South America that has resulted in the Atlantic Ocean as we know it today.

The bottom of the ocean is a goal in itself, whether or not there is anything to find there. Most scientists now believe that the future lies in "tele-presence" as opposed to manned submersibles, but a Japanese quasi-governmental consortium of industrial corporations (Mitsui, Mitsubishi, and Kawasaki) and American inventor Graham Hawkes are competing to become the first to take a manned submersible to the oceans' greatest depth. (In a 1993 *Newsweek* article, Ballard is quoted as calling the race "a stunt; there's nothing there but mud.") The Japanese Marine Science and Technology Center (JAMSTEC) has launched the two-part unmanned submersible known as *Kaiko* (Japanese for "trench"), which is said to have cost 5.4 billion yen, or almost $50 million. Tethered to the support vessel *Yokosuka* by seven miles of cable, the 5-ton, 17-foot "launcher" is equipped with side-scan sonar, a sub-bottom profiler that can do geological research up to 30 meters below the sea floor, and various other sophisticated sensors. Attached by another cable to the launcher is the eyes of *Kaiko*, a 10-foot "roving vehicle" with color and monochrome television cameras, still cameras, depth sensors, and manipulator arms. In March 1994, a test dive took *Kaiko* to 10,911 meters (35,797 feet) in the Mariana Trench, only 3 feet short of the depth reached by the manned submersible *Trieste* in 1960. An "equipment failure" caused the Japanese to abort the mission, just feet short of the bottom, but before the failure of the video cable, pictures of the deepest part of the ocean were transmitted to the mother ship. (*Kaiko* and *Shinkai-6500* are both owned and operated by JAMSTEC.) From 1989 onward, *Shinkai-6500* dived at various locations in the Pacific and, using what is probably the most advanced equipment ever designed for this work, photographed (video and still) an astonishing array of creatures, many of whose images had never been seen before. On March 24, 1995, *Kaiko* descended to a measured depth

The remote-controlled deep-diving vehicle *Kaiko*, which the Japanese can send to the oceans' greatest depths. On March 24, 1995, *Kaiko* reached the bottom of the Challenger Deep in the Mariana Trench, 35,798 feet down.

of 35,798 feet at the bottom of the Challenger Deep, and planted a little sign to prove that she had been there.

Unlike the peak of Mount Everest, at 29,028 feet the earth's greatest terrestrial altitude, the deepest level of the ocean—the Challenger Deep in the Mariana Trench—is something of a variable. When the bathyscaph *Trieste* touched down in 1960, the depth gauge read 6,300 fathoms (37,800 feet), but according to a note in Piccard's *Seven Miles Down,* the gauge had originally been calibrated for freshwater, and corrections for "salinity, compressibility, temperature, and gravity" produced the new reading of 35,800 feet. This is not a particularly precise way to establish a record, so it is possible that *Kaiko* did break the record. Also, the configuration of the bottom of the trench varies enough to produce different depth readings at different locations.

Graham Hawkes, born in England in 1947 and now living in California, is the leading proponent (as well as designer and pilot) of exploratory manned underwater vehicles. His first innovations took the form of improved diving suits, in which the individual depth record for men (1,440 feet) and for women (1,250 feet) were set. In 1979, during the filming of a TV special, he met Sylvia Earle (whom he later married) and she dived to 1,250 feet in the "Jim Suit," a combination hard-hat diving costume and space suit. For this dive, which took place off Oahu, the suit (with Earle inside) was lowered to the sea floor aboard a Launch Recovery Transport (LRT), from which she took her record-setting solo walk on the ocean floor. Hawkes also experimented with mini-submersibles, including *Mantis* in 1978, a one-man sub powered by ten propellers, in which the operator sat inside a small cylinder and worked two mechanical arms. Next came *Bandit,* a two-man, 2,000-pound machine that was employed by the oil industry for pipeline work. (Hawkes also holds the individual record for a solo descent; in 1985, he dived to 3,000 feet off the coast of California in a miniature submarine.)

Hawkes is now at work on a miniature submarine that he hopes will take him to the bottom of the Mariana Trench. Dubbed *Deep Flight,* the prototype one-man sub is about 12 feet long and shaped like a miniature spaceship. The pilot lies facing forward in the plastic nose cone, controlling the sub's speed and inclination. Hawkes and Earle were divorced in 1993, but they are still working together on the *Deep Flight* project, hoping (according to an article in *The New York Times*) "to explore the deepest parts of the ocean, together. . . ." Whereas the Japanese entry has so far cost $50 million, Hawkes hopes to build *Deep Flight II* for less than $10 million, if a new battery is developed as a side effect of electric-car research. As to why they would want to descend in person to the oceans' greatest depths when an unmanned submersible could do the job in a much less risky and certainly less costly fashion, Earle says (in a 1994 interview in *Science News*), "Earth is a marine habitat. . . . [T]he ocean is home to the greatest diversity of the planet. It's still ironic that there are more footprints on the moon than there are on the bottom of the sea, and we're only 7 miles away. . . ."

In a 1994 article in *Currents,* the newsletter of the Woods Hole Oceanographic Institution, Bob Ballard discusses the video technology that now makes it possible to obtain high-quality, color television images from the floor of the ocean, and then writes:

> One of the major programs we're trying to work with now is the challenge
> of exploration in the Black Sea, the only major body of water in the world

This is what it looks like at 35,798 feet down. The Japanese deep-diving submersible planted this sign on March 24, 1995. The fish has not (yet) been identified.

that does not have oxygen on the bottom. It's anaerobic, which means wood-boring organisms are not there. The potential of finding bronze-age ships or even older ships preserved is ideal in the Black Sea.

In *Oceanus,* Dana Yoerger introduced the Autonomous Benthic Explorer (*ABE*), the latest development in deep-sea exploration. Developed by engineers at WHOI, *ABE* is untethered—that is, able to move without the restrictions of a cable. It is designed to spend months underwater, taking pictures, sampling water, and performing other chores as directed by its internal computer system. "*ABE* is designed for a wide variety of missions," wrote Al Bradley, Dana Yoerger, and Barrie Walden in 1995, "but foremost is monitoring geological and biological changes in hydrothermal vent regions." Albert Bradley, one of *ABE*'s designers, is quoted as saying, "Submarines only go forward; *ABE* can move up, down, left, right, back, forth and sideways." The three-bodied robot is about the size of a small car, and will be able to descend to depths of several thousand meters. It will also be able to "go to sleep" for months at a time to conserve battery power when not in use. In *Currents,* Yoerger (the designer of *ABE*'s control-system software) said, "You can't go back to the seafloor with *Jason* or *Alvin* every month to get data. There's only one *Alvin* and only one *Jason.* They can't be all over the world and back at the same experimental site every month." But there can certainly be more than one *ABE*; by becoming a part of the environment we wish to investigate, rather than an awkward, alien presence, we may be looking at a new age of undersea exploration.*

This history of submersibles—indeed, the history of any technological advance that presumes to be up to date—will be obsolete as soon as it is published. New developments in the conquest of inner space are constantly taking place. *Kaiko*'s landing on the floor of the Challenger Deep differed dramatically from the 1960 dive of *Trieste* because the Japanese submersible is an advanced vehicle, capable of moving around and sending back images, while in *Trieste*, Piccard and Walsh just sat there and looked out the window. There may be nothing but mud at the bottom, but that hardly demystifies the journey—what, after all, is at the top of Everest but snow and ice?

* The British are also planning to participate in the autonomous underwater vehicle (AUV) race with the planned development of DOGGIE (Deep Ocean Geological and Geophysical Instrumented Explorer) and DOLPHIN (Deep Ocean Long Path Hydrographic InstrumentatioN), two robotic vehicles whose acronyms must have taken almost as much time to create as the vehicles themselves.

By Submarine
Across the Atlantic

The wrecks dissolve above us; their dust drops down from afar—
Down to the dark, to the utter dark, where the blind white sea-snakes are.
There is no sound, no echo of sound in the deserts of the deep,
Or the great gray level plains of ooze where the shell-blurred cables creep.

Here in the womb of the world—here on the tie-ribs of earth
Words, and the words of men, flicker and flutter and beat—
Warning, sorrow, and gain, salutation and mirth—
For a Power troubles the Still that has neither voice nor feet.

They have wakened the timeless Things; they have killed their father Time;
Joining hands in the gloom, a league from the last of the sun.
Hush! Men talk today o'er the waste of the ultimate slime,
And a new Word runs between: whispering, "Let us be one!"

RUDYARD KIPLING
"Deep Sea Cables" (1893)

From 1520, when Ferdinand Magellan's ropes dangled overboard and never touched bottom, to the time Matthew Maury collected data from sailing captains, to the echo-sounders of the 1960s, we have tried to gain an image of the floor of the ocean, forever hidden from our eyes. Marie Tharp and Bruce Heezen painstakingly drew every known ridge, rise, canyon, and seamount on their maps of the sea floor, and while their pioneering cartographic efforts exponentially expanded our understanding of the physiography and mechanics of the sea floor, recent technological advances have given us a picture of the face of the earth heretofore unavailable, even to those who saw it firsthand through the portholes of research submersibles.

Space satellites equipped with radar altimeters are able to measure every bump and depression on the earth's surface—including those on the bottom of the ocean. Mountains, ridges, canyons, and other features create depressions or swellings on the sea's surface, and these can be calculated to such a fine degree that hundreds of previously unknown seamounts, rifts, ridges, and fracture zones have now been added to our maps. In 1990, the National Geographic Society issued a map of the floor of the Atlantic that contained more detail than any such map before it, revealing a world that was completely unknown to our ancestors, and even today, unsuspected by almost everyone except professional oceanographers.

It is a fascinating and instructive exercise to compare the earlier maps with the most recent ones. When Maurice Ewing wrote about the Mid-Atlantic Ridge in a 1949 *National Geographic* article, his map showed a soft ridge bisecting the ocean, with no fracture zones and very few seamounts except those associated with island groups like the Azores or the Canaries. Subsequently, Bruce Heezen and Marie Tharp would draw physiographic maps of the sea floor, with every known seamount, ridge, rise, and rift laboriously inked in by hand. The 1990 *Geographic* map reveals the complex, jagged nature of the Ridge, and fracture zones, rises, plains, and tablemounts that Ewing, Heezen, and Tharp may have suspected, but which would not be revealed until NASA's eyes-in-the-sky, the Seasat and Geosat systems, reported their existence. "For lack of proper tools," wrote Rear Adm. Richard Pittinger on the 1990 map, "this vast undersea frontier has defied exploration until very recently. Now that new technology is at hand, slowly, the earth's underwater realm is beginning to emerge."

By 1992, Woods Hole scientists were using "Sea Beam," a high-resolution sonar system capable of mapping a two-kilometer-wide swath of the sea floor in a single pulse, and powerful computers were used to model the data in unprecedented detail. No sooner had this wealth of information become available to the oceanographers than a whole new raft of questions arose. As posed by Jian Lin in a 1991 article in *Oceanus,* they include: Why do slow-spreading ridges differ from fast ones? How do spreading segments evolve in time over tens of millions of years? Why are transform faults longer and stable while nontransform faults are shorter and nontransitory? Does the segmentation in the volcanic ridge correlate with changes in ridge-crest hydrothermal vents, or even with the biological population at the ridge crest? A cooperative study known as RIDGE (Ridge Inter-Disciplinary Global Experiments), funded by the National Science Foundation, will attempt to answer these and many other questions.

Using the latest in hydrographic and bathymetric information as our road map, we are about to embark on a cruise of the Atlantic—underwater.

Our vessel is named *Navegador* for Henry the Navigator (1394–1460), the Portuguese prince who founded a school of navigation and cartography at Sagres on Cape Saint Vincent, and our cruise—conducted in a manner that he could not have imagined, and encountering phenomena that his wildest dreams could not have encompassed—is an *hommage* to the history of Atlantic exploration. In our modern version of Verne's *Nautilus,* we will traverse the breadth of the Atlantic, looking out the viewing ports as we head eastward. Except at the start, when we cruise along the continental shelf, no sunlight will penetrate these depths—nor has it ever—so we must provide illumination for our hypothetical cruise, enabling us to see the sediments, canyons, and cliffs—and the occasional representatives of the world of living things. We are lucky that the abyssal ocean water is usually much clearer than that near the surface; there are no waves to roil the waters, and for the most part, the currents are comparatively gentle. If the sediment is disturbed, it will probably be our own fault.

We plan to start in New York and fetch up at Sagres, where Atlantic exploration began. Our journey begins just off the beach, where the bottom is made up of sand and gravel, much of which has been produced by the abrasive action of waves on shells and rocks. We descend below the surface onto the flat plain that marks the continental shelf of North America, cruise along the sandy, featureless seascape for about a hundred miles until it drops precipitously to the abyssal plain a mile and a half below. The beveled edge of the shelf is scored with vertical gullies and ravines, the largest of which is the Hudson Canyon, one of the many canyons that mark the continental slope from Maine to New Jersey. Hudson Canyon begins as a shallow channel in about 300 feet of water at the mouth of the Hudson River and gouges a 1,600-foot cleft into the seaward face of the upper continental slope, but like all submarine canyons, it narrows and completely disappears as it approaches the boundary of the slope and the abyssal floor. The canyons funnel sediments from terrestrial sources to the continental rise, which consists of debris which has accumulated at the floor of the continental slope.

Early oceanographers puzzled over the origin of submarine canyons, venturing opinions ranging from muddy-water avalanches to rivers that carved the land when the level of the sea was much lower. (To carve the Hudson Canyon, a river would have had to be a mile and a half lower than present sea level, a somewhat unlikely proposition.) They are puzzling still. Dutch oceanographer Philip Kuenen first identified "turbidity currents," but he originally believed that they were isolated phenomena restricted to lakes and ponds. Subsequently, he came to realize that turbidity currents are among the most powerful of undersea forces, capable of altering the topography of the ocean floor on an enormous scale.

A graphic demonstration of this phenomenon can be seen on the continental rise south of Newfoundland, where, on November 18, 1929, a huge earthquake rumbled beneath the sea under the Grand Banks, creating a turbidity current that carried a thick layer of sediment over a bottom formation known to geologists as the Laurentian Fan. The precise date is known because six telegraph cables lay athwart the path of the current, and each broke and cut off service as the current rolled over it. In their analysis of this event, Heezen and Ewing (1952) wrote: "Each successive cable was broken by a turbidity current originating as a slump along the continental slope in the epicentral area and traveling downward along the continental slope, continental rise, and ocean basin floor, and continuing far out on the abyssal plain well over 450 miles from the continental shelf." In waters that range from 2,000 to 4,800 meters deep (6,560 to 15,744 feet), this earthquake—measured at 7.2 on the Richter scale—redistributed gravel, boulders, and sediment, and carved massive channels and valleys in the ocean floor. Heezen and Ewing calculated that the torrent of turbid water traveled at a speed of more than 50 miles per hour and carried about 24 cubic miles of sediment—according to Kuenen, "enough to load a row of tankers 20 ships wide running round the equator."[*]

We know that these canyons exist all over the world—usually, but not always, in conjunction with a terrestrial river delta—but because so much of the sea floor is hidden from human eyes, we cannot easily see what is there, and even if we could, it is not easy to figure out how it got there. Turbidity currents are generally believed to be the cause of submarine canyons, but no naturally occurring one has ever been seen—which may be just as well, since proximity to such a powerful event might be too dangerous.[†] Our shipboard library has the best possible field guide for the trip, Heezen and Hollister's *Face of the Deep*, where we read, "It is hard to discover a more hotly debated subject in geology or one that offers such a wide variety of theories as the origin of submarine canyons."

As our voyage continues, Heezen and Hollister would have us abandon the conundrum of submarine canyons and "turn away from the lush gardens and fertile pastures of the sun-nurtured sea and begin our visual journey to the underlying vast, black, and frigid watery Hades. We will search through the

---

[*] In a report published in the journal *Nature* two weeks after the event, C. Davison described some of the effects of the earthquake. The White Star liner *Olympic* was about 300 miles from the spot at which the cables were broken, and the captain "felt the vessel suddenly quiver, as though she had cast off a propeller blade, and this movement was followed by vibrations lasting for two minutes." The tremor was felt in Boston, 700 miles from the epicenter, and in Nova Scotia, where "chimneys were thrown down." A sea wave 15 feet high swept away houses in the Newfoundland towns of Burin, Lord's Cove, and Lamaline, killing twenty-six people.

[†] Diving in the French bathyscaph *FNRS-3* in 1954, Jacques Cousteau started an avalanche in the Toulon Canyon of the Mediterranean. *FNRS-3* had inadvertently settled on a ledge at 4,920 feet, and when the aquanauts tried to move off, they loosened blocks of mud which tumbled toward the bottom of the canyon, creating a cloud of mud that rendered them blind. They hung motionless for an hour, unable to determine if they were stuck in the mud or the victims of a mechanical failure. When they realized that they had been down so long that their gasoline had cooled, making them heavier, they ejected their ballast and came safely to the surface.

nearly barren abyss for those few sparks of life which have somehow found a way to survive in a dark, bitter-cold environment." Keeping the Bermuda Rise and its attendant islands to starboard, we then encounter the New England Seamounts and the Sohm Abyssal Plain, a thousand miles of flat sediment under 17,000 feet of ocean. Most of the familiar animal forms are absent here; we see few fishes, mostly grenadiers and rattails, a single octopus, a scattering of sponges and gorgonians (sea whips and sea fans), and many different echinoderms—starfishes, feather stars, and brittle stars. In some areas, the starfishes are widely scattered, but occasionally we pass over a dense congregation of stars, a living mound of slowly moving arms. We have no idea what they are doing. Many species of deepwater invertebrates have never been collected, so we may be seeing creatures unknown to science.

Seventy-one percent of the earth is covered with water, and 80 percent of that is the sediment-covered sea floor. The predominant life form on the floor of the deep sea appears to be holothurians, commonly known as sea cucumbers. Different types can be seen, sometimes moving very slowly, sometimes half buried in the ooze. Some are fat, shapeless tubes, while others have leglike protrusions (known as podia) with which they move. The genus *Psychropotes* may reach 18 inches in length, but others are only 3 or 4 inches long. They ingest the ooze like vacuum cleaners for detrital sustenance, probably rained down from above. While most shallow-water holothurians are brown, olive, or black, the ones we see in the abyssal depths are often purple, maroon, or violet, and those that are half buried in the sediment are yellow, red, or orange. We pass over an unusual congregation of multicolored holothurians, a veritable herd of massed orange and yellow bodies assembled for reasons known only to them.

The ocean floor appears featureless until we get close to it, but then we see that it is marked with tracks, trails, burrows, and other evidence of life on the bottom. Indeed, the very bottom itself varies from place to place, and every location is covered with a particular sediment; there is nothing that is just plain old "mud." Here we are floating over a plain of "red clay," not really red, but a chocolate-brown, fine-grained sediment that covers much of the floor of the Atlantic. The great majority of bottom sediments are composed of the shells of countless protozoans, such as the foraminifera (commonly called "forams"), bottom-dwellers with calcareous shells, and silicate-shelled radiolarians, components of the planktonic community. The *Globigerina* species have formed great deposits, covering more than a third of the ocean floor. Globigerina ooze can be milky white, ocher, or brown, and it is a chalky material found mostly at depths of 4,000 meters or less. The yellowish or straw-colored stuff is diatom ooze, made up of somewhat larger particles than glob ooze, and the greenish material is deepwater radiolarian ooze.

Heezen and Hollister wrote, "It must be stressed that it is not the living organisms themselves, but the effect they have had on the sediment during the course of their lives that is the principal thing to be seen on most of the deep sea floor." During our voyage, we will be on the lookout for "footprints, plow marks, excrement, holes, and mounds that comprise nearly all there is to see in the vast majority of abyssal photographs." These tracks have been laid down as long as there were animals to lay them, so we are looking at the top layer of thousands—often hundreds of thousands—of years of geological history. (No part of the Atlantic Ocean floor is very old; no bottom samples have ever been found that predated the Cretaceous period, 135 million years ago.) But since the abyssal red clays are laid down at a rate of perhaps one or two millimeters per thousand years, the tracks we see might have been made last week, or five hundred years ago. We can identify some of the tracks—there is the multilegged trail of a brittle star; and the treadlike spoor of a holothurian—but even our guidebook does not help us with that meandering plowmark that terminates in a burrow. What creature wandered here until it decided to bury itself?

We are in the Atlantic's primary traffic lanes, where, for half a millennium, ships have traversed the ocean. It is therefore not surprising to see assorted human discards on the ocean floor, such as an old-fashioned Coke bottle, a shoe, and what looks like a toilet, half buried in the sediment. Other foreign objects are spotted: there are large rocks that were probably transported by icebergs, which subsequently melted. And because we are traveling the route of the transatlantic cables, we see what Kipling referred to as "the shell-blurred cables," their twisted strands tracing long lines across the ocean floor. We espy an enormous skull entangled in a cable thrown in loops around its toothed lower jaw. Scattered around it are hugely curving ribs and numerous smaller bones, picked white by the crustacean scavengers of the bottom. It is the remains of a sperm whale that became entangled in the cable and drowned while it was plowing through the sediment, or perhaps it mistook the strands of cable for the tentacles of a squid.

As *Navegador* cruises along the bottom of the abyssal plain, we watch sea pens and sponges bowed over as if by a gentle breeze. There is a steady movement and mixing of cold bottom waters along abyssal contours; we can see ripples on current-swept ridges, like those formed on sand by the wind. And just ahead, there is an immense field of what looks like coal-black potatoes. They are manganese nodules, more common in the Pacific but also present on the Atlantic floor. Found on the flat plains, they vary in size—according to the oceanographers who described them—from grapes and potatoes to grapefruit and cannonballs. Most nodules are no bigger than a potato, but occasionally a larger specimen is brought up. The largest on record, collected by a British cable-salvage ship in 1955 from 17,000 feet in the Philippine Trench, was three feet in diameter and weighed 1,700 pounds.

During the *Challenger* expedition of 1873–76, in addition to samples of various substances that comprised the sea floor (red and gray clays, globigerina ooze, diatomaceous ooze, and radiolarian ooze), the scientists collected the first manganese nodules. In his 1876 report, John Murray wrote:

> The nodules vary from little pellets to masses of a large size and of several pounds in weight. In some regions every thing at the bottom, even the bottom itself would appear to be overlaid by and impregnated with this substance [manganese]. . . . The varieties most commonly procured may be here mentioned: Nodules of a black-brown colour throughout, the manganese being laid down in concentric layers, which are evident from their enclosing lines of red clay; Nodules having a nucleus of pumice which is surrounded by concentric layers, the original nucleus being often very deeply impregnated by spider-like ramifications of manganese, or nearly the whole pumice being replaced by manganese. When pieces of bone have formed the nucleus we have much the same state of things. The compact bone of the tympanics of cetaceans does not, however, appear to alter so rapidly as other bone; and hence it may not be that we get earbones in such great numbers.

They are formed by the gradual accretion of minerals around a core, such as rocks, pumice, sharks' teeth, or whale earbones, but just about any hard object can serve as a nucleus, and most nodules form around microscopic grains of sediment or sand. If we were to examine a nodule in detail, we would see alternating atomic layers of manganese oxide and iron hydroxide, with in-between layers of nickel, copper, cobalt, and zinc. The actual source of the manganese is still not clear, but it might come from decomposing igneous rocks, volcanic emanations, or from land rivers or streams carrying minerals to the sea.

Since Murray's original description, the mysteries of the nodules have not been solved, and there are still more questions than answers. In a 1978 article, G. Ross Heath (an expert on the subject) asked, "Why are nodules found in some areas but not in others?"; "Where do the metals come from?"; "Why do nodules from different locations have different compositions?"; and "Why are nodules concentrated at the sea floor, rather than buried in the sediments?" In his article, Heath discusses possible answers to these questions, but he does not solve the problems he poses.

To get from a grain of sand to a grapefruit-sized nodule must take an enormous amount of time, and indeed, Heezen and Hollister tell us that "the growth of nodules is one of the slowest chemical reactions in nature, rates of accumulation being atomic layers per day . . . [resulting in] a rate of growth of two to four millimeters per million years." That they are not covered with sediment—and that they are usually concentric—indicates that they must be frequently rolled, and the only agent capable of doing that is the deep currents. Heath, the author of the above-mentioned discussion, suggests that "large foragers could easily roll a nodule while searching beneath it for food," but notes that "we have never actually photographed or observed an animal rolling a nodule." (Heath was director of a National Science Foundation program called MANOP, the Manganese Nodule Program, created to solve the mysteries, and also to "focus on the major processes that lead to mineable nodules in one place and worthless deposits in another.")

Heezen and Hollister give the estimate of 2 billion tons of manganese nodules on the floor of the ocean, "and it is clear," they wrote, "that these nodules comprise the largest mineral deposit on the planet." According to John Mero's 1965 *Mineral Resources of the Sea,* the manganese cobbles contain enough titanium to fulfill our needs for 2 million years, enough nickel for 150,000 years, cobalt for 200,000, manganese for 400,000, and aluminum for 20,000.* Some attempts have been made to mine this vast mineral wealth, but the combined problems of locating the fields and then collecting the nodules make it almost impossible with today's technology.

Most of the mysteries of the nodules are still unsolved, but there is no shortage of theories. One theory holds that the nodules contain bacteria that can extract manganese from seawater, and that the process is a biotic rather than an inorganic one. Enough of the material can accumulate in the oceans from rivers, continents, volcanoes, and hydrothermal vents, but this does not explain the shape of the nodules. It may be that the ocean is saturated in iron and manganese, and these elements precipitate as colloidal particles that gradually increase in size and filter down to the sea floor. Colloids of manganese and iron oxides may collect many metals and bear an electric charge, which would explain their agglomeration as nodules on the sea floor rather than particles in the general sediments.

The Mid-Atlantic Ridge is almost continuous except for a break near the Equator called the Romanche Trench. Fracture zones offset the Ridge for its entire length, giving it the appearance—if anyone could see it in its entirety—not of a single serpentine outcrop but rather of a sinuous set of zigzagging

---

* Manganese is a chemical element (symbol Mn) that occurs in nature as a gray, brittle metal. It is an essential trace element in higher animals and is a component of the reduction of nitrates in green plants and algae. It is critical in the manufacture of steel, where it is combined with iron ores in blast furnaces to create ferromanganese, which gives steel its strength. The United States, western Europe, and Japan have no minable manganese deposits; more than 70 percent of the world's terrestrial supply is found in Russia and South Africa, the remainder being in Zaire, Cameroon, and Morocco.

stairs. (Because most American research ships sailed east to west, parallel to the fractures, they did not notice them. It was Soviet oceanographers, prohibited from using American ports, who first discovered these enormous anomalies.) Fracture zones sometimes displace the axis of the Ridge, often cutting for many miles across the ocean basins. They mark the lines along which there has been a horizontal displacement, so that points which were once adjacent can now be hundreds of miles apart.

Our journey takes us south of the Laurentian Fan, a wide, sloping plain at the foot of the continental shelf, where the great earthquake occurred in 1929. The only evidence of the turbidity current that roared across the ocean floor is a smooth, slightly inclined field of gravel, vanishing into the gloom that is not illuminated by our portside lights. In this bathypelagic landscape, we have done little to change the face of the deep (although we have done terrible things to the water itself, and have treated the ocean as a dumping ground for our unwanted, and often dangerous, refuse), but all along the ocean floor are reminders of the frailty of man's designs. For centuries, ships have been wrecked by nature or sunk by warfare, and their hulks lie scattered on the bottom, mute testimony to the power and indifference of the enveloping sea. The colossal avalanche that severed telegraph cables and moved millions upon millions of tons of sediment barely missed the wreck of the *Titanic*. On April 14, 1912, the "unsinkable" White Star liner, the largest ship in the world, on her maiden voyage from Southampton to New York, collided with an iceberg and sank to the bottom in 13,000 feet of water. In September 1985, some 350 miles southeast of Newfoundland, the resting place of the wreck was found by a French-American consortium led by Robert Ballard of Woods Hole and Jean-Louis Michel of IFREMER, the Institut Français de Recherches pour L'Exploration des Mers.

Equipped with the latest search technology, including side-scan sonar, underwater video cameras, and computer timing equipment, the French research ship *Le Suroît* and the Woods Hole vessel *Knorr* crisscrossed a 150-square-mile area southwest of Newfoundland for weeks, an operation the crews called "mowing the lawn," hoping to pick up an image that would identify the *Titanic*. The searchers were flying blind, since they had only imprecise coordinates of the wreck's location, and they did not know what direction she had taken on her two-and-a-half-mile trip to the bottom. On September 1, 1985, the video camera sled *Argo* returned an image of one of the liner's huge boilers that had burst through the hull upon impact with the bottom, lying in a gravel-floored canyon.

The catastrophe in which 1,522 out of the 2,227 crew and passengers died is probably the most heavily documented shipwreck in history, with hundreds of pages of testimony, any number of books, and more than one society dedicated to the preservation and analysis of its history. There were many controversies surrounding the event, such as why they didn't see the iceberg until it was too late; why there were not enough lifeboats; and what happened to the ships that were supposed to rescue the passengers.

The ice struck *Titanic*'s starboard bow, and we do not know if the rivets holding the hull plates popped, or if the ice actually ripped a gash in the hull. When the water poured into the ruptured forward compartments, she went nose down, and the 882-foot-long ship broke in half. The bow sank through two and a half miles of the frigid North Atlantic and plowed into the bottom, raising a bow wave of mud that suggests she hit at considerable speed. She sits in an upright attitude with her bow buried in 50 feet of mud. The puncture that actually caused the ship to sink is hidden in the mud, and the question of what actually happened will probably never be answered. The first person to see her on the bottom (after *Argo*'s television images had verified her existence and location), was Bob Ballard aboard *Alvin*. He wrote, "My first direct view of *Titanic* lasted less than two minutes, but the stark sight of her immense black hull towering above the ocean floor will remain forever ingrained in my memory." She had been launched as the largest and most luxurious ship in the world, but *Titanic* is now a deepwater spectre, with rows of blind portholes staring out of her rusting hull plates.

At ground level *Navegador* takes us the length of the once-black hull, now mottled yellow, ocher, and red with rust. The guardrail at the bow is festooned with "rusticles," hanging dribbles of oxidized iron that soften the towering, sharply pointed prow into a multicolored sculpture. The hard metallic surfaces are softened by rust, corrosion, and a thin dusting of "snow"—the constant fall of tiny particles that eventually constitute the sediment. Protruding from the hawsehole, the flukes of the great bow anchor are streaked with ferrous ribbons of rust. Our lights reflect off myriad falling particles; it looks as if it is snowing. The indented letters that spelled out "Titanic" have been corroded over. As we make our way slowly sternward, we see the litter that fell to the bottom as the ship plunged downward: teacups bearing the emblem of the White Star Line (a white star within a red burgee); a chair; wine and liquor bottles; pots and pans; ladders; unidentifiable pieces of machinery; a sink. Perhaps attracted by our lights, a grenadier hovers over an encrusted bathtub. We ascend 50 feet so that we can cruise the length of the forecastle deck toward the bridge.

It is covered with a film of sediment, but all the features are clearly visible. The massive anchor chains, with their 175-pound links, are in place, rust-frozen forever around the capstans. Stretching from its step on the foredeck is the great hollow foremast that toppled onto the bridge when the ship hit the bottom. Still visible on the now-horizontal mast is the crow's nest, where look-

outs Reginald Lee and Frederick Fleet were stationed to watch for ice. At 11:40 p.m. on the cold, clear night of April 14, Fleet rang the alarm bell three times, then telephoned the bridge and shouted, "Iceberg right ahead!" (The call was taken by Sixth Officer James Moody, who said "Thank you" and informed First Officer William Murdoch, who immediately ordered "Hard a-starboard," which meant that he wanted the ship's head to go to port. Murdoch then ordered, "Stop. Full speed astern," but less than a minute later, the ship felt the impact. There is a strong possibility that the order to turn caused the disaster. "Had she rammed the berg head-on," wrote Ballard, "she would likely have flooded only two or three compartments and remained afloat.") The *Titanic* sank two hours and forty minutes after the collision with the ice.

We cruise over the starboard foredeck of the *Titanic*, passing over the bollards that were used for securing the great ship while she was docked. Unfortunately, she never docked again after her maiden voyage; she sank in the North Atlantic on April 12, 1912, after colliding with an iceberg.

The four huge funnels were apparently ripped loose during the descent, and their location is marked by torn flanges of metal. Guy wires and telegraph cables thickened with a coating of muddy sediment dangle from the fallen masts. The pine decking is gone, eaten away by wood-boring organisms, leaving only the bare metal underlayment. In fact, everything that was made of wood is gone, including the walls of deck structures, masts, chairs, and handrails. Many of the steel plates used in the construction of the ship were torn upon impact and are twisted grotesquely, like a badly opened tin can. The huge square cargo hatches, their covers ripped off, yawn beneath us. The roof of the first-class lounge collapsed on top of the decks below, leaving a sloping mass of wreckage. On this incline, just aft of the site of the number two funnel, now gone forever, there is nothing. The rest of the *Titanic* is not here. As the forward portion of the ship plummeted like a 30,000-ton arrow to the bottom, the stern section tumbled crazily, spewing machinery, furniture, plumbing fixtures, *objets d'art,* and other items loosened by the sudden and unexpected downward voyage.

To get to the stern, we must cross the so-called debris field, about 2,000 feet of litter. We see a boiler, then another. Mangled metal plates lie all around us, and there are smaller objects of all sorts scattered about. A champagne bottle, still corked. Dozens—maybe hundreds—of dinner plates. A bedspring. A shoe. Metal stanchions. A crumpled silver tray. Three lamps. A porcelain doll's head with its eyes open. A spittoon. A large square box that may be a safe. What looks like rocks litter the field, but we know that they are lumps of coal, showered down to the sea floor when the ship's bunkers burst open. Even though coal, dolls, and silver are not supposed to be the same color, this landscape is almost monochromatic. Because of the film of sediment, everything is a pale grayish-brown, like a faded sepia print.

The stern faces in the opposite direction from the bow; somehow it twisted around almost 180 degrees on its voyage to the bottom. Ballard wrote that it "looked as though it had been alternately torpedoed, bombed, and shelled." It is barely recognizable as part of a ship, since it collapsed and crumpled when it hit, peeling the poop deck back like the skin of a banana, but smashing and compressing everything beneath it. Like its forward counterpart, the rear mast fell, and it lies bent and twisted across the wreck. We can make out a cargo crane, which is being visited by several pale crabs, and there the number eight lifeboat davits arch silently into the icy water. We look for the propellers, each 23 feet across, but they have either come loose or are buried deep in the mud. In this tangled mass of wreckage and mangled metal, we can see certain elements that remind us of the catastrophe that befell those thousands of people on that cold April night, such as that stoker's shovel lying next to a single rubber boot.

The wreckage of the *Titanic* is not for us to remove and place on our mantels to prove we have been here. ("Take nothing but pictures," as the backpackers say.) It is not to be brought up to be sold to collectors. Rather, it is a memorial to those who died in April of 1912. *Titanic* will not be raised, but only viewed in the eerie silence of the illuminated abyss, either by travelers in hypothetical submarines like ours or by viewers of the photographs and videos

that were brought up at such great risk and with such dedication by the people who respect her history.*

In a statement before the U.S. House of Representatives in October of
1985, Ballard said, "I strongly believe that if the *Titanic* is left alone that within
the next few years, beginning as early as next year, robotic vehicles will be able
to enter its beautifully designed rooms and document in color its preserved
splendor. No salvage operation in the world could duplicate this feat." Indeed,
the "next year" Ballard brought the *Jason Jr.*, a robotic television camera, down
with *Alvin*, parked the sub above the grand staircase, and obtained spectacular pictures of the ship's interior. Its "preserved splendor," however, was a
shambles of broken furniture and dangling light fixtures, everything overhung
with a cascade of rust stalactites. In his epilogue to Ballard's 1987 article, the
editor of *National Geographic* wrote, "Robert Ballard's hope that the *Titanic*
should remain undisturbed was not realized. Last July, a French expedition
began to retrieve artifacts from the wreck site. Its actions were roundly criti-
cized as grave robbing—justifiably, for the line between curiosity and acquisi-
tiveness seems to have been crossed."

There is another major historic shipwreck, also in the North Atlantic,
and also discovered by Ballard. The *Bismarck* was sunk by the Royal Navy
about a thousand miles off the coast of Normandy in 1941. Like the *Titanic,*
the *Bismarck's* first voyage was her last. Almost as large as the *Titanic,* the
German battleship was 823 feet long and 118 feet wide. (*Titanic's* beam was 92
feet.) She was launched on February 14, 1939, in the presence of Adolf Hitler,
Hermann Goering, and Adm. Erich Raeder, and by May 1941, she had sunk
the proudest ship in the British navy, the battle cruiser *Hood.* After a chase
that took them all over the North Atlantic, she was attacked by the battleships
Rodney and *King George V,* and the cruisers *Norfolk* and *Dorsetshire.* A total of
2,876 shells were fired at her by the British. The *Bismarck* was sinking as a result of so much damage, so to keep her from falling into enemy hands, she was
scuttled by her crew. On May 27, 1941, she went down somewhere over the
Porcupine Abyssal Plain at the foot of the British continental shelf, with most

---

* It will probably come as no surprise to learn that almost as soon as Ballard had come up,
a team of divers was preparing to descend to the *Titanic* for commercial purposes. No one actually
has jurisdiction over the wreck, so there was no way to stop anyone who wanted to desecrate the
remains. In the summer of 1987, French and American divers made thirty-two dives in the submersible *Nautile* and grabbed whatever they could, destroying precious mountings and artifacts in
the process. (In their attempt to wrest free the bell that Frederick Fleet had rung when he sighted
the iceberg, they destroyed the crow's nest.) They put on a tasteless television show—the only
record of this debacle—where they opened a safe with great fanfare, claiming that it contained the
valuables that the passengers had given to the purser. It contained some coins and jewelry belonging to one man.

of her crew of two thousand aboard. In 1989, using many of the same techniques that he employed to locate the *Titanic,* Ballard found the German battleship resting upright in 15,000 feet of water.

Leaving the remains of the *Titanic,* we pass the Corner Seamounts, another range of drowned volcanoes, and soon we are beginning to see what amounts to the foothills of the Mid-Atlantic Ridge; low, jagged peaks rising before us and getting increasingly steep as we continue our eastward journey. Strange formations greet us here; ropy tubes and pillows of solidified lava testify to the volcanic origins of the Ridge, but the ever-present coating of manganese makes precise geological identification difficult. There are also "sheet-flows"—slabs of lava that are swirled and wrinkled like a messy tablecloth, formed when bursting tubes spewed forth liquid lava that formed ponds that were then cooled by overlying seawater. We can see further evidence of strong currents along the slopes of these mountains in the polished lava and current-rippled sand pockets in the eroded rock. Sea fans spread their nets across the moving waters, and urchins and holothurians march deliberately across the patches of sand.

We follow the Oceanographic Fracture Zone, which runs parallel to our itinerary, one of the deepest of all the east-west fissures that cross the Ridge. Its walls are steep and bare, and pebbles are strewn along the bottom. The precipitous rock walls appear to be composed of materials drawn directly from the earth's mantle: serpentine (a common rock-forming mineral), gabbro (a coarse-grained rock formed deep down under heat and pressure), and basalt (a rock which originally poured out in molten form). We are climbing now; although we hug the bottom, we have to thread our way through steep-sided mountains whose bases force us upward. We encounter the rift valley about two-thirds of the way across the Atlantic; the abyssal plains on the western side of the Ridge are far larger than those to the east. It is a landscape like no other on earth, with high mountains flanking an enormous chasm, 6,000 feet deep at this point. (Just as the mountains of the Ridge system are higher than the earth's highest terrestrial peak, so too are the subaqueous canyons deeper than comparable fissures on land. The average depth of the Grand Canyon of the Colorado is 4,000 feet, while the mid-Atlantic rift averages more than 6,000 feet in depth.) We are going to descend to the floor of the rift valley.

Only twenty-two years after Rachel Carson wrote that "most of the Ridge lies forever hidden from human eyes" (in her 1951 classic, *The Sea Around Us*), French and American oceanographers would prove her wrong. Scientists participating in Project FAMOUS would become the first men to view the heretofore hidden wonders of the Mid-Atlantic Ridge. "Although much has been learned about the mid-ocean ridges by remote sensing techniques, by drilling and by random sampling from surface ships," wrote James Heirtzler, the scientific leader of the 1973–74 project, "it finally became obvious that direct manned observation, by means of special submersible vessels, would ultimately be essential for any real understanding." For this cooperative venture, the bottom charts were updated by American and French hydrographers; the British contributed a seven-ton, side-scan sonar system named GLORIA (Geological LOng-Range Inclined Asdic), and the U.S. Naval Research Laboratory added a new underwater photography system called LIBEC (LIght BEhind Camera). Woods Hole provided a camera sled they named ANGUS (Acoustically Navigated Geological Underwater Survey), which could be controlled from the surface, and which would prove to be indispensable in the collection of photographic data.

The most important elements in the project, however, were the three submersibles: *Alvin* of Woods Hole, fitted with a new titanium hull that withstood test pressures of 22,500 feet, far greater than the depth of the rift; the French *Archimède*, a 69-foot-long bathyscaph that had been to 32,000 feet in the Pacific; and the newly built *Cyana*, a descendant of Cousteau's diving saucer (*"la soucoupe plongeante"*) and, at a length of 20 feet, a little smaller than *Alvin*. Like its predecessor *Trieste*, *Archimède* employed a gasoline-filled

The French bathyscaph *Archimède* was one of three submersibles engaged in Project FAMOUS, the 1974 undersea investigation of the Mid-Atlantic Ridge. (The other two submersibles were *Alvin* and the Cousteau diving saucer, *DS-2*.)

hull (which accounted for her immense size), but *Alvin* and *Cyana* relied on the weight of their ballast to bring them down; compared to the ponderous *Archimède,* they were as handy as bicycles. Altogether, the three submersibles made a total of forty-seven dives to depths of approximately 3,000 meters. (Project FAMOUS turned out to be the last voyage of the *Archimède;* she was too large, too unmaneuverable, and too expensive to run.) On August 2, 1973, some 400 miles southwest of the Azores, *Archimède* carried the first human beings to the floor of the Atlantic rift valley.

In *The New York Times* for May 21, 1974, Walter Sullivan wrote, "In the most ambitious exploration effort ever to be undertaken with deep sea submersibles, three of the world's deepest diving craft are to make some 60 penetrations this summer into the so-called 'navel of the world'—the volcanic rift valley beneath the Mid-Atlantic." And in the *National Geographic's* 1975 article celebrating the first year's accomplishments, Heirtzler wrote, "For the first time in history, men have gone down in the sea to prowl and study firsthand the largest mountain range on this planet—a system greater than the Rockies, the Andes, and the Himalayas combined."

Our journey will replicate theirs, but unburdened by the cumbersome baggage of reality, we can perform feats they could only dream of. (We also have their published accounts; so, unlike the pioneers in *Alvin* or *Cyana,* we know what we are looking for.) We descend along the west wall of the valley, a sheer drop of terraced steps marked by nearly vertical fault scarps. (The east wall rises much more gradually, and consists of short slopes covered with broken, fragmented lava.) At the point of our descent, the floor of the rift valley is nearly ten miles wide, and marked by recently formed volcanic hills named Mount Jupiter, Mount Venus, and Mount Pluto. We cruise slowly over the bottom, two miles down, picking out tumbled, conical structures resembling 15-foot-high volcanic spatter cones. Nicknamed "haystacks" or "flow-cones," they were formed when molten lava flowed from vents and cooled in an irregular pyramid that looks like a pile of melted boulders. There are bloated pillows formed when the hot lava was quenched by the chilling ocean waters, the burst ones looking like gigantic black eggshells. Some show striated "growth rings," resulting from the intermittent cooling of lava that flowed from the earth at 2,200° F (1,204° C). The pillows in the rift valley may be weeks old (some are still warm) or five hundred years old. There are also ropy, toothpaste-like lava tubes, many broken open to reveal their hollow, layered structure, and cascades of hardened lava that look like solidified intestines, formed when a tube burst, spewing its fluid contents down the steep sides of the slope. Most common is the jumbled debris of volcanic action, easily visible because there is so little sediment on the valley floor. Many of the basalt samples collected by *Alvin* were very young, as shown by their glassy surfaces, formed when the lava erupted and was cooled so quickly that it did not have time to crystallize into rock.

The floor is also cut by numerous fissures, some 40 feet deep. Fissures are extensive cracks in a rock formation, probably caused by mini-earthquakes that occur regularly along the seismically active rift zone. Some of them are small, while others have opened to a width of 30 feet. Seawater might percolate into these cracks and then be heated by the hot magma below, rising with a suspension of dissolved minerals. For about two hours, *Alvin* was wedged into a fissure that the pilot had wanted to investigate: only the most careful backing maneuvers averted a major disaster.

Life forms on the floor of the rift were sparse; the camera captured a few crinoids and gorgonians, and a species of anglerfish identified as *Chaunax pictus*. The nearest hydrothermal vent animals were found on the rift at a location known as the TAG (Trans-Atlantic Geotraverse) Hydrothermal Field, far to the south of our route, so we will not see any of the unusual creatures of the rift on this cruise.

We can see what could only be suggested in the more than 100,000 photographs taken (mostly by *Alvin* and ANGUS) during Project FAMOUS: the incredible steepness of the vertical walls of the rift. One of the scientists aboard *Alvin* when she descended into the rift was Tjeerd Van Andel, who wrote (in *Tales of an Old Ocean*), "The sea floor is so beautiful, so out-of-this-world beautiful. The misty, grandiose, mysterious landscape of craggy black and snowy, pillowy white set in the foreground with brilliantly lit small, sharp, and perfect vignettes of rock, coral, and sponge is unforgettable and I cannot do justice to it. I wish I could draw, it would be so superior to photography."

Emerging from the rift, we float over the eastern wall of the Ridge, a towering mountain range that replicates its western counterpart. We glide down the gradual eastern slope of the Ridge, over much the same topography as we saw on the valley floor. The slopes are covered with the shards of shattered pillows, now dusted with a light manganese coating, but those on the flanking rift mountains may be thousands of years old. Some of the flatter areas are dusted with volcanic sand and gravel, forming black ripples over the blanket of globigerina ooze. It is among the most irregular and tortured landscapes in the world; Heezen and Hollister tell us that "flows beneath the sea must be quickly quenched and the resulting submarine topography must thus be rougher than that of the land."

On a heading toward the western plain, we are aware that a range of undersea mountains looms ahead. It is the Azores, most of which are submerged, but nine of the peaks rise above sea level, including Pico Island, 27,000 feet above the plain, but only 7,750 feet above the surface. *Navegador* cruises over the Hirondelle Deep at the base of the islands, which Ewing described in 1949 as "a great hole dropping down to 1,809 fathoms, as if a volcano had caved in there at some time in the past." As the plain flattens, the sediments thicken, until we are over a featureless plain closely resembling the Sohm Plain, now 2,000 miles aft. "If the mid-oceanic rift is indeed the womb of the ocean floor," wrote Heezen and Hollister, "then one should expect accumulated sediments to thicken gradually from the recently formed flanks of the rocky rift towards the continents and this is approximately what has been found to be the case."

We cruise the length of the Azores-Gibraltar Ridge, an anomalous rocky spur that snakes from the Oceanographic Fracture Zone toward the Strait of Gibraltar, a little south of our destination. (Because of the increased accumulation of sediment, fracture zones usually disappear as they approach the continental margins.) Within 300 miles of our destination, we pass over a jagged ridge that includes the Josephine Seamount and the Ampere Seamount, a 15,000-foot peak rising from the depths to within 132 feet of the surface—almost an island. (To the south there is Madeira and the Canaries, which successfully emerge from the Atlantic to become *terra firma*.)

Our lights pick up the steadily falling "snow," always visible as we sail silently through the empty blackness, but when the lights are doused, all we can see is our own faces, reflected in the luminescent dials of the instrument panels. As we hover in the blackness of mid-water, our lights pick up a flicker of movement aft. *Navegador* turns quickly, and with our light slicing a brilliant white beam through the darkness, we head for the last place the movement was seen. There is nothing there. A siphonophore drifts by, a gelatinous illumination in the brightness, then passes out of the light and disappears. There are no directions here, not even up and down. It is black above and below us; black all around us. The black is the absence of light, the dense absence of everything we know. Only gravity—something that seems to have nothing to do with us, far below the familiar and reassuring landforms—holds us in our seats and reminds us of our connection with the earth. Something round reflects our light, looking for an instant like a polished chrome hubcap. It flickers and disappears. We move slowly toward the last sighting, knowing that if it is a living creature, it might very well have moved somewhere else by the time we get there.

Something moves in the blackness. It looks like some sort of snake, or several. But it is not a cluster of snakes; it is the arms of a squid. (In *Moby-Dick*, Melville—who never saw a giant squid—described its arms as "curling and twisting like a nest of anacondas. . . .") The "hubcap" is its eye, the largest eye in the animal kingdom. Our narrow beams cannot encompass its length; it extends beyond the illumination on either side. In the glaring beam of our lights, we see that the animal's color seems to be flashing, as if it were com-

This giant squid was seen at the surface from the French warship *Alecton* off the Canary Islands in 1861. The squid was harpooned, but all they got was the tail.

posed of a battery of strobes: it is now dark red, now bone-white, now dark again. The color does not change gradually, but instantaneously. How does it do that?

Squid can move just as easily forward as backward. They propel themselves by ejecting water from a rotating funnel on their underside, and therefore they can move just as easily in the direction of their tentacles as in the direction of their tail. This one has a pointed tail, flanked by two small fins, but the head, which we usually think of as being at the forward end of an animal, is sort of in the middle, neither at the front nor at the back. In the center of the circle of writhing arms (we count eight) there is a horn-colored beak, not unlike that of a parrot, but much larger, and with an upper mandible that fits into the lower. (Jules Verne, for some reason—probably because he never saw a giant squid either—likened it to the beak of a parakeet: *"comme le bec d'un perroquet"* in the original French.)

It moves in a strangely graceful manner, undulating through the water, its arm tips wriggling gently before it. The arms are equipped with hundreds of little suckers, which appear to be on stalks and individually movable. Suddenly two enormous tentacles shoot out: the missing two arms. (Squid have

ten arms in all; octopuses have only eight.) With the club-ends of the tentacles it touches the submarine, feeling the titanium hull and sending messages
to its brain, 40 feet from the tentacle tip. We can only guess, but this creature
would probably measure 60 feet from tail tip to the tip of the flattened, leaf-
shaped clubs at the end of the tentacles. (It is the end of that tentacle, expanded like the hood of a cobra, that probably gave rise to many "sea serpent"
stories if the squid had brought it above the surface.) At a distance of 50 feet,
just at the limit of our lights, this apparition turns and glides alongside our submarine, staring at us with its gigantic, unblinking eye. There is something
weirdly intelligent about the staring black eye of the squid—it somehow suggests another level of sentience.

Perhaps *Architeuthis* is common here in the eastern Atlantic; if so, their
presence might explain the sperm whales that were hunted by the Azoreans.
If only we could see it feed, or even see it jet away. Nobody knows what they
eat, how fast they can go, or how deep they normally live. (Rarely, Yankee
whalers would see a sperm whale in a battle with a giant squid, but more frequently, after they had harpooned the whale, they would see it regurgitate
hunks of squid, usually sections of the arms.) As if to signal that its perfor-
mance is concluded, the giant cephalopod ejects a cloud of ink, darts off, and
disappears into the abyss. For a brief, spectacular moment, we were vouchsafed a sight that no humans before us had ever experienced: we have seen the
living *Architeuthis*.

The continental shelf of the Iberian Peninsula is much smaller than that
of eastern North America. Only 30 miles from shore we are in water 17,000 feet
deep. Silt washing down from the Tagus and the Guadiana rivers for hundreds
of thousands of years has deposited sloping fans of gravel at the base of the
cliffs and the seamounts. Navigating our way through the steep-walled range
of seamounts at the base of the peninsula, we will have to climb steeply before leveling out for our arrival at Sagres.

The light is beginning to change. Before, we could see only that which
was illuminated by our powerful halogen spotlights, but now the water around
us is beginning to appear dark blue instead of black. Luminescent fishes appear, but only as glinting lights in the darkness. A small shark with bright green
eyes swims slowly past the viewing port. Foot-long squid with glowing photophores drift by like glittering ghosts. We are rising through the water column
surrounded by a dense school of lantern fishes, flitting in all directions and
flashing like fireflies. Microscopic creatures of the plankton swirl around our
vessel like moths around a candle. We no longer need our lights. The water is
greener now, and we can see shadows of some larger fishes. They are swift,
bullet-shaped, and glittering like quicksilver. . . . Are they tunas of some kind?
Sunlight penetrates in shafts illuminating the phytoplankton; the water is

clouded here by living creatures, unlike the clear sterility of the deeper water. The bottom is sand and gravel, littered with rocks that have been exposed by the tidal currents.

We have witnessed monumental evidence of the earth's power; we have seen the outcome of millions of years of specialized evolution; we have visited the sunken remains of the greatest ship of her time. Our guides have been geophysicists, historians, oceanographers, ichthyologists, paleontologists, meteorologists, geologists, magneticians—a faculty of the greatest scientific minds of the past two centuries, dedicated, as we have been, to finding out what lies beneath all that water.

Hydrothermal Vents

Discovery of deep-sea hydrothermal vents and the associated biological communities on the Galápagos Rift in 1977 profoundly and permanently changed our view of the deep sea. In addition to the typical, sparsely populated, vast deep-sea habitats, we learned that there were small "oases" around the vents where the density of animal life was extremely high. While the vent communities were initially viewed as isolated, rare phenomena, ensuing geological expeditions have found them to be associated with virtually all areas of tectonic activity throughout the deep sea.

JAMES J. CHILDRESS
Deep-Sea Research (1988)

Prior to 1977, every popular or technical book that had as its subject the fauna of the deep sea was written with the assumption that even if all of its subject matter was not yet known, certainly the major classifications were. Moreover, while the lifestyle of creatures that lived in the deep sea varied from one phylum to another—some were sedentary, some swam or floated around, some burrowed in the bottom layer—the basic mechanics were the same. In one way or another, all life as we knew it was dependent upon sunlight; photosynthesis fueled everything in the food chain, from the tiniest bacteria to the largest whale. The submersible *Alvin,* diving in the Galápagos Islands, changed all that. From the submersible's viewing ports, scientists observed what was probably the most unusual collection of living creatures ever beheld by the eyes of man. John Corliss, Tjeerd Van Andel, John Edmund, and Robert Ballard were the first humans to see what appeared to be gigantic tube worms with vivid red gills emerging from thick, ghostly-white tubes that were as much as ten feet long. They also saw blind white crabs, pink fishes that resembled no known species, and clams that were as big as footballs.

First identified from the Galápagos Rift System, what became known as "hydrothermal vent animals" were subsequently discovered in numerous other locations, including scattered locations along the Pacific coast of North and South America, from Vancouver Island to the coast of northern Chile, and most recently in the Atlantic, first in the Gulf of Mexico and then along the Atlantic Mid-Ocean Ridge. The location of these vent systems is always associated with hot springs.* The "springs" themselves are a far cry from the cool, groundwater emanations that the word first brings to mind, but are caused by cold seawater seeping into cracks in the sea floor and coming into contact with the molten material from the earth's mantle, raising the water temperature to unexpected levels.

Where the sea floor actually pulls apart (the phenomenon known as sea-floor spreading), cracks or rifts are created in the crust of the earth. This activity usually (but not always) takes place along the Mid-Ocean Ridge, a 40,000-mile-long undersea mountain range that is the largest single feature on the earth's surface. The rifts mark the edges of the lithospheric plates that bear the continents in their inexorable movement on the outer 100 to 250 kilometers of the surface of the planet. The plates such as those of North America and Africa drift over the less rigid athenosphere, much like giant icebergs in the ocean. The formation of the plates occurs at the mid-ocean ridges, and they are consumed at "subduction trenches," where one plate slides under the lip of another. Where plates interact, earthquakes occur, volcanoes erupt, and mountains are pushed up. (All three were manifest in November 1963, when the Icelandic island of Surtsey was born in a spectacular cataclysm of fire, lava, and steam.) The rifts caused by the separation of the plates fill up with lava that wells up from within the earth, flowing outward from the center and moving across the ocean floor. As described by J. R. Heirtzler and W. B. Bryan in 1975, "Bizarre as the idea seemed at first, it was becoming evident that the mid-ocean-ridge system was nothing less than a vast unhealed volcanic wound."

As seen by the crew of *Alvin,* and subsequently by other scientists in other submersibles, the landscape of the thermal vents is one of the most amazing sights on earth. It is also one of the least-viewed directly by human eyes; from the submersibles, only a handful of people have ever seen the pil-

---

* There are also hot springs on land, including the eponymous Arkansas spa and Warm Springs, Georgia, where President Franklin Roosevelt built the "Little White House" because he believed the warm waters were therapeutic. Terrestrial hot springs are essentially the same as the subaqueous versions, with water heated by molten-rock vapor rising to the surface through faults or other natural conduits. When there is a steady emission of heated water, it is referred to as a steam vent or fumarole, and when the accumulated water is ejected forcibly, it is known as a geyser. The largest and most dramatic geysers are those in Yellowstone Park, Iceland, and New Zealand, where the irregular eruptions can be hundreds of feet high.

The workhorse *Alvin* at work. Since her launching in 1964, the Woods Hole manned submersible has made almost three thousand dives, in every ocean. She has now been reconfigured to reach depths of 14,764 feet.

low lava, black and white smoking chimneys, and the hot, shimmering water of the vents. The Mid-Ocean Ridge is far too large to be seen as anything but isolated geological formations, but when lit by the lights of a submersible or camera, it reveals recently erupted volcanoes with hardened lava tubes, basaltic rocks stained orange or yellow by mineral emissions, and the characteristic feature of the hydrothermal vents: the "black smoker chimneys."*

The chimneys are formed by the minerals spewing hot water from the cracks in the earth's crust; some of this metal-rich water has been measured at 350° C (662° F). The particulate matter from the fissure forms a tube that is composed of fine-grained sulfides and oxides, which can build to a height of 20 feet. Because each vent differs in its mineral content, temperature, geologic

---

* Photography has revealed some aspects of this mysterious world to millions of people. Some of the first stories of the Galápagos hydrothermal vents ran in one of the most popular magazines, *National Geographic,* with a worldwide readership that numbers in the tens of millions. The National Geographic Society—a partial sponsor of some of the earliest dives—produced a television film called *Dive to the Edge of Creation,* first aired in January 1980, which contained some of *Alvin's* more spectacular images of tube worms, black smokers, and vent fauna. Since the first dives, images of the vents have been featured in every magazine and on virtually every television station, whether educational or commercial.

setting, and size, the chimneys—which eventually collapse from their own weight—form deposits on the valley floor. For the first time, we can see the actual formation of mineral deposits. At approximately 8,000 feet down, the landscape looks like—because it is—the side of a recently erupted volcano. Some of the lava surfaces are wrinkled like the hide of an elephant; others are glass-smooth because they have not yet been covered by the constant rain of sediment. Mounds of black manganese and yellow iron oxides from deep in the earth have been formed by the metallic eruptions into the sea.

A recent study by a team of French, Portuguese, and American geologists (Fouquet et al. 1995) has reported the existence of "lava lakes" atop submerged volcanoes on the Mid-Atlantic Ridge. These lakes—first reported from the Galápagos Ridge and the East Pacific Rise—were discovered by scientists aboard the French submersible *Nautile* during a series of cruises in 1994 near the Azores hotspot at the site known as "Lucky Strike." They are not liquid, since the seawater cools the lava as it emerges, but they consist of several generations of very fresh lava that have recently crusted over, creating a flattened area at Lucky Strike that is approximately one thousand feet (three hundred meters) in diameter.

Throughout the vent fields, organisms are scattered around, completing the otherworldly aspect of this heretofore unsuspected landscape, a landscape that was lit before only by the glow of underwater sizzling lava eruptions. Before the arrival of the submersible, this world, and everything in it, had never been subjected to the one thing that surface creatures (like ourselves) take so much for granted: light. And even more astonishing, the absence of light, rather than being a handicap, is the *modus vivendi* of many of the hydrothermal vent creatures. Most of the "vent animals" discovered in 1977, such as crabs, clams, mussels, and shrimps, are related to known species, and to the untrained eye, they resemble the more familiar forms. But there are some, like the vestimentifarian worms, that presented a major taxonomic problem to the scientists: they are different from any other creatures above or below the surface of the sea. Their discovery, according to Ann Bucklin of the Scripps Institution of Oceanography, "added an entirely new and unexpected element to deep-sea biology."

As first seen in the *Alvin*'s lights, these worms were four to six feet long: white tubes with blood-red, feathery plumes emerging from the top. At first they were believed to be related to the thread-sized pogonophores, worms that also live in self-secreted tubes, but further examination indicated that they ought to be placed in a new and distinct phylum: the Vestimentifera. (The name comes from the *vestimentum*, a unique, collar-like arrangement at the head of the tube.) Like the pogonophores, the vestimentifarian worms have no gut and no mouth, structures their discoverer, Meredith Jones, calls "of more

A fish swims among the tube worms of a hydrothermal vent zone, an environment and *modus vivendi* that was completely unexpected until it was discovered in the Galápagos Rift Zone in 1977. The worms, which can reach a length of ten feet, do not depend on oxygen but synthesize hydrogen sulfide.

than passing import . . . in other animals." They were named *Riftia* (for the rift) *pachyptila* (from the Greek *pachys*, which means "thick," and *ptilon*, which means "feather," referring to the plumes). These worms are found densely packed together, always associated with mussels and less frequently with clams, which are affixed to crevices.

The pogonophores themselves are only a recent discovery. Although the first specimens were dredged up in Indonesian waters in 1900, it took another fourteen years before a description was published, and it was not until 1937 that a Swedish zoologist named Johansson designated them as a new class and gave them the name "pogonophores," which means "beard-bearers." After further study, mostly by Soviet scientists, it became apparent that they were not only a new class of animals but a new phylum. Like the Vestimentifera, they live in tubes; they have no digestive tract, mouth, anus, or intestine, and digestion takes place through small structures in the tentacles. In *Living Invertebrates of the World*, Ralph Buschbaum and Lorus J. Milne described them as "among the most astonishing discoveries made with deep-sea dredges in the twentieth century," and in *Abyss*, C. P. Idyll quoted Libbie Hyman of the American Museum of Natural History as saying: "The finding of an entirely new phylum of animals in the twentieth century is certainly astounding, and ranks in zoological importance with the finding of the coelacanth fish and the archaic gastropod [*Neopilina*], both belonging to groups believed to be extinct for hundreds of millions of years."

It was startling enough to see ten-foot worms with bright red plumes densely clustered around the vents, but when specimens were brought up for examination, it was revealed that they were more than a little unusual. *Riftia pachyptila* lived at great depths—not in the superheated water of the smoking vents, but alongside—in water that is never visited by light. Virtually all the photosynthesis in the ocean occurs in the upper 100 to 200 meters of the water column, by one-celled plants that fix oxygen. To be available to these bottom-dwelling creatures, sufficient foodstuffs would have to fall through 2,500 meters (approximately 8,000 feet) of water, an unlikely proposition. But if photosynthesis was not the main source of energy for life in these deep-sea oases, what was?

The waters flowing from the vents are rich in hydrogen sulfide, a substance highly toxic to most living things, but the vestimentifarian worms were not only not adversely affected by this toxic substance, they existed on it. Not directly, of course, but their guts were found to be packed with bacteria that could "eat" the inorganic chemicals like hydrogen sulfide, fix the carbon dioxide, and synthesize reduced carbon compounds (e.g., sugars) and thus provide nourishment for the host organisms.*

Some vent animals, such as crabs, can "graze" on the bacteria fields, much as a cow grazes in a pasture, but the immobile tube worms were found to contain colonies of the bacteria in their gut, which, in a purely symbiotic relationship, process the chemicals that provide nourishment for the worms. The proper scientific terminology for this phenomenon (according to Childress) is: "major sessile animal species had sulfur-oxidizing chemoautotrophic bacteria as endosymbionts." Where both partners benefit from a symbiotic relationship, it is known as mutualistic. (When it is harmful to one of the partners, it is parasitic.) But if the trophosome ("feeding body") that occupies most of the worm's body cavity has no channel through which particulate food might enter, how does it feed? Through the branchials (the plumes), the worm absorbs the raw materials needed to fuel its metabolism (carbon dioxide, oxy-

* More recently, bacteria have been found deep below the ocean floor. From the examination of samples brought up from the earth's crust under the Pacific Ocean, investigators discovered colonies of microbes that live in a completely anaerobic (oxygen-free) environment, at temperatures that may reach 167° F, feeding on methane and other hydrocarbons. The proposed name for these unexpected bacteria is *Bacillus infernus* ("bacillus from hell"). In the *Proceedings of the National Academy of Sciences,* Thomas Gold of Cornell University wrote that there were "strong indications that microbial life is widespread at depth in the crust of the earth."

gen, and hydrogen sulfide), which are transported to the trophosome by the host's circulatory system. In most animals, hydrogen sulfide inhibits respiration by blocking the oxygen's binding sites on the hemoglobin molecule, but the tube worms are able to resist the toxic effects by binding the oxygen molecules and the sulfide molecules simultaneously and separately, thus preventing the sulfide from combining with oxygen, which is ordinarily a poisonous combination.

This means of earning a living is known as chemosynthesis and is utilized by the tube worms and certain clams, mussels, and crabs. The uniqueness of their adaptations is summed up by George Somero:

> These animals have one of the most stressful habitats imaginable: high pressures, no light, therefore no photosynthetic productivity; and waters laden with toxic substances. Through evolutionary changes, the vent animals have met these challenges, and can tolerate and even thrive in their unusual environment.

As C. L. Van Dover wrote, "The implications of these findings are stunning: they suggest that hydrothermal vents support life in the absence of sunlight— without the photosynthesizing bacteria that provide most sea creatures with food."

The rift clam, *Calyptogena magnifica,* is clam-shaped, with a hinged pair of shells, but there the resemblance to other bivalves ceases. The shell of *Calyptogena* is white, and the animal inside is a deep, rich red, making the opened clam look not unlike a large piece of beef liver on a small plate. The largest rift clam measures almost a foot in length. Because of the hydrogen sulfide in its tissues, the vent clam gives off an overwhelming smell of rotten eggs, much to the consternation of the oceanographers who brought up the first samples. *Calyptogena* has a large foot that is usually inserted into a crevice, but the clam can also use the foot to change locations. The giant white clams, clustered around the active vents, have been responsible for some of the more fanciful names employed to identify individual oases in the Galápagos Rift, including Clambake I and II and the Garden of Eden.

Most benthic fauna is sparsely distributed, but the rift clams and mussels (*Bathymodiolus*) form dense aggregations that are most uncharacteristic of deep-sea animals. Clambake II differed from other oases in that all the clams were dead. They probably died when the hot-water vents shut down, cutting off the supply of life-supporting hydrogen sulfide. Because it has been demonstrated that rift clam shells dissolve in about fifteen years, the presence of such shells indicates that the hydrothermal circulation ceased within that period of time. The vents themselves are unstable, and therefore the vent communities are relatively short-lived, perhaps lasting no more than a few decades.

The mussel *Bathymodiolus thermophilus*, while not quite as large as the clam, is another large bivalve mollusk that inhabits crevices in the hydrothermal vents. It was first described from specimens collected by *Alvin* on dives at the Galápagos Rift in 1977. At the Galápagos sites, the mussels are always found nestled in among the tube worms, attached to each other and to the tubes. Like the tube worms and vent clams, *Bathymodiolus* has symbiotic intercellular bacteria, but because the mussel also has a functional mouth and gut (which the worms and clams do not), the role of these bacteria in the nutritional process is unclear. It may be that the mussels are able to process nutrients chemosynthetically, and can also filter feed on nutrients not produced by the vents. *Bathymodiolus* has not been found outside the vent areas, and if they are removed, they exhibit a marked decline in nutritional state, which strongly suggests that they are dependent on the vent effluvients. From 60 to 80 percent of the mussels of the Galápagos vent sites were found to be accompanied by a polychaete scale worm (*Branchipolynoe symmytilida*), which appears to be involved in a commensal relationship with the host mussel, but the nature of the commensality is not understood.

The worms, clams, and mussels usually remain in one place, feeding on suspended bacteria in the water and processing them chemosynthetically, but the vents are also the home of several species of crabs that can and do move around. Except for the waving motion of the tube worms, the predominant movement around the vents is the scuttling of crabs. The crabs are white, and when seen in a submersible's lights or on film, they add an eerie quality to an already supernatural tableau. (Where there are crabs, there are likely to be octopuses, and the vents are no exception. There are photographs of an unknown species of octopod hunting crabs in the vicinity of Clambake I.) The brachyuran (true crab) genera *Bythograea* and

Cyanograea are usually seen in the vicinity of the tube worms and bivalves, scurrying over the fissures and crevices. *Cyanograea praedator*, as its name implies, is a predatory species, feeding on the annelid worm *Alvinella* (a new species, named for the submersible), which has been found living close to the vents in superheated water of 285° C (545° F). The galatheid crab *Munidopsis subsquamosa* is found in abundance around the vents, but it is not unique to the vent systems and is found in other deep-sea habitats.

If sulfur-digesting worms and foot-long clams characterize the Galápagos (and other) Pacific vent fauna, a most unusual shrimp dominates the fauna of the North Atlantic vents. *Rimicaris exoculata* was discovered in 1985 at the 3,600-meter-deep vent site known as the TAG (Trans-Atlantic Geotraverse)

Vent shrimp, *Rimicaris exoculata,* swarming over the chimney of a black smoker in the TAG Hydrothermal Field on the Mid-Atlantic Ridge. Each shrimp is about two inches long.

Hydrothermal Field by Peter Rona, swarming in dense schools at springs spewing forth water that may reach 350° C (662° F). *Rimicaris* means "rift shrimp," and *exoculata* means "without eyes." In the first photographs, these swarming two-inch-long shrimp each showed a bright, reflective spot on the back. When examined by Cindy Van Dover and her colleagues, these spots turned out to be "paired lobes of very large and unusual organs just beneath the thin, transparent carapace." The organs contained no image-forming devices, meaning that the shrimp could only distinguish light and dark, but they did contain a light-sensitive visual pigment. Since it is permanently pitch-black at the depth the shrimp inhabited, what was the purpose of these photoreceptors?

Van Dover guessed that *Rimicaris* was detecting low-level gradients of light emitted by the thermal vents themselves. Such a conjecture presupposed a light source certainly invisible to human eyes, and barely photographable even with the most sophisticated equipment. Using cameras developed by Marine Imaging Systems to detect light from distant galaxies, pictures were taken of a black smoker, and the results were surprising. Cindy Van Dover: "I expected to see some ambiguous hint of a fuzz which, if one was willing to stretch the imagination, might be called a glow; I doubt I was alone in that expectation. Instead, what came up on the screen was a dramatic, unequivocal glow with a sharply-defined edge at the interface between the sulfide chimney and the vent water." The Atlantic rift shrimp may be able to locate thermal vents by sight.*

The stomachs of rift shrimps are packed with sulfides, but they also contain the symbiotic bacteria that characterize the tube worms and bivalves of the Pacific. *Rimicaris* feeds by scraping the sides of the chimneys with specially adapted claws and drawing the minerals directly into its mouth.[†]

Because of the unique nature of the vent environment, many creatures have been discovered that are found only in the vicinity of the hydrothermal springs. This high degree of endemism is clearly demonstrated by the previously unknown clams, crabs, and shrimp, and, of course, the completely unexpected giant tube worms, which are found nowhere else *but* around thermal vents. In their 1983 summary of the fish fauna of the Galápagos Vent Region, Daniel Cohen and Richard Haedrich list some twenty species that were found to live around the vents at depths of about 2,400 meters (7,800 feet). The samples consisted of pictures taken by deep-sea 35-mm cameras that photographed fishes attracted to baited traps, fishes actually caught in the traps, and observations made by scientists aboard the submersible *Alvin*.

Of the twenty species described by Cohen and Haedrich, the most frequently observed were an unknown species of pale halosaur, a narrow-tailed spiny eel; various species of rattails (Macrouridae), mostly not specifically identified, some of which were observed swimming head down above the vents; and eelpouts (Zoarcidae), which are predators and are most commonly seen among the *Calyptogena* aggregations.[‡] At least three species of fish—all previously unknown to science—have been observed around the vents, and

* In 1994, however, experiments—some of which were conducted by Van Dover—seemed to disprove the idea that the light coming from the geysers' heat was strong enough to provide the glow. The problem has not been solved, but suggestions as to the light source include luminescence created when chemicals crystallize (crystalloluminescence); sonoluminescence, created by the sound of bubbles collapsing; triboluminescence, the result of rock crystals cracking; and luminescence caused by the radioactive decay of elements in the vent water.

† In the spirit of scientific inquiry, Van Dover and J. R. Cann boiled one of the shrimp over a Bunsen burner and ate it: "It did not turn an appetizing pink. If anything, it turned a still more unappealing shade of gray. As we might have expected, given the sulfide environment of the shrimp, the flesh tasted of rotten egg, and if that were not enough, the texture of the beast was as I imagine a rubber band might be. Perhaps it was overcooked. We concluded from our experiment that there will be no market for these shrimp among the gourmandizing public."

‡ In 1986, Rosenblatt and Cohen described a new genus and two new species of eelpouts from the Galápagos Rift; one they named *Thermarces cerberus,* from the Greek *thermos,* meaning "heat," and Cerberus, the three-headed dog that guarded the gates of hell, and the second was christened *Thermarces andersoni,* after Eric Anderson, a student of the Zoarcidae.

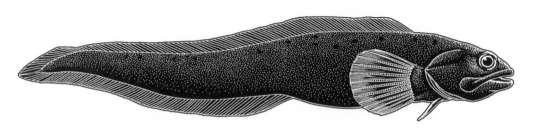

The eelpout *Thermarces cerberus* was discovered inhabiting the Galápagos Rift. *Thermarces* is derived from the Greek *thermos,* meaning "heat," and in mythology, Cerberus was the three-headed dog that guarded the gates of hell.

nowhere else. A small pink fish named *Bythites hollisi* (after Ralph Hollis, the pilot of the *Alvin*) is the most common in the eastern Pacific locations and is often seen hovering head down above the vent, with its tail undulating to keep it in position. As many as eight have been seen together at a single vent, but they are usually seen one or two at a time. Many of the other rift species have no common names, and fish named *Bassozetus, Acanthonus,* and *Porogadus* would be recognizable only to ichthyologists. Skates have been seen gently gliding from light into darkness, and on one occasion, through the viewing ports of *Alvin,* the mysterious "tripod fish" *Bathypterois* was seen perched on the tips of its fins.

Until March 1984, the rift fauna—with the obvious exception of *Rimicaris,* the Atlantic rift shrimp—were known only from the various Pacific locations. On a geological dive to 3,266 meters at the "Florida Escarpment" in the Gulf of Mexico, the submersible *Alvin* encountered "the same types of organisms that characterize the Pacific vent communities—white bacterial mats; large dense beds of mussels; numerous small gastropods; the shells of live mussels; thick patches of 1-meter-long tube worms; red-fleshed vesicomyid clams; galatheid crabs; and eel-like zoarcid fish." But where the Pacific vent communities were always associated with hot springs, the Florida Escarpment communities exist in a completely different geological environment. At the base of the escarpment, a limestone cliff that rises some 2,000 meters above the 3,280-meter-deep floor of the Gulf, the Atlantic vent fauna proceeds chemosynthetically, but in the absence of hot springs, upwelling lava, or black smoking chimneys. The sulfide compounds to fuel this process seep out of the adjacent Florida platform as black sediments, and demonstrate that while heat dependence is not a necessary component of chemosynthesis in the depths, a steady source of inorganic compounds is. Vent communities are no longer believed to be isolated and rare phenomena located only at vent sites, but have been found to be associated with virtually all deep-sea tectonic activity, including vents, subduction zones, fracture zones, and spreading centers in the deep trenches.

It would seem that the "vent biota"—clams, crabs, tube worms, etc.—are more common than scientists first believed. In August 1985, shortly after the discovery of the Florida Escarpment cold seep community, the NOAA vessel *Researcher* was cruising over the Mid-Atlantic Ridge at 26° 08′ N, a location approximately midway between Brazil and Cuba. Using a combination of sampling techniques, the staff identified thermal venting, black smokers, and, for the first time on the Ridge, the now familiar—but still unexpected—vent animals. Conditions at this site are similar to those of the early eastern Pacific sites, but different from those at the Florida Escarpment.

On November 18, 1929, a huge earthquake created a turbidity current that carried a thick layer of sediment over a bottom formation known to geologists as the Laurentian Fan, south of Newfoundland (see p. 97 for details). Evidence of a powerful underwater avalanche also came from the successive rupture of cables as far as 300 miles from the epicenter. Because the date of the disturbance is known, the appearance of chemosynthetic biological communities along the ridges can be accurately dated, and therefore, the growth rate of the communities can be estimated. Geologists diving in the *Alvin,* seeking only to explore the effects of the earthquake, encountered "four expansive occurrences of dense biological communities comprising vesicomyid and thyasirid clams, gastropods, pogonophoran tubes, galatheid crabs, and unidentified branched organisms" (Mayer et al. 1988). Because *Alvin* was not expecting to do any collecting on these dives, she was unequipped to recover much of the biological material, and therefore, only a small amount could be brought to the surface for examination. From the submersible's viewing ports, however, dense fields of clams were seen, along with many empty shells. There were no mussels and no vestimentifarian worms.

But it is not the absence of mussels or worms that makes this site particularly interesting, nor is it the redistribution of sediments by an underwater earthquake. Like the Florida Escarpment, there was no hydrothermal vent associated with these animals. The geologists theorized that the original valley floor was scoured by gravel waves, exposing "previously buried horizons that are enriched in reduced compounds, or permeable enough to permit the migration of reduced compound-rich fluids." In the fifty-eight years from the earthquake to the discovery of the vent fauna without any vents, a full community of chemosynthetic organisms established itself on the floor of the deep

Atlantic, indicating that whatever we thought we knew about the creatures of the hydrothermal vents is marginal at best, and that our knowledge of these phenomena is still in its infancy.

In 1988, a group of European scientists (see Fricke et al. 1989), using the submersible *GEO*, discovered "a new type of Atlantic vent community in shallow water" off the island of Kolbeinsey, north of Iceland on the Jan Mayen Ridge. At a depth of only 90 meters, they observed fissures, chimneys 30 meters high, and "large, crater-like dips, 1.5 to 2 m deep, with powerful outflows of hot water." While the ambient seawater temperature was 2.6° C (36° F), the temperature at the fissures was 89° C (192° F), and they also saw bubbles of boiling water issuing from the openings of craters. ("At this depth," wrote the authors, "the boiling point of seawater is 180° to 182° C [356° to 359° F].") The living creatures at this site consisted mostly of bacteria, but there were also sponges and hydrozoans that appeared to be filtering the hydrothermal water. (Crabs and a single sea bass were seen in the vicinity of the vents, but they were believed to be visitors.) In a southern California vent community (discussed by Stein, 1984), the abalone *Haliotis cracherodii* was seen foraging opportunistically on mats of sulfur-oxidizing bacteria, deriving nourishment from geothermal matter.

A question still unanswered by vent biologists is: How do the animals get to the sites in the first place? (In the Kolbeinsey communities, the bacteria were believed to have developed from surrounding cold-water fauna.) The vents, while more common than originally believed, are widely scattered and spring up along the fissures, in (so far) unpredictable locations. It is even more difficult to predict the eruption of an underwater hot spring than it would be to predict an earthquake, and so far, it has been almost impossible to predict a terrestrial disturbance. On land, various seismic devices have been employed, more or less unsatisfactorily, but the sea floor affords even fewer such opportunities.* The sea-floor vent appears, and is somehow colonized by the rift animals. Of these creatures, however, only the crabs are mobile; the tube worms, clams, and mussels are what the biologists call "sessile," meaning that they are more or less attached to the substrate. (The fishes are mobile, but very few species are considered endemic to the rift environments.) In any event, it is unlikely that a clam or a crab would leave one thermal vent in search of an-

---

* It has recently been revealed that the U.S. Navy has been seismically monitoring the sea floor with a sophisticated array of underwater hydrophones that were installed over the years to track the ships and submarines of potential enemies. In June 1993, geologists were able to monitor a deep-sea volcanic eruption as it was occurring along the Juan de Fuca Ridge, some 400 kilometers off the coast of Oregon. Sites on the Juan de Fuca Ridge (part of the San Andreas Fault), such as the "Endeavor Segment," are known locations of hot springs.

other, so it is up to the larvae to disperse themselves. Passive dispersal, where the larvae of many marine invertebrates become part of the plankton and drift about at the mercy of deep-ocean currents, is the strategy whereby most species colonize new areas. The larvae of vent animals might ride upward on the rising, heated plumes until they encounter horizontally moving currents, where they drift until they drop down to a new vent site. Some biologists subscribe to the "founders" theory, which holds that the free-floating larvae of the various rift animals happen upon an erupting vent and colonize it. The species that arrives first and in the largest numbers becomes the dominant form at that location, which explains why some sites are dominated by tube worms, others by clams, and still others by mussels. (In the Pacific, a vent community was found on the skeleton of a gray whale, suggesting to C. R. Smith and his colleagues [1989] that "whale skeletons may indeed provide persistent and abundant 'stepping stones' for the dispersal of deep-sea chemosynthetic communities. . . .")

In June 1993, scientists Charles Langmuir of the Lamont-Doherty Earth Observatory and Gary Klinkhammer of Oregon State, investigating hot-water vents along the Mid-Atlantic Ridge, discovered the largest hydrothermal vent in the Atlantic, consisting of seven sites covering some 15 acres, 200 miles west of the Azores. As described (but not yet published) by Langmuir and Klinkhammer, these vents, marked by 600- to 1,000-foot-high cones, were inhabited by yellow mussels (a form of bivalve not seen at previous vent sites in the Atlantic or the Pacific) and pink sea urchins. Once again, the surprising finds were made from the *Alvin,* which has already become the premier investigative tool in the search for thermal vent animals.

In 1991, researchers in *Alvin* off the west coast of Mexico witnessed a volcanic eruption that effectively killed all the vent animals at that site. A year later, brachyuran crabs had recolonized the site—dubbed "Tube Worm Barbecue" because of the charred remains of the worms—and less than two years later, new worms had grown to four feet in length, covering the site with their white tubes and feathery red gills. In April 1991, the fissure site dubbed "Hole to Hell" was devoid of life, but only twenty-one months later, a thicket of four-foot-long worms had appeared, making them possibly the fastest-growing of all marine invertebrates. In a 1994 *National Geographic* article, researchers Richard Lutz and Rachel Haymon commented on the unsuspected rapidity of the growth of the mineral chimneys and the speed with which the tube worms recolonized the site. *Alvin* accidentally knocked down one of the chimneys; it took only three months for it to grow another 20 feet. In a 1994 *New York Times* article, William Broad wrote, "Traditionally, the ocean abyss has been thought of as a slow-motion world where all development is frustrated by low temperatures, perpetual darkness and pressures so great as to defy comprehension." As a result of *Alvin*'s 1991–94 expeditions, we will have to rethink our ideas about life in the depths, especially at the mysterious vent sites.*

In addition to the unsuspected animals and behavior associated with the hot springs, oceanographers also noticed yellow and orange stains on the basalts, which were shown to be a result of powerful seepages of hydrogen sulfide. The creatures of the vent systems make a living in a totally different way than any other creatures on earth, suggesting—at least to some imaginative researchers—that life may have begun in these deep-sea vents.

Jack Corliss, one of the discoverers of the Galápagos rift animals, was among the first to suggest the possibility of life having started in conditions similar to those found in the vents. (Corliss, who was then at Oregon State University, became obsessed with the possibility that the vent systems were the source of life, and left the university to devote himself full-time to working on the problem. By 1991, he had moved on to become chief scientist of *Biosphere 2*, the closed-system environment built in the Arizona desert.) Working with Corliss and John Baross, graduate student Sarah Hoffman formulated a theory that life had originated in the Archean period, about 4.2 billion years ago, on the sea floor, which was probably much more hydrothermically active than it is today. The authors suggested that the water issuing from the Archean vents was so hot—600° C (1,112° F)—that it cracked the molecular bonds of the rocks and released carbon and carbon compounds (such as methane) into the solution. Then simple organic molecules form out of the newly formed chemical elements, and while some of them rise into the water column, some adhere to the rock faces, and form a clay that provides a safe haven for these molecules, giving them the opportunity to form more complex organic molecules. Out of this jumble of molecules, argued the authors, "biopolymers" can be formed, producing fragmentary nucleic and amino acids, which, in a system far from equilibrium, can organize themselves into new forms, i.e., primitive living cells. In 1985, Baross and Hoffman wrote that the hydrothermal activity "provided the multiple pathways for the abiotic synthesis of chemical compounds, origin, and evolution of 'precells' and 'precell communities,' and ultimately, the evolution of free-living organisms." (One of the problems with this suggestion is that even if sulfur-based life did develop at the vents, it would have had to metamorphose into a photosynthetic form before it could give rise to the carbon-hydrogen-oxygen-nitrogen system currently in use.)

---

* We might also have to reevaluate our theories about octopus sex. For the most part, male octopuses transfer sperm to a female of the same species by using a specially modified arm, known as a hectocotylus. On *Alvin*'s video monitor, researchers spotted two male octopuses of different species, apparently having sex. Until this time, no one had ever observed the mating behavior of deep-sea octopuses, nor had anyone ever seen homosexual behavior among octopuses.

Obviously, nobody has come up with an answer to the question of how life began. In 1988, Stanley Miller and Joseph Bada wrote a paper in which they refuted the suggestions of Corliss, Baross, and Hoffman, claiming that "the proposal for a hydrothermal-vent origin of life fails each of the three proposed steps involved in the origin of life." The debate about the origin of life—certainly one of the most intriguing problems in all of science—continues, but it is fascinating to consider at least the possibility that the hydrothermal vents, unknown and unsuspected until the 1970s, might provide some clues.

Part Two

Creatures
of the
Abyss

Introduction to Deep-Sea Biology

I f there is magic on this planet," wrote Loren Eiseley, "it is contained in water." Ours is the only planet in the solar system that contains water. It is because of this fortuitous combination of hydrogen and oxygen that the earth can support life as we understand it; there is no life form that does not depend directly upon water. Ninety percent of the living space on earth is underwater. Of the 197 million square miles of the earth's surface, 139 million are covered by ocean, and of this 139 million, 85 percent, or 118 million square miles, are more than a mile deep, making the deep ocean by far the earth's predominant habitat. Most of this water is perpetually dark, illuminated only by the scattered flickers and flashes of bioluminescent organisms that generate their own biological light.

Most oceanic life can be found in the uppermost 600 feet, where sunlight penetrates with sufficient intensity to ensure the growth of plants. Some greatly diminished light may reach as deep as 1,000 feet, but without sunlight to promote photosynthesis, there will be no plants. Everything that lives below 1,000 feet is an animal. Animal life of one sort or another has populated virtually every available habitat on earth, from the peaks of the highest mountains to the polar ice caps; from the hot, vacant Sahara to the dank, polluted alleys of urban centers. But there is no habitat on earth that equals the oceans' cold, black density for sheer inhospitability. A mile below the surface, the pressure is more than a ton on every square inch. Beyond two miles of depth, the temperature remains only a couple of degrees above the freezing point of sea-water. In 1851, the oceanographer Edward Forbes wrote, "As we descend deeper and deeper . . . the inhabitants [of the sea] become more and more modified, and fewer and fewer, indicating our approach towards an abyss where life is extinguished. . . ." It was not until the surprisingly successful deepwater trawls of the research vessel *Challenger* in 1872 that the presence of life in the abyss was universally acknowledged. No food that is not animal matter, living or dead, is available in the depths of the ocean, and the food chain depends upon the constant rain of minuscule particles ("undersea snow") from the surface layers, usually the remains of animals that have died.

Because there have been so few human visitors to the uninviting world of the deep sea, scientists have had to rely on trawled specimens, photographs taken by robotic cameras, or, occasionally, observations from deep-diving submersibles to get even the vaguest idea of the nature of life in the abyss. So far, even our most elaborate efforts to penetrate the blackness have produced only minimal results. It is as if someone lowered a collecting basket from a balloon high above the tropical rainforest floor, and tried to analyze the nature of life in the jungle from a couple of random hauls. The deep sea, the largest environment on earth, is the least known.

There are about a million kinds of animals known, and of these, about three-quarters are insects. Indeed, insects are the predominant life form on earth. But in the sea—where the joint-legged phyla are represented by crustaceans—there are fewer species and lesser densities, but more animals. In the depths and on the sea floor, there are sponges, fans, pens, anemones, corals, mosses, lilies, starfish, brittle stars, urchins, cucumbers, squid, octopuses, crabs, spiders, acorn worms, eels, and approximately two thousand species of fishes.

Life in the ocean is conducted by a completely different set of rules than on *terra firma*. Because water is eight hundred times more buoyant than air, marine creatures are less affected by gravity than their terrestrial cousins, and they are free to assume weird and wonderful shapes. Consider the jellyfishes or the siphonophores, gelatinous, floating creatures with no visible means of internal support. Strong skeletons and muscles are not required for support, which means that many marine creatures have developed strange and marvelous shapes that would be totally impractical in air. It is not an accident that the sea is the home of the largest animal that has ever lived: the 100-ton bulk of the blue whale needs the support of water.*

Despite its mountains and valleys, the surface of the land can be described as a two-dimensional environment, but the deep-sea world is very much three-dimensional. Terrestrial animals, such as ourselves, can occasionally operate in

* In recent years, paleontological discoveries have been made that appear to dispute the blue whale's title as "the largest animal that has ever lived." In 1985, in a New Mexican cliff face, researchers found the fossil evidence of a dinosaur (*Seismosaurus*) that may have measured 150 feet in length. Even at this astonishing size, these gigantic herbivorous dinosaurs were mostly long neck and long tail, and would not have weighed much more than 50 tons, a quarter of the weight of a full-grown blue whale.

three dimensions—when we ride in an elevator, fly in an airplane, or scuba dive, for example—but compared to the three-dimensionality of the oceans, our surface movements are largely restricted to forward and back, north and south, east and west. In the sea, movement is also forward and back, but "up and down" play much more important roles. (Birds, insects, and flying mammals live in a more three-dimensional world than we do.) The average depth of the ocean is 2.4 miles, or 12,566 feet. By and large, the salinity, temperature, and oxygen content of the vast deep sea are homogeneous, but the most important variable is pressure—the accumulated weight of all that water.

Unlike the waters of the surface, where wind, weather, tides, and other influences create variations that can range from glassy calm to force-10 gales, the "weather" under the sea is comparatively tranquil. The temperature of the deep sea varies from 4° C to −1° C (39° F to 30° F). There are currents that circulate deep within the ocean that affect the appearance of the bottom and, more important, transport deeper, colder water from the poles around the world. There are even "benthic storms" that can last anywhere from a few days to several weeks which can alter the temperature balance of the abyss, and can stir up bottom sediments to a substantial degree. Activity of the sea floor, affected by volcanic action where the bottom is opening up, is another factor that affects the weather on the bottom. In some areas, this activity takes the form of hydrothermal vents, where superheated water (and occasionally lava) is spewed from cracks in the sea floor. There are also geological activities that can change the face of the deep, such as landslides, "slumps" (where a large section of a wall collapses), and "turbidity currents," where earthquakes deep within the earth trigger landslides of huge quantities of bottom sediment.

The depths of the sea truly represent the last frontier on earth. Even now, we know more about the back side of the moon than we do about the bottom of the ocean, but that is because the surface of the moon is not hidden under miles of impenetrable water. Living in this inaccessible medium are some of the most fascinating creatures on earth, adapted for life in an environment that is as foreign to our understanding as another universe. In this sunless world, miniature monsters chase and are chased by diminutive dragons; fishes flash, sea cucumbers light up, and giant squid, with eyes as big as dinner plates, lurk at the fringes of our consciousness. Superheated minerals bubble out of cracks in the sea floor, and unexpected animals subsist on a diet of sulfuric acid, eschewing the oxygen dependence that fuels every other form of life on earth. The deep sea is a world as old as time, as recent as technology.

A NOTE ON NOMENCLATURE

Many of the creatures mentioned in this book are rare, exotic, or very poorly known; some are all three. Since some are represented in scientific collections by only a couple of specimens and are not well known even to scientists, they would not be readily recognizable to laymen. Because of their rarity and unfamiliarity, many of the species have no common names, and I have made liberal use of their scientific names in these discussions. Although Latin and Greek names can appear intimidating at first, they are actually more useful in species identification than their vernacular counterparts.

As developed by the Swedish botanist Carl von Linné (1707–1778), commonly known as Linnaeus, the system of binomial nomenclature makes it possible to assign a name to any living creature and, to a lesser extent, to recognize its immediate affiliations. Prior to Linnaeus, various names were given to various creatures, but there was no coherence to the naming system, and animals often acquired any number of different names. This made it difficult, if not impossible, for one writer to know which animal another writer was referring to, and therefore, it was impossible to communicate within a unified framework. Linnaeus was a botanist, so he first classified the plants, in the *Species Plantarum,* 1753. For the animals, he published ten editions of the *Systema Naturae,* the last dated 1758.

"Binomial nomenclature" refers to the two names that he gave to every plant and animal known to him (he also classified the mineral kingdom). Those who specialize in naming and classifying organisms are known as taxonomists—from the Greek *taxo,* "to arrange," and *noma,* "name." Animals are now named in accordance with the regulations set forth in the International Code of Zoological Nomenclature, which, among other rules, mandates that the official scientific name of an animal must have two parts (hence "binomial"), the *genus* and the *species.* The generic name always comes first (and begins with a capital letter), and identifies the affiliations; the specific name comes second (and begins with a lowercase letter), and identifies the species. "Genus" comes from the Greek *genos,* which means "race" or "kind," and refers to closely related species, and its plural form is "genera." The word "species" is taken directly from the Latin, and means "a particular kind." The plural of "species" is "species" (just as the plural of "deer" is "deer"); *specie* means "coined money," and has nothing to do with the naming of animals. Your scientific name is *Homo sapiens;* you are a member of the genus *Homo,* which means "man," and you are the only animal that can read this book, hence *sapiens,* which means "wise."

Let us look at a typically difficult scientific name: *Grammatostomias flagellibarba.* This is a small deep-sea fish that actually has no common name, so its binomial is particularly important. *Grammatostomias* is the generic name, and is used for every member of the genus. Thus, we have *Grammatostomias circularis, Grammatostomias dentatus, Grammatostomias paucifilus,* and so on. (To save space when listing members of the same genus, the generic name can be represented by its initial letter, e.g., *G. dentatus,* etc.) Even though it looks like a tongue twister, *Grammatostomias flagellibarba* does an excellent job of identifying and describing the fish. It is a member of the order Stomiiformes, which word is derived from the Greek *stoma,* meaning "mouth." (The stomiiformes are characterized by large mouths filled with nasty-looking teeth.) *Grammatostomias* means "lined stomiatid," referring to the pattern of lines on the side of the fish, and *flagellibarba* means "whip-barbel," describing the extremely long chin barbel of this species. (Wherever possible, I have tried to translate the Greek or Latin roots, to demonstrate the descriptive value of scientific nomenclature.) Since the fishes in this family have no common name, they are referred to in the literature as "stomiatids." (In some reference works they are called "dragonfishes," but this name is used for many types of deep-sea fishes, and does not help in identifying the particular fish in question.) Without the scientific name, then, we would have no way of differentiating one species from another. *Grammatostomias flagellibarba* may be hard to say, but "lined stomiatid with a whiplike chin barbel" is much clumsier, and even if it were easier, it would work only in English. Scientists who speak other languages might have to refer to *Grammatostomias flagellibarba,* and they cannot be expected to use some complicated English sequence. Therefore, regardless of the language in which the discussion is printed, whether it is German, French, Japanese, Russian, or Sanskrit, the scientific name always appears exactly the way you see it here: *Grammatostomias flagellibarba.* This guarantees that wherever the scientists are, and whatever language they speak, they will know which species is being discussed.

Finally, the scientists who first gave this little fish such a big name were E. W. L. Holt and L. W. Byrne, who described it in 1910 in the British journal *Annals and Magazine of Natural History.* They published their description in an article entitled "Preliminary Diagnosis of a New Stomiatid Fish from South-west of Ireland." The names of the person (or persons) who first describe an animal—as well as the year of first publication—become an integral part of its official name; therefore, the full and complete name of the little sto-

At a depth of 2,470 feet, Beebe sighted *Bathyceratias trilychnus* from the bathysphere. In a 1934 *National Geographic* article, he wrote, "The three-starred anglerfish, new to man, is six inches long. . . . It showed a trio of tall, light-tipped masts. . . . [T]he light was pale yellow, and so strong that it was clearly reflected on the dark skin of the back."

Beebe named this fish *Bathysidus pentagrammus* ("five-lined constellation-fish"), and claimed that it was "one of the most unexpected and most gorgeous deep-sea inhabitants I have ever seen." No one has seen or collected any-thing like it since its original description in 1934.

Beebe described the "pallid sailfin" (*Bathyembryx istiophasma*) as "at least two feet in length, wholly without lights or luminosity; the body rather elongate. . . . [T]he color was peculiar, an unpleasant, pale, olive drab, like water-soaked flesh, an unhealthy-looking buff."

miatid with a whip-barbel is "*Grammatostomias flagellibarba* Holt and Byrne 1910." (The fish is discussed on p. 241.)

Some scientists enjoy giving fishes common names, especially if they are writing for popular magazines. William Beebe, who published more than eight hundred articles in everything from the *Bulletin of the New York Zoological Society* and *National Geographic* to *Ladies' Home Journal* and *Harper's*, evidently took pleasure in making up elaborate names, for his popular articles ring with such appellations as "golden-tailed serpent dragon," "double-bulbed dragon fish," and "beacon-finned dragonfish," names that did not perdure, and no longer appear in anything but Beebe's articles. (All the foregoing "dragons" are stomiatids, and are represented by actual specimens with proper scientific binomials.) Beebe also coined "pallid sailfin," "five-lined constellationfish," "three-starred anglerfish," and "untouchable bathysphere fish," which were names he invented to describe fishes he observed from the bathysphere. (He also gave them scientific names because he was introducing new species.) Alas, no one has had the opportunity to use either the common or the scientific names of these esoteric creatures, because there are no specimens, and no one has seen any of them since Beebe's original descriptions in the 1930s.

THE ILLUSTRATIONS

Because of the enormous discrepancies in the size of the animals drawn for this book, hardly any of the drawings are done to the same scale. As they appear, the drawings of the sperm whale and the shrimp are approximately the same size, as are the illustrations of the giant squid and the tiny squid *Heteroteuthis dispar*. The former can be 60 feet long; the latter does not exceed three inches in total length. Obviously, I could not maintain a proportionate scale for all the illustrations, so I have tried to indicate the actual size of the creature in the caption for each drawing.

I wanted the drawings in this book to appear in contrast to the black of the deep sea, so I had to find a way to draw white on black. I first tried scratchboard, and in fact, the drawings on pages 246, 270, and 277 were laboriously carved into a black-inked board with a scratchboard tool. Scratchboard is an enormously painstaking and meticulous process, and if I had done all the drawings that way, I would still be working on them. In the end, I drew all the pictures in reverse—that is, I drew them in black ink on white illustration board, but in such a way that they could be shot as negative photostats, thus appearing white on black. This required thinking negatively: I had to put in the highlights as shadows and vice versa. As a demonstration of this peculiar (and probably unique) art form, I have reproduced one original drawing, along with its negative version, on this page. Because they are of light-colored fishes, the drawings on pages 239, 254, and 284, and the squid on page 181, were not done this way; they are reproduced as they were drawn—that is, black on white. I then painted a black background around the white drawing.

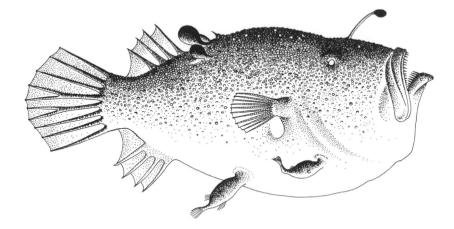

The original drawing of a female *Cryptopsaras couesi* was drawn in black ink on white illustration board. A negative photostat was then made from the original, resulting in a white drawing on a black background. This anglerfish, shown with two parasitic males attached, is discussed on pages 273–74.

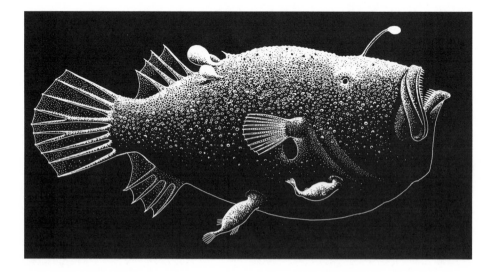

Invertebrates

The smallest life forms in the ocean are microscopic algae, first identified by Joseph Hooker, naturalist on James Clark Ross's Antarctic expedition of 1839–43. Hooker saw evidence of this microscopic life in the water as cloudy blooms, discolorations on the ice, and as a mucus scum on the surface. Following the lead of the German investigator Christian Ehrenberg (who found terrestrial evidence of diatoms in "rotten stone"), Hooker recognized that the siliceous coverings of the tiny plants and animals must sink to the bottom to form sediments on the sea floor. The floor of the ocean is covered with them—in fact, in many places, the deep-sea floor *is* them. Depending on variables such as the age of the underlying crust and the sedimentation rate, the layers may be miles deep. In *The Sea Around Us,* Rachel Carson wrote, "When I think of the floor of the deep sea, the single, overwhelming fact that possesses my imagination is the accumulation of the sediments. I see always the steady, unremitting, downward drift of materials from above, flake upon flake, layer upon layer—a drift that has continued for hundreds of millions of years, and will go on as long as there are seas and continents."

There is, of course, no logical or biological progression—except in the mind of man, who usually nominates himself as the culmination of a process designed to produce him—from simple to complex creatures, although single-celled animals and plants are certainly more rudimentary than multicelled organisms. A horse, considered one of the "higher" vertebrates, is no more complex than a shark, or even a sea cucumber. Although it does not have a brain, or eyes, or opposable thumbs, the starfish is every bit as intricate an animal as *Homo sapiens.* Most texts, however, have arranged the seas' wildlife on a scale that runs from the simple to the complex, and, coincidentally, from the smallest to the largest. (The smallest animals are the single-celled protozoans, part of the ocean's plankton, and the largest animal that has ever lived is the plankton-eating blue whale.)

"Plankton" is an all-purpose term that is used to describe the small plants and animals that are found in the "euphotic zone," the upper reaches of the ocean where sunlight provides the energy for the photosynthesis that fuels almost all life in the ocean. (There is a region, discussed on pp. 110–25, at depths never reached by the sun, where the predominant source of energy is chemical, but this is an exception to the prevailing rule.) Most planktonic plants (known as phytoplankton, from the Greek *phyton,* for "plant," and *planktos,* meaning "wandering") are too small to be seen by the naked eye and were almost unknown until the middle of the nineteenth century, when scientists began to tow bags of muslin or silk through the water to trap what they could find.* Most marine plants are small, but there are some, like seaweeds and kelp, that grow very large indeed. (The giant kelp, *Macrocystis pyrifera,* found off the west coast of North America, can reach a length of 100 feet.) But numerically and in terms of organic productivity, the most important plants in the ocean are the microscopic diatoms and dinoflagellates. They account for most of the photosynthesis in the pastures of the ocean, and therefore provide the broad base for the marine food pyramid.

Diatoms are an extraordinarily large and diverse group, of which there may be as many as twenty thousand species. For the most part, they are tiny "pillboxes" of silica, which contain minute masses of protoplasm, in which are found the chloroplasts that contain chlorophyll, the green building blocks of photosynthesis. And at the base of this oceanic pyramid, the number of these diatoms almost defies description, as does the number of grains of sand on the beach. In the Gulf of Maine, for example, a single square meter of water was estimated to contain between 7 and 8 billion diatoms. One step above the diatom in size is the copepod; a single individual is capable of consuming hundreds of thousands of diatoms in a day. According to C. P. Idyll, "It has been estimated that 4 million tons of copepods exist at one time in the Gulf of Maine, and over a season, the quantity is many times more." Imagine the number of diatoms required to feed 4 million tons of copepods.

The other group of phytoplankton is known as the dinoflagellates. These are unusual one-celled plants that have the power of movement, because they all possess one or two whiplike appendages that propel them jerkily through

---

* According to Alister Hardy in *The Open Sea* (1956), "in nearly all the text-books of oceanography, it is stated that the tow-net was first used in 1844 by the German naturalist Johannes Muller," but, Hardy says, this is an error. It appears that the first man to use a tow net was J. Vaughan Thompson, collecting plankton off Ireland in 1828, and Hardy then mentions no less a naturalist than Charles Darwin, who referred in his journals to an occasion on December 6, 1833, when he "often towed astern a net made of bunting and thus caught many curious animals."

the water. They come in every conceivable shape and form, some resembling Chinese hats, others children's tops, urns, pots, war clubs, hand grenades, lances, and balloons on strings. Even though they can move, they are considered plants because they have the green, yellow, or brownish pigments of chlorophyll, which means they are not animals. They are not exactly plants either, but the distinctions interest primarily zoologists and botanists, because their photosynthetic functions are far more important than their taxonomy. Because diatoms are, on average, larger than the dinoflagellates, they were long considered more important in the chain of life in the ocean, but now that more sophisticated collecting gear has been developed, it has been shown that the flagellates are even more numerous than their cousins. In a quart of water taken in the Gulf of Mexico, some 60 million individuals of the species *Gymnodinium brevis* (the red-tide organism) were caught. It is the skeletons of the diatoms and the flagellates that fall to the bottom in such great profusion that they form a sediment that is in some places several miles thick.

It is the dinoflagellates that are mostly responsible for the phenomenon known as phosphorescence.* When fishes, boats, oars, or other objects move through the water at night, they often leave trails of what looks like ghostly greenish fire. These displays are usually caused by the glowing of millions of luminescent dinoflagellates, each one stimulated by an oxidation process as it is agitated in the water. The commonest species involved in phosphorescence are *Noctiluca,* the "night-light," and *Pyrodinium,* the "fire-whirler." Aboard the *Beagle* in December 1833, Charles Darwin recorded a famous observation of phosphorescence:

> While sailing south of the Plata on one very dark night, the sea presented a wonderful and most beautiful spectacle. There was a fresh breeze, and every part of the surface, which during the day is seen as foam, now glowed with a pale light. The vessel drove before her bows two billows of liquid phosphorus, and in her wake she was followed by a milky train. As far as the eye reached, the crest of every wave was bright, and the sky above the horizon, from the reflected glare of these livid flames, was not so utterly obscure as over the vault of heaven.

Swimming along in vast swarms with the diatoms and flagellates are the smallest one-celled animals: the foraminifera and the radiolarians. Most species are visible only under a microscope, but some are pinhead-sized, and

---

* Although the terms "phosphorescence" and "luminescence" are used interchangeably to describe chemically generated heatless light, "phosphorescence" is more accurately applied to the combustion of the chemical element phosphorus—not found free in nature—which glows in the dark, and takes fire spontaneously upon exposure to air.

some may be as large as peas. These creatures cannot photosynthesize; they must capture their food by means of the sticky protoplasm outside their skeleton. The skeletons of the "forams" are made of calcium carbonate and, even more than the phytoplankton, fall to the ocean floor in prodigious quantities. (The white cliffs of Dover are composed of the tiny shells of trillions upon trillions upon trillions of forams.) The most prominent foram genus is *Globigerina,* an amoeba-like protozoan with a perforated "basket" shell through which protrude the pseudopods, little leglike extensions of the inner cell material. (*Globigerina* was named by J. M. Brook in 1854 for the spherical shape of the calcareous shells he found in a sample from the bottom of the deep Atlantic.) As a component of the sea floor, globigerina ooze is second only to "red clay"— which is neither red nor clay—as the most common sea-floor sediment. (The red clays are composed mostly of inorganic matter, such as terrestrial silt from river runoffs, volcanic ash, and perhaps chemical precipitates from seawater.)

Because there is more available oxygen in temperate and colder waters, the ooze is composed of diatom shells (also known as "tests"), and a large proportion of coccolith material. Smaller than the diatom tests, coccoliths are microscopic shells of tiny flagellates known as coccolithophores ("coccolith-producers"). The coccolithophores are among the smallest known flagellates, which can pass through the finest meshes and can only be collected by special filters and centrifuges. The radiolarians are named for the threads radiating from a perforated central skeleton, which is often a thing of astonishingly delicate beauty. Radiolarian ooze accumulates in colder, deeper waters than the diatomaceous ooze, because the tiny skeletons are made of opal, which is resistant to dissolution in cold water.

Barely visible (even under a microscope) as participants in the swarming world of the zooplankton are tiny transparent worms known as *Tomopteris,* and the larger, slender creatures called arrowworms (Chaetognatha), which range in size from less than a quarter of an inch in length to several inches, but average less than an inch long. Arrowworms are aggressive feeders, grasping their prey in their mouth, which is surrounded by bristles ("Chaetognatha" means "hairy jaws"), and they are further identifiable by their rapid, darting movements. They are so transparent as to be virtually invisible, but they are numerous enough to be considered the dominant species of animal plankton.

Snails are also represented in the plankton, but not in the traditional format with a heavy shell and a muscular foot. Planktonic mollusks are delicate little creatures with wings; hence their name: pteropods ("wing-feet"). Some have shells (*Limacina*), and some do not (*Clione*), but both types—now believed to be unrelated—"fly" through the water by the undulation of their wings, which are actually extensions of the foot. The tiny coiled shells of the shelled varieties fall to the bottom when their occupants die, in such profusion that there are regions of the sea floor blanketed in what is called "ptero-pod ooze."*

They do not look like animals as we know them; rather, they look like transparent cylinders, open at both ends. Bluish bands of muscle fibers circle each individual like the hoops of a barrel. They are the salps, citizens of the plankton, and among the strangest animals in the sea. (They are also referred to as "salpas"; the terms are interchangeable.) Water flows through the animal to provide food in the form of diatoms and other minute creatures that adhere to the salp's mucous network; it provides oxygen; and it also moves the animal through the sea. At 1,400 feet, through the quartz portholes of the bathysphere, William Beebe saw salps that were "four or five inches in length and perfectly transparent except for the translucent vertical bands and the small brown gut at one end."[†]

Salps are mostly warm-water inhabitants, occasionally carried into the North Atlantic by the Gulf Stream. These fragile creatures range in size from one to six inches, but a relative, the colonial *Pyrosoma* ("fire body") can get considerably larger. Both salps and *Pyrosoma* are tunicates, referring to the exterior integument, or tunic. Salps are open at both ends, but *Pyrosoma* is open only at the rear, and moves by ejecting water out of the opening. The scientific name refers to its ability to luminesce, and Beebe wrote (in *Half Mile Down*) that they had seen a half dozen colonies, "completely aglow with tiny pin-points of light." Crew members of the *Challenger* discovered that they also luminesced when touched, as they calligraphed their names with their fingers on the flanks of the colonies. In the South Atlantic, Hans Hass dived with (and photographed) "a large, gelatinous body floating just below the surface. It was a good five feet long and eighteen inches thick, in the shape of a spiraled cylinder. . . . There was not the slightest sign of any organ. I tried to touch it with my finger, but the finger passed through without resistance."

In *Twenty Thousand Leagues Under the Sea,* Professor Arronax takes an

---

* In May 1952, aboard the research vessel *Galathea,* in a trawl pulled up from 11,878 feet in the Mexican Pacific, Danish malacologist Henning Lemche found several specimens of a segmented, limpet-like mollusk with gills—a combination that had been observed only in fossils of the Cambrian period, 350 million years ago. A true "living fossil" (of equal zoological importance, but less showy than the discovery of the living coelacanth in 1938), *Neopilina galatheae* consists of a single spoon-shaped shell about an inch and a half long, and an animal with five pairs of gills, a radula, and, around the mouth, fleshy structures that are thought to assist in bringing food in. Neither a clam nor a snail, *Neopilina* is one of two living members of the Monoplacophora ("one-plate-bearers"); another similar species was hauled up from almost 20,000 feet off the coast of Peru in 1958.

[†] The two-inch-long fish commonly known as the squaretail (*Tetragonurus* spp.) lives inside salps, biting off chunks of the guts and the gill bar of its host with its mandibular teeth. The salp's only defense against this predation from within appears to be to close itself up when the little fish is not inside (Janssen and Harbison 1981).

underwater stroll and finds "creatures with umbrellas of opal or rose pink, touched with a tint of blue; fiery pelagiae, which light our path through the waters with their phosphorescence." We are not sure what Jules Verne meant by "pelagiae," but the description fits the larvaceans, also known as Appendicularia. They are tiny, finger-shaped creatures that spin "houses" of mucus around themselves that serve as traps for the tiny organisms on which they feed. The miniature food organisms were unknown until they were discovered, trapped by larvacean filters, by the nineteenth-century biologist Hans Lohmann. "Man has not yet succeeded in devising suitable means for the capture and estimation of these tiny members of the plankton," wrote Alister Hardy in *The Open Sea*. "That larvaceans should have solved the problem so efficiently makes one marvel all the more at the astonishing powers of adaptation through natural selection." (In a footnote, Hardy wrote that "Millepore filters" have now been developed "for collecting these small flagellates from sea water.") Most larvacean houses are small, about the size of a walnut, but the deepwater species *Bathochordaeus charon* spins a web that may be the size of a pumpkin.

The best-known of the larvaceans is *Oikopleura,* but there are two other appendicularian families, the Kowalevskiidae and the Frittilaridae, both of which build houses, and about which less is known. *Oikopleura* is a tadpole-shaped creature less than a quarter of an inch long (not counting the inch-long tail) that builds a cellulose "house" around itself that Alice Alldredge has described as "one of the most complex external structures built by any organism other than man." From within an exceedingly thin envelope that it secretes, *Oikopleura* undulates its tail to inflate the envelope like a tiny balloon. There are two openings at the hind end, which are covered with threads so minute that only the smallest particles can enter, and toward the front are two conical nets, which lead to the mouth of the inhabitant. The undulating tail draws water (and food) into the house through the fine-mesh grids at the rear, and circulates the water and food items into the miniature tow nets, and thence to the mouth. At the rear of the "house" is an escape hatch, through which *Oikopleura* can wriggle out in times of danger, and go on to build another of these miraculous structures. (The tiny creature may build a house several times a day, a process that takes only a few minutes.) And if this were not complicated enough, *Oikopleura*—and its house, even when abandoned—is luminescent. In a 1978 article in *Science,* C. P. Galt wrote, "The luminescence is intrinsic to the animals and their houses. Field observations suggest that, because of this dual method of light production, larvaceans may contribute substantially to surface coastal displays of marine bioluminescence." Their cast-off houses also contribute to "marine snow," the constant fall of detritus from the surface waters to the depths, a major source of nourishment for creatures of the benthos.

One group of simple animals attach themselves permanently to the ocean bottom, their immobility a seeming contradiction of the definition of animals. Moreover, they have no muscles or bone; no mouths or teeth; no brain or nervous system; and they cannot see or hear. When dissected, they reveal no hearts, glands, or gills. Why should such creatures, defined more for what they lack than for what they have, be considered animals and not plants? Because they do not carry on photosynthesis, and their cells do not have a cell wall, but instead are surrounded by a thin membrane. What are these plant-like animals? They are sponges, of course, the most primitive of the common multicelled animals.

Members of the phylum Porifera ("pore-bearers"), sponges are more complex than the protozoans, since they are composed of many differentiated cells, arranged in layers. The body is made up of a supporting meshwork surrounding tiny pores, through which water is drawn by the beating of tiny whips (flagella) that line the inner cavity. Water is expelled through a large opening known as the osculum, leaving behind the minute organisms on which the sponge feeds. This process also brings in oxygen and eliminates waste products. Shallow-water sponges usually have a powerful mechanism by which they pump water in and out of their bodies, but the deep-sea varieties have no such hydraulic efficiency and depend on the steady currents to move the water through them. Some sponges reproduce asexually, by releasing masses of cells enclosed in resistant cases that can attach to a solid object and become new sponges, but they can also reproduce hermaphroditically, where a single individual releases eggs and sperm into the water—but not at the same time—to prevent self-fertilization.

We tend to think of sponges as being shapeless blobs full of holes, but the familiar bath sponges are only the soft skeletons of shallow-water species of the genera *Spongia* and *Hippospongia*. Shallow-water sponges, like those that have been collected commercially for centuries by sponge-divers in Greece and Florida, are especially useful for bathing because they have skeletons of soft, resilient fibers instead of the tough spicules that the deep-sea sponges have to strengthen their body walls. (The protein spongin predominates in the skeleton of the softer, shallow-water species, while mineralized skeletons characterize the sponges of the cold depths.) The soft and friendly bath sponges (now mostly replaced by synthetics) are nothing at all like their deep-sea relatives. Consider the Hyalospongiae (*hyalos* is Greek for "glass"), for example. They would make very poor bath sponges indeed, since they have a skeleton composed of six-rayed spikes, which are sharp and actually made of silica or glass. These render the otherwise defenseless sponge unpalatable to most predators, and if this isn't enough, many species secrete venomous toxins.

The Porifera of the deep may be vase-shaped, funnel-shaped, cornucopia-shaped, cactus-shaped, tulip-shaped, or, in the case of *Cladorhiza,* shaped like "a space-age microwave antenna" (Heezen and Hollister 1971). Many species of glass sponges are rooted to the sea floor by an extension of the body composed of long spicules, giving it the appearance of a vase, a funnel, or a tulip on a long stem. The most diverse group is the Demospongia, represented in the deep by the genera *Chondrocladia, Cladorhiza,* and *Abyssocladia,* seen at depths up to 6,000 meters. Observing from the submersible *Deepstar,* Ron Church (1971) remarked, "When a sponge dies, the glassy stalk remains. I have seen eerie forests of them rising from the sea floor like the stems of so many gigantic champagne glasses." The watering-can sponge (*Euplectella* spp.), also known as "Venus's flower basket," develops basal spicules that are twisted together to form a short stem. *Euplectella* is a complex organism that is prized as a curio in Japan, where it is often given as a wedding present because in life, the sponge often houses

a pair of crustaceans. Vase-shaped sponges (like *Euplectella*) often tend to point downcurrent, so as to carry away the waste matter expelled from the ocsulum.

The phylum Coelenterata consists of the hydroids and siphonophores, the jellyfishes, the anemones, and most of the corals. All the coelenterates are radially symmetrical and have a single, hollow body cavity, called the coelenteron; hence the name. A single opening to the central cavity serves as both the mouth and the anus, and is surrounded by one or more circlets of food-capturing tentacles. Stinging cells on the tentacles paralyze the prey be-

Jellyfish, like this *Dactylometra quinquecirrha,* are animals characterized by a translucent, gelatinous body that can be as much as 99 percent water, and tentacles that are armed with stinging cells known as nematocysts.

fore it is drawn into the mouth. Jellyfishes and siphonophores are included in the myriad, floating world of oceanic plankton, and are similar in general form, but the jellyfishes are single animals, while the siphonophores are colonies of differentiated cells, each with a particular function. There are over two hundred jellyfish species (Scyphozoa), ranging in size from less than an inch to several feet in diameter. (The largest is *Cynaea arctica*, a resident of the deep North Atlantic from Greenland to North Carolina, which may achieve a diameter of 7 feet and have tentacles over 100 feet long.) Although they are capable of directed movement, jellyfishes (also known as medusae, because of the purported resemblance of the tentacles to the snakelike coiffure of Medusa) are mostly carried by currents, much in the way parachutes are carried by the wind. For this reason, they are considered members of the plankton, even though many species get to be quite large. They feed by trapping their prey in their tentacles as they swim or float along, and then transferring it to the mouth. Most deepwater medusae are luminescent, and many are deep maroon or purple in color.

According to N. B. Marshall's 1979 *Deep-Sea Biology,* "Siphonophores . . . are among the most abundant of the larger forms of zooplankton. They are so transparent and elusive that it takes some time before one realizes that a catch is full of the smaller kinds. In their natural surroundings they must be invisible. When they luminesce, a bluish glow lights up the glassy bells of the colony." The best-known of these creatures is the Portuguese man-of-war (*Physalia*), whose purplish, inflated float is often seen on the surface in tropical waters. Beneath the float are the tentacles, which carry batteries of stinging cells (nematocysts) and may trail 100 feet behind. When the prey—usually small fishes—comes in contact with the stinging cells, a trigger mechanism is activated and shoots a toxin into the victim. Depending on the size, the victim may be irritated, wounded, paralyzed, or killed. (Although a limited exposure is not normally potent enough to kill a man, multiple stings from *Physalia* can result in nausea, vomiting, loss of speech, respiratory difficulties, paralysis, convulsions, and even death.)

Many smaller siphonophores are found from the surface to the deep sea and come in a dazzling array of combinations of floats, tentacles, and digestive and reproductive organs. An animal composed of an assortment of differentiated cells is a complicated zoological puzzle. In *The Open Sea,* his book on plankton, Alister Hardy wrote, "Nowhere in the animal kingdom do we get the extraordinary integration and coordination of persons [Hardy's term for the functional cell groupings] that we find in these composite siphonophores. The whole colony now appears to act as one, as if it was endowed with some new and higher individuality greater than that of the component persons." Some have multiple bells, which pulse in unison to move the organism, but can also operate asymmetrically to effect a quick course change. Siphonophores are hermaphroditic, with the fertilized eggs developing into a larval form which produces the large colony by asexual budding.

The continued investigation of the deep-sea fauna has generated a classification of the vertically defined environments, ostensibly to assist in describing them and identifying the species that live there. But whereas there is an International Code of Zoological Nomenclature to set the rules and adjudicate disputes over the scientific names of animals, there is no such system to determine what a particular area of the ocean should be called, or, for that matter, where it should begin or end.

The top of the ocean is the surface, of course, and the first 100 meters below that is referred to as the epipelagic zone, derived from the Greek *epi,* which means "upon" or "over." (Another term for this zone is "euphotic," since it gets the most light.) Below that, for another 1,000 meters or so, is the mesopelagic (*meso* = "middle"), the lowest level of which is marked by the absorption of all surface light. From 1,000 to about 6,000 meters is the bathypelagic zone. The word *benthos* means "depths of the sea" in Greek, and therefore, its adjectival form, "benthic," refers to the flora and fauna of the depths. Animals that live on the sea floor, such as asteroids, crinoids, gastropods, and many holothurians, are sometimes known as "benthopelagic" forms, or sometimes "creatures of the benthos." (Various fish species, with the exception of those that perform daily vertical migrations, are generally restricted to specific environments.) Add "abyss"—from the Greek for "bottomless"—and we get "abyssal," "abyssopelagic," or "abyssobenthic," referring to the deepest parts of the ocean, except for the great Pacific trenches. (The deepest place in the Atlantic is the Puerto Rico Trench, a mile shallower than the Mariana Trench.)*

In 1960, Torben Wolff of the *Galathea* expedition wrote "The Hadal Community: An Introduction," in which he attempted to describe the extent of what he referred to as "life in the trenches."† The greatest depths—from 6,000 to 11,000 meters—are all at the bottom of trenches, and these are mostly in the Pacific. The pressure at these depths also contributes to the quality of life there; Wolff wrote that "organisms from the greatest depths have special physiological adaptations to determine the upper limit of their occurrence."

---

* As an example of an alternative system, consider Sanders and Hessler (1969), who wrote, "The bathyal region encompasses depths from 200 meters to 2000 or 3000 meters and includes the continental slopes; the abyssal zone covers from 2000 to 3000 meters to 6000 meters; the hadal zone is at depths greater than 6000 meters and includes the deep-sea trenches."

† Anton Bruun of the *Galathea* expedition coined the term "hadal" in 1956, referring to Hades, the Greek underworld. Other authors, such as Menzies and George (1967), preferred "ultra-abyssal" or "trench floor fauna," but Bruun (1970) believed that this zone, like the littoral, bathyal, and abyssal zones, "deserves" its own name.

The very inaccessibility of the hadal zone makes collecting difficult, and relatively few samples have been collected from the trench floors. (Trawling in the trenches requires tremendously long cables, controlled by powerful winches and engines. In one instance, the *Galathea* put out nearly seven and a half miles of cable—an operation that took six hours—and the trawl touched bottom almost a mile and a half behind the ship.) In the Pacific trenches (Kurile-Kamchatka, Philippine, Banda, New Britain, Kermadec, Sunda, Mariana, and Tonga), the macrofauna collected by the *Galathea* consisted of polychaete worms, crustaceans, anemones, holothurians, bristle worms, crinoids, starfishes, sea urchins, fishes, and assorted invertebrates. At depths greater than 7,000 meters, some 58 percent of the species were endemic—that is, they are found only at those depths, and nowhere else. Under "special peculiarities," Wolff writes that "hadal species show the same adaptations to life in eternal darkness as many abyssal and even bathyal (and cave-dwelling) species: greyish or whitish colours . . . and probably always total blindness."

Knowledge of the deep-sea fauna does not depend exclusively on sampling; as early as 1932, William Beebe was aiming his camera through the portholes of the bathysphere, and a decade later, when Maurice Ewing was investigating the floor of the Atlantic, he and his colleagues relied heavily on photography as an adjunct to geological sampling. In the late 1960s, John Isaacs of Scripps employed a baited robotic camera to photograph life in the depths, and he was amazed at the results. "The thousands of pictures make it clear," he wrote in 1975, "that much of the deep-sea floor teems with numerous species of scavengers; vigorous invertebrates and fishes, including some gigantic sharks, that are supported by a marine food web whose extent and complexity is only beginning to be perceived." Robotic cameras were deployed to photograph every sort of benthic creature, and the results were examined, analyzed, and published. Heezen and Hollister's 1971 *Face of the Deep* was an annotated compilation of these photographs; Clyde Roper and Walter Brundage's 1972 study revealed heretofore unknown aspects of the lives of deep-sea cephalopods, and the same can be said for David Pawson's review of thousands of photographs of holothurians. From the various submersibles, such as *Alvin* and *Deepstar*, scientists photographed every sort of sea creature, including some—the hydrothermal vent animals—whose existence and lifestyle were totally unanticipated and surprising. By the mid-1980s, advances in technology made it possible to send more sophisticated equipment to the bottom, perhaps best exemplified by the "bathysnap," a time-lapse system developed by the Institute of Oceanographic Sciences (IOS) in Surrey, England.

Responding to the limitations of one-shot photography of the deep-sea fauna, IOS technicians developed a system that would photograph a patch of seabed repeatedly over periods of several days or even months, to obtain a record of the normal behavior of animals dwelling on the sea floor. "Bathysnap pho-tographs are providing a wealth of information on the behavior of deep-sea ani-mals," wrote Richard Lampitt of IOS. "Some species have never been seen in their natural environment nor collected in trawls or dredges." They were not sur-prised to learn that "deposit feeders" (like holothurians) predominate on the ocean floor, but pictures of 20-inch-long burrowing worms were completely unexpected. (Of these worms, Gage and Tyler wrote, "Most belong to the fam-ily Bonelliidae, possessing a long, tongue-like flattened food-gathering proboscis that is extended, ventral side up, over the sediment in different directions from the short, fat body that lies completely buried within a 'U'- or 'L'-shaped bur-row in the soft sediment." In other words, the "worms" photographed by the bathysnap may be only their tongues.) Lampitt and his colleagues wanted to photograph the undisturbed behavior of the sea-floor animals, but on one occa-sion, they baited the camera array with a "juicy cod steak"; the amphipods (usu-ally the first creatures attracted to a food source) were almost immediately attacked by predatory fish and shrimp that were also drawn to the bait. In recent years, robotic television cameras have been added to the oceanographer's arse-nal, and we can expect more exciting revelations about life in the unexplored (and mostly unexplorable) depths.

Those creatures large enough to be photographed or captured in trawls and dredges—as opposed to fine-mesh nets—are known collectively as the mega-fauna. The phylum that dominates the sea floor is the Echinodermata ("spiny-skins"), including the starfish, brittle stars, basket stars, sea urchins, sea lilies, and sea cucumbers. All echinoderms have a body plan with five-part (pen-tamerous) symmetry, obvious in the five arms of the starfish and the five "petals" of the sand dollar, but not so obvious in the sea cucumbers. In fact, holothurians have five internal muscle bands and other structures that con-firm their pentamerous nature. Five-part symmetry is unique to the echino-derms, and occurs nowhere else in the animal kingdom.

The bodies of the echinoderms are protected and supported by skeletons composed of calcium carbonate plates, or by granules embedded in the skin. Echinoderms move with the aid of a hydraulically operated water-vascular sys-tem, a series of canals that extend to little tube feet (podia) which form five rows on the outside of the body. Each foot has at its base a muscular bulb that contracts to extend the foot—rather like squeezing one end of a sausage-shaped balloon. Sucker disks on the end of the feet can adhere to the sea floor and enable the animal to slowly pull itself along. Movement is aided by spines and plates of the skeleton that are under muscular control.

Starfish have no gills, but breathe through dermal branchiae ("skin gills"), which are outpouchings on the spiny skin that absorb oxygen and give off carbon dioxide, rather like the way the blood flows past the air sacs in the lungs of air-breathing vertebrates. Echinoderms have a definite top and bottom (dorsal and ventral surface), however, with a mouth on the bottom at the center of the star, where all the arms come together. Many starfish are carnivores, and capture their prey—usually bivalves, such as clams or mussels—with their arms, pry open the shells with the constant pull of the suckered tube feet, and then evert their stomachs into the bivalve to devour the soft tissue. It is believed that all sea stars can regenerate lost arms, and an arm that has become detached can often grow a whole new animal.*

The sea stars (Asteroidea) are the best-known echinoderms. Most have five arms; others have ten or more. Starfish of the depths conform to the basic five-rayed plan, but many lack suckers on the tube feet and live their lives burrowed into the soft sea-floor sediments, swallowing their prey whole. The spiny cushion stars (Pterasteridae) have an inflatable respiratory chamber, and they look like fat little pillows with short, stubby arms. Cushion stars have been taken as deep as 6,700 meters (21,976 feet) in the Kermadec Trench.

The brittle stars (Ophiuroidea) are among the most abundant inhabitants of the sea floor, and they occur as far down as 6,270 meters (20,565 feet). The species known as *Ophiacantha bidentata* is bioluminescent. Much of what is known about these creatures has come from examination of deep-water net hauls in which great numbers of them have been brought up; in Heezen and Hollister's collection of deep-sea photographs (*The Face of the Deep*), there are numerous pictures of brittle stars, and the authors write that they "are second in importance only to holothurians in the visible abyss."

With their arrangement of thin, flexible arms around a central, disklike body, brittle stars (sometimes known as serpent stars) are very active, moving rapidly along the sea floor. Some deep-sea species can actually swim for short distances. While shallow-water brittle stars often burrow in the sediment, deep-sea forms rarely burrow. Some species are often seen raised up on the tips of their arms with the central disk off the bottom; the reason for this behavior is unknown. In a few species, the arms can be as much as 15 inches long, resulting in a total spread of 30 inches or more. Invertebrate biologist Libbie Hyman wrote that the sixteen hundred existing species of brittle stars "may be regarded as the most successful echinoderm group living today, and this is probably to be attributed to the smaller size and greater agility of the members."

Even though the reasons for such arrangements are not clear, many

---

* Commercial oyster-growers learned this to their dismay. When starfish were found to be preying on their oyster beds, the oystermen often mopped up the offending echinoderms, cut them up, and threw them overboard. Most of the arms regenerated into new starfishes, so instead of decreasing the predators, they actually increased them.

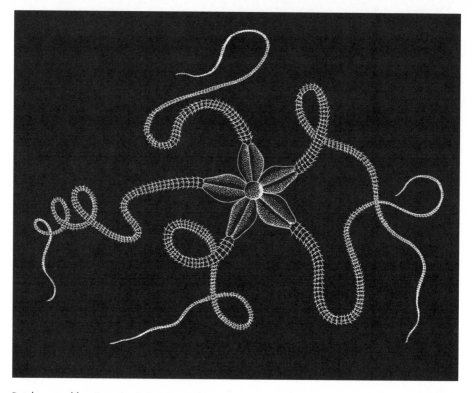

Brittle stars like *Asteronyx excavata* have five long, flexible arms that they use to entrap food items, and also to locomote along the bottom. They can cast off an arm if they are in trouble, accounting for their common name.

echinoderms possess bioluminescent capabilities. Peter Herring of the Institute of Oceanographic Sciences at Wormley, Sussex, examined two species of ophiurids, six asteroids, nine holothurians, and two crinoids. All were bioluminescent. Why an eyeless creature that hugs the bottom and feeds on animals of the sediment would need to draw more rather than less attention to itself is a mystery. As Herring wrote, "The functions of the bioluminescence of echinoderms remain a matter for conjecture. It may be that these animals are unattractive prey by nature of the spines or poisonous secretions which many possess, and the bioluminescent response merely advertises the fact to a potential predator."

Imagine a brittle star whose arms have branched at the base, then branched again, and again and again, and you will have an image of one of the most unusual creatures of the abyss: the basket star. (The notorious "crown-of-thorns" sea star [*Acanthaster*] that has wreaked havoc with Pacific coral reefs is not a basket star, even though it has more than five arms—usually ten to thirteen—with nasty-looking spines all over them.) Basket stars belong to the family Gorgonocephalidae ("Gorgon-headed"), a name based on the resemblance to the head of the Gorgon—in Greek mythology, a woman with snakes for hair. (The branching corals known as gorgonians get their name from the same figure.) Using the web of branching arms like a net, basket stars capture pelagic organisms such as copepods and appendicularians, which they transfer to the mouth on the underside of the disk. The best-known of the basket stars is the North Atlantic *Gorgonocephalus arcticus*, found in the shallows and at depths of 4,000 feet from the Arctic to Cape Cod. In the 1927 *Handbook of the Echinoderms of the British Isles*, Mortensen wrote, "The species of this genus live rather gregariously; on rocky ground swept by currents they may

The basket starfish *Gorgonocephalus arcticus* traps floating plankton in its web of branching arms. The name *Gorgonocephalus* is derived from the Gorgons, sisters of Medusa, women in Greek mythology with snakes for hair.

be found in great numbers, covering the ground, clinging to one another, their branching arms forming a dense network in which are caught the pelagic organisms on which they feed." In mature adults, the body disk can be 4 inches across, and the arm span, 20 inches.

The sea urchins (echinoids) take the term "spiny-skinned" to the extreme. Most of them seem to be composed only of spines, but in fact, there is a more or less spherical body, thickly covered with movable spines, with a centrally located mouth on the underside. They move along the sea floor by means of podia (tube feet) similar to those of the starfishes, but they can also use their spines to assist in locomotion, since the spines are individually equipped with a ball-and-socket joint. Sea urchins feed by moving over the food item and chewing it to bits with an organ known as "Aristotle's lantern," which consists of an ingenious arrangement of five teeth, arranged radially around the mouth and worked by a complex set of muscles and calcareous plates. Their food consists mostly of mosslike animals like hydroids, but they may also ingest large quantities of mud and sand to extract small food particles.

The name *Cucumis marinus*—"sea cucumber"—was bestowed upon them by Pliny the Elder, for what appeared to be obvious reasons, based on their familiar shape.* Only recently, however, has the true nature of these curious animals begun to reveal itself. In a 1986 article, D. S. Billett wrote, "Sea cucumbers are supposed to be long and cylindrical and live at the bottom of the sea. Marine biologists are now finding that in the deep oceans these animals break all the rules and swim high above the ocean floor. . . ." As echinoderm specialist David Pawson has written, "Knowledge of the deep-sea benthic fauna has increased tremendously in recent years, not only as a result of the fact that new collections of organisms have been described, and that several studies have been conducted on population structure and patterns of distribution, but also as a result of the increasing use of underwater cameras and manned submersibles to record the habits and interrelationships of living organisms *in situ*." By 1989, Pawson himself had "studied approximately 80,000 photographs of the deep-sea floor" and had "made probably 200 dives in manned submersibles, and always there are beautiful holothurians to be seen."

Known officially as holothurians, sea cucumbers are echinoderms that have only the rudiments of the spines that characterize the rest of the phylum;

* In some parts of the world, the shallow-water species are prized as food items. Known as trepang or bêche-de-mer in the Indo-Pacific or along certain Oriental coasts, the animal is eviscerated, boiled, then dried or smoked. The meat is rich in protein, and highly favored in Chinese cuisine.

the spines have been replaced by minute calcareous deposits (known as "spicules" or "ossicles") of various shapes embedded in the body wall, which can be used to differentiate the species. According to dredged samples and the photographic record, these soft-bodied echinoderms are the dominant life form on the deep-sea floor. They are found at almost every level of the ocean, from the shallows to the abyssal depths. (The "fish" that was spotted swimming away from the *Trieste* at the ocean's greatest depth is now believed to have been a holothurian, perhaps *Galatheathuria aspera*. In 1960, when the dive was made, very few people were familiar with even the *idea* of swimming sea cucumbers.) Many varieties are as unadorned as pickles or potatoes, but others have a profusion of protuberances, the functions of which are not clearly understood. For example, *Scotoplanes globosa*, brought up from 32,800 feet in the Kermadec Trench, is described by Idyll (1971) as "about three inches long and . . . rather like little pigs with strange protrusions growing from their backs."

"Most abyssal holothurians," wrote Heezen and Hollister, "do not exceed the size of a mouse, but a few of the largest reach the size of a kitten." Some of the deep-sea species have a tail-like appendage, which is often elevated.

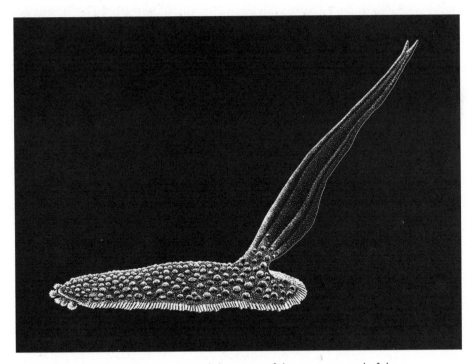

The sea cucumber *Psychropotes mirabilis* is one of the most unusual of the holothurians. The purpose of the "sail" is unknown.

One of the largest and most spectacular of the holothurians is *Psychropotes longicauda*,* which can reach a length of 20 inches, and is usually seen with its "tail" raised. The *Galathea* expedition collected eight specimens of *P. longicauda* ("long-tail") with "delicate reddish-violet hues, one having a lemon-yellow back." *Psychropotes mirabilis* is even more dramatic, with a single dorsal papilla, or "sail," longer than its body. (In 1989, Eric Foell and David Pawson published the preliminary findings of their examination of some 250 hours of videotape, taken in the northeastern Pacific, which included footage of *Psychropotes semperiana*, another related species with an unmistakable dorsal appendage; these animals almost always faced into the current, with their appendages recurved overhead.) Some species, such as *Molpadia*, live head down in the sediment, while others, like *Echinocucumis*, are horseshoe-shaped and spend their lives with most of the body buried and only the mouth and anus sticking out of the seabed.

There are more than twelve hundred holothurian species, classified into six orders: Apodida, Molpadiida, Dendrochirotida, Aspidochirotida, Dactylo-chirotida, and Elasipodida. A majority of the three hundred known deep-sea forms belong to the Aspidochirotida and the Elasipodida, but the other orders are also represented in the deep-sea fauna. (The Elasipodida are unique in being confined to the deep-sea environments.) In Heezen and Hollister's photographic survey of benthic animal forms, they found—not surprisingly—that "the large elasipods have been seen most frequently." David Pawson wrote, "As the holothurians comprise more than 95 per cent of the total biomass over large areas of the deep-sea floor, I'm always trying to point out their importance to doubting colleagues." From their examination of deep-sea photographs, Heezen and Hollister also found that "deep-sea elasipods are vividly colored in bright translucent shades of purple, maroon, and violet. . . . [D]ull shades of gray, brown, olive, or black are characteristic of shallow-water holothurians."

The bottom-dwellers plow along the sediments like vacuum cleaners, hoovering up muddy sediments that include bacteria, diatoms, and other microscopic organisms that make up their food supply. The mouth is typically at the front end of an elongated or flattened body, surrounded by a corona of oral tentacles, and the anus is at the other end. In order to extract nourishment from sand or mud, they have to process considerable amounts of inorganic matter; W. J. Crozier estimated that a single ten-inch-long *Stichopus* (a shallow-water species) ingests and egests two and a half pounds of bottom sediment every day.

* With the exception of the all-purpose "sea-cucumber"—which does not have much to do with an animal that may be shaped like a Frisbee—most holothurians have no common names. For the most part, the holothurians are known only to scientists, who usually discuss them with their peers or in scientific publications, so any discussion of the life and times of these curious creatures is perforce replete with scientific names.

The sea cucumber *Scotoplanes globosa* is a deepwater species that often occurs in "herds." One author described them as "about three inches long . . . rather like little pigs with strange protrusions growing from their backs."

(He also estimated that in the 1.7 acres of Harrington Sound, Bermuda, the *Stichopus* population processes between 500 and 1,000 tons of bottom material per year.) Many holothurians breathe with a pair of "respiratory trees" in the body cavity that extend forward from the cloaca and keep the internal organs aerated and the body plump. Others lack trees and respire through their body walls. They move by means of podia, which are usually disposed on the underside in rows down the mid-line, and on each edge of the outer margin, but there are many variations on this theme. As it "walks," the animal makes identifiable tracks in the sediment, some of which have been illustrated in the chapter called "Footprints" in *The Face of the Deep*. (In it, Heezen and Hollister wrote, "Holothurians feeding on the bottom sediments mix and till the surface muds on an enormous scale, producing features more widespread and more visibly evident than those produced by any other animals on earth.) According to Marshall (1979), *Scotoplanes*, "with a few extra pairs of tube feet to lurch over the sediments, has been photographed in herds on the continental slope off California and New England."

It was long believed that all holothurians stuck to the bottom. As recently as 1975, Bent Hansen, even though he included some records of their swim-

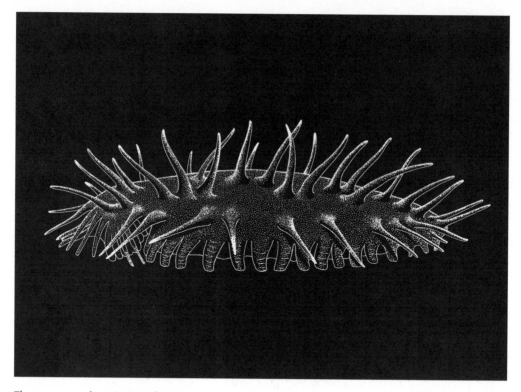

The sea cucumber *Oneirophanta mutabilis* is a deepwater species that moves along the sediment on its podia, or tube feet. The function of the numerous dorsal protrusions is a mystery.

ming, wrote, "the majority of deep-sea holothurians seem to spend their life on the surface of the bottom. . . ." The advent of submersible research revealed that there are some species that swim, or at least locomote through the water. Swimming sea cucumbers have evolved shapes that are more conducive to a pelagic existence; some are shaped more like jellyfishes, while others have developed a "brim" that is a fusion of their tube feet at the outer margin. The large, pancake-shaped *Paelopatides grisea* was seen from the *Alvin* swimming over the bottom with undulating movements of its crenellated brim, something like a cuttlefish.

Billett (1986) wrote that "*Scotothuria* seems capable of migrating vast distances vertically. Why it bothers to, and how often it goes travelling remain a puzzle." John Miller, David Pawson, and other scientists, in their research dives aboard the submersibles *Johnson Sea-Link* (off the Bahamas) and *Pisces* (off the Galápagos), observed four swimming species, including *Hansenothuria benti,* a new species that they described in 1989 and named for the Danish researcher Bent Hansen, "in recognition of his superb contributions to our knowledge of deep-sea holothurians." (The late Dr. Hansen, an invertebrate specialist, wrote—among other things—the comprehensive "Systematics and

Biology of the Deep-Sea Holothurians.") In their 1990 paper ("Swimming Sea Cucumbers . . . : A Survey, with Analysis of Swimming Behavior in Four Bathyal Species"), Miller and Pawson wrote that "the true natatorial acrobats among the class Holothurioidea are the deep-sea species of the orders Aspidochirotida and Elasipodida. Approximately 20 species . . . have been captured or observed near the bottom or at depths several hundred to several thousand meters above the seafloor. A few deep-sea species have even been found in surface waters."

The "reasons" for sea cucumbers' swimming are unknown, since most of the pelagic varieties appear to be adapted for feeding in the sediments. They may range upward for breeding purposes, or they may even have developed some method of filtering particles from the water, but not enough is known about the lives of most of the deepwater holothurians to determine exactly what they are doing off the bottom. Miller and Pawson identified "possible reasons for swimming behavior," including "predator avoidance, escape from physical hazards, locomotion, seeking out suitable substrata for feeding, and dispersal of juveniles or adults." They identified *Pelagothuria natatrix* ("pelagic swimming holothurian") as the only known species to spend its entire life "swimming and drifting in the water column, feeding on re-suspended sediments or on the rain of detrital material from the shallower depths." *Hansenothuria benti,* on the other hand, "has been found to swim only in response to a disturbance," flexing through a series of S curves to propel itself away from the offender. *Paelopatides retifer,* a sweet-potato-shaped animal with a wide brim, flexes its body and pulsates the brim, like its relative *P. grisea.* Surprisingly, the barrel-shaped *Enypniastes eximia* locomotes on a vertical orientation with its feeding tentacles uppermost. *Pelagothuria natatrix,* they wrote, "is perhaps the most bizarre holothurian species in existence. Its shape is more reminiscent of a medusa, and it bears no obvious resemblance to most sea cucumbers." At the anterior end of the body is an enormous, umbrella-like web of feeding tentacles that may be as long or longer than the slender, conical body, and which the animal pulsates to move through the water. When scientists attempted to capture a specimen of *Benthodytes* from the submersible *Archimède* off Madeira, "the movements of the grab made the holothurian expand very rapidly to three or four times its original volume. It thus became loaf-shaped instead of sausage-shaped, and its colour changing at the same time from dark brown to reddish violet . . . it escaped the grab" (Wolff 1971).

Diving (separately) off southern California in the submersibles *Sea Cliff* and *Turtle,* scientists (see Barnes, Quetin, Childress, and Pawson 1976) were "surrounded by living hordes" of the swimming elasipod holothurian *Peniagone diaphana,* which they described as a small, flattened holothurian, averaging

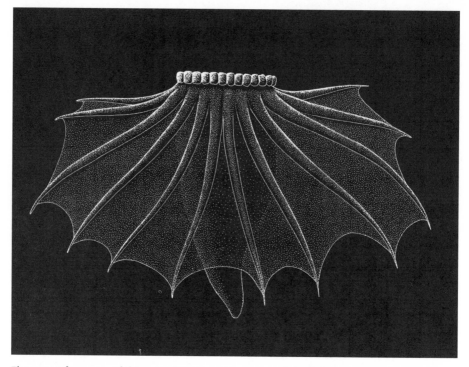

The scientific name of this swimming sea cucumber, *Pelagothuria natatrix,* means "pelagic swimming holothurian," and describes its lifestyle perfectly. Unlike most of its relatives, this animal never settles on the bottom, and spends its entire life suspended in the water column.

about three inches in length, with a tentacled mouth at one end and a paddle-like postanal fan at the other. (This species is also known from the Atlantic at depths of from 2,550 to 5,600 meters.) Originally, they were never seen "in contact with the substrate" (they never rested or crawled on the bottom), but even more surprising, they were always swimming vertically. (There are very few marine animals other than sea horses and their relatives that maintain a constant vertical orientation.) Later studies showed that this species also lives on the sea floor. *Peniagone diaphana* may feed on suspended detritus, but examination of captured specimens revealed "sponge spicules, holothurian spicules, diatom frustules, foraminiferan shells," indicating some sea-floor feeding. (Not all *Peniagone* holothurians swim; nothing researchers in *Alvin* did could make one western Atlantic species leave the bottom, but other closely related forms were observed *only* off the bottom. In their 1989 paper, Foell and Pawson wrote that *P. leander* "may only spend about 25% of the time on the seafloor, presumably feeding on the sediments, while the remaining time is spent swimming or passively drifting at heights of up to at least 250 meters above the bottom.")

And not only do some of these "natatorial acrobats" swim in unexpected regions and unpredicted orientations, some of them glow in the dark. In the above-mentioned study by Herring of the bioluminescent qualities of various echinoderms, several species of North Atlantic holothurians were collected and produced a dazzling array of luminescent effects, but as with the starfishes, the "reason" for the display is by no means obvious. (In a 1961 study, J. A. C. Nicol suggested that sedentary animals might "flash or twinkle . . . when touched, and thus warn would-be settlers that the territory is already occupied.") The species *Kolga hyalina* "gave a bright blue light when handled," and the small orange species *Ellipinion* "emitted a brilliant blue light from a great many minute sparkling points all over the whole dorsal and lateral surface."

"There may not be as many different kinds of crustaceans as there are insects," wrote C. P. Idyll, "but there certainly are vastly more individuals." In fact, there are no real insects in the sea at all, but there are enough arthropods ("jointed-legs") to make up for the omission. In *Deep Oceans,* Peter Herring and Malcolm Clarke wrote, "The crustaceans are the insects of the sea in their successful colonization and spread in the marine environment, and comprise at least 70 per cent of almost any haul of marine animals." In addition to the crustaceans (branchiopods, ostracods, copepods, isopods, amphipods, euphausiids, and decapods), there is a small group of marine arachnids (the group to which spiders belong), including the shallow-water horseshoe crab, deepwater mites, and the sea spiders (pycnogonids), benthic creatures whose gut extends into their legs.

Ostracods are tiny animalcules with a bivalved shell, from which fewer legs protrude than in any other crustacean—only two pairs—along with the antennae. They inhabit the bottom sediments, where they feed on detritus. Although most species are blind, many emit a luminous secretion whose chemistry is the best-known of any such system. The Pacific ostracod *Cypridina hilgendorfi* gives off brilliant blue sparks when disturbed, and can repeat the act many times. (Other species emit green or yellow light.) So powerful are the substances that engender this light, according to Waldo Schmitt, "that in water a proportion as minute as one part in 1,700,000,000 parts of water will still give off a visible light." In his 1952 study of bioluminescence, E. Newton Harvey wrote that during World War II, Japanese officers were able to read documents in the dark by the low intensity light given off by a bit of dry *Cypridina* powder moistened in the palm of a man's hand. Larger ostracods live in deeper waters; *Gigantocypris* (also said to be luminescent) is a globular orange creature about the size of a cherry with paired eyes facing forward like the headlights of a car. It has been collected at depths of 600 fathoms.

The Peracarida (from the Greek *pera*, a "pouch," and the Latin *caridis*, a "shrimp") are a large group of shrimplike crustaceans that carry their eggs and young in a protective brood pouch. Included in this large and diverse group are the Tanaidacea, the Cumacea, Amphipoda, and Isopoda. (The Mysidacea are another Peracarid order; delicate shrimplike creatures sometimes called "opossum shrimps" that are found at depth and near the surface, and sometimes serve as the food of whales.) Cumaceans are tiny animals that burrow into the ooze and sort through the surface layer, apparently eating whatever organic material they encounter. Tanids—like the Cumaceans, they have no common name—are even smaller, and are differentiated from other peracarids by crablike claws and the lack of a fanlike tail. There are hundreds of species (of the 262 found between the Bay of Biscay and the Rockall Trough in the North Atlantic, 58 percent were new), some of which swim off the bottom or build tubes in the sediment. One species, *Neotanis serratispinosus*, was collected from the Kermadec Trench at a depth of 8,200 meters.

Of the myriad life forms that inhabit the world ocean, the copepods are considered "the most important single group of marine animals in the economy of the seas, often making up 70 to 90 percent of the biomass of a plankton sample, and not infrequently occurring in vast swarms" (Herring and Clarke 1971). In his study of plankton, Alister Hardy wrote, "Not only are there a great many different species [there may be more than ten thousand], but the number of individuals of some of the commoner kinds is beyond calculation. It has been suggested that there must be more copepods than all other multicellular animals put together; I think this is probably no exaggeration." Copepods are found at every depth of the ocean. They are the predominant grazers of the phytoplankton, the animals mostly responsible for converting the photosynthetic process to animal energy. Their countless numbers form the broad base of the food pyramid of the sea.

They have no carapace, but they are equipped with a pair of long, feathery antennae that resemble a handlebar mustache, and six pairs of legs, including a pair of oarlike thoracic limbs to propel them forward. ("Copepod" means "oar-footed," from the Greek for "oar" (*kope*), and *pous*, "foot.") Typically, copepods have a single eye located in the middle of the head. Ranging from a couple of centimeters to a foot in length, and from insect- to eel-shaped, all copepods pass through a stage called the nauplius, in which the rhomboidal body is unsegmented and has only three pairs of limbs. As it molts, it elongates and adds segments (somites), passes through a stage known as the metanauplius, and finally arrives at its "copepodid" form, molting four more times and adding segments until it achieves its adult state. The average copepod is about the size of the head of a pin, but the larger ones, such as *Calanus finmarchicus* of the North Sea, can be as big as a grain of rice, and some are even larger. (*Calanus* is the principal food of herring, one of the most numerous fish in the ocean, and it also serves as the food of the right, bowhead, and sei whales. In the whaleman's parlance it was known as "brit.") Many species are parasitic, and they parasitize virtually every group of animals in the sea (and fresh water as well), taking up residence in the eyes and nostrils, and even burrowing into the flesh. (*Somniosus*, the Greenland shark, is almost always found with a copepod parasite on each eye.) The largest of the copepods is *Penella* (diminutive of the Latin for "feather"), which parasitizes swordfish, shark suckers, ocean sunfishes, and even baleen whales.

With copepods so numerous and so important to life in the sea, it is not surprising to learn that they exist in great profusion at every level. "The relative proportions of copepods in the total zooplankton increases with depth," wrote Georgina Deevey and Albert Brooks in 1977, "from 73.5 percent in the upper waters to 91 per cent between 1,500 and 2,000 metres. . . ." (The numbers of species, however, also declines with depth.) There are even copepods to be found near the deep-sea floor; the Spinoclanidae have been recorded from 4,000 meters. And "at depths below 12,000 meters there is a distinct and rather diverse bathypelagic fauna of calanoid copepods. . . ." (Marshall 1979). From the *Alvin* in 1968, in the North Atlantic south of Woods Hole, G. D. Grice captured several copepod species (genus *Xanthocalanus*) that he described as "planktobenthic"; they seemed to occupy a zone that was near, but not on, the ocean floor. Some were found in the gut of tripod fishes, which stand clear of the bottom on elongated fin spines. Although most species are transparent—perhaps with a faint iridescence or occasional spots—some of the deepwater varieties assume vivid colors, such as *Euchaeta*, which is a clear red, and *Candacia*, which is black. Some of the benthic copepods are light-producing, such as *Gaussia princeps*, which has a profusion of light glands that can produce a luminous blue discharge which lasts for one to three seconds, probably permitting the animal to escape from predators. In a series of experiments on the luminescence and behavior of *Metrida lucens*, it was seen that the copepod luminesced only when threatened by a predator (the euphausiid *Meganyctiphanes*, itself bioluminescent), and emitted a large flash when trying to escape, and a series of smaller flashes during its struggle to get away from the euphausiid.

There have been more than four thousand marine species of isopods recorded, many of them from the abyssal depths. They usually have seven pairs of legs of about equal size, hence the name "isopod," which means "equal feet," but otherwise, the morphological range is tremendous. Some are segmented like chitons; others elongated like worms; still others have attenuated bodies and long legs, giving them the appearance of stick insects. They walk along the bottom, dig into the sediments, and some are capable of swimming. They attach themselves to fish, often in the mouth cavity and even on the eyes. The Isopoda are represented on land by wood lice, pill bugs, and sow bugs, little fellows that are about a quarter of an inch long. In the sea, they get much larger than their terrestrial relatives, and become vicious parasites on fishes and many other crustaceans—including other isopods. Gigantism prevails in the depths, and isopods such as *Bathynomus giganteus* can get to be 14 inches long.

Another order of marine crustaceans is the amphipods, similar in most respects to isopods, but whereas isopods are compressed dorsolaterally, amphipods are arched and flattened from side to side. (The prefix *amphi* means "both"—as in "amphibian"—and refers to the shallow-water or terrestrial species that can use their feet to walk or swim.) Amphipods exist in countless numbers and also in great variety: there are some 4,600 species. When we see them on sandy beaches, they are known as sand hoppers or sand fleas, but there are thousands of species that are purely aquatic. Like their cousins the isopods, amphipods come in a great variety of shapes and sizes, but the largest, *Alicella gigantea* (which is known as a "supergiant" among amphipods), gets to be about seven inches long, only half the size of the largest isopod, but still quite large indeed.

The caprellid amphipods are sometimes known as skeleton shrimps, be-

Amphipods—like *Hirondella* shown here—are decapod (ten-footed) crustaceans that occur in almost all marine environments, from beach wrack to the depths. The prefix *amphi* means "both"—as in "amphibian"—and refers to the shallow-water or terrestrial species that can use their feet to walk or swim.

cause they appear like meatless shadows of crustaceans, and in fact, they use this skeletal conformation to blend their inch-long bodies with branched seaweeds, bryozoans, or hydroids, looking exactly like short branches of these marine growths. (Whale lice are flattened caprellid amphipods that live only on whales. They are "host-specific," which means that each species lives only on one species of whale: *Cyamus scammoni* on the gray whale, *C. physeteris* on the sperm whale, etc.) Amphipods are part of a highly motile, scavenging fauna that is quickly drawn to large food falls on the ocean floor, and therefore, many bottom-dwelling species have mouth parts that are adapted for slicing, biting, and chewing. Indeed, John Gage and Paul Tyler (1991) have written, "Baited traps set in deep trenches tend to confirm that the hadal environment is the exclusive preserve of crustacean scavengers, mainly amphipods. . . . [T]he rapidity with which bait attracts scavenging amphipods suggests that these animals are much more common than their rarity or absence from seabed trawl catches suggest." In addition to the ability to locate carrion, deepwater amphipods have developed other modifications for life in the dark; *Cytosoma neptuni* has enormous red eyes that presumably enable it to see in the dim light of the deep sea, but the deeper-water *Lepechinella* has no eyes at all.

The most familiar of the crustaceans—the euphausiids, shrimps, crabs, and lobsters—are classified as Eucarida, from *eu,* which means "true," and *karis,* "shrimp." These decapod (ten-footed) crustaceans can be further subdivided into the suborders Macrura ("large-tailed"), Anomura ("irregular-tailed"), and Brachyura ("short-tailed"). Lobsters and shrimp are macrourids; hermit crabs and coconut crabs are anomurids; and the true crabs are brachyurids.

What the whalers know as "krill" (a Norwegian word that means "young fish"), the invertebrate biologist knows as euphausiids. Krill—singular and plural—is the principal food of whalebone whales in the Antarctic; the predominant Antarctic species is *Euphausia superba,* which can reach a length of two and a half inches. (The largest euphausiid is *Thysanopoda cornuta,* a deepwater form that can be almost four inches long.) Next to the copepods, which are also eaten by some species of whales, euphausiids are among the most numerous creatures in the ocean. In the North Atlantic, they are represented by *Meganyctiphanes norvegica, Nyctiphanes couchi,* and *Thysanoessa raschii,* all of which serve as food items for fishes, and for baleen whales. They are generally shrimplike in appearance with a rigid carapace that shields the base of the swimming legs and large, stalked eyes, but they differ from true shrimps in that their feather-like gills are exposed, whereas in shrimps, all the gills are covered by the carapace. Most euphausiids are transparent or translucent with touches of pink or red; some are completely red.

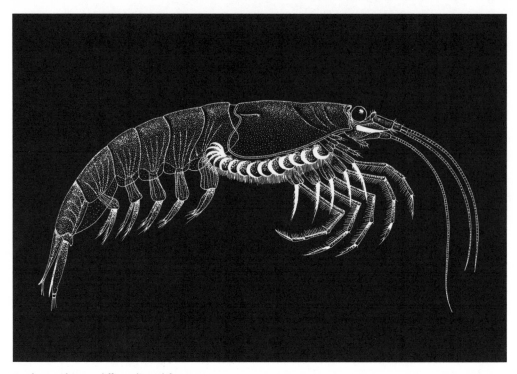

Euphausiids are differentiated from true shrimps by their exposed gills. The two-inch-long *Euphausia superba* is the species eaten in countless numbers by baleen whales. (In this lateral view, only one of each pair of legs and antennae is shown.)

All euphausiids except a few of the deep-water species (such as *Bentheuphausia*) are bioluminescent, and N. B. Marshall calls them "among the brightest midwater animals." ("Euphausiid" can be roughly translated as "true shining light.") They are equipped with rows of prominent red spots along the thorax and abdomen, and a pair on each of the eyestalks, which shine steadily rather than blinking on and off. (Like most bioluminescent animals, euphausiids glow with a blue light.) The compound eyes—which can look upward at other krill and downward at food simultaneously—are also equipped with photophores, and Buschbaum and Milne (1966) wrote, "It seems likely that the animal actually jacklights its food (copepods) at night." Other authors have assumed that the ventral position of the photophores means that the euphausiids are camouflaging themselves, but Peter Herring, one of the world's foremost authorities on bioluminescence, is not so sure: "Little is known of the ecological value of the luminescence," he wrote in 1990. "It is widely presumed that the light acts as a counter-illumination system, eliminating the animal's silhouette against downwelling daylight, though the evidence on which this is based is still circumstantial." It is also possible that the flashing lights provide a way of cohering the large swarms, or serve some sort of a communications function in sexual interactions. In *Half Mile Down*, William Beebe differentiated between euphausiids and shrimps and wrote:

> Luminescence was repeatedly observed. Two general kinds were produced, one type, by the photophore-like luminous spots characteristic of all euphausiids and a few shrimps, and, another, by a discharge of luminous fluid. As is well-known, the Hoplophorid *Systellapsis* [a shrimp] is capable of producing both kinds, but in most other deep-sea shrimps luminous spots are almost, or completely, lacking. Shrimp-like animals with characteristically arranged light organs were observed several times from 650 feet downward; in one case the glow was distinctly greenish. These were unquestionably euphausiids.

According to Herring and Locket's 1978 study of euphausiid luminescence, "Individual specimens may luminesce spontaneously from some or all of their photophores. The flash begins abruptly, remains steady for some seconds, and dies away gradually. . . . Euphausiids flash in response to light stimuli, including that from another specimen." Whereas many light-producing animals harbor colonies of luminescent bacteria (see p. 208), in euphausiids (and copepods and shrimp), the system is intracellular, whereby the animal employs special light organs or lanterns to generate the light, and reflectors to disseminate it. The chemistry of this system is not completely known, but it involves a photoprotein that fluoresces in contact with oxygen. "Our interpretation of the structures," wrote Herring and Locket, "suggests that light generation is probably controlled by alteration of the blood flow through the lantern, and that this in turn is under nervous control."

Shrimps are crustacean decapods that are characterized by a semitransparent body that is flattened from side to side; whiplike antennae; a carapace that juts forward as a prominent saw-toothed rostrum; and a flexible abdomen and a fanlike tail which are flexed to enable the animal to swim in its customary direction: backward. There are some two thousand species, divided into two groups, differentiated by the plates of the second abdominal segment, which overlap in the *Caridea,* and not in the *Penaeidea.* Deep-sea penaeids have extremely long antennae, which may be tactile or olfactory in nature. Shrimps range in size from a few millimeters to giants almost a foot long, and are found from the surface waters to the abyssal depths. (At a hydrothermal vent site along the Mid-Atlantic Ridge, a new species of eyeless caridean shrimp was discovered. Austin Williams and Peter Rona [1986] published the first descriptions of *Rimicaris exoculata* and *R. chacei,* whose unusual lifestyle is discussed on pp. 118–19 of this book.) Of the two-hundred-odd known species of pelagic shrimps, the largest is *Hymenopenaeus;* a specimen col-

The deepwater shrimp *Systellapsis debilis* reaches a length of 2.5 inches. It is characterized by the profusion of light organs, shown here in white. (For clarity, only one of each pair of legs and antennae is shown.)

lected by the *Galathea* expedition measured 11.7 inches in total length—not including antennae.

"If they succeed in catching anything at all," wrote Idyll in 1971, "scientists dragging deep nets in mid-water can usually rely on capturing brilliant scarlet shrimps and prawns."* In the era preceding deep-sea flash photography, observers like Beebe had their descriptions translated into illustrations, so his "scarlet shrimp (*Acanthephyra purpurea*) shoots forth a cloud of luminous fluid to blind its assailant" in a painting in the 1934 *National Geographic* story of the descents in the bathysphere, "A Half Mile Down." (In the book with the same title, Beebe wrote, "A rocket-like burst of fluid was emitted with

---

* The terms "shrimp" and "prawn" are usually interchangeable, but in Britain, "shrimp" refers to the smaller animals, and "prawn" to the larger varieties. Americans consistently use the term "shrimp," regardless of size.

such violence that the psychological effect was that of a sudden explosion." What Beebe first took for an explosion turned out to be "a large red shrimp and an outpouring fluid of flame . . . the abyssal equivalent of the sepia smoke screen of a squid at the surface.")

Deep-sea shrimps are almost always red. (Euphausiids may show some red, but are rarely completely scarlet.) To be brightly colored in a world of total darkness reminds some of the lines from Thomas Gray's *Elegy Written in a Country Churchyard*:

> Full many a gem of purest ray serene,
> The dark unfathom'd caves of ocean bear:
> Full many a flower is born to blush unseen,
> And waste its sweetness on the desert air.

In fact, it is probably the "intention" of the deep-sea shrimps to "blush unseen": no good can come of drawing attention to yourself if you are such a tasty morsel. Since the red wavelength is the shortest, it is the first to be absorbed, and therefore, a red animal will appear black in dim light. Why not simply be black? It appears that the red pigments (carotenoids) are much easier to produce than the black (melanin). When lit by artificial lights from a submersible or robotic camera, or brought on deck in a collecting trawl, the red-colored shrimp are being seen as they have never been seen before. Having developed the pigmentation that renders them invisible in their environment, many species of shrimp, such as *Hoplophorus,* confound the issue by displaying luminous organs. Along with their relatives the euphausiids, shrimps can light up in addition to discharging the "cloud of luminous fluid" described by Beebe.*

If it is a ten-footed animal that swims, such as a shrimp, it is known as a "natantid" decapod; if it crawls, we call it "reptantid," in which category are lobsters, crabs, and crayfishes. Lobsters have a rigid, segmented body covering (the exoskeleton) and five pairs of legs, one or more pairs of which are modified into pincers (technically known as chelae or chelipeds), with one usually larger than the other. The eyes are on movable stalks, and there are two pairs of long antennae. A flipper-like tail is used for swimming.

Most of us are familiar with the American lobster (*Homarus*), the Norway lobster or slipper prawn (*Nephrops*), and the spiny lobsters (*Palinuridae*), but the lobsters of the deep sea are quite different. Known as Polychelidae

---

* Despite its prominent mention in Beebe's immensely popular book—or perhaps because of it—his description of the luminous discharge of *Acanthephyra* was omitted from a 1962 discussion of luminescence in various pelagic creatures by Clarke, Conover, David, and Nicol, who wrote, "Luminescence in *Acanthephyra* has been overlooked hitherto, despite the fact that specimens frequently are caught alive."

("many claws"), they are soft, weak animals that are often blind. The squat lobsters (*Galatheidae*) resemble crawfish, and are differentiated from the Brachyuridae (true crabs) in having the elongated abdomen—popularly called the "tail" in a lobster—curved forward under the carapace. A well-known galatheid is *Pleuroncodes planipes,* better known as "lobster krill," though it is neither lobster nor krill. It is a little crab that occurs in vast swarms in the eastern Pacific, where it sometimes provides sustenance for California gray whales. (It is also eaten by various fishes, especially the yellowfin tuna.) One estimate (quoted in Schmitt 1965) held that there were some 200 billion *Pleuroncodes* present in the offshore fishing grounds of Baja in 1959. Named for the *Challenger*'s biologist Rudolf von Willemoes-Suhm, *Willemoesia indica* is a five-inch-long blind lobster that was collected by the *Galathea* expedition at 3,170 meters (10,397 feet) in the eastern Pacific. Photographs show that *Willemoesia* lies in furrows in the sediment, suggesting a scavenging or predatory lifestyle.

There are sand crabs, land crabs, king crabs, porcelain crabs, stone crabs, rock crabs, fiddler crabs, ghost crabs, robber crabs, hermit crabs, spider crabs, pea crabs, mole crabs, shallow-water crabs, deepwater crabs, crabs that climb trees, crabs that can weigh as much as 30 pounds, and crabs that can measure 13 feet across their outstretched claws.* All crabs are decapods; they are further classified as short-tailed (brachyurids), because the abdomen is reduced to a small flap curled under the carapace. In most species, the first pair of legs is modified into pincers.

Although there are some 3,500 known species of brachyuran crabs, only about 125 have been found below 200 meters. "Perhaps," wrote Gage and Tyler, "their more selective carnivorous/scavenging mode of life offers fewer opportunities here than the primarily deposit-sifting feeding method of hermit crabs and squat lobsters. . . . One of the more impressive crabs of the North Atlantic is the formidably-spined, pink-colored stone crab, *Neolithodes grimaldi,* found in the Rockall Trough." Other crabs of the northeastern Atlantic continental slopes are species of *Geryon* and *Chaceon,* large and robust animals that can reach a weight of two pounds or more. The *Galathea* expedition collected "typical deep-sea crabs (*Ethusa*), blind and pallid," which are often found clinging to sponges or tunicates.

Along with the other surprises confronting biologists who visited the hy-

---

* The heaviest of the crabs is the Tasmanian giant crab, *Pseudocarcinus gigas;* the 13-footer is the Japanese spider crab, *Macrocheira kaempferi.* Neither of them is found in particularly deep water, and certainly not in the Atlantic. Except on menus, there is no such animal as a "soft-shelled crab." The term is used to describe the two-day stage (usually of the Atlantic blue crab, *Callinectes sapidus*) after the animal has shed its old shell, and before the new one has hardened.

Crustaceans of the genus *Munidopsis* have been collected at hydrothermal vent sites in the Atlantic and the Pacific. Because of its long tail section, *Munidopsis* is classified was a lobster.

drothermal vents were several previously unknown species of crabs, described thus in 1979 by Ballard and Grassle: "Brachyuran crabs, though resembling the cancer crabs of the shallows, are blind. Of 150 collected, all were sexually mature adults. They scramble everywhere, like free spirits, scavenging from the periphery to the base of the chimneys where toxic minerals may discourage settlement." Photographs show them among the tube worms, poised over the smoking vents, and climbing the mineral-encrusted walls. In 1980, A. B. Williams identified and described a new family of brachyuran crabs, the Bythograeoidea, which were seen "grazing" on the tubes of the *Riftia* worms and even scavenging on the exposed plumes without the plume being withdrawn. *Cyanograea praedator* is another new crab species from the vents that seems to feed exclusively on the polychaete worm *Alvinella. Munidopsis sub-*

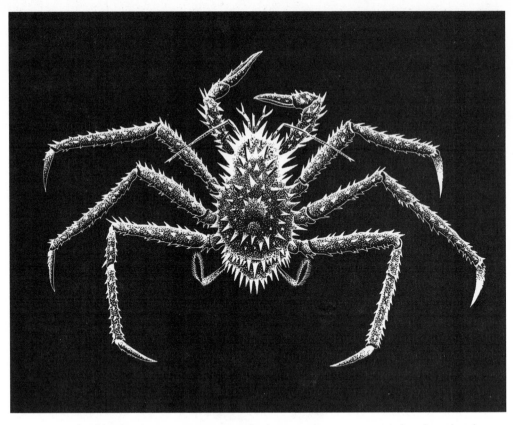

Crabs, like the deepwater species *Lithodes agassizii*, are assigned to the suborder Brachyura, which means "short tails." (Lobsters are also decapods, but are classified as Macrura, which means "large tails.")

squamosa is a deep-sea species that is bleached white in color and has been photographed and collected at hydrothermal vent sites, often in proximity to the tube worms. Viewers in the *Alvin* saw brachyuran and galatheid crabs together; they would appear to be able to coexist in what is certainly one of the harshest environments in the world. A new species of *Munidopsis* (called *lentigo*, which means "spotted") was collected from vents along the East Pacific Rise, and was described by Williams and Van Dover in 1983.

Deep-Sea Cephalopods

Although they share some fundamental cephalopod characteristics, the body plan of the squid is quite different from that of the octopus. The squid is basically a spindle-shaped animal with arms at one end and a tail at the other, while the octopus consists of a baglike head mounted on a ring of arms. Both have a horny beak at the center of the arms, and both have well-developed eyes. Octopus and squid have a funnel (also called a siphon) which is used to eject water taken in through the mantle opening and can propel the animal through the water. All cephalopods have suckers on their arms, but the structure of these suckers is a differentiating factor between octopuses and squid. In octopuses, the suckers are smooth like suction cups and are attached directly to the tentacle, but those of the squids are on short stalks and are often equipped with a ring of horny teeth. (In some species, the suckers of the tentacular clubs are armed with claws as well.) Octopuses often "walk" along the bottom, but squid, which are equipped with a pair of flexible fins at the posterior end of the mantle, rarely establish contact with the ocean floor.

Squid and octopuses are agile, flexible animals, more than capable of eluding or escaping from nets and trawls. For this and other reasons, the vertical distribution of cephalopods—particularly the deepwater species—is poorly known, and as G. L. Voss wrote in 1967, "It is not remarkable that the numbers of cephalopods available for study . . . decrease rapidly with increasing size due to their greater ability to dodge the net; the adults of many species are rare in collections and in a number of species completely unknown." Information on the squids—if not their lifestyle—can be gathered from specimens washed ashore, found in the stomachs of predators, dipnetted at the surface, jigged, seined, and trawled. In recent years, there has been a marked improvement in mid-water nets and trawls, where the actual depth at which a particular animal was collected can be ascertained.

The analysis of bottom sediments has also proven to be a useful method of identifying squid species. In a 1962 study, the Soviet teuthologist I. I. Akimushkin (in a summary by Belyayev) analyzed an enormous number of cephalopod rostra (beaks) dredged up by the oceanographic expedition vessel *Vityaz* on numerous voyages. The predominant species were *Gonatus* and *Taonius*, although the records also showed single beaks of the giant squid (*Architeuthis*) as well. Curiously, some of the samples showed a preponderance of the beaks of immature squid, which led Akimushkin to suggest that "it seems probable that the young squid, developing en masse in the spawning areas and fattening on the abundant plankton there, last for a long time, and in their turn are devoured in enormous quantities by larger animals."

Roper and Young (1975) introduced the problem of identifying deep-sea squids with the words "Information concerning the vertical distribution of pelagic cephalopods is relatively sparse. . . . Often the bathymetric range will extend over a great vertical distance, but the vast majority of a population will occupy only a restricted depth zone." In other words, we have only the vaguest idea of which species live where. We cannot readily sample the population at various depths because we cannot determine if a particular species was caught on the way up, down, or at the downward limit of the sample. We will probably never know about the species that are able to avoid conventional sampling gear. Despite the inadequacy of collecting techniques, we can safely assume that various species live at various depths, some of them identified (often by fortuitous accidents) from an occasional specimen brought to the deck of a research or fishing vessel. By the examination of the anatomy of various species, however, we can make some educated assumptions about their distribution and lifestyle.

We know that some species, such as *Loligo,* are not found over deep water, occupying continental shelves and coastal margins, but many other species perform a daily vertical migration, spending the nights close to the surface, and the days at depth. Were it not for the occasional trawl capture, or the even less frequent sightings from submersibles, we would know even less about the lives of deepwater teuthids. In a 1957 discussion of a camera that enabled scientists to photograph deepwater squid, A. de C. Baker wrote, "Very little is known at present about the habits, distribution, numbers, or even the species of oceanic squid, but it is apparent that these animals must play an important role in the economy of the ocean both as prey and predators. The world population of squid must be extremely large, for they form the major part of the diet of sperm and other toothed whales, and in certain areas are also eaten by great numbers of seals and birds." Up to this time, the only way to identify the species (but certainly not their abundance) was to hang baited hooks on the wire used to tow a plankton net, and hope that something took the bait. The drawbacks of such a system were obvious—one might never know what took the bait—so a camera was designed that would be triggered when an animal pulled at the bait. Several clear pictures of *Ommastrephes* were taken at depths between 600 and 1,000 meters, indicating that this species of squid could be found at these depths off the Azores.

Other teuthid species are found in the North Atlantic, but the majority have not been seen except at the surface, revealing little about their habits. In his comprehensive "Review of the Systematics and Ecology of Oceanic Squids" (published in 1966), Malcolm Clarke discusses what was known at that time, and even includes a couple of photographs of *Todarodes sagittatus* taken "with a deep sea camera at a depth of 1000m and 700m" in the North Atlantic. He writes, "The species comes to the surface at night but apparently prefers to stay on the bottom in daylight . . . where it is caught with trawls at depths between 70–800m." World maps with the recorded locations of the various species supplement Clarke's text, but except for trawl records, there is little information on depth. The lives of deepwater squids are still a mystery. It would be another nine years before Roper and Young would publish their synopsis of "Vertical Distribution," but even they admitted that "information concerning . . . pelagic cephalopods is sparse. . . ."

Octopuses are usually shy and elusive creatures, and they are not likely to be attracted by the lights of submersibles. Nevertheless, a member of the genus *Graneledone* was photographed by the *Alvin*'s camera at a depth of 8,000 feet at the Galápagos Rift Site in the Pacific. Because they are soft-bodied with tissues that are made up mostly of uncompressible liquid, the deep-sea octopods are not affected by the tremendous pressure at these depths. There are authenticated records of octopuses trawled from depths of 2,425 fathoms (almost 15,000 feet), and one record of an octopus egg that was recovered from the stomach of a bottom-dwelling fish that was brought up from 7,200 meters (23,000 feet). If the shallow-water species are delicate, the deepwater octopods are almost insubstantial. Their bodies have a jelly-like consistency, and are so fragile that they are usually badly damaged by the act of bringing them up.

Before exploration in submersibles (and certainly before robotic cameras), the only way to investigate life in the depths was to drop a net of some sort and, when it was retrieved, examine what was caught in it. That was the methodology of the *Challenger*'s scientific collecting from 1873 to 1876, and it was employed in most subsequent expeditions. Sponsored by the Carlsberg Brewing Company, the Danish research vessel *Dana* conducted several round-the-world expeditions, collecting various deepwater invertebrates and fishes, which were subsequently described in the *Dana Reports*. (Among the more dramatic of the *Dana*'s finds was the giant leptocephalus discussed on

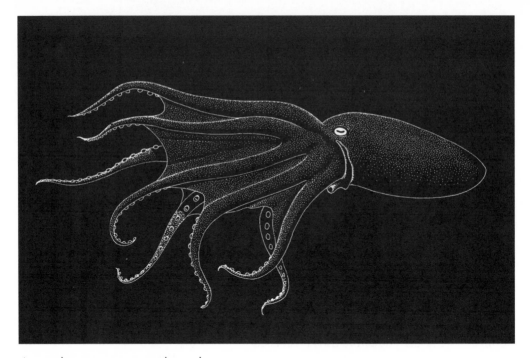

A rare deep-sea octopus with an almost transparent, gelatinous body, *Vitreledonella richardi* reaches a maximum length (including the arms) of about 18 inches.

pp. 218–19.) In 1937, Louis Joubin published an extensive discussion of the octopuses collected during the *Dana's* 1921–22 cruise. This cruise was restricted to the Atlantic and the Mediterranean, and deepwater collections were made at locations off Morocco, the Canaries, the Azores, Bermuda, the Antilles, Mexico, and the United States.

Joubin described several rare octopuses, including *Vitreledonella richardi,* a creature described (by Nesis, 1982) as "transparent as glass [with] an almost colorless gelatinous body," that reaches a maximum known length of 18 inches. The *Dana's* specimen was dredged from a depth of 2,000 meters. Also mentioned in Joubin's paper is the mysterious *Vampyroteuthis,* a cephalopod that is usually classified between the squids and the octopuses. (It has eight arms, but also two tiny tentacles that can be withdrawn into pouches, and were not noticed in the first specimens.) On the subsequent *Dana* expeditions (1928–30), many more specimens of *Vampyroteuthis* were collected, and were described by Grace Pickford of Yale University. (Originally, there were thought to be several different kinds of *Vampyroteuthis,* but on the basis of her examination of the fifty-three *Dana* specimens, Pickford showed that there was only one species.)

The order Octopoda (all octopuses) is subdivided into two suborders:

Cirrata and Incirrata. The Cirrata—commonly known as "cirrate" octopuses, from the "cirri," or filaments on the arms—are gelatinous, flattened animals, with a deep web that often reaches the arm tips. (All other octopus species are classified as "incirrate," because they lack the fingerlike cirri on the arms.) The function of the cirri is not known, but various suggestions have been advanced, including that they serve to set up currents to direct food to the mouth. The most likely explanation is that they are "tactile-sensory," and add another component to the sensory capabilities of an animal that lives in darkness and depends heavily on its ability to sense movement around it. The Cirrata are also known as "finned" octopuses, because there is a pair of fins located about midway on the mantle. The animals are usually dark-colored, ranging from purple to chocolate-brown, often with transparent elements. There is no radula and no ink sac.

The number of cirrate octopus species is small compared to the incirrate, but within that number are some very unusual animals indeed. Although they are very poorly known, it is believed that most, if not all, species are deep-water inhabitants. At 12,000 feet in the Cayman Trough, scientists aboard the *Alvin* saw "a large pink octopod" pass one of the viewing ports, and a lucky color photograph showed it to be a brownish cirrate octopus of an unidentified species. In the *National*

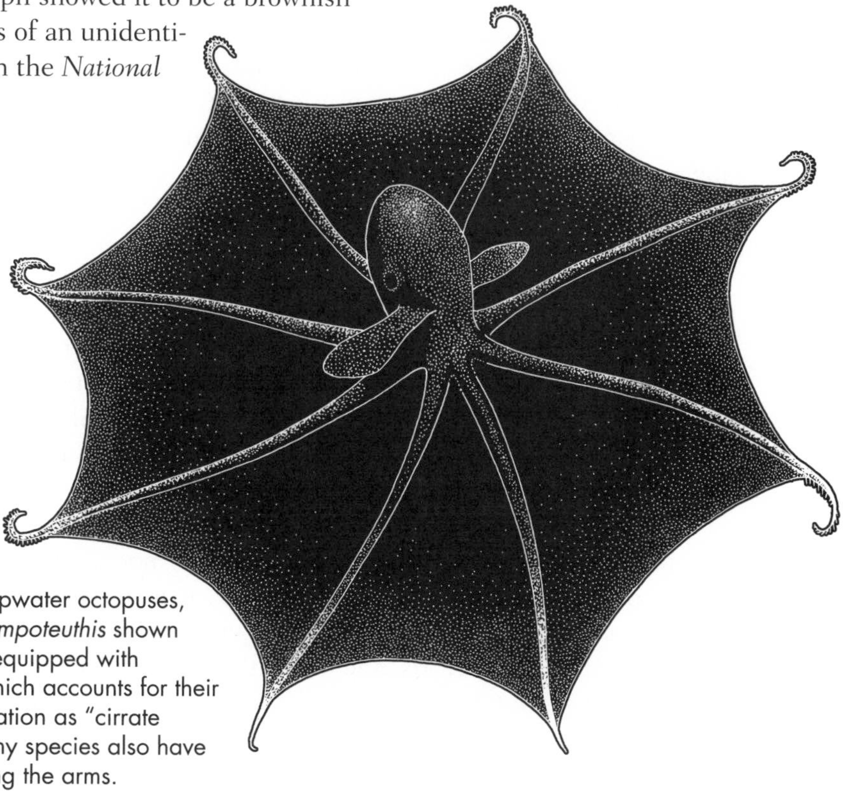

The arms of deepwater octopuses, like those of *Grimpoteuthis* shown here, are often equipped with sensory cilia, which accounts for their common designation as "cirrate octopuses." Many species also have a web connecting the arms.

Geographic photo caption, it was described as an " 'eared' apparition, more than a meter long . . . [I]ts curious fins help it to swim." (Ballard 1976). An unidentified cirrate octopod was photographed by an unmanned camera some 325 miles northeast of Barbados. One lucky frame out of a total of 340 exposures showed (what was then considered) "the deepest photographic observation yet made of a marine cephalopod," a cirroteuthid seen with its arms trailing as it headed in the direction of the surface—16,875 feet away. The depth record, however, appears to be held by a cirrate whose portrait originally appeared in Heezen and Hollister's *Face of the Deep* (1971), where it was misidentified as a "vampire squid" (*Vampyroteuthis*). Roper and Brundage later identified it as a cirrate octopod, whose picture was taken at a depth of 5,200 meters (17,506 feet).

The web may be a useful component of life in the depths, since it enables the cirrate octopuses to float or hover just over the bottom. The gelatinous consistency of these creatures may contribute to their neutral buoyancy, and they may be designed to "float" above the bottom, rather than to creep along in the sediments. In a remarkable series of photographs, included in Clyde Roper and Walter Brundage's 1972 "Cirrate Octopods . . . Data Based on Deep Benthic Photographs," various species are shown with their webs fully extended, looking for all the world like open umbrellas. (This position has been referred to as the "droguelike or umbrella phase, utilizing outstretched web and arms.") They are thought to assume this position while hovering over the bottom, but they can also close the webs and propel themselves by shooting water from the funnel, and they can move in the direction of the arm tips, steering with their fins. The smallest cirrate octopus photographed measured 4 inches across, and the largest 67 inches.

All the photographs in the Roper and Brundage study were taken in the Atlantic, some in the vicinity of the Virgin Islands, others in the Canaries Basin, south of the Azores. The species are not easily identifiable, but the authors suggest that most of the photographs show *Cirroteuthis*. An additional set of pictures, taken from *Alvin* at 1,300 meters, 90 miles south of Martha's Vineyard, show what the authors describe as "a different species," but it remains unidentified.

Then there is *Cirrothauma*, the blind octopus, known from only a few specimens caught at depths of 1,500 meters or more. (*Thauma* is Greek for "wonderful"; there is a deep-sea anglerfish named *Thaumatichthys,* and a holothurian called *Galatheathauma.*) The eyes of the blind octopus are much reduced, with no lens or iris, and only a thread of an optic nerve. During two research cruises in the North Atlantic, twenty-two cirrate octopods were collected, most of which were *Cirrothauma murrayi,* the remainder tentatively identified as *Grimpoteuthis,* a poorly known species found in the Atlantic and the Pacific (Vecchione 1987).

Another cirrate octopod is *Opisthoteuthis,* nicknamed the "flapjack devilfish" because it is a thick, flattened creature, with the mantle reduced to a hump on the dorsal surface, and the short, muscular arms extended from the heavy webbing. This genus is best known from California waters, but *O. agassizi* is found in the Atlantic. (One was photographed sitting on the bottom at 2,000 feet off Saint Vincent in the Bahamas.) When nine specimens of cirrate octopods were captured in an otter trawl of the Spanish research vessel *Chica Touza* in the South Atlantic in 1981, they turned out to be a new species, and were named *Opisthoteuthis vossi* in honor of the late teuthologist Gilbert Voss of the University of Miami. Studies of two kinds of opisthoteuthids off South Africa indicated that they feed on polychaete worms, copepods, mysid shrimps, amphipods, and isopods. Because there is no radula to grind the food, the prey items were easily identified.

As another example of the mysterious nature of the deepwater octopods, consider *Vampyroteuthis infernalis,* whose name can be translated as "vampire squid from hell." About eight inches long, this deepwater denizen is among the most fascinating animals on earth. It was first described in 1903 by Carl Chun, a German teuthologist who identified it as an octopus because it had—he thought—eight arms. Then another pair of thin arms was discovered, tucked into pockets outside the web that connects the eight arms. Taxonomically speaking, it hovers between octopus and squid in its own order, the Vampyromorpha.

The type specimen was taken on the *Valdivia* expedition in the Atlantic Ocean, and was illustrated by the expedition's artist, a man named Rübsamen. Subsequent specimens have been collected from tropical and subtropical waters all over the world, usually from depths of 3,000 feet or more, in the abyss where no light penetrates. The first specimens seemed to have two pairs of paddle-like fins, but when one with a single pair appeared, it was believed to be a separate species. Rübsamen's drawing, now in the Zoological Museum of the University of Berlin, showed only two fins, so the original description was of a two-finned animal. Further study (mostly by Pickford) revealed that in the original drawing, one of the pairs of fins was erased, so it has now been concluded that only a single species exists. The very young forms have two fins; the intermediate stages have four; and when the animal reaches maturity, it reverts to its two-finned form.

For its size, *Vampyroteuthis* has proportionally the largest eyes of any animal in the world. A six-inch specimen will have globular eyes an inch across, approximately the size of the eye of a large dog. At the end of its body away from the tips of its arms, *Vampyroteuthis* has two retractable fins that have reflective surfaces, but the rest of its body is a brownish or black. (Between Panama and the Galápagos in 1925, William Beebe's *Arcturus* expedition hauled in "a very small but very terrible octopus, black as night, with ivory white jaws and blood-red eyes." Beebe refers to this creature as "*Cirroteuthis* spp.," but it appears to have been *Vampyroteuthis*.)

Vampyroteuthis may compensate for the blackness of the abyss in which it lives by being equipped with an astonishing series of photophores—lights all over its body (except for the inner surface of its web) that it appears to be able to turn on and off at will. In the back of the "neck" are clusters of more complex photophores, and behind the base of the paired fins, there are two more light organs, equipped with a sort of "eyelid" that the animal can close to shut off the light. "The lack of an ink sac," wrote Pickford, "is also in accordance with the bathypelagic habits of the species, although it strongly suggests that the animal must have other means of masking its own phosphorescence."

Until very recently, it was thought that the vampire squid was a weak swimmer, and its weak-muscled, gelatinous body suggested that drifting rather than darting was its primary method of locomotion. It has a highly developed statocyst, the organ that controls its balance, which indicated that it descends slowly, further backing up the idea that *Vampyroteuthis* was an almost passive predator. Imagine the surprise of

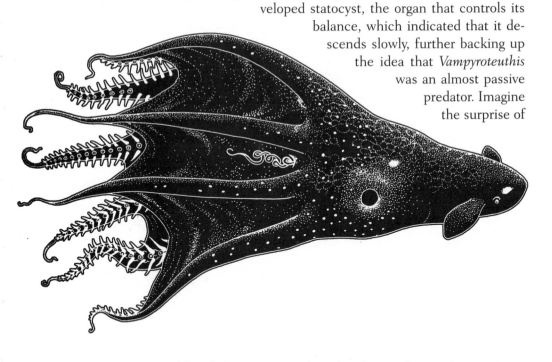

The "vampire squid from hell," *Vampyroteuthis infernalis* is neither squid nor octopus. It is a monotypical deepwater cephalopod that has recently been observed to move quickly, rather than passively hovering. It reaches a maximum length of 12 inches.

researcher Bruce Robison, watching the transmissions of a robotic camera deployed in Monterey Canyon off the coast of California, when a specimen of *Vampyroteuthis* darted into view. Discussing their observations in an article in *The New York Times* (Broad 1994a), Robison, Michael Vecchione, and James Stein Hunt were absolutely amazed. "The images completely blew my mind," said Vecchione. "Nobody suspected it acted like that—buzzing around in circles and swimming rapidly. Usually they've been pictured as drifting with their arms spread out." The article continued:

The brownish-red creature swam with great dexterity, flapping its large thin fins that looked like wings. It trailed a long thin filament, whose function is unknown but probably sensory. A close-up view showed the animal perfectly still, slowly opening and closing its large arms with a sinuous rhythm, revealing them to be joined by thick webbing. Visible at the animal's front was a huge eye, eerie and blue. At the center of its web was a beady [*sic*] mouth, held motionless.

Research from submersibles, manned or unmanned, continues to reveal heretofore hidden and often totally unexpected aspects of the lives of these creatures. "Everything that was written about this animal was that it was a slow, sluggish sort of cephalopod," said Hunt. "But when you actually see it alive, doing flips and carts and trailing that thing and moving all over, it's clear that it has to be rewritten. We have to rethink the animal."*

In a 1995 *Scientific American* article, Robison described *Vampyroteuthis* as being "the size and shape of a soft football," and then recounted another observation calculated to redefine our perceptions of this most unusual cephalopod:

My colleagues and I have discovered that this strange animal has a bioluminescent organ at the tip of each of its arms. *Vampyroteuthis* somehow uses these light sources by swinging its webbed arms upwards and over the mantle, which turns suckers and cirri outward and changes the animal's likeness from a football into a spiky pineapple with a glowing top. This maneuver covers the animal's eyes, but the webbing between the tentacles is apparently thin enough for it to see through. We have observed this transformation frequently but remain at a loss to explain exactly what function this unusual behavior might serve.

---

* One of those who has had to "rethink the animal" is me. In my *Monsters of the Sea* (Knopf, 1994), I wrote, "Based on the careful analysis of its morphology and knowing the depths at which it can be found, we can only speculate on the life-style of the vampire squid. It appears to be a weak swimmer and may not even swim at all. Instead, its gelatinous body is weak-muscled, which suggests drifting rather than darting, and its web may serve as a 'parachute' to enable it to float downward in search of prey."

The three-inch-long squid *Heteroteuthis dispar* is one of the few animals that eject a bioluminescent fluid as a decoy. Another is the fish known as the "tube-shoulder" (*Searsia koefoedi*), shown on page 237.

Very few octopuses have bioluminescent structures, but most squids have light-producing organs known as photophores. There are two distinct types of luminescence: symbiotic (also known as bacterial) and intrinsic (intracellular). In symbiotic luminescence, the light organs contain symbiotic luminous bacteria that glow inside the glands of the animal, but most teuthids have, as Malcolm Clarke has written, "special photogenic cells, often equipped with a reflector that can point the light in one direction, redirect it to an area remote from the source, or spread it out over a surface. . . . These devices can impart a variety of effects, from an overall dull glow or a bright wooly, ethereal effect, to sharp pinpoints of light or a torch-like beam." (The light organ of *Heteroteuthis dispar* consists of a large saclike gland situated on the ink sac; this species can eject a bioluminescent cloud of ink, a process that has been called "fire-shooting.")

Depending upon the species, the photophores can range in size from tiny pinpoints of light to a glowing disk the size of a quarter. Sometimes the photophores are simple structures, but in other cases, they are almost unbelievably complex. According to Frank Lane, "Some have reflector mechanisms, pigment cups, lenses, mirrors, and color screens," and there is at least one

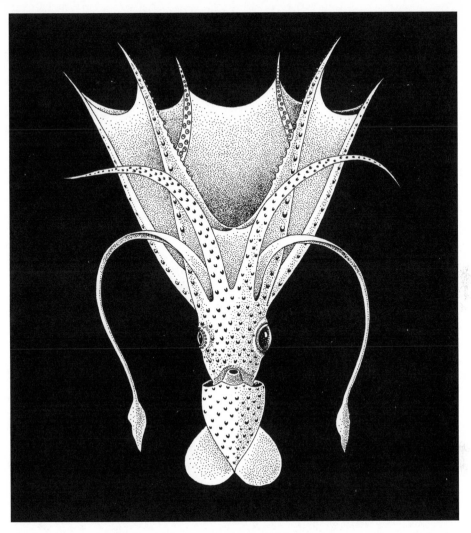

The foot-long umbrella squid (*Histioteuthis bonnellii*) has light organs all over its body, around its right eye (which is much smaller than its left), and even on its arm tips. In this ventral view, the funnel is visible.

species (*Histioteuthis*) that has mirrored searchlights. Photophores appear in every imaginable location, sometimes distributed all over the mantle and arms, sometimes appearing only on the ends of the tentacles. Some species have eyes that light up, and in the transparent squid *Megalocranchia,* the photophores are on the liver.

Animals with lights are truly extraordinary. Aboard the *Valdivia* expedition in 1899, the German teuthologist Carl Chun (who published some of the most important and comprehensive studies of squid ever written, including the first description of *Vampyroteuthis*) was observing some individuals of the small squid *Lycoteuthis diadema* in a container on deck:

> Among the marvels of coloration which the animals of the deep sea exhibited to us nothing can be even distantly compared with the hues of these organs. One would think that the body was adorned with a diadem of brilliant gems. The middle organs of the eyes shone with ultramarine blue, the lateral ones with a pearly sheen. Those towards the front of the lower surface of the body gave off a ruby-red light, while those behind were snow-white or pearly, except the median one, which was sky-blue. It was indeed a glorious spectacle.

But as with so many aspects of teuthid biology, luminescence is still poorly understood. In a 1977 essay on this subject, Peter J. Herring of the Institute of Oceanographic Services in Surrey, England, wrote, "Any purpose that is fulfilled by colour or pattern in the illuminated terrestrial or coastal environment can also be achieved by luminescence in the dark of the deep sea. The cephalopod inhabitants of this environment almost certainly make far more extensive and varied use of their impressive luminescent abilities than we can presently envisage."

Roper and Young list some of the possibilities in a 1976 article on bioluminescent countershading, including "camouflage [which] would seem especially important in the open ocean, where an animal has no holes in which to hide. An opaque animal in the dimly lit midwaters, silhouetted against the highly directional downwelling light, will be visible to predators below." To investigate this phenomenon, they placed several specimens of the mid-water species *Abraliopsis* in a tank with rheostatically controlled overhead lighting:

> The silhouettes of the squid were distinct when the overhead light was on and when the photophores were not yet lighted. With photophores dimly glowing, the contrast between silhouette and background was greatly diminished, and the squid was difficult to see. A squid would disappear from view completely when it swam beneath light of the same intensity as its luminescence. On one such occasion a glowing squid flashed its armtip photophores brilliantly, revealing its location, although nothing but the flashing lights could be detected.

To accomplish this ventral bioluminescent countershading, all cephalopods are equipped with light-sensitive organs known as "extraocular photoreceptors," which enable them to respond to ambient light in the water, even at depths where very little light penetrates. The actual function of these photoreceptors is not clear, but since they are found in all octopuses and all squids, they must be a part of the animals' *modus operandi*. Richard Young of the University of Hawaii has studied these photosensitive vesicles in various cephalopod species, from the deepwater squid *Bathyteuthis* to the mysterious *Vampyroteuthis infernalis*. Hardly anything about *Vampyroteuthis* conforms to the cephalopod norm—if there is one—and its photoreceptors are designed to read its own bioluminescence, in what Young suggests is a device to respond to the glowing of the prey it is consuming, to ensure that the vampire squid does not emit any light that would attract predators.

In the other teuthids, the light-sensitive photoreceptors, usually located near the optic lobe, transmit information to the brain via the optic nerves. Translucent "windows" in the skin enable the dorsal and ventral surface receptors to "see" daylight from above, or luminescent organisms—including themselves—from below, in order to adjust their own luminescence accordingly. In his discussion of these receptors, K. N. Nesis (1982) has written:

> There is no doubt that the functions of the light-sensitive vesicles in cephalopods are diverse and probably differ in different species, but it is most probable that their main function is to give the animal an idea of the general level of illumination in the surrounding water and of long-term changes (seasonal, for example) of illumination.

In the early history of submersible exploration, various observers had spotted cephalopods through the portholes. William Beebe, describing a dive in the bathysphere in 1930, wrote that he had seen "a school of large squids. . . . Their great eyes, each illuminated with a circle of colored lights, stared in at me—those unbelievably intelligent yet reasonless eyes backed by no brain and set in a snail."* Diving in the French submersible *FNRS-3* in the Mediterranean in 1954, Jacques Cousteau saw "a beautiful squid, which stops for a second, as if dazzled by the searchlight beam. . . . I see clearly its rocket-like head and its 10 arms. It is about 1½ feet long, and it leaves a blob of ink. The ink is white."

By 1991, Clyde Roper had managed to wangle submersible time (primarily aboard the *Johnson Sea-Link*) to seek his subjects, for, as he wrote, "Ultimately, the goal of any discipline in biology is to understand organisms as they occur in nature." (As in all fishing expeditions, however, "you shoulda been

---

* Although he was technically correct about the brainlessness of the squid—rather than a brain, squid have a concentration of nerve fibers—Beebe was dead wrong about their lack of intelligence, since even at that time, the teuthids were known to exhibit remarkable cognitive abilities. In 1917, Paul Bartsch, curator of Marine Invertebrates at the Smithsonian, wrote, "The largest, the most highly organized, as well as intelligent, and therefore, most interesting invertebrate creatures of the sea belong to the class of organisms known as cephalopods. . . ." As a zoologist, Beebe should certainly have known that while a squid is indeed a mollusk, it is certainly not a *snail*.

here yesterday." As Roper writes, "The most interesting or spectacular sightings of cephalopods seem to occur on the dives preceding or following the teuthologists' dives.") This observation notwithstanding, Roper and Vecchione recorded 158 observations of thirty-three species of cephalopods, and along the way managed to accumulate still photographs, videotapes, and fifty-eight specimens "in nearly perfect condition." Multiple sightings of *Illex, Ornithoteuthis,* and *Teuthowenia* indicated the abundance of these species, and encouraged further underwater studies. *Ornithoteuthis antillarum* (the generic name means "bird-squid," and refers to its recognized flying ability) was previously considered rare on the basis of net sampling, but underwater observations showed that it was an extremely common species, and that it simply swam too fast to be captured in a net. They saw the actual behavior of some of the cephalopods, including the unexpected posture of the cranchiid squids that "hold their arms and tentacles in a tight straight bundle above the head," leading the crew to refer to them as "cockatoo squids." Of course, in situ observations of free-swimming squids presuppose the ability to identify the species, and specimens are still required for taxonomic and morphological studies.

Between 1982 and 1989, teuthologist S. I. Moiseev made several dives in Soviet submersibles, looking for squid. He made a total of 186 dives, mostly in the Atlantic Ocean, from the mid-North Atlantic to Patagonia. As expected, *Gonatus fabricii,* a cold-water form that reaches a total length of about two feet, was most abundant in the higher latitudes. (This species was known to be the main food of the bottlenose whale [*Hyperoodon ampullatus*] a species heavily hunted in the Norwegian Sea in the nineteenth century.) Moiseev reported that *Gonatus* was observed during the day between 420 and 1,200 meters, and at night, at approximately the same depths, indicating an "insignificant" vertical migration. Most observations of the wing-armed squid (*Sthenoteuthis pteropus*) occurred in conjunction with the creatures of the deep-scattering layers, since this species is known to feed on the euphausiids, shrimps, and fishes that migrate toward the bottom during the day and toward the surface at night. Many species (including *Todarodes* and *Ommastrephes*) were observed at the surface at night, which may have something to do with their attraction to ships' lights.

The lives of deepwater squids are still almost a complete enigma. We have seen and even photographed some of them, but most of their natural history remains hidden. (In an article discussing a fortuitous photograph of *Octopoteuthis* at 1,000 meters, the authors [Roeleveld, Augustyn, and Melville-Smith] wrote, "The rarity of photographs of oceanic squid is clearly shown in Nesis's *Cephalopods of the World* . . . [T]he collection of 16 pages of full colour photographs includes only two . . . of oegopsids, although the group constitutes 23 of the 25 squid families.") They are numerous almost beyond counting, but their speed and "intelligence" renders most species uncatchable by humans. Certain cetaceans and fishes do not share our problem, and appear to exist almost exclusively on a diet of squid. As Malcolm Clarke (1988) has written, "Although squids are extremely difficult to catch . . . we know that they are extremely important in the food webs of all oceans because of their ocurrence in the stomachs of oceanic birds, fish, seals, and cetaceans. . . . The largest toothed whale, the sperm whale, consumes well over 100 million tonnes of squid each year. This compares with the 70 million tonnes of fish that man catches for all purposes and is about half the weight of mankind."

The giant squid is usually the first animal that comes to mind whenever the subject of mysterious or threatening inhabitants of the abyss is raised, but except for where they strand, and some general morphological details, hardly anything is known about the life of *Architeuthis*. In their 1982 *Scientific American* article, Clyde Roper and Kenneth Boss wrote, "On other matters, such as its habitat and method of reproduction, one can offer only educated guesses based on what is known of related oceanic squids." It is the largest invertebrate in the world, reaching a known length of 60 feet and a maximum known weight of about two tons. Despite its reclusive habits and enigmatic status— or perhaps because of them—it has been in the forefront of sea-monster lore since the days of Homer. Giant squid (also known as kraken) are believed to be responsible for a large proportion of sea-monster stories, including several that originated in Europe during the seventeenth and eighteenth centuries.

The real kraken did not reveal itself to science until 1853, when a Danish zoologist named Johann Japetus Steenstrup examined a six-inch beak. (Squid have beaks like parrots, only the upper mandible fits in the lower.) But it was not until twenty years later that a scientist would actually examine the animal. For reasons that will probably go forever unexplained, giant squid began appearing off the beaches of Newfoundland during the decade 1870–80. As many as sixty of these beasts were found on the beach or floating offshore. *Architeuthis,* therefore, is the quintessential deep Atlantic monster; since it made its debut in Newfoundland, and although it has been recorded from other locations, such as New Zealand (where a late nineteenth-century invasion occurred of a magnitude almost equal to that of Newfoundland's), it is best known from both sides of the North Atlantic.

The giant squid is also known from British and European shores, but again, only from stranded specimens. The earliest record seems to be of a carcass that washed ashore at Thingøre Sand, in Iceland, in 1639. It was introduced to the world by Professor Steenstrup, a lecturer in geology, botany, and zoology at Copenhagen University. In a paper read in 1849, he quoted a 1639 description that appeared in *Annalar Björns á Skardsa* (in Danish), which was translated as follows:

In the autumn on Thingøresand in Hunevandsyssel a peculiar creature or sea monster was stranded with *length and thickness like those of a man; it had 7 tails and each of these measured approximately two ells.* These tails were densely covered with a type of button, and the buttons looked as if there was an eye ball in each button, and round the eye ball an eyelid; these eyelids looked as if they were gilded. On this sea monster there was in addition *a single tail* which had grown out above those 7 tails; *it was extremely long, 4–5 fms* [7.50 to 9.40 meters]; *no bone or cartilage were found in its body* but the whole to the sight and to the touch was like the soft body of the female lumpfish (Cyclopterus lumpus). No trace was seen of the head, except the one aperture, or two, which were found behind the tails or at a short distance from them.*

Even though the annalist managed to read the animal upside down, confusing the head with the tail(s), it is quite obvious that the "monster" was a giant squid that had lost one of its arms and one of its tentacles.

In 1673, a 19-footer was found on the beach of Dingle Bay, County Kerry, Ireland. It was displayed for all to see, and a broadsheet was printed up in Dublin, which announced the exhibition of

A Wonderful Fish or Beast that was lately killed, by James Steward, as it came of its own accord to Him out of the sea to the Shore, where he was alone on Horse-back at the Harbour's Mouth of Dingle-Icoush, which had two heads and Ten horns, and upon Eight of the said Horns about 800 Buttons or the resemblance of little Coronets; and in each of them a set of Teeth, the said Body was bigger than a Horse and was 19 Foot Long Horns and all, the great Head thereof Carried only the ten Horns and two very large Eyes, and the little head thereof carried a wonderful strange mouth and two Tongues in it, which had the natural power to draw itself out or into the Body as its own necessity required, there is several other very remarkable things to be observed in the said Monster, and in particular it had a Redish Coloured wrapper or Mantle growing and Sticking fast to the back thereof, and the Laps on both sides were loose, which was white within and Red without. Therefore all persons who desire to be further satisfied in the truth hereof, may see the said little head and two of the said Horns with the Coronets thereon, and a draft of the whole as it appeared altogether alive, with a certificate from responsable hands, and

---

* Translation from a publication entitled *The Cephalopod Papers of Japetus Steenstrup,* by Agnete Volsøe, Jørgen Knudsen, and William Rees, published by the Danish Science Press in 1962.

a real Relation of all the passages, witnessing the truth thereof, to their further admiration, at the Three Castles on the Lower end of Cork Hill.

The broadside is one of a number of documents that are included in an 1875 study by A. G. More, who takes the description and the accompanying drawing almost literally, and says: "I do not see why the extensible proboscis should not be accepted as correct, though the little eyes may have been added as ornaments by an enterprising showman." He then proposes to name the Kerry "monster" *Dinoteuthis proboscideus,* which can be roughly translated as "terrible squid with a big nose."* W. J. Rees, a biologist with the British Museum of Natural History (and one of the "authors" of the Steenstrup papers), quoted this broadsheet in an article about giant squid that appeared in the *Illustrated London News* in 1949, and explained, "The 'little head,' of course, refers to the siphon through which water is pumped out to propel the squid through the water."

In December 1853, a gigantic cephalopod washed ashore at Raabjerg beach, on the Jutland Peninsula of Denmark. It was cut up for fish bait, but the beak, which measured approximately three by four inches, was the basis for Steenstrup's designation of a new species, *Architeuthis monachus.* His description of the Raabjerg specimen, based on eyewitness accounts and the impressive beak, was published in 1857 and marked the official transition of the giant squid from the realm of fable into the scientific literature. Three years later, Steenstrup described another new species of giant squid, *A. dux,* from the remains of another carcass that a Captain Hygom had brought from the Bahamas to Denmark. Another North Atlantic stranding took place in 1860, when a 23-footer with a 7-foot-long head and mantle came ashore on the Scottish coast between Hillswick and Scalloway.

No one has ever seen a healthy giant squid—especially in its native habitat—but we think they live at considerable depths. From the examination of the carcasses, we can extrapolate something about their lives in the icy blackness. First there are the eyes: the giant squid has the largest eyes in the animal kingdom, which can reach a diameter of 15 inches—the size of an automobile hubcap. And they are highly developed eyes, as complex and capable as those of the higher vertebrates, but adapted for seeing in very low light levels—and, of course, underwater as well. Like all squids, *Architeuthis* has eight arms and two greatly elongated tentacles, which may reach a length of 40 feet. The two tentacles are equipped with "clubs," which can grasp and hold the prey items,

---

* More ("Assistant-Naturalist in the Museum of the Royal Dublin Society") was acquainted with *Architeuthis,* as evidenced by his subsequent paper, "Some Account of the Giant Squid (*Architeuthis dux*) Lately Captured off Boffin Island, Connemara," which appeared in the same journal (*The Zoologist*) a month later.

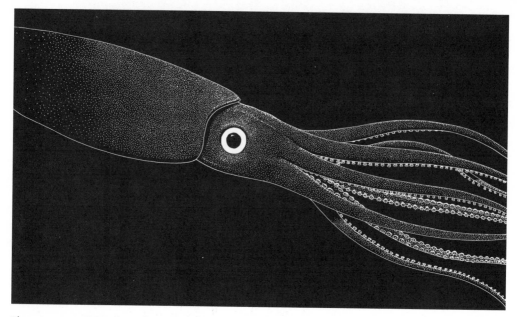

The giant squid (*Architeuthis princeps*) is the largest invertebrate in the world, reaching a known length of 57 feet. Many giant squid have been seen washed up on beaches around the world, but no one has ever seen a healthy specimen in its natural environment.

whatever they might be. The other eight arms have rows of suckers, each of which is individually movable and has a toothed ring around the perimeter, which digs into the flesh of its prey, holding on for eternity or death, whichever comes first. Unlike some other squid, *Architeuthis* has no hooks or "claws" on its tentacles. At the center of the corona of arms is the powerful beak, capable of ripping chunks of flesh from prey animals.*

We do not know why giant squids wash ashore at irregular intervals at apparently unrelated locations around the world. To date, the greatest known concentration occurred in Newfoundland, roughly between 1870 and 1880. During that decade, approximately fifty specimens washed up. (Many were recorded for science, but others were cut up for bait or dog food.) Since that time, specimens have come ashore elsewhere, but they have also continued to appear—albeit less frequently—on the rocky shores of Newfoundland. Either giant squid have a Newfoundland suicide wish, or some other forces may be at work that might explain this cycle. Frederick Aldrich, a teuthologist who

* Descriptions of titanic battles between giant squid and sperm whales are probably apocryphal, since the squid would be unlikely to attack an animal that might be fifty times heavier than it is. On the other hand, sperm whales are known to eat giant squid, so witnesses to the "battles" between these two giants were probably watching the desperate struggle of a squid trying not to be eaten.

specialized in *Architeuthis,* suggested that fluctuations in the Labrador Current were responsible for the appearance of giant squid off Newfoundland every ninety years or so. When the cold portion known as the Avalon Branch hits northeastern Newfoundland, the squid, following the cold mass of water, come close to shore, where, for unknown reasons, they die. He predicted that the next period of *Architeuthis* strandings would occur around 1960, and he was proven correct when six giant squid stranded between 1964 and 1966.

Recently, climatologist Michael Schlesinger of the University of Illinois has identified forces that affect the temperature of the North Atlantic, which may somehow be related to the life cycle of the giant squid. As warmer water flows north from the equator—in the Gulf Stream, for example—it cools and sinks, pulling more warm water northward, like a conveyor belt. As the warm water builds up, it begins to rotate clockwise, drawing in new, lighter water from the west. This water cannot sink until it cools, so the process is slowed down until the newer water is cooled and turns counterclockwise, bringing in denser, saltier water from the east. (The eastern Atlantic is saltier than the western, because the salty, shallow Mediterranean flows into it.) Schlesinger tentatively identified a seventy-year cycle for these changes, but physicists at the Geophysical Fluid Dynamics Laboratory at Princeton University created computer simulations of the cycle and suggested that the cycle took anywhere from forty to sixty years. Nothing in these studies mentions giant squid, but the movement of the water in which *Architeuthis* lives must have some influence on the lives (and deaths) of these perpetually enigmatic creatures.*

No other cephalopod approaches the dimensions of *Architeuthis,* but at various locations on the coasts of western European countries, a creature referred to as a "giant squid" washed ashore, to the consternation of fishermen and farmers, and to the eternal confusion of teuthologists. Depending upon the era in which it was described, this animal is known variously as *Sthenoteuthis, Stenoteuthis,* or *Ommastrephes.* (*Sthenos* means "strong" in Greek; *steno* means "narrow," and *Ommastrephes* means "eye-turner.") Because the taxonomy of this species is unresolved, it is not at all obvious—even to professionals—which animal is being discussed and, even more confusing, which animal was being discussed in the past.

The genus *Sthenoteuthis* was established by A. E. Verrill in 1879, "to include certain species of squids, remarkable for the large size and high devel-

---

* In December 1995, three specimens of *Architeuthis* were netted (intentionally) by deep-water trawls east of New Zealand. Squid-watchers around the world, including the Smithsonian's Clyde Roper, immediately began planning expeditions to New Zealand, not only to examine the newest specimens, but also to see if they might be able to catch a glimpse of a living giant squid from a research submersible. By the time this book is published, what I referred to (in the 1994 *Monsters of the Sea*) as "the last uncaptured image" might be uncaptured no more.

opment of their organs of locomotion, especially of the caudal fin and siphon, and for the presence of a broad, thin web along the lower side of the lateral arms, outside the suckers." The description is valid, but the name did not endure. In a paper devoted to the cephalopods of Scottish and adjacent waters, A. C. Stephen lists both *Ommastrephes* and *Sthenoteuthis*, treating them as distinct species and listing their appearances on Scottish coasts, but in his 1960 discussion of northeast Atlantic squids, Baker wrote, "There is considerable uncertainty regarding the use of the name *Ommastrephes* d'Orbigny 1835, and *Sthenoteuthis* Verrill 1880, and until this problem of nomenclature can be thoroughly investigated with additional material I follow the practice of recent authors in using the name *Ommastrephes* as the generic name of this common Atlantic form."*

Whatever we call them, these creatures are rapacious predators of the depths and the surface, capable of attacking fish or squids as large or larger than they are. W. J. Rees (1950) lists the British records from 1911 to 1941, and includes several specimens that were over 5 feet in total length. One that stranded at Withernsea, Yorkshire, in 1925, measured 7 feet 1.5 inches from tail tip to tentacle tip, and another, found dead on the beach at Looe, Cornwall, in 1940, was more than 6 feet in total length. The research vessel *Chain* out of Woods Hole hauled in a Nansen bottle south of Bermuda and found the end of a tentacle that had somehow been wrenched off. From the examination of the severed part, H. J. Turner (1963) tentatively identified it as *Sthenoteuthis*, and estimated its total length at between 8 and 10 feet. (The largest sucker on the *manus* was approximately the diameter of a nickel.)

The two species common to the Atlantic are *Ommastrephes caroli* and *O. pteropus.* They are also known by a variety of common names, including "orange-back squid," for a pattern of yellow or orange chromatophores on the dorsal surface, and "flying squid," a reference to their propensity to launch themselves out of the water. Unlike most other large squid species, we know something about their natural history, since they have been frequently observed at the surface (swimming or jumping), and Malcolm Clarke (1966) has written, "There can be no doubt that *O. caroli* and *O. pteropus* are present in enormous numbers in their areas of distribution as shown by their regular appearance at the surface at night." Unknown circumstances cause them to strand in large numbers, as demonstrated by the invasion that took place intermittently between 1922 and 1933, when thousands stranded on the coasts

---

* Although the taxonomy of these species is still unresolved (and mostly unpronounceable), *Sthenoteuthis* has now become *Symplectoteuthis,* so *Ommastrephes* (pronounced "o-mastruh-fees") is now the proper generic name of this large family of cosmopolitan squids—at least according to Nesis's 1982 *Cephalopods of the World. Ommastrephes* occurs throughout the temperate waters of the world, but *Symplectoteuthis* is found only in the tropical Atlantic and the Indo-Pacific regions.

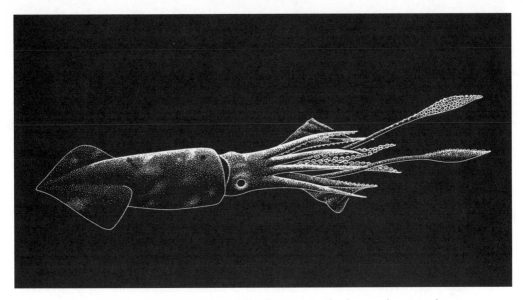

At a maximum length of ten feet and a weight of 250 pounds, the "jumbo" squid
(*Dosidicus gigas*) is a powerful and aggressive predator.

of Scotland. But for the most part, squid are not creatures of the surface (and
certainly not creatures of the beach), and through the deployment of deep-sea
cameras, we have an idea about their vertical distribution in the sea. (*Ommastrephes*, according to Roper and Young, "can roam from the surface to great
depths.") British scientists aboard the research vessel *Discovery II* in 1957 lowered pressure-resistant cameras to depths of 2,000 feet and obtained the first
pictures of *Ommastrephes* in its deepwater haunts. The known depth record
for this species is 1,490 meters (almost 5,000 feet), which was obtained when
a squid lost a tentacle to a piece of water-testing apparatus at that depth, but
that was a chance encounter, and we do not know if the species inhabits
deeper waters.

On exhibit in the National Museum of Natural History (Smithsonian
Institution) in Washington is an example of what Clyde Roper calls "the
world's biggest flasher." It is a specimen of the squid known as *Taningia danae*,
seven feet long and weighing 134 pounds. Unlike most other squids, *Taningia*
does not have two long feeding tentacles, but it does have something even
more surprising: on the ends of two of its arms are the largest light-producing
organs in any known animal. This one was caught in a fisherman's net off the
coast of Massachusetts, but they are world-wide in distribution, and live at
depths down to 3,000 feet.

Off the coast of Dakar in 1954, when the French submersible *FNRS-3* had descended to a (then-record) depth of 13,287 feet, crew members Georges Houot and Henri Willm spotted a shark through the porthole. In a *National Geographic* article, Houot described the experience:

> It would be odd to parachute aimlessly into mid-Sahara and land beside a lion; yet each time we have visited the bottom wastes in the bathyscaphe we have seen at least one shark. Unless our luck has been phenomenal this must mean there are thousands of them living in the world's dark basement. Willm's fish was about 6½ feet long. Though it must have known nothing but everlasting darkness, it swam without hesitation into the glare of our lights, and looked at the porthole with its great protruding eyes.

Not everyone seems to have encountered the profusion of sharks suggested by the *FNRS-3* dives. In fact, with a few notable exceptions, undersea observers rarely see sharks, and when they do, the sharks usually appear one at a time. (In the bathysphere, Beebe saw sharks that he could not identify at "100, 250, 650, and 850 feet.") In a 1958 article ("Four Years of Diving to the Bottom of the Sea"), Houot included a photograph of an unknown species of dogfish taken at 7,500 feet in the Mediterranean and wrote, "Such deepwater sharks inhabiting the realm of eternal night appear to the author to have lost the power of sight. . . . They have not the slightest reaction to our search-lights and flashes. That is why I think they are blind." (From the examination of the photograph and a reading of the literature on deepwater dogfishes, this would appear to have been one of the *Centrophorus* species of the Mediterranean, either *C. granulosus* or *C. uyato,* which Leonard Compagno says are difficult to tell apart, but neither of which is blind. There are no blind sharks.)

Evidently unaware of Houot's depth record, Eugenie Clark and Emory Kristof wrote (also in the *Geographic*) that they "found no evidence that [sharks] go much deeper than 12,000 feet." Oceanographer John Isaacs's robotic-camera pictures of a 12-foot-long Pacific sleeper shark (*Somniosus pacificus*) at 6,300 feet was described by Clark and Kristof as "the deepest accurate record of a living shark," but if the mention by Houot is accurate, Clark and Kristof cannot be correct. (Houot identified his only as "a shark," while the Isaacs film clearly shows the species, so perhaps the Isaacs record is for the deepest *identified* shark.) In Suruga Bay, Japan, observers in the French submersible *Nautile* saw (and photographed) a 23-foot-long shark of the same species, at a depth of approximately 4,000 feet. Portuguese commercial fishermen have hauled in a species of deepwater dogfish (*Centroscymnus coelolepis*) from 12,000 feet, but fishermen probably do not keep depth records as meticulous as those of scientists. According to Compagno's 1984 review of the sharks of the world, *Centroscymnus* is found "on or near the bottom . . . at depths below 400m, with a depth range of 270 to 3675m," so the *pescadores* are not far off the mark. Off Madeira, fishermen also haul in the four-foot-long catshark commonly known as the black shark (and scientifically as *Dalatias licha*), which is taken near the bottom in water known to be 6,000 feet deep. Compagno (1984) describes this species as "a powerful and versatile deep-sea

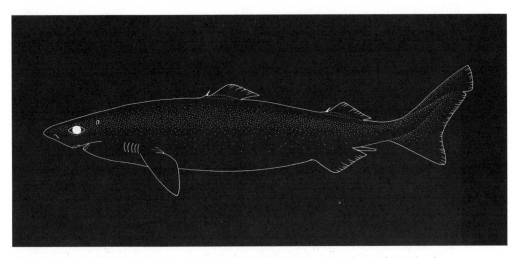

The deepwater dogfish (*Centroscymnus coelolepis*) has been hauled in from depths up to 12,000 feet from the continental slopes on both sides of the Atlantic. This three-foot-long shark is commercially fished in Portuguese waters.

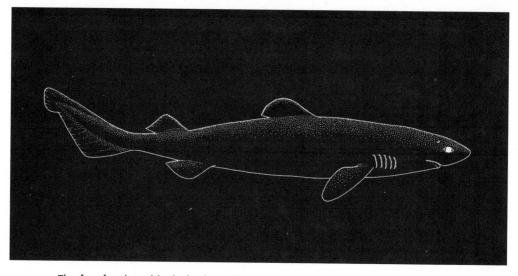

The four-foot-long black shark (*Dalatias licha*) is a deepwater predator that haunts the bottom at depths of 6,000 feet or more.

predator, equipped with huge serrated teeth and heavy jaws of enormous power. It feeds primarily on deepwater bony fishes, including deepwater smelt, viperfishes, scaly dragonfishes, barracudinas, greeneyes, lanternfishes, gonostomatids, cod, ling, whiting and other gadids, hake, grenadiers, deepwater scorpionfishes, bonito, gempylids, epigonids, and chaunacid anglers, but also skates, catsharks, spiny dogfish, squid, octopi, amphipods, isopods, shrimp and lobsters, and even polychaetes and siphonophores."

In the deep oceans there are certainly Houot's "thousands" of individual sharks (there are probably millions), but the number of species is more manageable. In the 1984 *Sharks of the World,* Leonard Compagno has listed all of the approximately 350 species. Many of these are objects of commercial fisheries, others are known because they occasionally attack people, and still others are famous simply for being sharks. In the depths, however, there are probably unknown species that have never been brought to the surface.*

For the most part, the deep-sea sharks have all the requisite components

---

* One might expect that these heretofore undiscovered species would be small, but in 1976, off the northern coast of Oahu, a 14.5-foot, 1,600-pound shark was hauled aboard a U.S. research vessel. The shark was captured at an approximate depth of 500 feet (it had swallowed a cargo chute that had been deployed as a sea anchor), and it was swimming in water that was 4,500 feet deep. A family, genus, and species had to be created for it, because no one had seen anything like it before. It was named *Megachasma pelagios* ("deepwater big-mouth") because of its huge mouth, and nicknamed "megamouth." Since its original appearance, six more specimens have surfaced in the Pacific (in California, Japan, and western Australia), and in 1995 the first Atlantic megamouth (a six-foot-long male) was caught by longline fishermen not far from Rio Grande in southern Brazil.

to qualify them as sharks: cartilaginous skeletons, multiple tooth rows, denticular skin, two dorsal fins, and so on. But with the obvious exception of *Somniosus,* which can get to be 23 feet long, they rarely exceed a couple of feet in length. Most of the sharks of the depths belong to the order Squaliformes, and can be generally characterized as slim animals, often equipped with spines on the dorsal fins and armed with a dizzying array of differentiated teeth. (The best-known of the Squaliformes is the spiny dogfish (*Squalus acanthias*), the bane of comparative anatomy students who have had to dissect one, and also of fishermen who find that the species chews up nets and generally interferes with more productive fishing operations. Since *S. acanthias* is a shallow-water species, we will say no more about it here.)

There is a large group of small, deepwater sharks, rarely reaching a length of 18 inches, that belong to the genus *Etmopterus,* commonly known as lantern sharks. They are usually dark brown or black, and have prominent spines in front of each dorsal fin (the second dorsal fin is usually larger than the first) and large eyes, presumably for better vision in the depths. Their teeth are completely different in the upper and lower jaws, those of the lower jaw being single-cusped and fused together to form a single cutting edge. Although it has never been witnessed by human eyes, the attack strategies of these little sharks may involve pack hunting, since their stomach contents often reveal evidence of assaults on comparatively large prey, such as cephalopod beaks that came from squids larger than the sharks themselves. Many of the lantern sharks have photophores on the underside of their body, and while no one has ever seen them employed in their natural habitat, it is believed that they serve to cohere the schools (if indeed these sharks actually travel in schools) or to counterilluminate the individuals. In a discussion of the social organization of shark species, Stewart Springer speculated on the behavior of *Etmopterus virens:*

> The cephalopod beaks and eyes commonly found in their stomachs were often so large that the sharks' jaws and gullet must have been stretched greatly when the parts were swallowed. I deduce that green dogfish hunt in packs and may literally swarm over squid or octopus much larger than themselves, biting off chunks with the razor-sharp band of lower-jaw teeth and perhaps maintaining the integrity of their school visually through their distinctive lighting system.

As with many deepwater genera, the lantern sharks are widely distributed throughout the world. Some have been found (so far) in limited areas: the comb-toothed lantern shark (*Etmopterus decacuspidatus*) appears only off the coast of Hainan Island, China, and *E. villosus* has been collected only in the deep waters of the Hawaiian Islands. The most common Atlantic species is *E. spinax,*

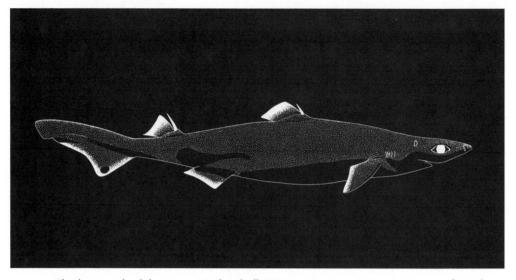

The lantern shark known as "velvet belly" (*Etmopterus spinax*) gets its name from the black markings on its underside. Its underside glows with a strong greenish light.

delightfully referred to as "velvet belly" because of the abrupt change from brown to velvety black on the belly. In 1900, Rudolf Burckhardt quoted a scientist named Beer who was engaged in ophthalmoscopic observations of *Spinax niger* (= *E. spinax*) in a darkened room, where its luminescence was vivid enough to enable him to see it at a distance of from three to four meters: "The whole of the ventral surface of the animal," wrote Beer, "from the snout to the root of the tail, was glowing with a feebly shining greenish lustre, as if it were impregnated with phosphorus or had been coated with luminous paint. . . ."*

Working at the Zoological Station in Naples in 1898, Burckhardt also noticed that a specimen of *Laemargus* (= *Somniosus*) *rostrata* contained luminous organs, but they were small, atrophied, and perhaps nonfunctional. In addition to *E. spinax* and *Somniosus,* he was able to find luminous organs in ten more species of sharks, and wrote, "I was greatly struck by the splendour of the spectral colours which these fish exhibited, and of which, so far as I am

* Although some sharks, like the tiger, the blue, or the great white, have familiar common names, some of the deep-sea sharks are known only from a couple of specimens, and might not have a common name at all. The beauty of scientific nomenclature is its simplicity: no matter what the local fishermen might call the green dogfish (it is *sagre vert* in French, *tollo lucero verde* in Spanish), whenever it is discussed in the scientific literature, its name will appear as *Etmopterus virens.* Because the scientific names are constantly being revised, one might see an earlier name used to denote a particular species, in which case, the "=" identifies the name now in use.

aware, no mention anywhere in the literature seems to have been made." Among the additional luminescent species were several varieties of the squaloid genus *Centroscyllium,* known as "black dogfish" to North Atlantic fishermen. In a 1960 study, Tamotsu Iwai of Kyoto University described the luminous organs of *Centroscyllium ritteri,* a species from the western Pacific but similar to other Atlantic versions. "The luminous organs," wrote Iwai, "are widely distributed over the body surface and some of the fins, though gradation is not uniform throughout the body. The organs are so numerous that their total number is difficult to estimate. . . . Of particular interest is the presence of luminous organs studded on the ventral surface of the upper eyelid." (The teleost *Chauliodus sloani* [see p. 239] has similarly located luminous organs, and although their function is unknown, Tchernavin suggested that the orbital photophores serve to illuminate approaching prey or to excite the eye.) Under a microscope, the organs look like small black spots, but no one knows if they are functional. Henry Bigelow and William Schroeder (1957) wrote that the thickenings of the skin on the ventral surface of *Centroscyllium* "presumably are luminous."

At a maximum length of ten inches, the pygmy or dwarf shark is the smallest in the world, and the only species that has a spine on its first dorsal fin and not on its second. The cigar-shaped (and cigar-sized) *Squaliolus laticaudus* has been collected at depths of up to 500 meters in the Atlantic, usually over the continental slopes. It has a dense network of well-developed photophores covering its ventral surface, which W. D. Clarke (1963) suggests might be "photophore countershading," in which the light-producing underside eliminates the shadow normally formed when the fish is illuminated from above, and hence makes it less conspicuous to potential predators (see pp. 211–12 for a discussion of this phenomenon).

Many lantern sharks have a pale yellow spot on top of the head, approximately between the eyes. This has been identified as a "pineal window," employed by the sharks to detect downwelling light. It has also been seen in lemon sharks (*Negaprion brevirostris*), sixgill sharks (*Hexanchus griseus*), and gulper sharks of the genus *Centrophorus*. (In a wonderfully simple experiment, Gruber, Hamasaki, and Davis [1975] put a lit flashlight in the mouth of a dead lemon shark to demonstrate the translucent nature of this "window.") Histological examination of the pineal organ (*epiphysis cerebri*) reveals that it is nearly as photosensitive as the retina, and can be affected by light levels as low as moonlight. The pineal window in sharks corresponds to the extraocular receptors in squids (see pp. 182–83). Although they approach the problem from completely different directions, the deepwater sharks, squids, and some bony fishes seem to have converged at the same solution for detecting ambient light

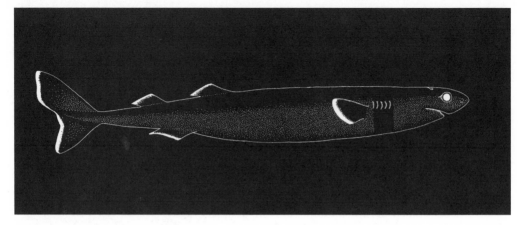

Known as the "cookie-cutter shark," *Isistius brasiliensis* takes corelike bites from large fishes, whales, and dolphins. The entire ventral surface of this foot-long shark is equipped with photophores, making it one of the most luminescent of all sharks.

to modulate their own levels of illumination and counterillumination.*

Another squaloid is the widely distributed *Isistius brasiliensis,* the "cookie-cutter shark." (It is also known as the "cigar shark" because of its elongated shape, and perhaps because of the dark "band" that circles the gill region.) Its curious common name comes from its habit of taking large, circular bites from much larger animals, including billfishes, tuna, large sharks, and even whales. The source of these "crater wounds" was long a mystery, but biologist E. C. Jones solved the mystery by holding the open mouth of a dead *Isistius* up to a nectarine and twisting it as he imagined the shark would do as it bit a larger animal. The result was a perfect pluglike core removed from the fruit, exactly like the piece that would have been removed from the living victim. (It evidently preys—or attempts to—on nonliving victims as well, as evidenced by the appearance of the same bites on the rubber coating of the sonar domes of submarines.)

Like many of its relatives, *Isistius* is bioluminescent. Its entire lower surface is covered with luminous organs that glow with a bright, ghostly green light. Victor Springer and Jon Gold call it "among the most luminescent of all sharks." These little sharks may use bioluminescence to locate each other in the dark, or it may serve a more devious purpose: to entice larger species to attack it, at which point it turns the tables and takes a bite. One of the earliest descriptions of this luminescence can be found in Frederick Debell Bennett's

---

* However strange the idea of a "third eye" might appear, it seems appropriate for animals that live in regions of low light. But the organ has also been found in tunas, fishes that spend most of their lives close to the surface. For them, the "pineal apparatus" may function as a light receptor that controls phototactic movement—that is, light levels that affect their vertical movements and migration patterns (Rivas 1953).

Narrative of a Whaling Voyage Around the World, published in 1840. When a specimen was brought aboard at night, "it afforded a very extraordinary spectacle. The entire inferior surface of the body and head emitted a vivid and greenish phosphorescent gleam, imparting to the creature by its own light a truly ghastly and terrific appearance."

In Jules Verne's *Twenty Thousand Leagues Under the Sea,* first published in Paris in 1870, Captain Nemo, Professor Arronax, Conseil, and Ned Land take a stroll on the ocean floor, and among the dangers they encounter are large sharks, which are described as "huge shapes leaving streams of phosphorescence behind them." He described "those terrible sharks . . . who secrete a phosphorescent substance through the holes around their snouts. They are like monstrous fireflies who can crush an entire man in their jaws of iron!" Whatever else sharks can do, they cannot emit "streams of phosphorescence," and it seems likely that Verne was combining the phosphorescence that is occasionally seen at the surface (caused by dinoflagellates, and described on p. 139) with the sensory pores—known as the Ampullae of Lorenzini—on the snout of some sharks. Although Verne does not identify the species, it seems likely that he was referring to the great white shark, a shallow- to mid-water species that has no bioluminescent capabilities.

At the opposite end of the scale from the little cookie-cutter shark is the gigantic *Somniosus,* known variously as the "Greenland shark," "sleeper shark," or "gurry shark." The "sleeper" appellation comes from its sluggish habits, and

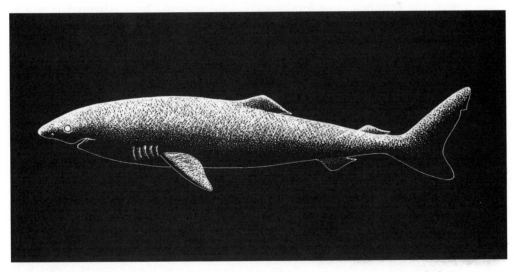

One of the largest deepwater fishes, the Greenland shark (*Somniosus microcephalus*) reaches a length of 23 feet. The greatest known depth for this species is 7,436 feet, recorded off Cape Hatteras in 1988.

"gurry" is the offal swept overboard after fishing or whaling operations, a reference to the sharks' habit of hanging around docks for scraps. It was this species that was photographed at 6,000 feet by Isaacs's remote camera, and the one that was represented by a 23-footer in Suruga Bay. (There are actually two species, *S. pacificus* and *S. microcephalus,* but except for their range, they are similar enough to be lumped together.) This is one of the largest sharks, and the largest of all deepwater fishes. (Only the whale shark, the basking shark, and the great white—all creatures of surface waters—grow larger.) During 1988 salvage operations for the SS *Central America* about 300 miles off Cape Hatteras, the unmanned submersible *Nemo* filmed a large shark at a depth of 2,200 meters (7,436 feet). It was a male, estimated to be 6 meters (nearly 20 feet) in length, and according to Charles Herdendorf and Tim Berra (1994), who analyzed the video transmissions, its eye was "distinctly white and luminous." Its size identifies it as *Somniosus;* the location makes it *S. microcephalus,* and the depth is a record for the species, and also a record for any shark other than the Portuguese shark, *Centroscymnus coelolepis.*

Greenland sharks are not exclusively inhabitants of deep water; in Greenland, the Inuit hunt them through holes in the ice, and the refuse from canneries and slaughterhouses will also bring them to the surface. It is believed that sleeper sharks feed mostly on carrion, although there has been little study of their habits. They are also known to feed on fishes, which usually appear in the stomach contents with their tails missing. Because *Somniosus* is often found with a parasitic copepod covering each eye, it has been speculated that the copepod is bioluminescent, and that the light attracts the fish to the shark, which eats them head first. The Greenland shark is found in the northern reaches of the Atlantic, occasionally straying as far south as North Carolina. The Pacific sleeper inhabits the deep waters of the northern rim, from Japan to Puget Sound. A smaller version, known as *Somniosus rostrata,* inhabits the Mediterranean and reaches a maximum length of four feet.

The squaloids are commonly known as dogfishes,* so it is not surprising (although the etymology is equally obscure) that there should be a group of sharks known as catsharks. For the most part, this large group (known collectively as the Scyliorhinidae) lives in the waters of the continental shelves, but there are some deepwater representatives. There are eighty-six recognized species, averaging about 40 inches in length, but many of them are known only

---

* In the past, sharks were generally known as "dogs of the sea" (*chiens de mer* in French), perhaps because of their habit of following ships. Since the most common shark in European waters is *Squalus acanthias,* which aggregates in large schools or packs, the squaloids acquired the popular appellation of "dogfish." Some other squaloids also have derivative canine names, such as spurdog and smooth hound.

The deepwater goblin shark (*Mitsukurina owstoni*) reaches a length of 15 feet, about 1 foot of which is the bladelike, overhanging snout. The function of this appendage is not known, although it is believed to be electrically sensitive.

from one or two specimens, and as with so many obscure sharks, they have not acquired a common name. For example, there is *Apristurus laurussonii*, a two-foot-long catshark found in water of 500 to 800 fathoms off Iceland and the Caribbean. Only one specimen of *A. profundorum* is known, and as might be expected from its name (*profundorum* means "deep"), it was collected at 816 fathoms (4,800 feet) in Delaware Bay. The false catshark (*Pseudotriakis*) is not a scyliorhinid, but monotypical (the only member of its genus), a slender, ten-foot shark that lives near the bottom of the deep Atlantic and Indian oceans.

Perhaps the strangest of all the deepwater sharks is *Mitsukurina*, the goblin shark. (When it was first discovered in 1898, it was believed to be synonymous with a long-extinct Cretaceous species known as *Scapanorhynchus*. More recently, it has been shown to be a distinct species, but many authors still use the earlier name.) A good part of its 14-foot length is tail, and a smaller proportion is the bizarre extension of its snout, a paddle-like blade that overhangs the protrusible jaws. The function of the snout extension is unknown, but it has been suggested that the goblin shark uses it to stir up the sediment in search of food. (Another possibility is that the snout—like the head lobes of the hammerhead—is rich in sensory receptors, enabling the shark to locate

Chimaeras are cartilaginous fishes distantly related to sharks. The deep Atlantic species *Harriotta raleighana* was named for Thomas Harriott, a seventeenth-century naturalist, and Sir Walter Raleigh.

prey buried in the sand.) Almost nothing is known about this creature, except that it inhabits deep waters around the world (Portugal, South Africa, France, Japan) and feeds on fishes and squids, and in one instance, a tooth belonging to a goblin shark was found embedded in a submarine telegraph cable in the Indian Ocean brought up from a depth of 750 fathoms.

While they have cartilaginous skeletons, the chimaeras have only a single external gill opening and are not closely related to the sharks. (They also have dermal denticles, but these are sparsely distributed along the head and claspers; the rest of the skin is naked and slippery with mucus.) They are not related to the bony fishes either, so these odd-looking creatures have been placed in a separate order, the Chimaeriformes.* All species are fairly small, rarely exceeding five feet, and are further characterized by large heads with disproportionately large eyes, and a tapering, pointed tail. Because of the tail, they are sometimes referred to as ratfishes, but in other parts of the world—

---

* In Greek mythology, the chimaera was a fire-breathing monster with the head of a lion, the body of a goat, and the tail of a serpent. In the *Iliad*, it is described as "a fearful creature, swift of foot and strong; whose breath was flame unquenchable," which Bellerophon kills with arrows while flying above the monster on the winged horse Pegasus.

particularly South Africa—they are called "ghost sharks." (Some chimaeras bear a marked resemblance to the macrourids, which also have large heads, large eyes, and a long, tapering tail that gives them their vernacular name, "rat-tails.") In place of the teeth that characterize many shark species, chimaeras have bony plates in the upper and lower jaws, which they use to grind their food, which consists of shellfish and crustaceans. There are some twenty-eight species of chimaeras, differentiated as three familes by the shape of the snout: the Chimaeridae have a rounded or cone-shaped snout (in *Living Fishes of the World,* Earl Herald described *Harriotta* as having a "stiletto-like nose . . . that reminds one of the nose contour of a supersonic jet aircraft"); the Cal-lorhinchidae are equipped with a hoe-shaped appendage on the snout (they are sometimes called elephant fishes); and the Rhinochimaeridae are known as long-nosed chimaeras because they have an extended, pointed snout. Various species are found throughout the world's oceans, but the Atlantic species are the Cuban chimaera (*Chimaera cubana*); the deepwater chimaera (*Hydrolagus affinis*); the elephant fish of the genus *Callorhinchus,* whose taxonomy is unresolved; and the long-nosed chimaera, *Harriotta raleighana.*

A deep Atlantic resident, *Harriotta raleighana* was named for Thomas Harriott, a seventeenth-century mathematican and naturalist, and Sir Walter Raleigh, who sent Harriott to Roanoke, Virginia, in 1585. (*Harriotta* was not known at that time, of course, but was named in 1895 by ichthyologists G. B. Goode and Tarleton Bean.) Earl Herald wrote that "the most startling feature of this group of fishes is the presence of a special clasper just in front of the eyes on the head of the male. Although it is thought to have some function in courtship, the actual method of using this clasper remains somewhat of a mystery." It is equipped with backward-pointing hooks (called "strong thorns" by Bigelow and Schroeder), which also "may have some function in courtship." Bigelow and Schroeder (1953) are somewhat more conservative, and refer to this appendage as a "frontal tentaculum," and since it does not occur at all in females, it appears to be a sexual characteristic—whatever its purpose. Male chimaeras, like sharks, have paired claspers located at the base of the pelvic fins and employed in internal fertilization. The eggs are laid in horny capsules. Chimaeras are equipped with a large spine at the front of the first dorsal fin, which is connected to a poison gland. The venom is powerful enough to cause severe discomfort and even death to a man unfortunate enough to be wounded, but because these fishes are not often seen alive, there is little likelihood of such an encounter. Like many other chimaeras, *Harriotta* is a deepwater species, having been recorded from depths in excess of 2,500 meters (8,200 feet).

Fishes of the Depths

When the great marine expeditions in the last century started the scientific exploration of the seven seas and the life they contain, the deep-
sea anglers or devilfishes were among the most amazing monsters to
be pulled out of the darkness of the vast depths. If their size had been
in any proportion at all to their ferocious appearance, these pitch-black
relatives of the ordinary angler or goosefish would have been truly horrifying with their tremendously oversized head in which a cavernous
mouth opens like a yawning trap beset with long daggerlike teeth.

ALBERT EIDE PARR, 1932

The abyssal zone is the world's largest ecosystem and covers more than
half the surface area of the planet. Almost 40 percent of the earth's surface lies under water masses that are from two to three miles deep.
Early deepwater trawls, such as those employed on the *Challenger* expedition of 1873–76, revealed an abundance of creatures whose existence was
completely unpredicted and unexpected. Previous concepts of ichthyology
were primarily concerned with fishes that could be seen or caught at or near
the surface, but the first tentative probes of the depths revealed such marvels
as miniature dragons with ferocious-looking fangs; pear-shaped fishes with luminescent fishing lures attached to their heads; fishes without eyes; fishes that
perched on elongated tripods made up of their fin spines; snakelike fishes that
were studded with colored lights; and fierce little predators that were able to
swallow creatures that were larger than they were.

N. B. Marshall (1965) estimated that the number of known deep-sea fish
species exceeds 2,000, and wrote that they are "more than ten times as diverse
as the surface dwellers." In a 1970 study, ichthyologist Daniel M. Cohen calculated that there were 1,280 recent species found on the continental slopes
and the deep-sea benthic environment, and another 1,010 species in deep

pelagic waters (below 200 meters), for a total of 2,290. (His estimate for the total number of bony fish species in marine and freshwater environments is about 20,000.) The deepwater denizens live at depths of 250 to 7,000 meters and can be roughly partitioned between the mid-waters (the mesopelagic species) and the deep-sea floor (the benthic fishes). The great majority of them are small—less than 6 inches in length—but some reach 2, 3, or even 6 feet. (The oarfish, a ribbonlike deep-sea species, may reach a length of 26 feet.) In the twilight zone between 200 and 1,000 meters live most of the stomiatids, the lantern fishes, the swallowers, and the lancet fishes; and in the sunless reaches below 1,000 meters dwell the deep-sea anglers, the gulper eels, the giganturids, and most of the bristlemouths. At the greatest depths of the oceans, often close to or on the bottom, can be found the halosaurs, tripod fishes, brotulids, rattails, and whale fishes. We can cover only some of the thousands of known species of deep-sea fishes. (There are more than a hundred species of deep-sea anglers, and even more stomiatids.) Most of our knowledge has been derived from the examination of trawled-up specimens or, occasionally, those that have been found in the stomachs of predators. Because of the inaccessibility of their habitat to humans, very few species have ever been seen alive—except for those that have been brought up in nets— and even fewer have been photographed.*

As contrasted with life at the surface, in which the primary requirements for prey capture are strength and speed, and where it helps the predator to be larger than its prey, feeding in the depths is often carried out according to a completely different set of rules. Speed and strength are not particularly useful attributes in circumstances where the prey can swim out of visual range in an instant. In the blackness of their habitat, bathypelagic hunters must be able to find their prey and, having found it, immediately capture it. To make sure the victim does not escape, most predators are equipped with ferocious-looking teeth that often point rearward, guaranteeing that a fish caught in the trap will not escape. And because prey items are, relatively speaking, few and far between, once caught, they have to be able to sustain the catcher for some time. Unlike some small terrestrial predators—shrews, for example—a predatory fish cannot take small bites from its prey, but has to be able to gain maximum nourishment as efficaciously as possible. To do this, the predator must keep the prey item from sinking, and what better place to store food than in

---

* Consider the Atlantic wreckfish, *Polyprion americanus*. Its common name comes from its inclination to frequent wrecks, usually at depths of 300 to 400 feet. In a series of time-lapse photographs taken at 445 to 740 meters (1,500 to 2,500 feet) on the Mid-Atlantic Ridge, wreckfish were attracted to the camera's flashes, and were photographed for the first time at these unexpected depths (Ryall and Hargrave 1984).

the stomach? This would account for the mouth design of many of the bathypredators, which allows them to open their jaws so wide that they can engulf victims larger than they are, and an expandable stomach, to hold the entire carcass. Because prey is spread out, predatory fishes cannot find something to eat all that often, so they have to be able to take advantage of the infrequent encounter or, in some cases, precipitate that encounter by attracting the prey instead of having to search for it.

Water is a particularly poor conductor of light, and much of the sunlight that enters the sea is extinguished in the upper layers. The Sargasso Sea, with no silt or other terrestrial detritus to cloud its translucency, is the clearest water in the world, but even there, most of the sun's light is absorbed within the first 30 feet. In a chapter of *Half Mile Down* (fittingly entitled "The End of the Spectrum"), William Beebe described his 1930 descent in the bathysphere thus: "The dimming of the light was more evident between the surface and fifty feet than anywhere else, for within this zone all the warm red rays are absorbed and the remainder of the spectrum, with its dominance of green and blue, reflected a sense of chill through our eyes long before the thermometer had dropped a degree." The shortest rays of the visible spectrum are gone by 300 feet, and with them, red, orange, and yellow, the colors we associate with warmth and sunlight. By 1,000 feet, the greens are gone too, leaving only blue and violet, the longest wavelengths of the spectrum. Below this is a black that only those who have seen it can imagine. Beebe was one of the first humans to descend to these depths, and was therefore the first to tell the world how it looked down there. Here are his observations about the blue-blackness of 800 feet, as he and Otis Barton were lowered in the bathysphere off Bermuda:

> The twilight (the word had become absurd, but I could coin no other) deepened, but we still spoke of its brilliance. It seemed to me that it must be like the last terrific upflare of a flame before it is quenched. . . . But only by shutting my eyes and opening them again could I realize the terrible *slowness* of the change from dark blue to blacker blue. On the earth at night in moonlight I can always imagine the yellow of sunshine, the scarlet of invisible blossoms, but here, when the searchlight was off, yellow and orange and red were unthinkable. The blue which filled all space admitted no thought of any others.

Many animals live at the low-light or no-light levels of these stygian depths, and they have evolved any number of solutions to the complicated business of earning a living in the dark. To begin with, how are they supposed to see anything? There is no standard solution to the problem of vision at great depths, since some deep-sea fishes see well, while others have small eyes (or even no eyes) and cannot rely on vision at all. As John Murray and Johan Hjort wrote in their 1912 *Depths of the Ocean,* "Nothing has appeared more hopeless in biological oceanography than the attempt to explain the connection between the development of the eyes and the intensity of light at different depths in the ocean. In a trawling from abyssal depths in the ocean we may find fishes with large eyes along with others with very small eyes or totally blind. Nowhere would a perfect uniformity be expected than in the dark and quiet depths of the ocean."

Regardless of the size of their eyes—or even the lack of them—all deep-sea animals have to find their food, avoid predators, and find mates in order to reproduce. Among the visual problems that must be solved by animals that live below 200 meters (according to E. J. Denton in 1990) are: holding an appropriate depth station in the daytime; being able to measure absolute light levels; camouflaging themselves, which involves not only countershading but also regulating their own light emissions; and detecting and identifying prospective prey, mates, or predators in daylight or in darkness.

BIOLUMINESCENCE

In the blackness of the abyss, a virtual firmament of tiny lights flickers incessantly, marking the location and activities of the myriad creatures that inhabit this sunless world. A great majority of deep-sea fishes have light-generating capabilities; Beebe estimated that of the fishes he caught down to 13,000 feet in Bermuda waters, more than 95 percent were bioluminescent. (J. E. Fitch and R. J. Lavenberg [1968] cited two other studies, in which bioluminosity was present in 96 and 98 percent of the species collected.) Some species have glittering rows of photophores along the sides; others are equipped with filaments that glow; there are some with light organs in their eyes, some have them on their tongues, one species has a glowing rectal gland, and on one occasion, a deep-sea fish was observed to be feeding by shining a two-foot beam of light into a swarming school of euphausiids. Bioluminescence has intrigued biologists for years, but there is still no agreement as to its function, or as to why so many different creatures (not only fishes but also certain sharks, squid, starfishes, sea cucumbers, and crustaceans) should have developed these structurally similar mechanisms.

Most deep-sea fishes are dark brown or black since there is obviously no need for bright coloration in a lightless world. (There are several species, particularly the whale fishes, that are red, but with no light to illuminate them, they appear black.) In most circumstances, the only part of the fish that can be seen in the darkness is that which lights up. There are three ways whereby marine animals can generate "living light." The commonest is intracellular, whereby certain cells are organized into special structures such as lanterns and photophores. In the cells of these organs, energy is released in the form of light when the oxidization (interaction with oxygen) of a substance known as luciferin is stimulated by the catalytic activity of an enzyme known as luciferase. (Because hardly any heat is generated by the luciferin-luciferase reaction, the "cold light" of chemoluminescence has become a subject of great interest to physicists concerned with the preservation of energy.) The organs that produce the light range from a simple luminous element surrounded by a layer of black pigment cells, to cups with a reflecting layer, and even to some complex structures with lenses and color filters. In some instances, the light is produced extracellularly, and can result in the discharge of a luminous cloud into the water.

Some fishes harbor luminescent symbiotic bacteria that provide a light source that glows from the fish's body but is not actually produced by the fish. Two strains of luminous bacteria are currently recognized: *Photobacterium* and *Beneckea*. In the deep-sea anglers, bacteria are usually maintained in the lure (also known as the "esca"), but in addition, the sea devils (*Ceratias* and *Cryptopsaras*) have additional bacterial bulbs in the form of caruncles, which are modified dorsal fin rays. One of the most intriguing problems in biology is that luminous bacteria must be transferred from generation to generation, or, as Peter Herring wrote in a 1977 study of bioluminescence, "the light organs of successive generations must be reinfected with the appropriate strain." Since the bacteria cannot exist outside the host, they must somehow pass to the offspring internally, but how this might work has not been explained. In 1993, Herring wondered "where the bacteria come from to reinfect successive generations of host. We know they can leak from the host into the surrounding sea water, but do they survive there? Adult and juvenile anglerfishes live at different depths; how does a larval female acquire the right bacterium, even if it is leaked by the adult, if the adult lives several hundred metres deeper?"

"Much research has gone into the bioluminescence of different marine creatures," wrote James Hamilton-Paterson, "a subject made more complicated because the light has no unitary function." Many species of deep-sea fishes have bioluminescent organs, but depending on their location, size, brilliance, and structure, they probably serve different purposes for different species. In a 1967 article entitled "The Significance of Ventral Bioluminescence in Fishes," D. E. McAllister listed the function of photophores for members of the same species, and for members of different species. In intraspecific interactions, he wrote, lights might be useful to attract potential mates, to serve as recognition signs for members of the same species, to indicate the sex of the possessor, to use in courtship displays, and to allow individuals to distribute themselves in space that provides no fixed reference points. The luminous organs might serve to lure prey within range, to illuminate the items of prey, to startle or divert predators, to reveal predators to larger predators, or to mislead predators through mimicry.

Given all these possibilities, it is obvious that more than one explanation might be applied, and that the organs probably have multiple functions. The lighted lures of the ceratioid anglers serve to attract prey items to the mouth of the predator, with the "mousetrap" arrangement of *Thaumatichthys* being the most sophisticated variation on this theme. Light organs around the eyes of some species of lantern fishes probably function as "headlights" to illuminate prey items immediately before they are consumed, but the illumination, even from a photophore the size of a pea, cannot show the fish where to go, but only what to do when it gets there. One of the most unusual demonstrations of bioluminescence has been observed in *Searsia,* a black, bathypelagic fish that can discharge a luminous secretion into the water from a subcutaneous gland just behind its head. (Members of the family are commonly known as "tube-shoulders.") *Searsia* appears to be the only fish that bioluminesces outside its body, but the squid *Heteroteuthis dispar* is also known to emit luminescent ink clouds, and is the only cephalopod to do so. In addition to photophores, the stomiatids *Stomias, Idiacanthus,* and *Chauliodus* can envelop themselves in a sheath of luminous, gelatinous tissue that glows bright pink when stimulated. As William O'Day (1973) wrote, this kind of luminescent silhouetting does the opposite of camouflaging the fish, and "may aid in mating, spacing themselves out as they hunt, maintaining conspecific aggregations, warning potential predators of their own formidable size, or perhaps allowing them to escape from predators by temporarily blinding them." He concludes by saying, "These functions, however, remain speculative."

In his 1983 overview of the general functions of bioluminescence, R. E. Young is careful to identify the possible dangers of lighting up underwater. He writes, "Attracting a mate with luminescence has a number of inherent drawbacks. An animal hoping to lure a mate may attract a predator instead, or an animal searching for a mate may be attracted to a predator instead." Furthermore, wrote Young, "even in the clearest oceanic water, fine detritus (marine snow) is abundant and light scattering by such molecules may well alert potential victims before they are exposed by the beam." Young concludes, "I view life in this dark environment as a peculiar battle in which stealth and luminescence are major weapons. It is a struggle unlike any found elsewhere on this planet. . . . While the complex rules of combat in this environment will be difficult to unravel, they should be entertaining and frequently surprising, and hopefully, their unique features will provide new insights into the ways nature operates." In an imaginative—and perhaps too convoluted—discussion of "a possible function of bioluminescence," M. D. Burkenroad (1943) suggested that the flashing might serve as a sort of "burglar alarm," attracting not only the first predator but another predator to prey upon the first, thus protecting the prey.

The Anomalopidae is a small family of shallow-water fishes, commonly known as "flashlight fishes" or "lantern-eye fishes." The four species all have an organ below the eye that contains luminous bacteria that can be exposed when the fish lowers a special opaque flap. Of the three genera, only *Kryptophanaron* is found in or near the Atlantic, the other two (*Anomalops* and *Photoblepharon*) being restricted to Indo-Pacific waters. Flashlight fishes, therefore, are well known, but nowhere else in the ichthyological literature do we encounter anything as astonishing as the description of a fish that uses a *searchlight*. Described as "an eel-shaped Stomiatoid fish with brilliant luminous organs and silvery scales," it was observed from the deck of the British research vessel *William Scoresby* east of the South Sandwich Islands, over water that was between 4,000 and 5,000 meters deep. As recorded in a note by E. R. Gunther (and repeated in R. Clarke 1950):

> From a pair of luminous organs in the orbital region, the fish (which was 9–12 inches in length) emitted a beam, of varying intensity, of strong blue light which shone directly forward for a distance of about two feet. The fish had a habit of lurking at a depth of 2–6 feet below the surface, poised at an angle of 35–40 degrees from the horizontal—this gave the beam an upward tilt: occasionally the fish swam round and with a quick action snapped at the cloud of krill above it.*

There are even some fishes that are not supposed to luminesce, but do anyway. The extensive literature on deep-sea anglers contains many references to luminescent lures and barbels, but no mention of the entire fish glowing. In their 1977 study of bioluminescent countershading, Richard Young and Clyde Roper examined various cephalopods and shrimp, and two specimens of *Cryptopsaras couesi*. They wrote, "*Cryptopsaras couesi* is a small, jet-black anglerfish

---

* In a 1961 discussion of bioluminescence, J. A. C. Nicol either identified the fish responsible for the "searchlight" or referred to another species with the same capabilities. In the caption for a photograph of *Stomias ferox*, he called it "a deep-sea fish . . . possessing three kinds of light organs, namely, a barbel under the chin, *a searchlight* [my italics], and a series of bull's eye lanterns along the flanks."

whose luminescence was thought to be limited to its esca and caruncles. To our vast surprise, this specimen was capable of luminescent countershading. . . . We could not detect the source of the luminescence, but it appeared to originate from the skin; where the skin was abraded or purposely cut, there was no luminescence. Except for the anteriorly placed, blunt lower jaw, all of the black skin, including that on the fin rays and on the dwarf male, luminesced."

While most luminous organs are located on the ventral surfaces of the fish, no simple explanation readily springs to mind as to why this location is so heavily favored. It has been proposed that ventral bioluminescence serves as a sort of "countershading" (although "counterlighting" might be a more appropriate term), in which the light organs offset the shadow that would be cast on the fish from surface illumination. (The characteristically dark coloration of the dorsal surface of most fish enable them to match the background when lit from above.) Many species of squid are equipped with an organ known as the "extraocular receptor," which enables them to read the downwelling light and adjust their luminescence accordingly, and there is a possibility that some fishes have a comparable apparatus, as J. V. Lawry suggested in 1974 with regard to the myctophid *Tarletonbeania* which "may see downwelling light and bioluminescence from a supra-orbital photophore and adjust the output of its ventral photophores to match environmental illumination."* In order for such a system to work, the fish has to be able to switch its photophores off at night, since in darkness, instead of camouflaging the fish, the luminous organs would draw attention to it. (In the above experiments with *Tarletonbeania,* Lawry observed that captured specimens kept in total darkness did not luminesce, but when they were illuminated from above, the photophores emitted a bluish light that was extinguished whenever the light source was.)

Marshall (1954) has indicated that piscene photophores are ventral so that they will not reflect sunlight when illuminated from above, but again, this would apply only during the day. Numerous authors have suggested that the ventral photophores disrupt the silhouette of the fish, but this occurs only when the predator approaches from below and does not explain why dorsal light organs would not serve the same purpose. In his discussion of the function of bioluminescence, W. D. Clarke suggested that since most fishes are nearsighted, they cannot see the photophores as separate lights, but from a distance, they appear as an indistinctly glowing, monochromatic cloud. In his survey, McAllister wrote, "As the specific functions attributed to biolumines-

* The supraorbital photophore in fishes appears to correspond to the extraocular receptor in squids, as well as the pineal eye in some species of deep-sea sharks. This is a good example of convergence, in which completely unrelated creatures have developed similar solutions to a particular problem—in this case, reading the ambient-light level in order to adjust one's own luminescence to it.

cence do not seem to require a predominately ventral position, one must look elsewhere for explanations of this pattern." It is clear that we, like the bearers of the light organs, are in the dark, and more *in situ* observations of living luminous fishes are necessary before we can understand the mysteries and miracles of bioluminescense.*

In his combined roles as ichthyologist, zoologist, writer, and adventurer, William Beebe was the first popularizer of deep-sea ichthyological research. His descents in the bathysphere in the 1930s allowed him a view of the creatures of the depths that had been vouchsafed to no other scientist before him. He described what he saw and collected in the scientific literature, but he was even more accomplished at writing for a popular audience in magazines (especially *National Geographic,* whose parent society sponsored much of his research), the *Bulletin* of the New York Zoological Society, and an enormously popular book, *Half Mile Down.* There are those who question a few of his unlikely descriptions, such as the six-foot-long "untouchable bathysphere fish" or the "five-lined constellationfish." Of the latter, an outraged Carl Hubbs, writing in the ichthyological journal *Copeia,* said that it was "so utterly at variance with any system of fish photophores that I am forced to suggest that whatever the author saw might have been a phosphorescent coelenterate whose lights were beautified by halation in passing through a misty film breathed onto the quartz window by Mr. Beebe's eagerly appressed face."

When Beebe and Otis Barton descended to 2,100 feet off Bermuda, they described a pair of fishes that passed within eight feet of the windows. According to Beebe's description (which appears in *Zoologica,* a technical journal of the New York Zoological Society, and also, along with an illustration, in *Half Mile Down*), *Bathysphaera intacta* (the "untouchable bathysphere fish") was "at least six feet in length. . . . [T]here was a single row of strong, pale blue lights along the side. . . . There were two ventral tentacles, each tipped with a pair of separate, luminous bodies, the superior reddish, the lower one blue. . . . [T]he position of the fish must be somewhere near the Melanostomiatidae, but the single line of large, lateral photophores and the two ventral tentacles set it apart from any known species or genus." In *Fishes of the Western North Atlantic* (where it is listed as *incertae cedis*—"relationships uncertain"), James Morrow and Robert Gibbs wrote, "As Beebe noted, the sys-

---

* One of the curious aspects of counterillumination is that it has never been observed from submersibles. "Indeed," wrote R. E. Young, "submersible observations suggest that counterillumination does not occur." In Beebe's dives, he could easily see various fish species that were supposed to be rendered invisible—or at least hard to see—against the ambient-light source. It may be that the presence of a large, strange, light-producing object in the fish's environment interferes with its coloration-control mechanisms.

The most spectacular of William Beebe's deep-sea discoveries was the six-foot-long "untouchable bathysphere fish" (*Bathysphaera intacta*), which he claimed to have seen from the bathysphere at 2,100 feet off Bermuda. In his 1932 description, he said it had "a row of strong pale blue lights along the side [and] two ventral tentacles, each tipped with a pair of separate luminous bodies, the superior reddish, the lower one blue."

tematic position of this fish is most uncertain. However, it is probably as near to the Melanostomiatidae as to any other group, and it is included here on the off chance that some day a specimen may be found."*

Another sight available to Beebe and no one else were the "rainbow gars," which he spotted in a group of four, swimming vertically, head up, off Bermuda, at a depth of 2,500 feet. Following his historic dive in the bathysphere, Beebe issued a stream of publications, many of which were in the scientific as well as the popular canon. The description of the "rainbow gars" (with an illustration by Else Bostelmann) appeared in the *National Geographic* for December 1934, and also in *Half Mile Down*, published in the same year. In many instances, he bestowed a scientific name on these hitherto unde-

* Volume 4 of *Fishes of the Western North Atlantic* was published in 1964, and in the ensuing years, no specimen of "*Bathysphaera*" has appeared. Although we cannot say with certainty that it will not, it seems somewhat unlikely that a six-foot-long stomiatid will appear when all the known varieties are less than two feet in length, and the majority much smaller than that. In his review of Beebe's *Half Mile Down*, Hubbs wrote that *Bathysphaera* was "twice as long as any known fish with this general type of illumination," and Beebe and Crane (in the same 1939 article in which *Bathysphaera* was described as "still uncertain") wrote that "the largest known melanostomiatid is the unique specimen of *Opostomias*, measuring 380 mm [15 inches] in length." The red and blue lights on the "tentacles" are another anomaly, but then, the only person ever to claim to have seen this creature in its natural habitat—or anywhere else—was William Beebe.

scribed species, but in this case he restricted himself to a common name. Here is his account from *Half Mile Down*:

> At 11:17 o'clock I turned the light on suddenly, and saw a strange quartet of fish, to which I have not been able to fit a genus or family. Shape, size, and one fin I saw clearly, but Abyssal Rainbow Gars is as far as I dare go, and they may be anything but gars. About four inches over all, they were slender and stiff with long, sharply pointed jaws. . . . There they stood, for they were almost upright, and I could see only a slight fanning with the dorsal fin. . . . [T]he amazing thing about them was their unexpected pattern and color. The jaws and head were brilliant scarlet, which, back of the gills, changed abruptly into a light but strong blue and this merged insensibly into a clear yellow on the posterior body and tail.

No one has ever seen or captured anything that remotely resembles Beebe's "rainbow gars," and the "unexpected pattern and color" have not been observed in any fish, at any depth, on the surface, or even among the usually bright-colored inhabitants of coral reefs.

Obviously, there is no preordained "order" in which various kinds of fishes should be discussed. In the case of deep-sea fishes, one is tempted to stratify the discussions by depth, beginning at the higher levels and working down to the abyss, but the fishes have not been so cooperative in their vertical distribution, and this system, while attractive, is unworkable, mostly because the fishes do not confine themselves to a particular depth. (Besides, some of them are so poorly studied that we are not at all sure of the depth they normally inhabit.) Various texts have classified the fishes according to their systematic positions, assigning "relationships" on the basis of anatomical similarities, a study known as phylogeny. (Many species deemed to be closely related do not look very much alike, and some species that appear similar are not related, so the physical aspect is not a very good guide.) The study of relationships has given us a framework for arranging the various species in a recognizable, although changeable, order and for identifying their phylogenetic affiliations. I have followed (with some minor variations) the classification and systematics of the 1993 edition of Joseph S. Nelson's *Fishes of the World*.

The basic unit of biological classification is the "species," consisting of organisms that can interbreed with each other and produce viable offspring. (If two closely related species interbreed, the result is often a sterile hybrid.) Nelson defines the species as "the only taxonomic unit with evolutionary reality." The evolutionary relationships between species (phylogeny) is expressed in hierarchical categories known as taxa, from which the word "taxonomy"—the study of relationships and classifications—is derived. Although there are many additional categories, such as superorders, subclasses, and subspecies, the basic arrangement of taxa is as follows, from the inclusive to the specific: Kingdom, Phylum, Class, Order, Family, Genus, Species. The classification of *Lipogenys gilli* (discussed below) is as follows:

Kingdom: Animalia
Phylum: Chordata (vertebrates)
Class: Osteichthys (bony fishes)
Order: Anguilliformes (eel-like fishes)
Family: Lipogenyidae
Genus: *Lipogenys*
Species: *gilli*

HALOSAURS, GULPERS, AND EELS

The order Anguilliformes (from *anguilla,* Latin for "eel") includes several families with long, thin bodies, such as the halosaurs and the spiny eels (notacanths), and also those fishes that look the way we expect eels to look: rather like underwater snakes. Eels may resemble snakes, but they are proper fishes, and some, as we shall see, are particularly interesting ones. Eels are also known as Apodes, which means "without feet" and refers to the absence of paired pelvic or ventral fins. The dorsal and anal fins lack spines and are continuous, including the tail, or caudal fin. They appear to lack scales, but microscopic examination reveals the presence of minute scales embedded in the skin—often hundreds to the square inch. Formerly, the gulpers were included in the Apodes, which consists of some twenty-two families of eels, but they have now been assigned to their own order, the Lyomeri. (The gulpers—Saccopharyngids—are also elongated fishes with no scales that pass through a leptocephalus phase and have no pelvic or ventral fins, but in other respects they are so distinctive that they have now been classified separately.) Among the better-known anguilliformes are the congers (Congridae), the morays (Muraenidae), and the snake eels (Ophichthyidae), but only the snipe eels (Nemichthyidae) and the cutthroat eels (Synaphobranchidae) regularly occupy the deep oceans.

The halosaurs are elongated fishes that swim close to the bottom with their narrow tails raised and their snouts plowing along in the sediments. They have spatulate, strengthened snouts and jaws on the underside of the head that facilitate rooting in the mud, although Samuel McDowell writes

The Atlantic halosaur (*Halosaurus guentheri*) has been collected from depths of 4,000 feet off the New York and New England coasts. It is believed that the lengthened snouts of these fishes are used for probing in the sediment for crustaceans.

that "the bone supporting the snout is quite delicate and thus quite unlike the rigid and sturdily built snout of the sturgeon. . . . More likely, the snout of halosaurs is used primarily as a sensory probe. . . ." In support of the "sensory" hypothesis, there is an elaborate pattern of neuromasts in the lateral line system, which extends to the gill covers and the exterior surface of the upper and lower jaws. (The lateralis system in halosaurs is characteristically present as a low course along the flanks.) As might be expected, halosaurs feed primarily on crustaceans that live in the mud. With its snout buried in the mud and its long tail waving in the currents, it would appear that this fish—or at least its empennage—would be fair game for passing predators, and indeed, the frequent appearance of a regenerated tail tip suggested to McDowell in 1973 that "the easy loss of the tail to predators may be a protective defense to these fishes, analogous to the easy loss of the tail in lizards and salamanders."

One noteworthy characteristic of the halosaurs is the modification of the olfactory organs of mature males. In all known species, males are identified by a modification of the exterior nostril, which, in *Aldrovandia** becomes a black fleshy tube, totally absent in females. Why this "olfactory dimorphism"? Males are probably attracted to females by scent, but this is hardly unique to the halosaurs, for as N. B. Marshall has written, "The females of all species [of bony fishes] have small or regressed olfactory organs, whereas the males of most species . . . are macrosmatic." ("Macrosmatic" and "microsmatic" refer to a well- or poorly developed sense of smell, from the Greek *osme* for "smell.") Since most fishes have a good sense of smell (Marshall writes that the common eel [*Anguilla*] "has the same olfactory sensibility as tracking dogs"), this dimorphism must be a form of sexual signaling, enabling males to find females in the blackness of their habitat. In most instances, the olfactory organs are hidden beneath the skin, but in *Aldrovandia* they are prominently exposed. Notacanths and halosaurs are deepwater species; one species, *Aldrovandia rostrata,* was caught by the *Challenger* at a depth of just over 5,000 meters. The neuromasts, particularly those of the lateralis system, may be luminescent, but the evidence is inconclusive. Observations from the French bathyscaph *FNRS*-3 indicate that these fishes are gregarious, "although they do not appear to show the close and orderly formation associated with schooling, as in mackerel" (McDowell 1973).

The gulper and pelican eels, the halosaurs, the notacanths, and—somewhat unexpectedly—the tarpons and bonefishes are sometimes grouped together because all of them share a unique developmental characteristic: they all undergo a leptocephalus larval stage. (The word "leptocephalus" means "small head," and refers to the size of the head relative to the body.) This phase, which begins when the fish hatches from the egg, takes the form of a transparent fish, completely different in shape from the adult. (For example, the leptocephalus of the snipe eel is leaf-shaped, as is the larval form of the gulper eel *Eurypharynx,* which metamorphoses into a six-foot-long fish that is all mouth with a tail attached.) Until the nineteenth century, leptocephali were treated as a separate group of fishes, and it was only in 1864 that Theodore Gill suggested that they might be larval eels. The duration of the leptocephalus stage varies from species to species, but it may last as long as

---

* This genus was named in 1896 by ichthyologists G. Brown Goode and Tarleton Bean for Ulysses Aldrovandi, an Italian naturalist of the late sixteenth century, who produced numerous illustrated books on animals, plants, and minerals. Goode and Bean were the authors of one of the most important texts of the nineteenth century, *Oceanic Ichthyology,* and both their names appear regularly in ichthyological nomenclature. For example, the lantern fish *Tarletonbeania* uses Bean's full name, one of the bigscales is *Scopelogadus beanii,* and one of the halosaurs was once known as *Halosaurus goodei.*

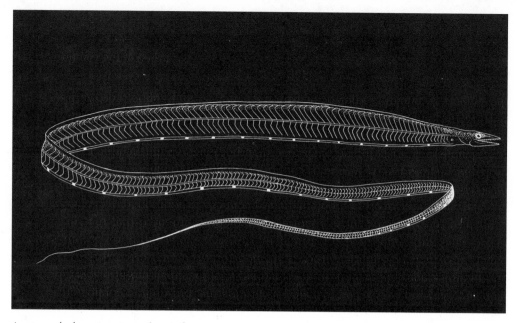

Leptocephalus giganteus, the six-foot larva caught at 1,000 feet off the coast of South Africa in 1930 by the Danish research vessel *Dana.* Is it an eel? How big would it get to be at maturity?

two or three years. In recent times, the study of leptocephali ("leptocephology") has become an important aspect of the study of certain fishes; as evidence of its importance, the 324-page volume 2 of part 9 of *Fishes of the Western North Atlantic* (1989) is devoted exclusively to leptocephali.

One of the great mysteries of ichthyology (and cryptozoology) concerns the discovery of a leptocephalus almost 6 feet in length, trawled up in 1930 during the *Dana* expedition from a depth of 1,000 feet off the coast of South Africa. Before it metamorphoses into an elver, the leptocephalus of the common eel reaches a length of about 3 inches. Extrapolating from the known ratio of the length of this leptocephalus to its adult size of about 3 feet—and even more dramatic, the conger eel, which grows thirty times longer than its 4-inch leptocephalus—those who would have us believe in sea serpents concluded that the *Dana*'s leptocephalus would have matured to a total length of over 100 feet. In *In the Wake of the Sea-Serpents,* Bernard Heuvelmans wrote, "There is no doubt that giant eels are responsible for *some* sightings of sea serpents," and Léon Bertin, one of the world's foremost authorities on eels, discussed this creature in a 1954 article he called "Les Larves leptocéphaliennes géantes et le Problème du 'serpent de mer,'" Bertin pointed out that there are many other species of eels where the ratio of leptocephalus to adult is much less than 1/12 (or 1/30!), and in fact, he wrote, "If the two giant leptocephali . . . belong to the *Nemichthys* group it is therefore very likely that the adult is no more than 16 to

20 feet long and not 100 feet as has been suggested." Twenty feet is still twice as long as the longest known conger eel, and monsterologists were not willing to let the subject of the giant leptocephalus drop so easily. In 1957, zoologist Maurice Burton incorporated these data into a book called *Animal Legends,* and proposed that the Loch Ness monster was "a giant eel, one of greater proportions than any known to science."

The odds of finding a 100-foot eel (or even a 20-footer) are approximately the same as finding the Loch Ness monster, and it turns out that the giant leptocephalus is very likely the larval form of an unspecified notacanth. In collections around the world there reside other elongated, unidentified leptocephali, some of which were collected in the early twentieth century, and one may have been described by Constantine Rafinesque in 1810. When leptocephali were believed to be distinct species and not the larval forms of other fishes, there was nothing particularly unusual about these specimens (except that they were considerably longer than any similar species), and they remained in their jars, specifically unidentified. In 1911, the French ichthyologist Léon Roule called them *"larves Tiluriennes,"* and they were variously named *Tilurus, Tiluropsis,* and *Tilurella.* (According to David Smith's 1970 discussion, "*Tilurella* was later identified as a post-larval *Nemichthys* . . . and clearly does not belong with the others.") In 1959, an 893-mm (34-inch) specimen was collected off New Zealand and officially named *Leptocephalus giganteus* (Castle 1959). More recently, other larvae have been collected and examined, including two that were found in the stomachs of lancet fishes longlined in the Pacific (Haedrich and Nielsen 1966).

Sensational revelations, especially those that involve "monsters," are much more likely to be repeated and published in the popular press than arcane ichthyological theorizing, and it has been much easier—and a lot more fun—to write about 100-foot-long monster eels than the speculations of Monsieur Roule and Herr Professor Doktor Kölliker. (Kölliker described the first elongated larva in 1853.) The real story is fascinating, but quite complicated, and includes not only several unidentified large leptocephali but also several papers in which possibilities other than monsters were suggested. In 1970, David G. Smith published an article in *Copeia* ("Notacanthiform Leptocephali in the Western North Atlantic") in which he proposed that the very large larvae (there are other problematical specimens in addition to the *Dana's* mystery specimen) were notacanths or halosaurs, but although "*Tiluropsis* was probably a halosaurid, *L. giganteus* cannot be identified to family. . . ." Also in 1970, Danish scientists Jørgen Nielsen and Verner Larsen published their "Remarks on the Identity of the Giant *Dana* Eel Larva," in which they discounted Bertin's 1954 suggestion that it might be a 20-foot-long *Nemichthys* (to date, the longest *Nemichthys* known measured 57 inches) and supported Smith's contention that the *Dana*'s larva was indeed *L. giganteus*. In his 1932 discussion of the *Dana*'s collections, Å. V. Taning did not give the giant leptocephalus a name; it was not officially christened until 1970, when Smith affiliated it with the New Zealand specimen.

Finally (or, more accurately, most recently), in the 1989 leptocephalus volume of *Fishes of the Western North Atlantic*, Smith lists *Tilurus* and *L. giganteus* as notacanthiform (which includes the halosaurs) leptocephali, but he modified his conclusion by writing that "*Leptocephalus giganteus* may represent a species group within the Notacanthidae or Halosauridae, or it may represent a group yet unknown as adults." As for the 6-foot larva maturing into a 100-foot-long eel, Smith wrote, "In reality, the relationship between the size of the leptocephalus and the size of the adult varies widely among elopomorph fishes, and there is no way to predict it beforehand. Indeed, the evidence suggests that halosaurids, at least, undergo a drastic reduction in length at metamorphosis."

Larval notacanths thus appear to be much more interesting than the adults, which are elongated and generally eel-like, characterized by a row of isolated spines along the back that are not connected by a dorsal fin, and are therefore named "spiny eels." They are believed to inhabit waters down to 3,000 feet, where they swim head downward, just off the bottom, at an angle of about 30 degrees. From the examination of stomach contents, it has been learned that the notacanths' primary food is sea anemones, but they also nip off bits of bryozoans and sea pens. In the Atlantic, the genus is represented by

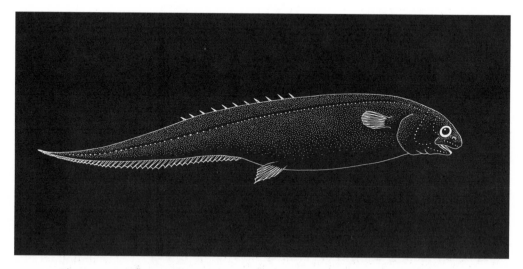

The spiny eel *Notacanthus chemnitzi* is not a true eel but a relative of the halosaurs, differentiated from them by the unconnected spines on its back.

A relative of the notacanths (spiny eels), *Lipogenys gilli* is a bottom feeder, scooping up detritus with its suckerlike mouth.

Notacanthus chemnitzi, one of the largest notacanths at a maximum of 36 inches (McDowell 1973). This species has been collected from Labrador to the Gulf of Mexico, and a related species, *Polyacanthonotus rissoanus*, has been found at depths close to 10,000 feet in the Mediterranean and the North Atlantic.

The genus *Lipogenys* contains only a single species, *L. gilli*. In shape it resembles the notacanths (to which it is related), with a long, tapered body and rounded head, but unlike the spiny eels, *Lipogenys* has no teeth. It is believed to feed on detritus such as plant fibers, crustacean parts, and sponge spicules, by vacuuming them up from the ocean floor with its suckerlike mouth. In his discussion of the genus (in part 6 of *Fishes of the Western North Atlantic*, where he wrote about all the Notacanthiformes), S. B. McDowell wrote, "None of the specimens had an empty stomach, suggesting that *Lipogenys* may feed almost continuously on a diet of low nutritional value, rather than selectively on items of high nutritional value." The specimens referred to were all collected from Nova Scotia to Cape May, New Jersey, off the bottom in water as deep as 5,000 feet. (*Lipo* means "without," and *genys* is "chin"; *Lipogenys*, therefore, is named for its chinless profile.)

In his introduction to the order Lyomeri (Saccopharyngiformes) in *Fishes of the Western North Atlantic*, James Böhlke wrote that

the deep-sea gulpers are perhaps the most extremely modified species of vertebrates anatomically. . . . In the main [they] grow to about six feet, are black, flabby, bathypelagic fishes with enormous mouths, distensible guts, long tapering tails, and long vertical fins supported by numerous rays. They pass through a typical eel-like leptocephalus stage in their early life history, during which their bodies are deep, laterally compressed, relatively short and transparent—that is, leaf-like. The bones have cells. There are no scales, ventral fins, pelvic girdle, pyloric appendages, or swim bladder.

Ichthyologist Giles Mead observed that "the Order Lyomeri [is] a small group of deep-sea inhabitants so bizarre in form that they bear little resemblance to any other living creature—a tribute to nature's ingenuity in the deep-sea environment." And in the discussion of the relationships of *Eurypharynx* and *Saccopharynx* to other fishes, Böhlke wrote, "The gulpers are so aberrant that they have been treated as a group apart from the bony fishes by several students, especially by Nusbaum-Hilarowicz."*

They are deepwater fishes that are practically all mouth, exemplified by the amazing gulper (or pelican) eel *Eurypharynx pelecanoides,* which is found in all the world's oceans at depths of 6,500 feet or more. At a known maximum length of two feet, a good proportion of which is the whiplike tail, *Eurypharynx* ("wide-gullet") *pelecanoides* looks like a cartoonist's nightmare version of a deep-sea fish. Its "body" consists almost entirely of mouth, and its jaws are loosely hinged and enormously expandable. Despite its fearsome appearance, the pelican eel (which is sometimes known as the "umbrellamouth gulper") is weak-muscled and flabby, and depends on its ability to engulf, rather than to attack, prey items. To do this, it does not swallow them outright, but expands its mouth—probably using water pressure to force it open—and draws itself around the prey until the victim is enclosed in the pouchlike lower jaw (hence the name *pelecanoides*). The eyes of *Eurypharynx* are located at the very anterior point of the head, and they are tiny, about the size of the head of a pin in a ten-inch specimen. The end of the tail is equipped with a luminous lure, but it is difficult to imagine how the fish uses a lure that is so far from its mouth, unless it swims in circles, chasing fishes that are chasing its tail.

Another "gulper" is *Saccopharynx* ("sack-gullet"), larger than the pelican eel but with many of the same components, somewhat differently organized. We see the same underslung jaw, but its proportions are not so exaggerated as in *Eurypharynx*. Both species are black, but whereas *Eurypharynx* has no teeth, *Saccopharynx* has a proper mouthful. Where *Eurypharynx* reaches a length of two feet, six-foot *Saccopharynx* have been collected. And where there

* In 1915, Joseph Nusbaum-Hilarowicz actually proposed that fishes without opercular bones, such as *Saccopharynx* (which he knew as *Gastrostomus bairdii*), be classified as a separate order to be known as "Teleostomi anoperculati."

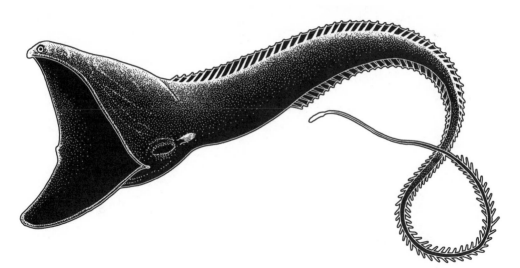

One of the strangest of all deep-sea fishes is the pelican eel, *Eurypharynx pelecanoides*. (It is also known as the "umbrellamouth gulper.") Found at depths of 6,500 feet or more, this two-foot-long fish is almost all mouth. It feeds by expanding its mouth and engulfing its prey, which usually consists of small fishes.

is but a single species of *Eurypharynx*, there may be as many as four of *Saccopharynx*, differentiated by a plenitude of unusual luminous organs.

The type specimen of *Saccopharynx harrisoni* was collected at 900 fathoms (5,400 feet) off Bermuda by Beebe's 1931 expedition. Of the luminous structures of *S. harrisoni*, Beebe wrote that toward the tip of the tail there were thirteen scarlet papillae, six on the dorsal and seven on the ventral profile, and "at an equal distance beyond these begins a most amazing LUMINOUS ORGAN, a leaf-like compressed, almost transparent zone, traversed with a network of large blood vessels," which he described as equipped with purple and scarlet "fingers" that tapered to the end of the tail. This creature, nearly six feet in length and the largest specimen of the genus ever examined, also had a bluish-white bioluminescent trough running along its back from a couple of inches at the head to about two feet from the origin of the tail. When it was examined, this specimen had two large, undigested fish in its stomach, which gave it, according to Beebe, "the shape of an elongate black sausage."

In 1884, Theodore Gill wrote of the saccopharyngoid fishes, "Whether any of the other known types of fishes belong to this order is very doubtful, and, in fact, we have sufficient data respecting them to be tolerably certain that none do." While none of the "known types of fishes" could be assigned to the order, a fish was discovered during the 1920–22 *Dana* expeditions that was

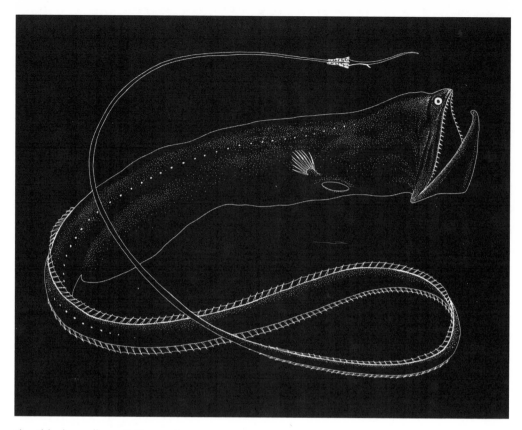

The "black swallower" (*Saccopharynx harrisoni*) grows to a length of six feet, and is therefore considerably more formidable than its only relative, the pelican eel. Also, *Saccopharynx* ("sack-gullet") has a mouthful of teeth.

completely unsuspected, and was indeed aligned with the Saccopharyngids. After four specimens were brought to the deck of the Danish research vessel, Léon Bertin described them in a 1938 paper and erected the genus *Monognathus*. In 1987, Erik Bertelsen and Jørgen Nielsen of the Zoological Museum in Copenhagen examined all the known specimens and produced a monograph on these heretofore unsuspected deep-sea inhabitants. "The monognathids are among the strangest of all fishes," they wrote; "they resemble the other gulpers, particularly *Saccopharynx*, but they lack all trace of an upper jaw and they have no caudal organ." (The other gulpers have a unique luminous organ at the end of the tail.) As of 1987, seventy specimens were known, ranging in size from 1.56 to 6.20 inches.

The name *Monognathus* means "one-jaw," and indeed, these creatures have no upper jaw whatsoever. As part of the skull, however, *Monognathus* has "a fang-like downward projection . . . which is hollow and connected to a pair of glands on each side." It is not known if these glands contain poison, but in their 1989 summary of the species, Bertelsen and his colleagues wrote:

> The method of feeding is unknown, but it seems logical to assume that the rostral fang is involved somehow. An injection of venom could immobilize a shrimp that might otherwise easily escape the grasp of a seemingly feeble predator. How the monognathid finds and captures its prey in the first place is not clear. It is virtually blind, has no lateral line, and only a weakly developed olfactory organ.

Since it is clear that such a helpless creature could not hunt down its prey, perhaps the prey is attracted to the predator. Bertelsen and Nielsen found no indication of luminescence, but they did locate a pair of glands whose purpose is unknown, and suggested that "the prey is lured inside reach of an attack by release of secretions of attractive smell." (To explain away the possibility that such a secretion might attract predators instead of prey to *Monognathus,* the authors opined that another gland might secrete a repellent to ward off an attack.) In the post-metamorphic specimens that were examined, several had entire shrimps in their stomachs, which "appeared to be very close to the maximum capacity of the predator." This led the authors to write, "With the no doubt irreversible degeneration of the lower jaw, the sexually mature *Monognathus* lose the ability to feed and will die after spawning. In other words, they are 'one-time spawners,' and as mentioned above, may be 'one-time feeders' as well."

Monognathus has no common name. Bertelsen and Nielsen list some fourteen more or less similar species, from oceans all over the world, but so little is known about these fishes that the actual number of species is unresolved. Indeed, two specimens are described "that have not even tentatively been referred to as species," because both of them were in such poor condition that the specific characters could not be checked, but it was clear that they did not belong to any of the fourteen known species.*

Is it possible that the monognathids are simply larval forms of *Saccopharynx* or *Eurypharynx*? Bertelsen and Nielsen answered, "All the monognathid specimens are small; most hardly seem more than postlarvae. This would ordinarily raise the suspicion that they are merely postlarval saccopharyngids, but individuals have recently been observed with ripe ovaries

---

* The names of the fourteen species contain a veritable hall of fame of deep-sea ichthyologists and other authorities. The list includes *M. bertini* (for Léon Bertin), *M. bruuni* (for Anton Bruun), *M. herringi* (for Peter Herring), *M. rosenblatti* (for Richard Rosenblatt of Scripps), *M. isaacsi* (for John Isaacs, also of Scripps), *M. nigeli* (for Nigel Merrett), and several others named for scientists associated with these rare creatures: *M. rajui, M. smithi, M. ozawai, M. jesse, M. taningi, M. boehlkei, M. ahlstromi,* and *M. jesperseni.*

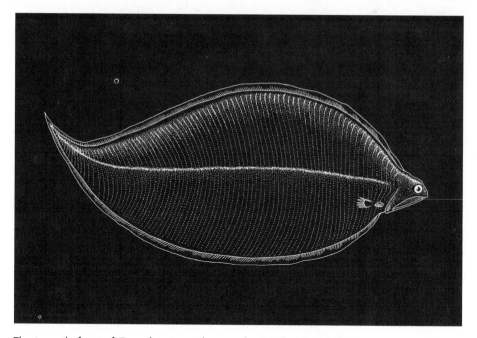

The juvenile form of *Eurypharynx pelecanoides* is a leptocephalus, a tiny, transparent creature that bears hardly any resemblance to the bigmouth gulper it will eventually become.

and testes." Only one "ripe" male has been examined: a 64-mm (2.5-inch) specimen of *M. herringi*. While all the females had an expanded stomach, this male had no abdominal pouch. The head was nearly completely covered by a layer of spongy tissue, "of a remarkably stiff and fragile structure." Probably the most unusual development, however, was the presence of enlarged olfactory organs, which completely covered the side of the head, totally obscuring the tiny eyes. (The highly developed olfactory organs suggest that the males locate prospective mates by smell, and that some of the otherwise unidentified glands in the females might produce specifically characteristic pheromones.) Like their larger relatives, the gulpers, mature individuals of both sexes of *Monognathus* resorb their lower jaws and lose their teeth, suggesting that they will mate and die. Bertelsen and Nielsen have suggested the term "nuptial metamorphosis" to describe the final phase of their lives.

In the North Atlantic there lives a fish so remarkable that its life cycle was unknown for most of recorded history. Although the rivers of Europe teemed with eels (*Anguilla*), their origin remained a mystery. Early observers, such as Aristotle, believed that eels originated in the center of the earth, and Pliny wrote that baby eels came from the sloughed-off skin of adults. Some thought that eels were formed from horsehairs that fell into the water and then

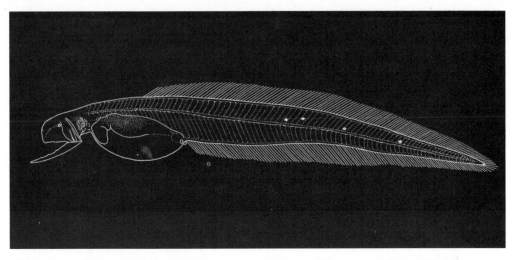

The species of the genus *Monognathus* are among the world's strangest fishes. They are related to the gulper and pelican eels, but they only reach a length of six inches. They have no upper jaws, but they do have a fanglike projection in the roof of the mouth that is believed to be venomous.

came to life. These early mysteries attended *Anguilla* because no reproductive organs could be found in dissected specimens, until a concerted but discontinuous effort across Europe eventually solved the mystery. In 1777, a Bolognese scientist discovered the ovaries, and a hundred years later, a Pole named Syrski found the testes of the male. But since no baby eels (known as elvers) had been identified, their method of propagation remained a mystery. In 1856, the German naturalist Johan Jacob Kaup examined a strange, flattened, leaflike, transparent fish that he named *Leptocephalus brevirostris,* or "short-beaked slender-head." Although it bore little resemblance to the snakelike *Anguilla,* it indeed proved to be the juvenile form of the common eel. As the eel grows older, the leaf shape changes into a narrow, eel-like form, the elver, and it eventually grows into the snakelike adult. The discovery was made in 1904 by two Italians, Giovanni Battista Grassi and Salvatore Calandruccio, who kept the leptocephali in an aquarium and watched them mature and become rounder, change color, and metamorphose into the eels that we are all familiar with. But where this transformation took place in nature still remained a mystery.

From 1905 to 1930, the Danish biologist Johannes Schmidt examined thousands of larval eels, most of which he collected by towing nets all over the Atlantic, in a massive attempt to solve the mystery. He recognized that the species dispersed itself transatlantically, and that the European eel (*Anguilla anguilla*) and the American eel (*A. rostrata*) both breed in the deep water at the northern edge of the Sargasso Sea, and then (no one knows how they decide which way to go), they head for Europe or America. (There are minor differences between the species, but some ichthyologists still believe that there is only a single species.) Both species—if indeed they are distinct—utilize the Gulf Stream to reach their goal, but while the American form spends one year at sea before it arrives off the American coast, the European version takes three years to make its journey. Upon reaching their mystifyingly programmed destinations, the elvers head for the same area their parents inhabited, often swimming upstream or, in some instances, wriggling across land to get to the fresh water in which they will spend their adult lives. After their first summer in fresh water, the elvers acquire the pigmentation—dark backs and greenish-yellow undersides—that gives them the name of "yellow eels," and after another six or seven years, they mature into "silver eels," with a more streamlined head, and eyes that grow to twice their previous size. Some signal then tells them that it is time to head back to the sea, so the eels swim downstream to the Atlantic, heading for the Sargasso Sea.

In the depths of the sea, each female lays as many as 20 million eggs, which are fertilized by the males. Upon spawning, males and females die. The eggs float upward and hatch into leptocephali, which drift and then swim the ocean currents, each population heading for its "home" in Europe or America. The journey of the eels is comparable to the migration of the salmon, but it is performed in reverse. Salmon are characterized as "anadromous," which means that they grow up in salt water and spawn in fresh, while the salt-to-fresh-water spawning pattern identifies the eels as "catadromous." Even though millions of mature eels migrate to the Sargasso in the autumn, not one has ever been observed making the passage, and even more surprising, not one individual has ever been caught there. The Sargasso Sea breeding ground is only conjectural, since neither eggs nor adult eels have been collected from that region. It has been suggested that they inhabit mid-water or even bottom water as they begin their migration. Moreover, because the Sargasso is remarkably devoid of endemic species, it is rarely fished. (Not much meat on a four-inch sargassum fish.) Eels are not a particularly popular food in America, so their arrival in American waters goes largely unnoticed, but they are among the most widely consumed of all food fishes in Europe, and upon their return to Continental streams and rivers, they are fished by the ton.

There is no way of knowing *why* eels make the epic journey to the Sargasso Sea, or Tongue of the Ocean (a deep-sea trough in the Bahamas), and thence to their Continental destinations, but, according to Teal, there are those who believe that their spawning behavior might be related to the widening gap between the continents. Perhaps the eels bred between what would come to be known as North America and Africa, and even as the spreading sea floor pushed the continents farther and farther apart, the eels instinctively retained their traditional breeding site.

In 1977, researchers aboard the submersible *Alvin,* diving to 2,000 meters in Tongue of the Ocean saw and photographed through the porthole an adult eel of the genus *Anguilla.* The eel was a healthy female, identifiably swollen with eggs, but what she was doing at that depth in that location is a mystery. According to the authors, "The supposed spawning depth for *Anguilla* in the Sargasso Sea is 400 to 700 meters in midwater. Hence the discovery of a mature or near mature *Anguilla* on the bottom deeper than 2,000m is in itself a surprise," but ". . . it creates new rather than solving old problems" (Robins, Cohen, and Robins 1979).

Snipe eels (Nemichthyidae) pass through a leptocephalus phase and are therefore true eels, but while the common eels have a blunt, rounded head, and the morays have those ferociously fanged jaws, snipe eels have beaklike upper and lower jaws, rather like those of a bird.* Unlike their avian namesakes, however, they cannot close their mouths, because the upper jaw curves upward and the lower curves downward. The inability to close its mouth would seem to present a problem for the fish, and although shrimps and other small crustaceans have been identified from the stomachs of these attenuated creatures, how they got there has been a subject of much debate. (Of the avocet eel *Labichthys carinatus,* Beebe wrote, "The slenderness of the jaws of this eel seems beyond all usefulness.")

During research dives in the *Alvin* in the western North Atlantic, Giles Mead and Sylvia Earle (1970) saw snipe eels below 300 meters, hanging vertically with their divergent jaws directed upward. (When photographer Ron Church descended into the Gulf of Mexico in the Cousteau submersible *Deepstar-4000,* he saw and photographed snipe eels swimming vertically, but head down.) Although they did not observe the eels feeding, Mead and Earle suggested that "these animals feed by entanglement," meaning that their jaws, studded with tiny, backward-pointing teeth, snag the long, threadlike antennae of passing crustaceans, whose struggles only serve to entrap them more securely, until they can be brought to the rear of the jaw for crushing and swallowing. "Assuming that the eel can disentangle the shrimp sufficiently to swallow it," wrote Nielsen and Smith (1978), "this theory is certainly plausible.

* Snipe are birds of the order Scolopacidae (hence *scolopaceus* for the snipe eel), related to sandpipers and woodcock. Another bird-named deep-sea eel is the avocet eel, *Avocettina* spp., which, like the bird, has particularly exaggerated mandibles, but whereas those of the fish diverge at the tips, those of the bird—whose charmingly descriptive scientific name is *Recurvirostra avosetta*—both curve upward, and the bird can close its mouth.

The snipe eel *Nemichthys scolopaceus* can reach a length of almost five feet. How this fish feeds with an upper and lower jaw that do not meet is not obvious—except perhaps to the fish. (One theory holds that the antennae of shrimps are entangled in the jaws, which are studded with tiny teeth.)

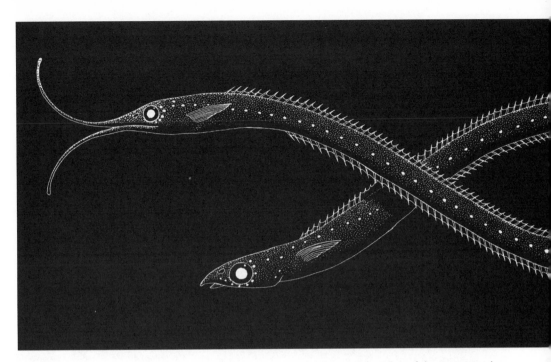

In a more general sense, though, the jaws seem well adapted for grasping and swallowing any large object." It might simply be the case that the widely separated mandibles give *Nemichthys* a much greater chance to snag a passing crustacean.

Males and females of the avocet eel (*Avocettina infans*) look like different species. Females have the jaws that are responsible for the fish's common name, but when the males reach maturity, their beaks disappear and their eyes become larger.

To achieve their great length, snipe eels have developed an increased number of vertebrae, rather than an increased length of each. A specimen of the cosmopolitan species *Nemichthys scolopaceus,* taken in the Indian Ocean, had 670 vertebrae—more than any other vertebrate. (*Nema* is "thread" in Greek, and therefore *Nemichthys* is "thread-fish," referring to the long, thin body.) This species is the longest of the snipe eels and can reach a length of 57 inches. Perhaps the most startling aspect of the biology of these remarkable creatures is the difference between males and females. This sexual dimorphism is manifest in mature males: when they reach sexual maturity, "the characteristic beak disappears and the teeth are lost. The anterior nostrils enlarge into forwardly directed tubes, the pectoral fin is displaced posteriorly, the eyes enlarge, and the color darkens" (Smith and Nielsen 1986). The differences were so great that early authors classified males and females in different genera, and even in separate families. As with the anglerfishes, where males and females are also dramatically dimorphic (and were originally classified as different species), there is probably a biological reason for the differences. In their discussion of the Nemichthyidae, Smith and Nielsen suggest that the degenerative nature of the changes (in the males) indicate that snipe eels die after spawning.

There is a related species that looks like a six-inch-long dart, also with long jaws that do not close. According to D. G. Smith (1989b), *Cyema atrum* "appears to be the deepest living of all pelagic eels," and has been collected from depths in excess of 1,500 meters. It has hardly any tail, and therefore Beebe called *Cyema atrum* the "tailless eel"; others refer to it as the "bobtail snipe eel" or "arrow eel." *Cyema* is Greek for "embryo," perhaps referring to its unfinished appearance, and *atrum* is from the Latin *ater,* which means "black," the color of the adult *Cyema.*

The synaphobranchids (*synaphe* means "joined" or "united"; *branchia* are gills), or "cutthroat eels," are dark-colored anguilliform fishes with tiny (but visible) scales, and jaws that look much more like those of other fishes. They are worldwide in distribution, and are "among the most numerous and most frequently

Variously called "bobtail snipe eel," "arrow eel," or "dart eel," *Cyema atrum* is a six-inch version of the much larger *Nemichthys,* but without the attenuated body and tail. It is worldwide in distribution, and is usually found at depths of 2,000 feet or more.

collected of the deep benthic fishes" (Robins and Robins 1989). The adults range in size from 20 to 40 inches. The leptocephali are distinguished from those of other eels by their telescopic eyes. They are exclusively deepwater species; as a rule, they live in waters that are 1,000 meters deep or more.* From the occasional captures in trawls, the species known to inhabit the North Atlantic are *Synaphobranchus kaupi* and *S. infernalis,* generally similar but differentiated by the number of vertebrae and dorsal spines. Their jaws are lined with small teeth, and there is another row of teeth on the vomer, a bone on the roof of the mouth. (A similar species is known as *Serrivomer,* the sawtooth snipe eel, with bladelike teeth on the vomer.) Because of their deepwater habitat, little of their natural history is known, although like other eels, they have a particularly well-developed sense of smell. Anton Bruun (1937) wrote that S.

* A synaphobranchid eel (identified as *Histiobranchus*) was photographed at Tongue of the Ocean at 2,837 meters (9,305 feet), and in *The Guinness Book of Animal Facts and Feats,* editor Gerald Wood writes, "There is a record of a deep-sea eel (family *Synaphobranchus*) in a state of metamorphosis being taken at a depth of 4040m (13,255 ft) in the Indian Ocean," but provides no source for this information.

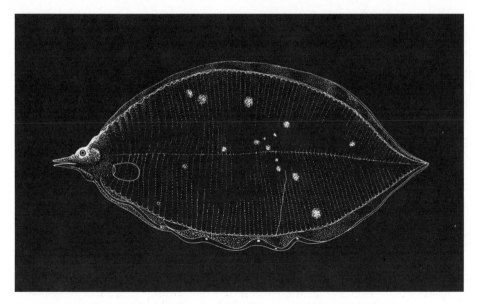

The juvenile form of the bobtail snipe eel (*Cyema atrum*) is a leaf-shaped leptocephalus about two inches long. One of the characteristics of eels is that they pass through a leptocephalus ("narrow-head") stage before assuming their attenuated form.

kaupi spawns in the Sargasso Sea, and the leptocephali drift at depths of 100 to 300 meters for eighteen to twenty-two months before metamorphosis. Recent underwater photographs have shown that these fishes swim just above the ocean floor.

D. M. Cohen (1964) called the Opisthoproctidae "the most specialized members of their suborder and . . . among the most bizarre of all teleost fishes." Some of them are compressed like hatchetfishes, but with upward-pointing tubular eyes. Members of the genus *Opisthoproctus* have a large anal light gland in which there are luminous bacteria. (*Opisthoproctus* means "behind the anus.") The ventral surface of this two-inch fish is flattened into a "sole," not unlike that of an old-fashioned steam iron, giving the fish a triangular shape in cross section. Light is transmitted from the anal gland to special cells in the "sole," giving this fish a luminescent base that cannot be seen from the side or from above. The relationship between upward-pointing eyes and a luminous ventral surface is not obvious, but it might be a way to maintain coherence in a group; the lowermost fishes recognize the illuminated flattened underbellies of their conspecifics above them.

The spookfishes or barreleyes (*Dolichopteryx*) are elongated, large-headed creatures with button eyes pointing upward but lacking the luminous

The ventral surface of the telescope-eyed, upward-gazing *Opisthoproctus grimaldii* is flattened like a steam iron and equipped with light organs. This allows the two-inch fish to cast a light downward, visible only to creatures underneath it—such as other upward-looking members of its own species.

sole of the other opisthoproctids. The genus *Dolichopteryx* is represented by three species: *D. longipes, D. brachyrhynchus,* and one discovered by Beebe in Bermuda waters in 1931, *D. binocularis. Dolichopteryx* means "bean-shaped eyes" (*dolichos* is "long," and also "kidney bean" in Greek), and it perfectly describes the optical equipment of these four-inch fishes. Their pealike eyes stare straight upward, looking for tiny animals on which to feed. On the supporting tube of each eye is a laterally facing photophore that may direct light to the eye, since these fishes live where there is little ambient light, at depths of 500 to 2,000 meters.*

The slickheads are so named because their heads are devoid of scales. (Their scientific name, *Alepocephalus,* means "head without scales.") Somewhat resembling the tube-shoulders (to which they are related, as well as to the salmons, trouts, and herrings), the slickheads are among the few soft-rayed fishes inhabiting the depths. (Most other deep-sea fishes are spiny-rayed.) Known only from deep-sea trawls, the alepocephalids are found at depths of 2,000 meters or more. An abyssal Atlantic species known as *Rinoctes nasutus* has been described as "scaleless and almost devoid of pigment" (Markle and

---

* In their 1968 book, Fitch and Lavenberg reported that "recently it was found that the barreleye and its family relatives (Opisthoproctidae) have two pairs of eyes—a large pair of telescopic eyes believed to function as light gatherers, and a small eye at the base of each large eye which probably focuses the image gathered by the large eye. Prior to this discovery the small eye was thought to be an orbital photophore."

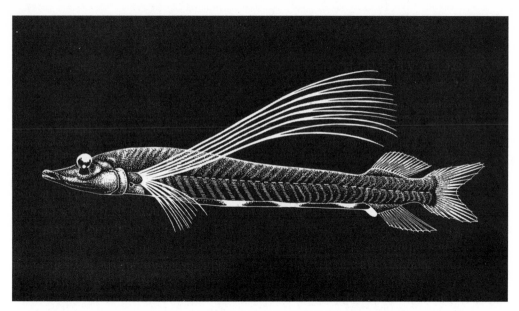

The four-inch spookfish or barreleye (*Dolichopteryx* spp.) has pealike eyes that stare straight upward. On the supporting tube of each eye is a light-producing photophore that may direct light into the eye, since there is little ambient light at depths of 500 to 2,000 meters.

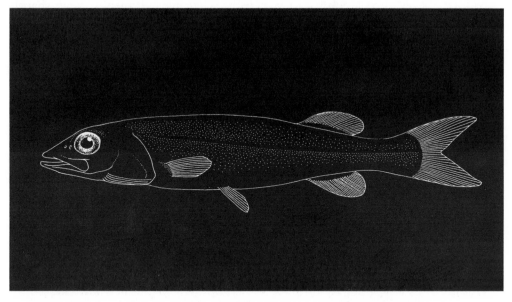

The slickheads are so named because their heads are devoid of scales. (Their scientific name, *Alepocephalus,* means "head without scales.") Known only from deep-sea trawls, the alepocephalids are found at depths of 2,000 meters or more.

Unlike the branchiostegal rays of other fishes, which are concealed by the gill covers, those of the bonythroat (*Bathylaco nigricans*) are fully exposed and account for its common name. *Bathylaco* means "deep hole," and *nigricans* means "blackish," a perfect description of the fish and its habitat.

Merrett 1980), but *Asquamiceps caeruleus,* collected from 2,000 meters deep in the Atlantic, has a black body and a "striking cobalt blue head" (Markle 1980).

Another alepocephalid subfamily includes the fishes known as "bonythroats," or technically, as bathylaconids. In the bonythroats, the branchiostegal bones, usually covered by the operculum or gill cover, have become platelike, and form part of the upper gill covers. *Bathylaco nigricans* is found in tropical and subtropical waters of the world's oceans, at depths of up to 2,000 meters. (*Bathylaco* means "deep hole," probably referring to the depths from which they have been collected, and *nigricans* means "blackish.") Specimens were discovered in the stomach contents of two cutlass fish (*Aphanopus carbo*) caught on a hook and line at about 1,000 meters off Madeira. A. E. Parr's 1948 description of *Bathylaco* identified a "comma-shaped preorbital luminous organ" forward of the eye, but later examination (Munk 1968) showed that this was merely whitish connective tissue, and that the species had no luminescent organs.

In 1951, A. E. Parr of the American Museum of Natural History in New York revised the family Alepocephalidae and introduced a new family which he called Searsiidae. As defined by Parr, the Searsiidae are distinguished by the presence of a shoulder organ, consisting of a "quite large sac underneath the skin" and an external tube through which the contents of the sac can be discharged. The shoulder organ is responsible for the common name "tube-shoulders," and these black fishes, usually less than a foot in length, are the only ones capable of excreting a luminous fluid, perhaps to distract predators at the moment of attack. (The squid *Heteroteuthis dispar* has the same unusual ability.) Many of the tube-shoulders, such as *Searsia koefoedi,* also have ventrally placed light organs.

Smelts are related to trout, salmon, and graylings, and, like them, have a small fin, known as the adipose fin, between the dorsal fin and the tail. Most of these fishes (all of which belong to the order Salmoniformes) are shallow-water species, but there is a family of deep-sea smelts known as the Bathylagidae. They are worldwide in distribution, represented in the deep Atlantic by *Bathylagus compsus, B. longirostris, B. bericoides, B. greyae,* and *B. euryops,* ranging in size from four to eight inches. (*Bathys,* of course, is "deep," and *lagos* is "hare" or "rabbit," making these fishes "deepwater rabbits," perhaps an allusion to their small mouths.) They have not been extensively studied, because they are not well represented in deepwater trawls. Their eyes are proportionally large (*euryops* means "big-eyes"), suggesting a deepwater environment, and those that have been collected have come from the surface down to 2,000 fathoms.

There is a group of small fishes that have protruding eyes that always face upward, so they are always staring at the surface—or at least in that direction. These are the hatchetfishes, named for their deep, laterally compressed bodies, which resemble the head of an ax. The best-known of these wondrous little creatures (rarely reaching a length of four inches) are those of

Of all the bioluminescent deep-sea creatures, only the squid *Heteroteuthis dispar* and the tube-shoulders, such as this *Searsia koefoedi,* are capable of emitting a glowing cloud into the water to distract predators.

The scientific name of this deep-sea smelt—*Bathylagus euryops*—can be translated as "deep-sea rabbit with big eyes," which refers to its habitat, and perhaps to its dentition.

the genus *Argyropelecus* (*argyros* is "silver"; *pelekys* is "ax" or "hatchet"). Paul Zahl photographed them for a 1954 *National Geographic* article, assuring that millions of people who had never heard of *Argyropelecus* (and probably couldn't pronounce it if they had) would now know what it looked like. Their bodies are silver and virtually scaleless, and the heads proportionally huge. The mouth is large, presumably to enable them to engulf their known prey items of copepods and small fishes, which they locate by using upwardly directed binocular vision. The various species can be distinguished by the arrangement of the abdominal photophores, which in some species form a continuous band of lights on the belly, while in others they are broken up into distinct groups. The silver hatchetfish was one of Beebe's favorites; he used a color painting of it as the frontispiece for *Half Mile Down*. In an article about the 1930 Bermuda expedition, he described one of the more familiar species thus: "A common but very marvelous inhabitant of the deep sea, *Argyropelecus hemigymnus,* the Silver Hatchet Fish, with its telescope eyes looking forever upward and the group of mauve and violet lights glowing downward. Although living in almost absolute darkness, its body is a mass of iridescent silver."

A spectacular fish whose picture appears regularly in books of deep-sea predators is *Chauliodus*, a diminutive creature of terrifying appearance with needle-like fangs so long that they do not fit in its mouth but project out of and above the lower jaw as far as the eyes. These photographs invariably show a museum specimen; the living *Chauliodus* has not been photographed. A typical species is the 10-inch *C. sloani,* which has been collected in the North Atlantic, the Mediterranean, the Caribbean, and the Gulf of Mexico. Commonly known as the viperfish, *Chauliodus* is well endowed with photophores—on its face, fins, spines, and serially along the ventral surface, as with the stomiatids. The first dorsal fin ray is greatly elongated and equipped with a luminous organ (although Morrow only says that it is "said to bear a light organ"), presumably to lure prey fishes toward its mouth. In *The Life of Fishes,* N. B. Marshall writes that *Chauliodus* has "a very long dorsal ray which bears a luminous tip," and then quotes a Dr. Peres who saw one from a bathyscaph off Portugal, "hovering head upwards, the long axis of its body making an angle of about 45° to the horizontal plane. The whiplike dorsal ray was inclined forwards so that the tip dangled in front of the mouth. Here, surely, is good circumstantial evidence for deep-sea angling."

Eight species of the genus *Chauliodus* are found throughout the world's oceans, preferring to lurk around depths of 8,000 feet during the day and ascend toward the surface at night, when the feeding is better. As with most

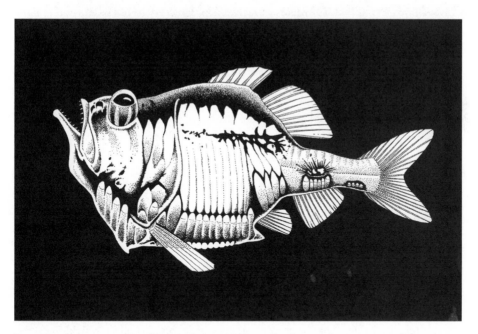

Because it was one of his favorite fishes, William Beebe used a painting of the silver hatchetfish (*Argyropelecus hemigymnus*) as the frontispiece for *Half Mile Down,* his 1930 account of the Bermuda deep-sea expedition.

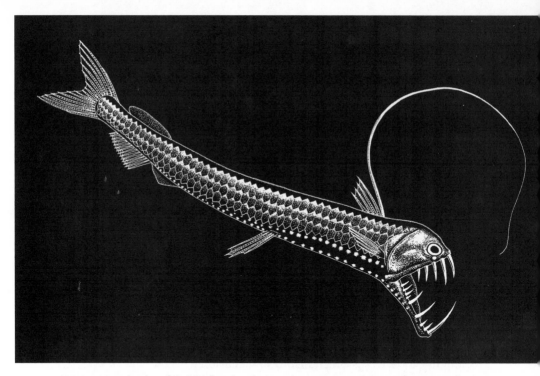

Hovering at depths of 8,000 feet by day, and rising toward the surface at night, the viperfish *Chauliodus sloani* is a consummate predator, able to throw its head upward and backward, and its lower jaw downward, in order to capture fishes larger than it is.

deep-sea predators, actual feeding has not been observed, but the exaggerated dentary equipment of these fishes has prompted Morrow (1964) to speculate that

> in order to ingest larger animals, *Chauliodus* must throw its head upward and backward and its lower jaw downward and forward, forming an angle of 90° or more between the upper and lower jaws. . . . Evidently the process of swallowing large prey is not an easy one, for the heart, ventral aorta, and branchial arches are moved briskly backward, downward, forward, and upward for a considerable distance in quick succession, and the gills are pulled downward and backward. It is likely that when *Chauliodus* swallows large prey its blood circulation and respiration become seriously upset. This extreme exertion suggests that large prey is not swallowed often, and that, when it is, the process is accomplished as quickly as possible.

THE SWALLOWERS

Few fishes can be designated exclusively as either a predator or a prey species, since in almost all cases, there will be a larger fish to prey on a smaller one. (There are some species that eat only plant matter or detritus, and therefore cannot accurately be called predators.) Even though they may sometimes be eaten by larger fishes, the stomiatids fulfill all of the requirements for a successful predatory life in the depths. They are terrifying in aspect, but diminutive in stature. In *Abyss*, C. P. Idyll offers a general description of the group:

> The mouth is deeply slashed into the big head, carrying the jaws far back and permitting the same kind of prodigious gape that we saw in the gulpers and the angler fish. Matching this capacity to open very wide, the jaws are equipped with strong muscles, giving them a vicious snap and bite, and the ability to hold tightly to any animal seized. The teeth are unequal in length, many of them are fearsome and the greatest of them are cruel-looking barbed fangs.

Sometimes known as dragonfishes or, occasionally, viperfishes, the stomiatids (*stoma* means "mouth") are usually black in color, with parallel rows of photophores along the ventral surface. In most species, the males have a luminous organ on the head behind the eye, known to ichthyologists as the "postorbital photophore." These little demons of the twilight zone are usually characterized by a large head armed with a formidable mouthful of sharp teeth that can accurately be described as fangs, wispy pectoral fins, and a dorsal and anal fin placed far back, almost next to the tiny tail. In addition to a fringed chin barbel, the monotypical genus *Chirostomias* has pectoral fins that terminate in fringes.* In the suborder Stomiatoidae there are six families and dozens of species, all of which have some sort of barbel attached to the chin, but these barbels differ widely and their design can be used to differentiate the species.

Consider the eight-inch-long *Grammatostomias flagellibarba*, a black fish with two rows of luminous organs along its lower flanks and a barbel that can be more than six feet long; or the marvelously named *Ultimostomias mirabilis*, a fish that only reaches a length of two inches but has a barbel ten times its body length. In these two extreme cases, the barbel is unadorned, but there

---

* In a wonderful example of descriptive nomenclature, the species is named *Chirostomias pliopterus*. *Chiro* is Greek for "hand," and *pliopterus* means "many-wings." Thus, *Chirostomias pliopterus* can be (loosely) translated as "stomiatid with many-winged hands," a direct reference to the unusual pectorals.

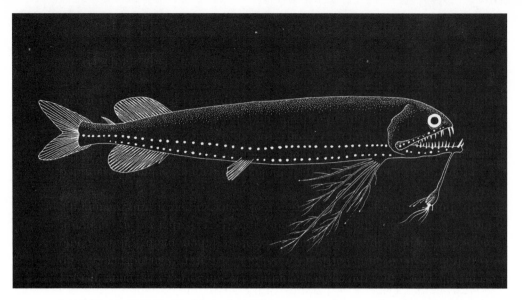

In addition to its fringed chin barbel, *Chirostomias pliopterus* has fringed pectoral fins. Its scientific name can be translated as "stomiatid with many-winged hands."

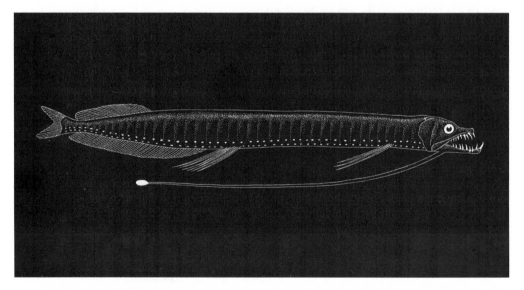

The stomiatids are sometimes known as dragonfishes or viperfishes, for obvious reasons. Shown here is *Eustomias longibarba,* a foot-long fish with a luminescent lure at the end of its chin barbel and a double row of photophores along its flanks.

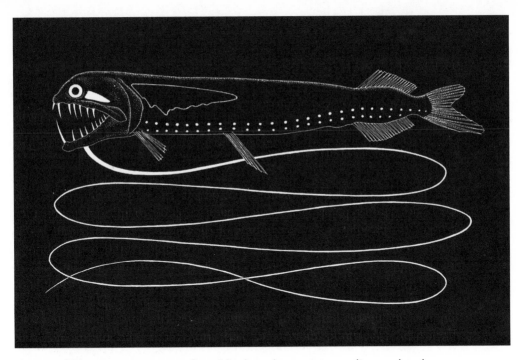

The incredible *Grammatostomias flagellibarba*, whose name can be translated as "lined stomiatid with a whip-barbel," is only six inches long, but the barbel can be six *feet* in length. The function of such a device is unknown.

are many species that have a luminous organ at the tip, and still others in which the barbel consists of a complicated collection of branches, filaments, and bulbs, as if the tiny fish had a miniature root system dangling from its chin. *Grammatostomias* ("lined stomiatid") is also characterized by a jagged loop of luminous tissue on the side of the body that glows blue-violet. In the various stomiatids, the bulbs may be pink, blue, violet, green, or yellow, and the serial photophores are purple. Not only do the barbels vary from species to species, they also vary between the sexes in the same species. The most populous genus is *Eustomias,* which at present contains some thirty-seven species, with the likelihood that more will turn up.

Adult specimens of *Eustomias* are unusual enough, with their luminous chin barbels, ferocious fangs, and dense black coloration, but the larval forms are so bizarre that a verbal description cannot possibly do them justice. They look nothing like the adult forms—in fact, these half-inch-long creatures do not resemble real fishes at all, but rather cartoons. Despite the inadequacies of the descriptive process, Beebe and Jocelyn Crane gave it a go in the interests of science: "The larvae of *Eustomias* are very distinct," they wrote, "bear-

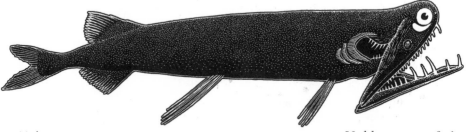

Looking for all the world like a badly drawn cartoon fish, the juvenile form of *Eustomias* has a flattened head with pop eyes and a tiny mouth.
At maturity, however, it will become a fiercely fanged, light-bedecked dragonfish.

ing a close resemblance to those of *Idiacanthus*, except that the eyes are not stalked and the pigment spots are fewer. . . . The snout is long and flattened, with a small terminal mouth; the head is correspondingly large; the fin-folds are small, and the gut is longer than usual, extending beyond the caudal fin when unbroken."

Distantly related to the stomiatids is *Malacosteus niger*, commonly known as the black loose-jaw or the rat-trap fish. At first glance, it looks more or less like the stomiatids, with a large head, a photophore under each eye, and small fins, but a closer examination reveals that there is no floor to its mouth. The lower jaw of this four- to six-inch creature is attached only at the hinge and by a modified tongue-bone, and since the open structure of the jaws eliminates water resistance, the "trap" can be sprung with great speed to engulf the prey. (Smaller fishes can probably escape through the trap mechanism, but larger animals have little chance, and therefore, this little predator probably feeds on fishes as large or larger than itself.)

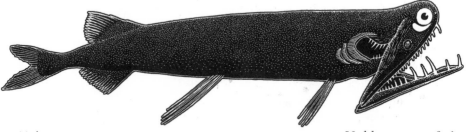

Malacosteus niger is commonly known as the "rat-trap fish" because of the unusual structure of its jaws. The mouth has no floor and can be sprung open to engulf prey items. The trap mechanism is believed to eliminate water resistance.

Unlike some of the stomiatids, *Malacosteus* does not have particularly large teeth, presumably because its jaw mechanism efficiently traps prey items without having to hold them with piercing fangs. *Malacosteus* has no serial photophores on

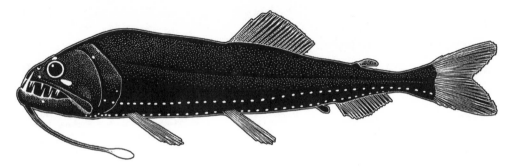

Commonly known as the "snaggle-tooth"—for obvious reasons—*Astronesthes niger* reaches a length of only four inches. Although it is equipped with two rows of photophores, this species can luminesce from its fins, back, and barbel.

its scaleless skin, but the comma-shaped light organ under the eye is red, an uncommon color for photophores, and below it is a bioluminescent green cheek organ.

Another genus of stomiatids is *Astronesthes,* commonly (and obviously) known as "snaggletooths." (Also included in this family are the genera *Borostomias, Diplolychnus,* and *Neonesthes.*) They are small, scaleless fishes, reaching a maximum length of about one foot. Found around the world at depths down to 3,000 feet, they often come near the surface at night. Most species have a barbel under the chin and a double row of photophores along the flanks and belly, but, according to R. H. Gibbs (1964), *Astronesthes niger,* the only species restricted to the Atlantic, is "apparently the only astronesthid on which observations of luminescence have been made." (*Astronesthes* means "covered in stars.") When captured specimens were manually stimulated by poking or shaking, the photophores did not luminesce, but rather, "all the fins light up, as does the entire barbel, and often the predorsal part of the back."

The adult form of *Idiacanthus* looks not unlike many of the other stomiatids; it is a long, thin, black fish with two rows of photophores and a chin barbel. As soon as we examine the sexes, however, things begin to look a little unusual, since the females are different in many particulars from the males. For one thing, they are larger: the largest known female measured a little over a foot in length; the largest male, a little over an inch and three-quarters. The males appear not to develop fully, since even when they are known to be sexually mature, they do not have a chin barbel; they have no teeth; and their digestive system is degenerate. Most of the body cavity is occupied by the testes, suggesting that the male *Idiacanthus* exists primarily to fertilize the female. Males are brown, females are black, and the colorless larvae are so different from their parents—or from any other fish, for that

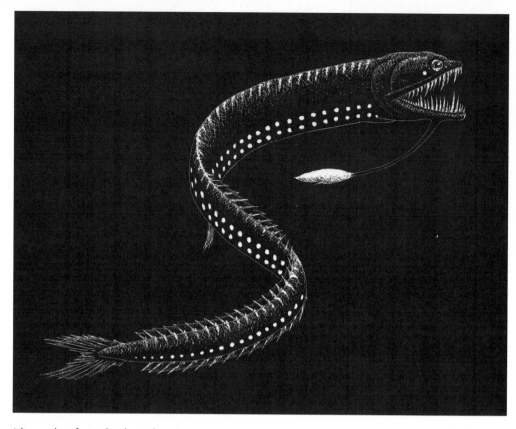

Idiacanthus fasciola, the "gleaming-tailed sea dragon." This is a female, approximately 12 inches long. Adult males have no teeth and no chin barbel, and only get to be about 2 inches long. Because most of the body cavity is occupied by the testes, it is believed that the males exist primarily to fertilize the females.

matter—that when they were discovered, they were thought to be a distinct species.

The first juvenile specimens were called *Stylophthalmus paradoxus,* a name that does a good job of describing the larval form. *Stylos* means "pillar," and of course, *ophthalmus* means "eye"; *paradoxus* is self-explanatory. In its early stages, the larval *Idiacanthus* is a tiny, transparent wisp of a fish, with a curious, spatulate head and eyes on long cartilaginous stalks, which can be a quarter of the length of the body. The eyes seem to be functional, since the muscle fibers and the optic nerve run the length of the stalk. It may even be that this miniature fish can turn its eyes in different directions to help it gather light. As it matures, the young *Idiacanthus* descends to greater depths, and the eye stalks begin to draw in. Even though the stalks are no longer needed, they do not disappear, but rather become knotted into capsules that remain embedded in the fish's head, just forward of where the eye ends up. The head

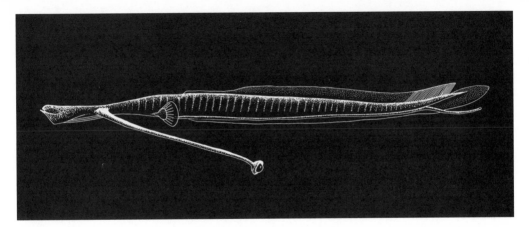

The half-inch larval form of *Idiacanthus* is so unlike the adult that it was originally believed to be a different species. Because its eyes are on long stalks, it was called *Stylophthalmus paradoxus,* the "stalk-eyed paradox."

and snout become proportionally shorter, and if the fish is a female, it develops pigmentation and grows larger. If it is a male, it grows very little, perhaps doubling its larval size. (The female increases her length tenfold.) Finally, the males develop the postorbital photophore, which may be as large as the eye itself.*

THE AULOPIFORMES[†]

In the *Challenger*'s trawls, there appeared several strange-looking fishes with extremely long fin rays. In the *Challenger Reports,* Sir John Murray wrote, "When taken from the trawl they were always dead, and the long pectoral rays were erected like an arch over the head, requiring considerable pressure to make them lie along the side of the body." It looked as if these fishes were

---

* In *Half Mile Down,* Beebe described the bathysphere's encounter with *Stylophthalmus:* "When we were both looking out, he [Otis Barton] saw the first living *Stylophthalmus* ever seen by man, which completely escaped me, although it must have been within a foot of the windows. This is one of the most remarkable of deep-sea fish, with the eyes on the ends of long, periscope stalks, almost one-third as long as the entire body. My missing the fish was all the more disappointing because I had recently been thoroughly studying these strange beings, and in fact had abolished their entire family, after proving that they were the larvae of the golden-tailed serpent dragons, *Idiacanthus.*"

† The Aulopiformes are named for the genus *Aulopus,* also known as "thread-sail fishes" (Herald 1961). *Aulopus* is a mid-water inhabitant that looks like a lizard fish, and the other genera in the order may have an adipose fin, but many of them do not. What characterizes the Aulopiformes? An anatomical modification of the second and third gill arches, described by Nelson (1993) as "second pharyngobranchial greatly elongated posteriorly, extending away from third pharyngobranchial, with uncinate process of second epibranchial contacting third pharyngobranchial."

equipped with specially adapted fin rays that they might use to probe the mud for food, and while this would have been a unique adaptation, the solution was not quite correct. The real reason for the long spines was much more unusual, but it would not be revealed until the "ray-fins" were observed and photographed at the bottom of the sea.

These remarkable fishes came to be known as bathypteroids, an obvious reference to the exaggerated pectoral fins. (In Greek, *bathys* means "deep," and *pteron* is "wing.") In the photographs, living *Bathypterois* are seen perched high off the bottom on stilts composed of one ray from each of the ventral fins, and one from the tail fin—hence the common name "tripod fish." The long pectoral fins are raised high and curved forward over the head. Histological examination of the fin rays of the pectorals has shown that they contain enlarged nerves and may therefore be used as sensors to detect the floating, microscopic plankton upon which the fish feeds (Sulak 1977a). But we don't know exactly how they feed, since none of the photographs show the fish with their mouths open. The stiff, elongated rays of the pelvic and caudal fins seem to serve only to elevate the fish above the ocean floor. Because they have only been seen immobile and facing into the current, we do not know if they hop like frogs, walk like storks, or launch themselves off the bottom and swim to their next destination.* From the submersible *Deepstar-4000* in the Gulf of Mexico, Ron Church photographed *Bathypterois* and wrote, "When a meal comes within range, the fish leaps from its three-point stance to snatch it," but we don't know if Church speculated on this behavior or actually witnessed it.

There are eighteen species of bathypteroids, differentiated mainly by the length and arrangement of the elongated pectoral fin spines. In *Bathypterois phenax* the pectoral spines split about halfway along their length; in *B. quadrifilis* they divide almost at the base, producing long, paired spines on each side and accounting for the name, which means "four filaments." The deepest-ranging species is *Bathypterois longipes* (= "long-legs"), found in the Atlantic at depths between 2,500 to 5,600 meters, and *B. bigelowi* has been observed in the Gulf of Mexico between 475 and 1,200 meters.† On a

---

* In one of the very rare eyewitness descriptions of this species (accompanied by a photograph), Lt. Comdr. Georges Houot, aboard the bathyscaph *FNRS-3* in the Mediterranean in 1958, wrote, "I do not wish to take a stand against the biologists who attribute to these filaments a tactile purpose, but I can affirm that the fish use them for supports—as legs! I have never observed them in any other posture than sitting on their three projections. I see them on the bottom, 'legs' wide apart, the head a little higher than the tail, the nose into the current, without moving, like a statuette on a mantelpiece."

† Because of its accessibility, *Bathypterois bigelowi* is the most photographed of the tripod fish. Aboard *Deepstar-4000* at 1,200 meters in the De Soto Canyon (Gulf of Mexico), Ron Church shot an excellent series of photographs of this surprising creature, its piebald coloration sharply vis-

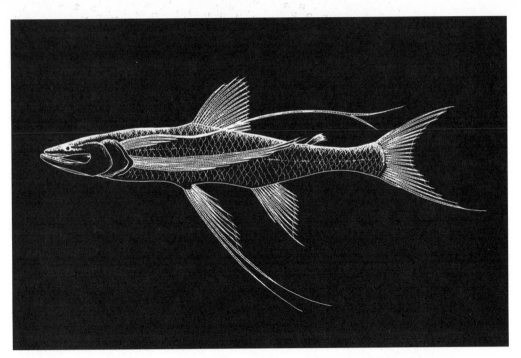

With its long pectoral fins held high and curved forward, the tripod fish (*Bathypterois bigelowi*) raises itself off the bottom on the rays of its ventral fins and its tail fin, waiting for food to drift by on the deepwater currents.

specimen from the Gulf of Mexico, the "landing gear" is almost half again as long as the fish's body, which puts this ten-inch fish more than a foot off the bottom.

In Giles Mead's detailed discussion of the genus (in *Fishes of the Western North Atlantic*), he writes, "Nothing is known of the development or life history of this bizarre species. The function of the greatly prolonged ventral and caudal fin rays has been determined by the use of recent developments in deep-sea photography, for two underwater photographs show this species resting on the ocean floor on the tips of the outer ventral and lower caudal rays, and it is said to hop along the bottom like a cricket." *Bathypterois* has tiny eyes, and even if there were anything to see at 5,000 feet (the average depth of the locations from which it was collected), it could not see it and would have to depend on its sense of smell, its neuromast system, or perhaps the vibrations transmitted along the elongated "antennae" of its fins.

---

ible as it perches high off the bottom on black fins, with its webbed pectorals aloft and arched forward like the wings of a bat. Some of the photographs appear on pp. 109 and 122 of Heezen and Hollister's superb 1971 collection, *The Face of the Deep*. (On p. 120 there are also two photographs of an unidentified bathypteroid deep in Bermuda waters.)

While most fishes have a lateral line system composed of hair-bearing sensory cells (neuromasts) that are sensitive to pressure and movement in the water, in the stygian darkness of the depths, some bathypelagic fishes (such as the bathypteroids) are even more sensitive, and they have neuromasts all over the head and body. Moreover, where the lateralis system of mid-water fishes is usually composed of mucus-filled canals, that of the deepwater fishes is undoubtedly more sensitive, consisting of "free-ending" neuromasts, directly exposed to the water.

Closely related to the tripod fishes is the equally weird *Ipnops murrayi*, first described by John Murray of the *Challenger* from a specimen dredged up from 1,900 fathoms. It is a tubular sort of fish, about six inches long, with a wide spatulate mouth, butterfly fins, and no eyes as we know them. In the *Challenger Reports,* it was described thus: "The structure of the eyes is quite unique. Externally they appear as a continuous, flat, cornea-like organ, longitudinally divided into two halves, which covers the whole of the upper surface of the snout and partly overlies the bone. The functions of this organ are difficult to determine." The difficulty does not inhibit scientists from speculating, however, and opinions have been published which suggest that the organs might be used in the detection of bioluminescent worms, or that the

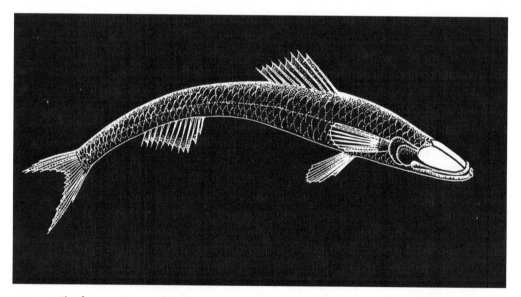

The first specimen of *Ipnops murrayi* was dredged up from 1,900 fathoms (11,400 feet) by the *Challenger* expedition of 1872–76. It has no eyes but rather a continuous, flat, cornea-like organ, divided into two halves, covering the upper surface of the flattened snout. The organ is light-sensitive, which means that *Ipnops* can only distinguish between light and dark.

organs themselves are bioluminescent and serve to attract prey animals which are then snapped up. In his discussion of the Ipnopidae (which include *Bathymicrops* and *Bathytyphlops,* about which more later), G. W. Mead wrote, "A suitably preserved specimen . . . has shown convincingly that the structure is a light-sensitive organ similar to the usual vertebrate eye in its retinal structure. . . ." Even though it looks more like the optical arrangement of an insect than that of a fish, the cephalic organs of *Ipnops* are highly modified light-sensitive structures. They are designed to respond to light, and while they are not exactly eyes, they serve the same purpose, albeit in a limited way.

No one has seen *Ipnops* in its deep-sea habitat, although a rare, robotic-camera photograph appears in Roper and Brundage's 1972 collection of deep benthic photographs. Based on its morphology, N. B. Marshall and Jon C. Staiger (1975) have speculated on its lifestyle. They suggest that since it obviously cannot see very well, and its olfactory sense is also limited, its dominant sense organ must be the lateralis system. "*Ipnops* may well rest on its pelvic and caudal fins," they wrote, "using its all-round system of mixed neuromasts . . . to localize the sources of nearby disturbances in the water. . . ." But in addition to finding food, these sensorily disadvantaged creatures also have to be able to find a mate. If they occur in aggregations, this would be less of a problem, but what if they are solitary? The surprising answer is that they are hermaphroditic, meaning that adults have both male and female organs, combined into the ovotestis. (Another term for animals that are male and female at the same time is "monoecious.") Hermaphroditism is a characteristic of all bathypteroid fishes, but it does not necessarily imply self-fertilization. It means that each fish can function either as a male or a female, as the situation demands, but it also makes clear that we do not know very much about reproduction in the bathypteroids.*

Bathymicrops and *Bathytyphlops* resemble their close relative in general morphology, but whereas *Ipnops* has those cephalic photoreceptors, they have hardly anything at all. "It is difficult to imagine," wrote Giles Mead (in his 1958 description of *Bathytyphlops marionae,* the first species known from the Atlantic), "a free-living fish more degenerate than the species of the genus *Bathytyphlops.*" As befits its name, *Bathymicrops* ("deepwater small-eyes") has minute, vestigial eyes, visible only by dissection, for they are embedded in the

* Many fishes are functionally hermaphroditic, but only one species is known to practice self-fertilization. A species of topminnow (*Rivulus marmoratus*) that lives in brackish water from Florida to the West Indies can produce eggs that it has fertilized itself. In the small sea perch *Serranus subligarius,* every adult bears ripe eggs and sperm, and as observed by Eugenie Clark (1959), each fish can alternately play the male and female roles. *Alepisaurus ferox* (pp. 290–91) is also hermaphroditic.

Bathytyphlops marionae has no common name—and not much else going for it either. It has no eyes (*typhlops* means "blind" in Greek), minute teeth, and ineffectual gill rakers. It is difficult to imagine how such a degenerate creature can earn a living.

head and completely covered by scales. *Bathytyphlops* cannot see (*typhlos* is Greek for "blind"); its teeth are minute denticles; and the gill rakers are also reduced in size, which suggests that it is not a filter feeder. Of these reductions, Mead wrote, "No explanation for these structural losses and modifications has been proposed." (From the Darwinian perspective, every modification must have evolved for a reason, but it is difficult to understand the adaptive value of these degenerate characteristics.)

The greeneyes (Chlorophthalmidae) are foot-long fishes of the deep sea, characterized by large eyes with keyhole-shaped pupils. The eyes include a modification that is extremely rare in bony fishes, a *tapetum lucidum*, which reflects light back to the retina. (It is often present in sharks, and in many mammals [such as cats] and birds [such as owls] that have particularly well-developed night vision. When seen by a human observer, the phenomenon is colloquially known as "eye-shine.") As their name implies, the chlorophthalmids have green eyes, but in his 1979 discussion of the vision of deep-sea fishes, Marshall wrote, "In certain species [of chlorophthalmids] the lenses are yellow. . . . [T]hus their users may well be able to 'see through' the ventral bioluminescent camouflage of euphausiids and prawns." The commonest species in the Atlantic is *Chlorophthalmus agassizi*. (As unpronounceable as its

The greeneye is technically known as *Chlorophthalmus*, from the Greek *chloros*, meaning "green," and *ophthalmus*, meaning "eye." Greeneyes are among the few fishes that have a *tapetum lucidum*, which reflects light back through the retina, creating the phenomenon known (in land animals, like cats) as "eye-shine."

generic name appears, it is simply "greeneye" in Greek: *chloros* is "green," and *ophthalmus* is "eye.")

Small aulopiform fishes with highly descriptive common names are the hammerjaws (Omosudidae) and the sabertooths (Evermanellidae). Both are voracious carnivores, given to attacking and eating fishes that are often larger than they are. (Earl Herald quotes a story of a larval *Omosudis* that swallowed a fish three times longer than it was.) The monotypical *Omosudis lowei* reaches a length of about a foot, and is found in temperate and tropical waters around the world, at depths ranging from 2,500 to 6,000 feet. It looks something like *Evermanella*, but its lower jaw, responsible for its common name, is proportionally larger. There are a half dozen species of *Evermanella*, all about six inches long, but differentiated by the angle of their eyes. One species—called, accurately enough, *Evermanella normalops*—has ordinary-looking eyes, but others have semitelescopic eyes, and *E. indica* has telescopic eyes that stare straight upward.

The fishes known as pearleyes also have tubular eyes, directed upward. The common name, however, is derived not from the shape of the eyes but from the presence of a glistening white spot on the side of each eye. There are some seventeen pearleyes, classified in four genera in the family

Commonly known as the hammerjaw, *Omosudis lowei* is a foot-long predator found around the world at depths ranging from 2,500 to 6,000 feet.

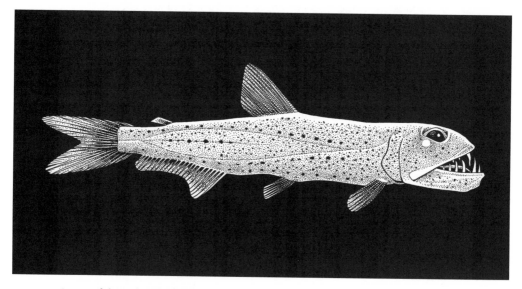

Some of the sabertooths have ordinary-looking eyes (one of them is known as *Evermanella normalops*), but *Evermanella indica* (shown here) has telescopic eyes that stare straight upward.

Scopelarchus of the shining eyes. *S. candelops* is a six-inch bioluminescent fish found in the North Atlantic. Adults are hermaphroditic, which means that they have both male and female sex organs, but do not fertilize themselves.

Scopelarchidae: *Scopelarchus, Benthalbella, Rosenblattichthys,* and *Scopelarchoides*. Because these six-inch fishes are rarely caught in nets, they are poorly represented in ichthyological collections. Found around 1,000 feet down in temperate and tropical oceans around the world, the species best known from the Atlantic is *Scopelarchus candelops*, whose specific name can be translated as "shining eyes." In their 1973 study of a related species (*Benthalbella infans*) from the eastern North Atlantic, Merrett, Badcock, and Herring revealed that *B. infans*—and presumably others of the genus—"is a hermaphrodite with simultaneous maturation of ova and spermatozoa, in common with other alepisaurid fishes." In the same study, this species was also shown to possess bioluminescent organs, a characteristic it shares only with the related genus *Scopelarchoides*.

Commonly referred to as "waryfishes," and sometimes as "paperbones," the scopelosaurids look like tiny barracudas. They are also Aulopiformes, which means that they are related to pearleyes, greeneyes, bathypteroids, and the ocularly deprived *Ipnops*. Also classified as Aulopiformes are the lancet fishes, sabertooths, hammerjaws, and the fantastic giganturids.

In the preternatural world of deep-sea fishes, it is difficult to name the weirdest fish of all. Is it *Ipnops* with platelike eyes, or *Bathypterois* perched on the tips of its stilts? Is it *Lasiognathus* of the fishhooks, or *Saccopharynx,* the degenerate gulper that is almost all mouth? We here introduce *Giganturus,* known variously as the "giant-tailed fish" or the "telescope fish." It is unconventional at both ends, with tubular eyes that point forward (suggesting binocular vision, a most unusual arrangement in fishes) and a tail fin in which the lower lobe is much longer than the upper, another unusual disposition. It reaches a maximum known length of five inches, with the long tail spines almost doubling that. There are two species: *G. chuni,* which is merely elongate, and *G. indica,* which has been described as "very slender." Unlike many deep-sea predators that are black, or at least dull-colored, *Giganturus* is burnished silver, but the gleam does not come from scales, since the genus is scaleless. When Carl Chun described the first specimen (collected on the *Valdivia* expedition of 1888–89), he wrote, "Its wonderful metallic lustre, its large fang-equipped gape, the fantastic elongation of the lower caudal fin rays, and finally, the horizontally-placed, forward-directed telescopic eyes denotes it as one of the most remarkable of the until now known deepsea fishes."

Giganturids (the name means "branched giant," referring to the tail) do not resemble any other species, and taxonomists are uncertain as to where to classify them. In their 1991 review of the family, Johnson and Bertelsen wrote, "Since their discovery in 1901, fishes of the family Giganturidae have constituted an ichthyological mystery. The morphological specializations of this

Giganturus chuni. When Carl Chun described the first specimen (collected on the *Valdivia* expedition of 1888–89), he wrote, "Its wonderful metallic lustre, its large fang-equipped gape, the fantastic elongation of the lower caudal fin rays, and finally, the horizontally-placed, forward-directed telescopic eyes denotes it as one of the most remarkable of the until now known deepsea fishes."

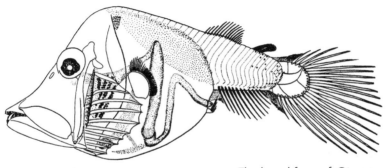

bizarre deepsea group are sufficiently divergent and numerous that their placement in the classification of teleosts has lacked stability. . . . Compounding the mystery was the larval form, *Rosaura rotunda,* described by

The larval form of *Giganturus* is a large-headed, round-bodied little creature that was originally called *Rosaura rotunda.* The chubby little fish looks hardly anything like the whip-thin *Giganturus* of the telescopic eyes. (After Tucker 1954.)

Tucker in 1954, and placed by him in its own monotypic genus and family." It is not surprising that the larval forms and the adults were classified separately; they differ in almost every characteristic. The larval form of *Giganturus* is a large-headed, round-bodied (hence *rotunda*) little creature, less than half an inch long, with a pointed snout and eyes that are laterally directed. (In his 1954 report, Tucker wrote, "Additional characters present in the young *Rosaura rotunda* which will become significant if it can be shown that they are carried through to the adult stage are: the short, stout body; the non-telescopic eyes; the undivided nostrils. . . .") From the catch records, it is known to favor the epipelagic zone, between 30 and 170 meters. Over time, the juvenile becomes transformed into a whip-thin, telescope-eyed predator that migrates to the lightless depths of 1,000 meters or deeper.

Examination of stomach contents has revealed that these miniature monsters attack and consume one large prey animal at a time, an observation borne out by their powerful jaws, curved fangs, and greatly expandable stomach. In one instance (described by C. Tate Regan in 1925), a giganturid measuring 80 mm (3.12 inches) in length had swallowed a *Chauliodus* 140 mm long, almost twice the length of the swallower.* Early writers believed that

---

* Regan wrote, "*Chauliodus* has so formidable a dentition that we cannot imagine a *Gigantura* venturing to attack one face to face, and if it seized one by the tail we should expect the large fish to turn and do the same to its opponent. An examination of the body of the victim enables us to reconstruct the crime. The *Chauliodus* was seized by the middle, and was swallowed double until it reached the posterior end of the stomach, when its head and tail protruded from the mouth of its captor; these were taken in and bent back until the whole fish, now doubly folded, was in the stomach of the Gigantura."

adult giganturids swam horizontally, like most fishes, but the forward-directed tubular eyes, along with the location and orientation of the pectoral fins, and the greatly prolonged tail, suggest that *Giganturus* might swim or hover in a vertical position, the better to pick out their prey silhouetted against the surface illumination.

BRISTLEMOUTHS, LANTERN FISHES, AND THE DSL

Before the advent of deep-sea exploration, the Atlantic herring was considered to be the most numerous fish, but the bristlemouths (Cyclothones) appear to have surpassed them in most population estimates, and they are now considered the most abundant fish in the world; Malcolm Clarke and Peter Herring (1971) wrote that "*Cyclothone* must be the vertebrate genus with the most individuals living." From the portholes of the bathysphere in deep Bermuda waters, William Beebe saw the silvery Cyclothones many times, but while he said that they were "by far the most numerous deep-sea fish in this area, and many were seen on every dive from 400 feet downward," he did not comment on their density. Although they are too small and flabby to be eaten individually by humans, they could be used in processed fish meal or fish pastes to provide protein to the world.*

Adult bristlemouths are equipped with a mouthful of tiny, brushlike teeth on the outer margins of their broadly rounded jaws, presumably to trap minute planktonic organisms on which they feed. (They are also known as "roundmouths.") These three-inch fishes migrate vertically from close to the bottom to close to the surface, some species having been recorded from depths of 2,000 meters or more. They are differentiated from similar species by the round mouth set with tiny teeth, the minuscule eyes, and the diagnostic pattern of photophores on the lower body. In *Fishes of the Western North Atlantic,* eleven species are listed, but the authors wrote, "Because the taxonomy of the genus is in need of revision, it is not possible at the present time [1964] to determine the number of species known in the western Atlantic, nor is it possible to prepare descriptions, or a key to the known species." Some of the species are transparent, while others are almost black, a variation that is related to the depth at which they live: the deeper the water, the darker the coloration. The name

* But, wrote Fitch and Lavenberg, "Before anyone decides to rush out and catch this untapped resource to start feeding the world's protein-starved multitudes, we would like to point out that even though a few kinds of lanternfishes might weigh four ounces each, a dozen other kinds never exceed a quarter of an ounce each when full grown, and a million bristlemouths would not keep a kitten in food for more than a week."

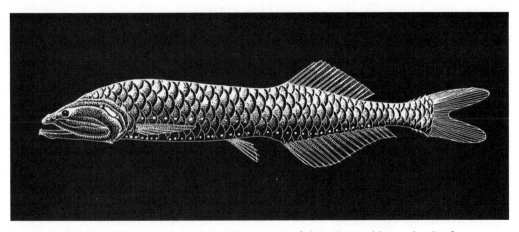

Bristlemouths (*Cyclothone* spp.) are the most numerous fish in the world. In schools of millions, they make daily migrations from the depths to the surface to feed—and to feed almost everything that is larger than a three-inch, quarter-ounce bristlemouth. Their common name is derived from the tiny, brushlike teeth on the outer margins of their rounded jaws, used to trap minute planktonic organisms.

Cyclothone means "circle veil," an apparent allusion to the parchmentlike skin.

Where the bristlemouths occur in vast numbers of only a few species, the lantern fishes, known collectively as myctophids, exist in huge numbers of many different kinds; there are more than 240 species in 30 genera. (The most populous genera are *Diaphus*, with 23 species; *Lampanyctus*, with 13, and *Myctophum* and *Lampadena*, with 6 apiece.) They are all small fishes, ranging in size from two to six inches, with a large head and large eyes. The diagnostic characteristic is the arrangement of fifty to eighty photophores on the head, belly, and sides. Lantern fishes are usually silvery in color, and the photophores emit a startlingly bright blue light, which has been likened to an electric spark. In addition to the photophores, some species have bioluminescent structures on the dorsal and ventral surfaces of the caudal peduncle (the tail stock), known as the supracaudal and infracaudal luminous glands. These glands have been nicknamed "sternchasers," because it is thought that the myctophids flash them to make a predator lunge for the tail as the fish darts away.*

---

* Rolf Bolin, an authority on lantern fishes, has suggested that for those species in which the luminous glands differ from male to female (in *Tarletonbeania*, the organ is supracaudal in the male, infracaudal in the female), they might serve to identify the sexes during breeding. He also wrote that the males might flash their sternchasers to draw predators away from the females. "In this manner," he wrote, "they serve as deflective individuals for the species as a whole and, although they may usually manage to escape because of the confusion engendered by intermittent flashes, they often pay with their lives for the protection of the other sex."

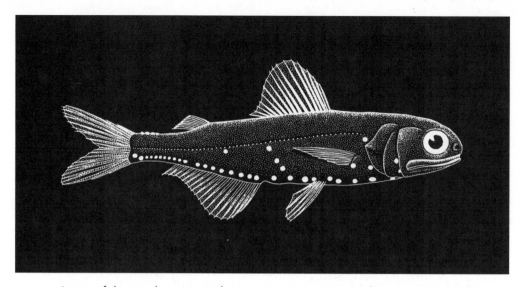

Lantern fishes, such as *Myctophum punctatum*, are among the most numerous fishes in the world. Their name is derived from the photophores along the sides, which glow with an electric blue light and may serve to keep the schools together, or to counterilluminate the fish from the downwelling light of the surface. Vast schools of myctophids are believed to be responsible for the false echo known as the "deep-scattering layer."

Other myctophid genera have specialized luminous tissues in particular locations, such as at the base of the fins, on top of the head, and in the front part of the head, like tiny automobile headlights.

During the 1949 *Atlantis* expedition to explore the Mid-Atlantic Ridge, Maurice Ewing wrote:

> Another mystery of the sea, as yet unsolved, showed up again on our fathometer, as it had the year before. This is a strange echo that in the daytime is reflected from about 300 fathoms (some 1,800 feet) down and is entirely separate from the echo sent back from the ocean bottom. At night this unusual echo comes from near the surface. Everywhere in the sea we found this echo. It may come from the plankton, vast hordes of small sea creatures which move up near the surface at night and sink during the daytime. It has been suggested, however, that the echo might come from the great schools of fish far out in the open sea where no one thought they existed.

Ever since we have been able to send sounds into the ocean and analyze the returning echoes, we have noticed an element that moves through the water column like a variable bottom. The existence of this phantom, sound-reflecting layer was not officially recognized until 1942, when Navy scientists, experimenting with underwater sound for detecting submarines, regularly encountered an echo from around 900 feet where no bottom existed; the water was actually several thousand feet deep. They knew it was not a submarine, because it was diffuse, rather like a moving shadow, and most curiously, it appeared only during the day. By evening, it would appear to rise toward the surface and disperse. Even before the nature of this layer was identified, it was christened the "deep-scattering layer," quickly abbreviated to DSL. Later, when it was learned that there were often multiple layers, the term was pluralized to "deep-scattering layers," or DSLs.

The first response—especially from fishermen, who had adopted the echo-sounder as a device for locating large schools of fish—was to assume that the DSL was composed of squid, vertically migrating through the water column. (The term "scattering" refers not to the actions of the animals that make up the DSLs, but to the acoustic diffusion of the returning echoes.) Nets towed through the DSLs failed to capture squid in commercial quantities, so someone then suggested that the layers might be made up of euphausiids, shrimplike crustaceans that school in vast quantities and were sometimes caught in the nets. Other candidates included myctophids, which are among the most numerous fish in the ocean, and also sergestid shrimps, which are tiny crustaceans known for their luminescence. It turned out that the DSLs did include some of the above creatures (squid, however, did not participate), but they were segregated by species. Thus, the lantern fish, which are more sensitive to light, move separately from the euphausiids, which in turn are segregated from the sergestids. The layers never crossed one another, but they merged into a single layer, sometimes 500 feet thick, at or near the surface. Eric Barham, of the Naval Electronics Laboratory in San Diego, diving aboard the *Trieste* off California, has seen relatively dense concentrations of sergestid prawns (at 1,200 to 1,500 feet) and lantern fish (at 1,700 feet), but he has also been quoted as believing that the DSLs are composed mostly of siphonophores with gas bladders that make them excellent echo-returners. Herring and Clarke (1971) concur, having written, "Those [siphonophores] with gas floats are believed to move up and down by varying the amount of gas, and are often implicated in deep-scattering layers, for their gas floats are excellent sound scatterers." The primary candidates for contributions to the DSL are, however, the myctophids. Not all fishes have swim bladders, but most of the myctophids do, and the presence of large numbers of small fishes, each equipped with a tiny air bubble, makes for an ideal sound-scatterer.

The swim bladder in fishes is a gas-filled organ that acts as a hydrostatic device; by adjusting to variations in pressure, the fish can remain poised at any depth without rising or falling. This equilibrium is achieved by making the density of the fish nearly equal to that of the surrounding water. Net hauls have shown that myctophids migrate vertically, rising toward the surface at night and descending during the daylight hours. As this movement coincides with the behavior of the DSL, it is not difficult to attribute these heretofore mysterious echoes to the lantern fishes. In 1954, when the role of the fishes in the DSL was still not clear, Hersey and Backus had written that "there is a strong indication that . . . migrating gas bubbles, probably the swimbladders of fishes, are responsible for a large part of the sound scattering in this area [the continental shelf off New England]. . . ."

Using a photometer to measure penetration of light into the sea and also the flashing of luminescent animals, Clarke and Backus (1964) demonstrated that these flashes were closely related to the vertical migration of animals in the DSL. The "flashiest" of these migrators are the lantern fishes. Furthermore, in order to qualify as a major component of the DSL, the sound-scatterers would have to be nearly worldwide in distribution, and the myctophids fill this re-

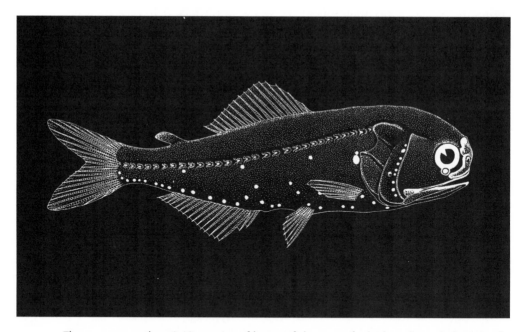

There are more than 240 species of lantern fish, most of which make a daily vertical migration of several hundred meters, rising toward the surface at night and descending during daylight hours. The four-inch *Diaphus metopoclampus* is characterized by the "headlight" photophores on the front of the head.

quirement quite nicely. They are found throughout the world's oceans, but not in the high latitudes of the Antarctic, and, perhaps not coincidentally, the DSL is not encountered there either. (Since squid and crustaceans are abundant south of the Antarctic Convergence, this discontinuity would suggest that these forms are not the scatterers.)

For years, Woods Hole scientists had been referring to the mysterious sound-scattering feature as "Alexander's Acres," after Sidney Alexander, the skipper of the Coast Guard cutter *Yamacraw,* a ship that had been used by the WHOI geophysics group in 1957 and 1958. They suspected that the peculiar blips on the echo-sounder were coming from some sort of animals, but they could not imagine what they might be. When it became clear that deep-diving research submersibles were not only feasible but were indeed a reality, Richard Backus, one of the WHOI biologists, decided to go down and have a look around. In 1967, scientists aboard the *Alvin* in the western North Atlantic descended through dense schools of the myctophid *Ceratoscopelus maderensis,* while echo-soundings of the DSL were being verified by the support vessel *Lulu* at the surface. In *Water Baby,* the story of *Alvin,* Backus is quoted as saying, "A tremendous cloud of Myctophids . . . Beautiful, beautiful fishes, silvery, head down, head up, swimming up, swimming down, lovely fishes . . . They're getting thicker and thicker. We are sitting motionless, right in the middle of a swarm of these fishes. You couldn't call it a school because they are all moving in different directions, but it's a fantastic aggregation, fantastic numbers. . . ." In a more reserved style, Backus wrote in 1968 that "not only does *C. maderensis* inhabit a wide range in the northern North Atlantic, but some, at least, of the dozens of species in the ubiquitous oceanic family Myctophidae (including the abundant, widespread *Ceratoscopelus townsendi*) might well be expected to cause similar acoustic effects in many or all parts of the world's deep ocean." The mystery of "Alexander's Acres" seems to have been solved.

As to why these fishes should rise and fall with such predictable regularity, the phenomenon probably has something to do with available food sources. In their 1974 study, John Isaacs, Sargun Tont, and Gerald Wick wrote that "their daily migrations lead the animals in the Deep Scattering Layer to food. The animals' response to light and their interaction with ocean currents maintain them within regions of high phytoplankton standing crop and transport them away from unproductive regions." It is unlikely that the vertical movement serves only one function, and W. D. Clarke (1963) believed that the vertical migrations occurred because the "organisms of the deep-scattering layer actively seek a certain light level to which they are best able to match their own luminescence for the purpose of concealment from predators." The lantern fishes and other creatures of the DSL move through the water column in order to maintain the luminescence that conceals them from predation. During the daylight hours they hide in the depths, but as night approaches, they begin to rise toward the surface, where their photophores will allow them to maintain the integrity of the massed aggregations, attract a mate, and feed on the zooplanktonic creatures of the pelagic zone.

THE DEEP-SEA ANGLERS

With most having gigantic heads all out of proportion to their tiny bodies, the deep-sea anglerfishes look more like children's bad drawings of evil fishes. But few children would equip their fishes with fishing rods, and even fewer would permanently attach miniature males to the bodies of the relatively enormous females. Some globular, some elongated, some pear-shaped, the ceratioids are grotesquely formed creatures that are among the most fantastic of all the deep-sea fishes. Were it not for the fact that most of them do not reach a foot in length, they most certainly would be listed among the most horrifying of sea monsters. They rarely have well-known common names, but the names that have been applied give a clue as to how they are regarded. For example, species in the genus *Ceratias* are "sea devils," *Cryptopsaras couesi* is the "triple-wart sea devil," and others have been called "netdevils," "whipnoses," and any number of descriptive, but generally pejorative, names. In a 1913 description of *Melanocetus johnsoni*, C. Tate Regan of the British Museum wrote, "This curious fish has an enormous mouth armed with slender pointed depressible teeth and an extraordinarily distensible stomach; it belongs to the order Pediculati and is a bathypelagic species, uniformly black in colour." Most of the anglers are black, and *Melanocetus* is no exception. In fact, even though the common name of *M. johnsoni* is "common black-devil," its name can be translated as "black whale," a curious appellation for a fish that reaches a maximum length of five inches.

The deep-sea anglers are so-called because of their habitat and their fishing equipment. Each species is equipped with a lure (illicium) that is a modified dorsal fin arising from the top of the head. Like the chin barbels of the stomiatids—and presumably functional in the same fashion—these lures come in all shapes and sizes, from short, stubby little buttons, to elaborate whiplike structures. (The luminous tip of the illicium is known as the "esca"—Latin for "bait.") Also like the barbels, the lures are decorated with filaments, tassels, branches, and, of course, lights. Of the anglerfish, only the genera *Centrophryne* and *Linophryne* have illuminated barbels like those of the stomiatids. As far as we know, members of the genus *Linophryne* (which means

The anglerfish *Linophryne arborifera* is well equipped for attracting food in its lightless environment. It sports a plumed lantern atop its head, and below its chin a hanging garden of branching filaments. The tiny male (not shown here) is parasitic on the female.

"toad that fishes with a net") are unique in having two distinct lighting systems: the esca harbors luminous bacteria, while the multirayed chin barbel generates its own light (described as "intrinsic, extracellular luminescence" by Hansen and Herring in 1977). Consider the tackle of *Linophryne arborifera,* a miniature ogre that is coal-black and about the size of a baby's fist, with a gigantic mouthful of frightful fangs. On the top of its head it sports a plumed lantern, and beneath its chin is a hanging garden (hence the name *arborifera*) of branching filaments.

Since escae and illicia (the plurals of "esca" and "illicium," respectively) are found only on the females and differ from species to species, they are probably helpful to the males in identifying the females of their own species in the dark

Shown here with an attached male, *Linophryne pennibarbata* ("feather-barbed") gets its name from the feathery nature of its chin barbel. Notice also the elaborate esca on this six-inch female.

water of their habitat. (The twinkling lights beneath the female might be effective in attracting prey.) There are twenty-one species in the genus *Linophryne,* all of them similar in shape, distinguished by geography, the design of the light organs and barbels, and size. (The smallest mature females are about the size of golf balls; the largest about the size of softballs.) Erik Bertelsen (1982) observed that in this species, the males always attach themselves to the females in the same place—"on the belly of the female, somewhat in front and below the sinistral anus. . . ." (In other anglerfishes, there is no such site specificity.)

No one has ever witnessed the actual spawning process of a deep-sea anglerfish, but in 1980, Bertelsen described a female *Linophryne arborifera* that had been brought to the surface with "a mucoid substance . . . hanging out of the greatly enlarged genital pore." When the fish was placed in a jar of seawater, the "mucoid substance" was seen to be a folded, gelatinous sheet containing a single layer of eggs. From observations of other, more accessible species, such as *Histrio* (the frogfish) or *Lophius* (the goosefish), it was seen that the egg veil is fertilized by the male as it is being released. It appears that this veil brings the eggs into contact with the male attached in the area of the genital opening, thus ensuring their fertilization.

The lovely anglerfish *Oneirodes eschrichtii*. Like its relatives, *Oneirodes* is a black fish, with a luminescent esca. The male doesn't look anything like this.

The name *Oneirodes* is derived from the Greek *oneiros*, which means "dream" or "vision" (there is also a holothurian known as *Oneirophanta mutabilis*, illustrated on p. 156 of this book), but the only kind of dream that one could associate with this five-inch fish is a nightmare. (Fitch and Lavenberg wrote that its name means "something out of a dream, in reference to its almost unbelievable shape.") The family Oneirodidae is the largest and most diverse of the suborder Ceratioidea; there are some thirteen genera and nearly fifty species. For the most part, they are no more nightmarish than the other deep-sea anglers, with a round, dark-colored body, a luminescent esca at the end of a crooked illicium, and well-formed spines on the head and jaws. (This, of course, is a description of the female; as in all ceratioids, the males are comparatively tiny and un-adorned, and serve primarily to fertilize the eggs of the females.) Using advanced electron microscopy, William O'Day (1974) examined the esca of *Oneirodes*, to see if the bacteria were bioluminescent, and indeed they are, but because he was unable to get the bacteria to luminesce in sea-water, he suggested that "the host provides certain nutrients required for luminescence."

While fishing for the "black sword" off Madeira, fishermen hauled in a black, strange-looking, eight-inch fish in which the stomach was so distended that it looked as if it had swallowed an orange. Protruding from its jaws was the tail of a fish considerably larger than it was. It resembled many of the ceratioid anglers in that it had toothy, gaping jaws; a lure atop the forward part of its head; fins with the long spines exposed; and a tiny male attached to the left side of its abdomen. Tate Regan of the British Museum (Natural History) described it as a new species and named it *Caulophryne polynema*, "stalked toad with many filaments," because it was covered with long, slender projections along the lateralis system, fringes on the illicium, and enormously elongated rays on the anal and dorsal fins. (In mature females, the fin rays are much longer than the fish itself.) The nonluminescent illicium is replaced by an extremely sensitive lateral line system with the free ends exposed on filaments, probably to sense prey rather than to attract it. The dwarf male, which lacked these filaments, was less than an inch long.

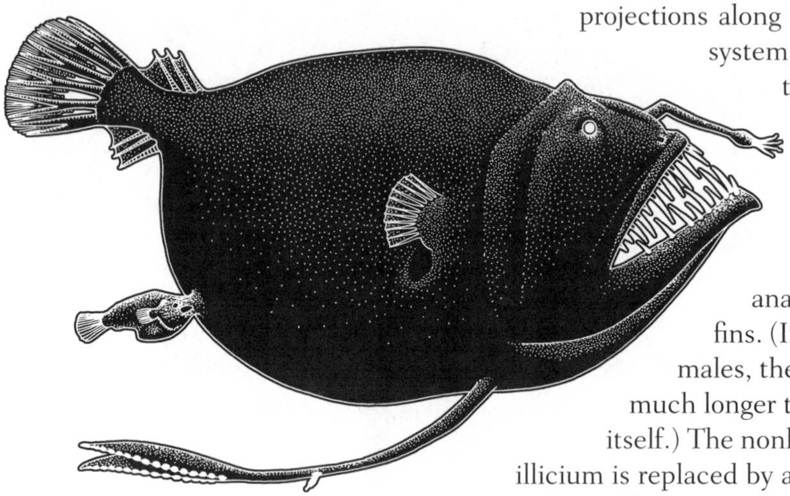

Commonly known as the "devil's anglerfish," *Linophryne lucifer* is equipped with a forked chin barbel and a luminescent lure on top of its head. A tiny male has attached himself to the four-inch-long female shown here.

Unlike most of the deep-sea anglers, *Ceratias holboelli* is not a small fish. Females have been measured at 40 inches and weighed at 20 pounds. (The males reach a maximum size of about 4 inches, and, because of the pronounced dimorphism between the sexes, will be described separately.) Writing in his nontechnical mode, William Beebe described a specimen that had fortuitously made its way to him from a Boston fishing boat:

> It is a great, unlovely-shaped fish with very small eyes, a large mouth well furnished with teeth, and coarse fins placed far back. From the crown of the head there sprouts a long slender tentacle tipped with a luminous lure. . . . In general shape this structure resembles a rod, line and bait, the latter suspended directly above the gaping mouth. Well behind it a second

ray arises, a mere bare lash directed backward. . . . Much of the surface of the body is covered with large, swollen, spine-tipped, hard, whitish tubercles.

In 1922, Icelandic ichthyologist Bjarni Saemundsson published a description of two small fish attached to the belly of a large female angler, *Ceratias holboelli*. (The fish had been named for Lt. Comdr. C. Holböll of the Royal Danish Navy, who found one washed up on the shore of Greenland in 1830, but it was not officially recognized until Kröyer published his description in 1844.) Saemundsson described his finds as juveniles, but wrote, "I can form no idea of how, or when, the larvae or young become attached to the mother; I cannot believe that the male fastens the egg to the female. This remains a puzzle for some future researcher to solve." Three years later, Tate Regan solved the puzzle when he dissected a small creature that had been attached to another female, and realized that it was a parasitic male, "merely an appendage of the female, and entirely dependant upon her for nutrition. . . . [S]o perfect and complete is the union of husband and wife that one may almost be sure that their genital glands ripen simultaneously, and it is not too fanciful to think that the female may possibly be able to control the seminal discharge of the male and to ensure that it takes place at the right time for the fertilization of her eggs."

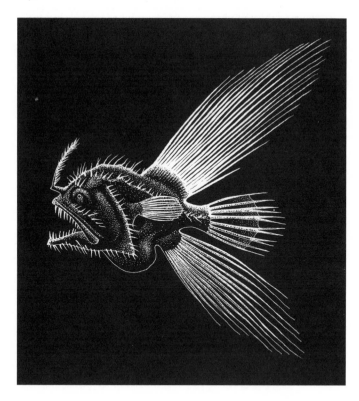

This wonderful-looking creature is a female *Caulophryne polynema*, whose name can be translated as "stalked toad with many filaments." It is one of the few lightless anglers, but like most of the others, the miniature males parasitize the females.

The female *Ceratias holboelli* is the largest of the deep-sea anglerfishes, and can reach a length of 40 inches and a weight of 20 pounds. The light-tipped tentacle protruding from the head is actually a dorsal spine that can be moved forward and back at will.

And so far as we know, this is exactly what happens. Free-swimming males are equipped with large, functional eyes and a well-developed olfactory mechanism that probably enables them to locate a female by smell, perhaps in addition to recognizing her luminous esca. They grasp the females with their jaws, becoming permanently attached as the mouth is gradually pushed backward, leaving a small opening for respiration. (Earlier studies suggested that the males' circulatory system became completely integrated with the females', but closer examination revealed that the males continue respiration on their own.) In one instance, a female *Ceratias holboelli* with an attached ripe male had nearly 5 million eggs in her ovary. The eggs are fertilized externally; the male must release his sperm when the female releases the eggs.

"It has long been assumed," wrote T. W. Pietsch in 1975, "that before acquiring a parasitic male, female ceratioids must mature to an adult stage." This seems not to be necessary, and in fact, wrote Pietsch, "gonadal development and sexual maturity of both males and females seems to be dependent on their mutual presence in an obligatory, sexual parasitic association." In other words, sexual maturity in either sex is brought on by the parasitic connection. No mature male (with developed testes) has ever been found that was not attached to a female, and females do not attain sexual maturity until parasitized by the male. In those cases where a male was found attached to an immature female,

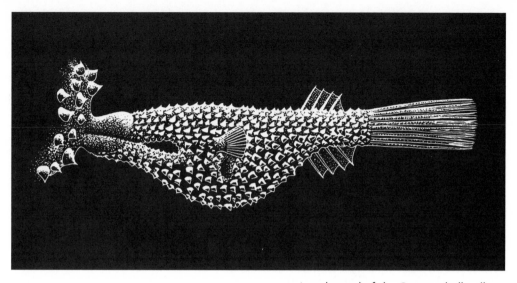

A male anglerfish, *Ceratias holboelli*. While the females can be almost four feet in length, the parasitic males are only four inches long. After permanently attaching himself to the female, their circulatory systems are united, and the male functions only as a reproductive organ.

it was assumed that the presence of the male would soon stimulate early maturity in the female. Pietsch points out that the reproductive strategies of ceratioid anglerfishes "can be understood when it is realized that population densities of these organisms are low and mobility restricted by a luring mode of energy capture and by an environment that is vast and productively poor. That parasitic attachment can take place at any time during the apparently long life of a ceratioid . . . makes this solution to the seemingly difficult problem of reproduction in the deep sea even more remarkable."

Pietsch and Basil Nafpaktitis declared that "sexual parasitism is certainly one of the most amazing reproductive strategies that has always attracted the interest and imagination of ichthyologists. . . ." One of the most preeminent of these was William Beebe, who most assuredly was a gentleman of the old school, and who wrote, "To be driven by impelling odor headlong upon a mate so gigantic as *Ceratias*, in such Stygian darkness, and willfully eat a hole in her barbed-wire skin, to feel the gradually increasing transfusion of her blood through one's veins, to lose everything that marked one as other than a worm, to become a brainless, senseless thing that was a fish—this is sheer fiction, beyond all belief unless we have seen the proof of it." Outdoing himself in romantically hyperbolic anthropomorphism, Beebe wondered, in an article called "*Ceratias,* Siren of the Deep," about the development of their most unusual strategy for procreation:

Did she know he was there? When did the last vestige of sight or smell, of heart-throb, or individual instinct and sensation leave the little being? What particular theory or combination of theories of evolution can explain the gradual development through past ages which has culminated in this self-immolation on the altar of generation?

Before they were recognized as parasitic on the females, the free-swimming males of *Ceratias* were classified as a distinct family: the Aceratiidae. It was a rather peculiar family—all known specimens were males—and unlike all other ceratioids, they had no illicium. (Even now, most of what we know about the males comes from the examination of those attached to females.) According to A. E. Parr (1930), it had been "modified into an internal rostral bone of a pincher-like structure, which, particularly in the genus *Rhynchoceratias,* may certainly be said to be strongly suggestive of an organ for attachment harmonizing remarkably well with the manner in which the parasitic male ceratioids have been attached to the females." (*Rhynchos* means "snout," and refers to the bone structure of the mouth.) Thus, Tate Regan's 1925 discovery of an "aceratiid" male attached to a female effectively eliminated the entire family, since its members were now recognized as being unattached males of the genus *Ceratias.*

Little about the ceratioid anglers is "normal"; Robert Clarke called the genus "the most peculiar and specialized of all fishes." Free-swimming males and juvenile females have functional eyes, but once they are united, the eyes of both sexes degenerate until both male and female are blind. Even the illicium differs from that of other anglers. The lure that dangles over the mouth is similar to the apparatus of other related species, but the rear "tentacle" that Beebe referred to as "a mere bare lash directed backward . . . the modified second ray of the dorsal fin" is nothing of the sort. It is the posterior portion of the illicium, threaded through the tissue of the fish's back and movable by a unique system of muscles. This unusual arrangement was discovered by Bertelsen (1943), who wrote, "The bone continues unbrokenly up to the joint of the illicium. In other words, the dorsal tentacle is neither a second or third isolated dorsal fin ray . . . but the posterior end of the basal bone of the illicium covered with a sheath from the skin of the back." As to why a bone would pass through the back of a fish, Bertelsen writes that "the cephalic tentacle in *Ceratias* can be very much displaced forwards or backwards. When it is fully exserted the dorsal tentacle is completely concealed. . . . When the cephalic tentacle is retracted the illicium is placed just above the mouth and the dorsal tentacle reached beyond the dorsal fin." By moving the lure back and forth, the angler can entice the prey fish closer and closer to its capacious mouth.

Given the darkness of their usual habitat and their limited visual acuity, it is difficult to imagine these fishes finding food or, even more problematical, finding a mate. Free-living adolescent males have large, functional eyes, but what do they look for in all that darkness? Close behind the dorsal tentacle, along the mid-line of the back, *Ceratias* females have a pair of small, club-shaped structures known as caruncles. "These organs," writes Robert Clarke, "probably have some kind of sexual significance." The caruncles are luminescent and may serve as a beacon to attract males, since a male drawn to the illuminated lure in front of the mouth would likely be perceived as prey and be eaten by the sightless female.

Ceratias is not an uncommon fish; it lives in deep temperate and cold waters around the world, usually close to the continental shelves. A specimen found by Robert Clarke in 1948 among various squids in the stomach of an Antarctic sperm whale being processed aboard the British factory ship *Southern Harvester* was originally thought to be *C. holboelli,* but has now been identified (by Pietsch, 1986) as the Southern Ocean species, *Ceratias tentaculatus.* The form endemic to the Southern Ocean differs from its northern relative by having two filamentous appendages on the tip of the esca, instead of *C. holboelli*'s single one. A third member of the genus, *Ceratias uranoscopus,* recently identified by Pietsch and nicknamed the "star-gazing sea devil," has an ovate escal bulb with no appendages.

Most known specimens of *Ceratias* have been caught by commercial fishermen, and the females were always relatively large, two to three feet in length. Since they could not be born at that size, ichthyologists wondered why they had seen no larval or juvenile females. (The tiny males were well represented in collections.) In their detailed review of the deep-sea anglerfishes, C. Tate Regan and Ethelwynn Trewavas had described various new genera, particularly *Mancalias,* that bore a superficial resemblance to the much larger *Ceratias,* which had come from different parts of the world's oceans. Bertelsen—who had already discovered the surprising nature of the illicium of this remarkable fish—realized that *Mancalias* must be the same species as *Ceratias,* and that the genus therefore had a much wider distribution than was previously suspected. The large females captured off Iceland and Greenland probably encountered the polar current at the northern limit of their range, and were forced upward by the cold bottom water, where they could be caught by commercial trawlers.

A smaller version of *Ceratias* is *Cryptopsaras couesi,* sometimes known as the triplewart sea devil. Whereas *Ceratias* females can be more than 3 feet in length, Mrs. Triplewart reaches a maximum length of about 18 inches. Like

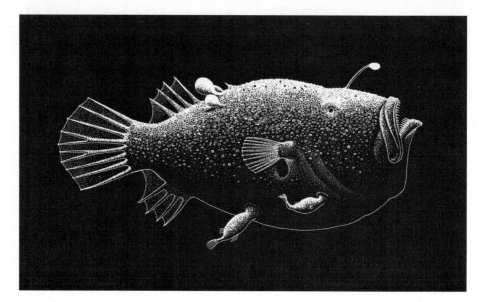

As with most anglerfish, the tiny males of *Cryptopsaras couesi* are parasitic, and permanently attach themselves to the females to facilitate breeding in the blackness of the depths. Perhaps to help him find her, the female is equipped with a lure and three caruncles that glow in the dark. (These bioluminescent structures may also be useful in attracting prey items.)

those of its larger relative, *Cryptopsaras** males are parasitic, and in this genus, there have been several instances in which more than one tiny male has been found attached to a female. Female sea devils are covered with tiny spines, and the common name "triplewart" derives from three globular caruncles just forward of the spiny dorsal fin. The caruncles, as well as the bulb on the end of the short illicium, are luminescent and are believed to have some function in attracting males to females.

When there is only one species in a genus, the term "monotypic" is applied. The fangtooth (*Anoplogaster cornuta*) is such a creature—a fish with no relatives except other fangtooths. And even other fangtooths don't look much like each other. Juveniles are so different from adults that it took fifty years for

---

* This is the correct spelling. It is so easy to get it wrong, however, that in Regan and Trewavas's 1932 report on the deep-sea anglerfishes, reviewed as "one of the most valuable reports in the history of oceanic ichthyology," the generic name is misspelled throughout as *"Cryptosparas."* In the authoritative *Catalog of Genera of Recent Fishes* (1990), W. N. Eschmeyer wrote that it was "misspelled or unjustifiably emended to *Cryptosparas, Cryptosaurus* and *Cryptosaras* by authors." The species was named in 1863 by T. W. Gill, who wrote, "The species has been named after the eminent ornithologist Elliot Coues. The name is derived from the Greek *cryptos* (concealed) and *psaras* (fisherman), and has reference to the concealed 'rod' or basal joint of the anterior spine or fishing apparatus."

Appropriately named "fangtooth" or "ogrefish," *Anoplogaster cornuta* is a deep-sea fish in which the juvenile form looks so different from the adult that it took ichthyologists fifty years to realize that *Caulolepsis* and *Anoplogaster* were the same species. Fangtooths are found in temperate and tropical waters around the world, at depths down to 16,000 feet.

ichthyologists to realize that the round-bodied little fish with a single row of small teeth was the same species as the big-headed creature with such a frightening array of teeth. (In *Fishes of the Western North Atlantic,* Loren Woods and Pearl Sonoda give "ogrefish" as another name.) Juveniles have several elongate spines on their heads, which disappear when the fish matures. The juveniles were first named *Anoplogaster cornuta* (*cornuta* means "crowned," and refers to these spines), and the adults, when they were believed to be a distinct species, were known as *Caulolepsis longidens.* Fangtooths are found in temperate and tropical waters throughout the world, at depths up to 16,000 feet. They are relatively hardy, and because they have no swim bladder to expand as the pressure is reduced, they can survive being brought to the surface better than most bathypelagic species. Fitch and Lavenberg wrote, "They are easy to keep alive in shipboard aquaria for as long as a week or ten days."*

* In a series of shipboard experiments published in 1973, R. P. Meek and J. J. Childress tested the feeding responses of specimens of *Anoplogaster* that had been brought up alive. When they touched the swimming fangtooth on its body with a forceps-held shrimp, the fish responded strongly, suggesting "that contact chemoreception may play a very important role in the feeding responses of *A. cornuta.* This role may be the primary system for sensing and locating prey organisms."

Deep-sea fishes appear so exotic that one expects to find them only in alien and mysterious locations. The deep ocean may indeed be the most mysterious environment on the planet—the term "unfathomable" is not inappropriate—but it is also true that the creatures of the abyss are likely to be found wherever the water is deep enough. William Beebe actually put this observation to the test. His home-based laboratory comprised the New York Zoological Society's Department of Tropical Research at the Bronx Zoo. In 1929, he wrote, "It has always been my desire to see how close to New York City the life of the deep sea is to be found." It turned out to be a mere 125 miles away.

From the seagoing tug *Wheeler,* Beebe lowered various nets and trawls into the mile-deep water of the Hudson Gorge (now known as the Hudson Canyon) and produced "fifty-five species of deep sea fish . . . of which five prove to be new." There were lantern fishes, bristlemouths, hatchetfishes, viperfishes, stomiatids, and anglerfishes; and two specimens of *Stylophthalmus,* the stalk-eyed creature that Beebe would later identify as the larval form of *Idiacanthus.* Among the new species was *Bathytroctes drakei,* a barracudina that Beebe named for a man named Drake who provided the tug; a stomiatid (*Stomias boa*); and a tiny anglerfish he named *Haplophryne hudsonius,* which was about half an inch long, and enclosed in a "very thick, balloon-like casing of skin." As he headed home on the *Wheeler,* Beebe reflected on the wonders brought up in the nets:

> With all this strangeness there is also beauty beyond words. In and out through the mass of life swim active opals—gleaming and scintillating as they twist and turn—tiny, oval, living tissues of flame and ash, which glow brightly after death, for their colors are due not to pigment, but, like a hummingbird's throat, to a myriad prisms.

Scientists who study deep-sea fishes often have relied on devices less complicated than nets and trawls to obtain their subjects. In the Municipal Museum of Funchal, Madeira, there is a significant collection of ceratioid fishes, which were catalogued by G. E. Maul in 1961 and 1962. Almost every specimen came from the stomachs of predatory fishes (the cutlass fish *Aphanopus carbo* and the lancet fish *Alepisaurus ferox*) that had been brought to the local fish market. Among the anglerfishes examined by Maul were several adult females of the genus *Himantolophus,* the first deep-sea anglerfish to be described, the original specimen having washed ashore at Godthaab, Greenland, in 1833, and been found there by the same Lieutenant Commander Holböll who introduced *Ceratias.* (Holböll delivered the 22-inch fish to Professor Reinhardt of Copenhagen, who eventually described it in 1837.)

Sometimes known as the "footballfish," *Himantolophus groenlandicus* was the first of the deep-sea anglers to be discovered. A 22-inch long female washed ashore in Greenland in 1833, but they are more likely to be found in the depths of the sea.

Like some of the other ceratioids, *Himantolophus* is a squat, rotund fish that appears to be mostly head and lure. (In *Fishes of the World*, J. S. Nelson refers to them as "footballfishes.") The illicium of *Himantolophus* is wondrous to behold; it is an intricate concoction of lights, filaments, and tentacles that can be as long or longer than the fish itself. (Based on differences in the illicia and other osteological determinations, Maul identified four new species in addition to the established *H. groenlandicus*.) The 22-inch female found by Captain Holböll is still the largest on record, but the males (which were among those previously believed to be a different species, *Rhynchoceratias*) do not get much larger than two inches. Since no females of this species have been found with attached parasitic males, it is assumed that *Himantolophus* is fertilized by free-swimming males.*

---

* Beebe recorded a type of anglerfish that no one ever saw before, and—not surprisingly—no one has seen since. From the bathysphere at a depth of 2,470 feet in Bermuda waters, he recorded a six-inch-long anglerfish with "three tall illicia, slender, apparently stiff, each about one-third the length of the fish. . . . [E]ach had a slightly enlarged tip [that] gave out a strong, pale yellow light, powerful enough to illuminate the adjacent dorsal skin when the fish was not in the path of my beam." He named it *Bathyceratias trilychnus*, the "three-starred anglerfish."

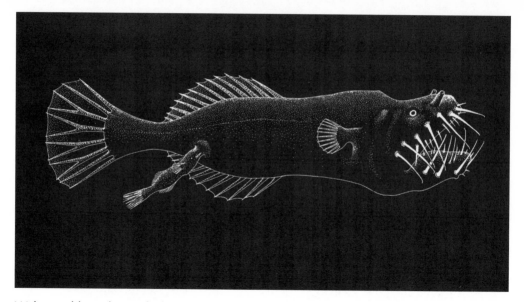

With movable teeth outside the jaws, *Neoceratias spinifer* (no common name) looks like an ichthyologist's nightmare pincushion. Males are much smaller than females, and are parasitic.

The sexual dimorphism in which the females can be as much as ten times the length of the males—and much more, if we consider their comparative volume—is unique to the deep-sea anglers, but not all species employ male parasitism as a breeding strategy. A study by Pietsch (1976) revealed that parasitic males are known from some genera and not from others. Male black-devils (Melanocetidae) are not parasitic, but *Ceratias* certainly is, as are the deep-sea anglers of the genus *Linophryne,* and those of the genus *Neoceratias,* generally considered one of the strangest-looking fishes in the world. The teeth of the adult females are inserted on the outside of the upper and lower jaws, making the fish look like an evil pincushion with fins. *Neoceratias* is also the only anglerfish that completely lacks an illicium.

These females are floating, baited traps, while the males are able swimmers, without light organs, but with large eyes and enormous olfactory organs, necessary for locating females. The tiny males attach themselves by grasping the female with their jaws (which are unsuited to the capture of prey, anyway), and metamorphose from a free-swimming little fish into a reproductive organ, sustained by a common circulatory system. "It is a marriage tie," wrote P. L. Kramp of the *Galathea,* "which cannot be broken." Reproduction where the male becomes permanently fused to the female is called "obligate parasitism," since it appears that these species cannot reproduce in any other way. (In some other species of anglerfishes, free-swimming males fertilize the females.)

There is no reason why more than one male should not affix himself to a female, and indeed, there have been several females examined with more than one little husband aboard. A female *Cryptopsaras couesi* was trawled up from 240 fathoms in the Gulf of Mexico with three males stuck on, and a scar indicating that a fourth had recently become separated. In Japanese waters in 1992, a female of this species was found with four males attached (Abe and Funabashi 1992). And although it is a completely nonproductive behavior, there is even the possibility of a male attaching himself to the wrong kind of female. A male *Melanocetus johnsoni* was found attached to a female of the species *Centrophryne spinulosa,* but there was no fusion of the tissue, suggesting that the attachment was a temporary one, perhaps even accomplished while the fishes were in the net. Pietsch and Nafpaktitis, who described this "mistake," wrote that "mistakes may be rare and their effect cancelled by genetic incompatibility. However, their evolutionary implications, especially among closely related species with temporarily attaching males, should not be disregarded. After all, our knowledge of speciation in the deep mid-waters is mostly, if not entirely, conjectural."

The three-inch-long *Lasiognathus saccostoma* (not much longer than its

Known as the "common black-devil," the anglerfish *Melanocetus johnsoni* is about the size and shape of a man's fist. *Melanocetus* can be translated as "black whale," an unusual name for a fish that reaches a length of five inches.

name printed here) is a grotesque among grotesques. Dubbed the "compleat angler of the abyss," this bizarre little creature is equipped with a fishing rod (illicium), a line, a luminescent lure, and, on the end of it, three bony hooks, the function of which is not known. At first glance, *Lasiognathus* ("hairy jaws") looks all wrong: it is not deep-bodied like most of the other deep-sea anglers, but depressed—that is, squashed flatter. Its head is enormous, about the same length as the rest of the body (excluding the tail fin), with a huge upper jaw that completely overhangs the lower.

As with so many aspects of this peculiar little creature, its feeding techniques are not clearly understood. From the stomach contents of the few specimens that have been examined, we know it eats small fishes, copepods, and shrimp, but not how it eats them. Beebe (1930) suggested that its fishing equipment might "be cast swiftly ahead, when the hooks and lights would so frighten any pursued fish that they would hesitate long enough to be engulfed in the onrushing maw," but this seems rather unlikely. It is also difficult to figure out the purpose of the hooks, but in a discussion of *Lasiognathus*, Nolan and Rosenblatt (1975) wrote that "squid tentacles could conceivably be impaled on the hooks and the prey thus secured." (In their own article, however, they did not list squid among the food items known for *Lasiognathus*.) In addition to the hooks, the tip of the illicium (the esca) has a bulb that is believed

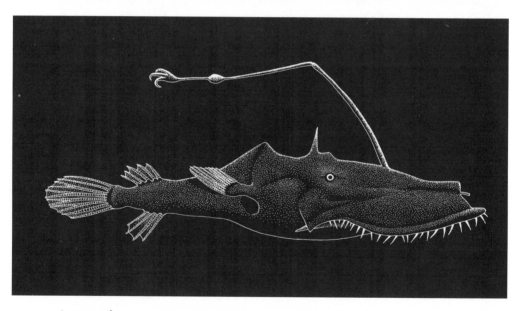

Lasiognathus saccostoma (no common name), a three-inch-long fish equipped with a fishing rod and a luminescent lure with three hooks at the end. Exactly how (or if) the hooks are used is not understood.

to be luminous, equipped with a flap of skin that may be used to cover the light when it is not needed. Although feeding has never been observed, one theory holds that the fish eats by forming its mouth into a sort of sieve that it uses to filter plankton organisms from the water, not unlike the baleen plates of whales. The twenty-seven known individuals have been divided into three species, principally because of differences in the esca and the location of the hooks.

With a huge head, gaping maw, and flattened body, the 18-inch long *Galatheathauma* ("Galathea's wonder")—now known as *Thaumatichthys* ("wonder-fish")—looks as if it might be related to *Lasiognathus*, and it is, but there are significant differences in body shape and illicium. (Both genera have denticles on the illicium.) Anton Bruun called *Galatheathauma* "unquestionably the strangest catch of the Galathea Expedition, and altogether one of the oddest creatures in the teeming variety of the fish world." (A portrait of this fish was used as the dust-jacket illustration for the 1956 popular book *The Galathea Deep Sea Expedition*.) Trawled up from 11,778 feet in the tropical Atlantic, it was a fish with the black, flattened body of a bottom-dweller, and an enormous head with a correspondingly large mouth, ringed top and bottom with teeth like those of a python. From the roof of its capacious mouth there hung a lighted bait that terminated in a pair of short, forked tendrils, resembling the egg case of a skate. It appears that this creature has taken the business of fishing with lights to abyssal perfection: what better place to attract the prey than into the mouth itself?

In his account of the *Galathea* expedition, Anton Bruun wrote, "We found that a small specimen [of *Galatheathauma*], eight centimeters long, of a similar type had been taken by an American expedition in 1908, in Indonesia in 1,385 metres of water. . . ." Since the *Galathea's* specimen was so much larger (47 centimeters compared to 8), Bruun said "we were justified in giving it the new generic and specific name *Galatheathauma axeli*, after the names of our ship and the Chairman of our committee, H.R.H. Prince Axel." The Indonesian specimen had been named *Thaumatichthys pagidostomus* ("trapmouthed wonder-fish"), and later examination (by Bertelsen and Struhsaker, 1977) showed that the thirty-two known specimens differed only in characters attributable to age, and therefore, there was only one genus containing three species: *Thaumatichthys pagidostomus, T. binghami,* and *T. axeli.* The stomachs of almost all specimens have been empty, so we still don't know what creatures might be attracted to the unique lure of *Thaumatichthys,* the trapmouthed wonder-fish.

The gigantactinids are a particularly interesting group of ceratioid anglers with the illicium protruding forward from a position just above the mouth; hence their common name, "whipnoses." Even though there has been exten-

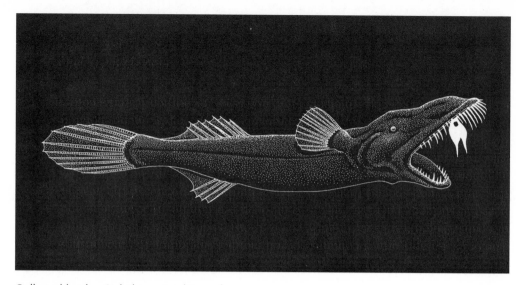

Collected by the *Galathea* expedition of 1950–52 from a depth of 11,778 feet in the tropical Atlantic, *Thaumatichthys axeli* ("Prince Axel's wonder-fish") has the ultimate refinement of the lumines-cent lure: the lighted bait hangs from the roof of its capacious mouth.

sive study of this group (Bertelsen, Pietsch, and Lavenberg 1981), they are still among the most mysterious of the anglers. They are much more elongate than other ceratioids, and although they will win no piscine beauty contests, they have been described as "slen-der, streamlined fishes." As with so many characteristics whose function seems obvious at first, closer examination pro-duces more questions than answers. For example, the illicium, often four to five times longer than the fish itself, looks very much like a fly rod (or perhaps a buggy-whip), but a fly rod without a hook is not particularly practicable. On one occasion, a captured gigantactid was observed in an aquarium, and "sev-eral whip-like, backward and forward thrusts of the entire illicium were fol-lowed by moderately strong vibrations of the esca" (Bertelsen et al. 1981), and the movement of the bioluminescent lure appeared to be a device for attracting prey. But because their eyes are small and weak, they probably cannot see the prey they have attracted, so the question of how these foot-long fishes (there are at least seventeen species) capture their food remains a mystery.

As with all ceratioids, female gigantactinids are enormous in comparison with the males, but since no female has been found with an attached male, it is believed that the tiny males never become parasitic. (The largest known fe-male is 15 inches long, while the largest mature male is only ¾ inch.) If the males are not parasitic, however, we do not know how they find or fertilize the females, but their relatively large nostrils suggest they may use olfaction to lo-

For obvious reasons, *Gigantactis* is called "whipnose." What is not so obvious, however, is what the fish does with this appendage, which has a bioluminescent tip. Does it whip it about like a fly rod? Troll for smaller fishes?

cate potential mates. Tiny male gigantactids have teeth, so it is presumed that they can feed, although not one has been found with food in its stomach. It is the teeth of the females that are a cause for amazement, consisting of several rows of fangs that can be used to seize the prey, and a full complement of pharyngeal teeth—that is, another set of teeth in the pharynx—which propel the prey to the stomach.

OTHER DENIZENS OF THE DEEP

The order Lampriformes contains several families, including the moonfishes or opahs, which are large, brightly colored, disk-shaped fishes usually found near the surface. There are also several deep-sea families that are long and thin, and several species that have a dorsal fin that culminates at the head in a pronounced crest. The most notorious of these creatures is the oarfish (*Regalecus glesne*), sometimes known as "king of the herrings." In *The Guinness Book of Animal Facts and Feats,* Gerald Wood calls the oarfish "the longest bony fish in the world"—which it probably is—but cites uncorroborated lengths of 45 and 50 feet, which are far in excess of any authenticated records.

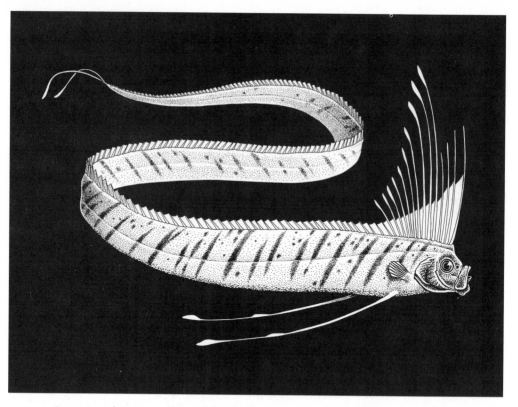

Sometimes known as "king of the herrings," the oarfish (*Regalecus glesne*) is known to reach a length of 26 feet, and is therefore the longest of all bony fishes. With its fragile, ribbonlike body, bright red dorsal fin, and "cockscomb," this fish, occasionally seen undulating at the surface or washed ashore, is believed to have been responsible for many "sea serpent" sightings.

J. S. Nelson's 1993 *Fishes of the World* and M. M. Smith and P. C. Heemstra's *Sea Fishes* give 8 meters (26.5 feet) as the maximum known length.

It has a silvery, ribbonlike body, a pair of long, slender pelvic fins with flattened tips (the "oars" of its common name), and a scarlet, cockscomblike crest (part of the dorsal fin) that it can erect above its head. Its size, undulating swimming motion, and red crest are believed to have been responsible for many "sea serpent" sightings, but with the rare exception of an occasional oarfish that washes ashore and can be examined, virtually nothing is known of its biology. (When examined, the stomachs were found to contain the tiny, shrimplike euphausiids known as krill, the predominant food of some baleen whales.) It is not even certain that it is a true deepwater inhabitant, since all known specimens have been observed at the surface or washed up on the beach. (A videotape shot from the Japanese submersible *Shinkai-6500* contains what is probably the first underwater footage of a live oarfish. It is swimming almost at the surface.)

The ribbonfishes (Trachipteridae) live up to their common name. They are incredibly thin, elongated fishes, usually silvery in color, with red fins, like those of the oarfish. Found at unknown depths throughout the oceans of the world, the polka-dot ribbonfish (*Desmodema polystictum*) is so-called because the juvenile form—which looks totally unlike the adult—is peppered with dark spots. According to Fitch and Lavenberg, "The largest complete specimen known, about 3½ feet long including the tail, weighed less than three-fourths of a pound." The name *Desmodema polystictum* means "many-spotted band-body," incorporating descriptions of the juvenile and adult forms.

With its telescopic eyes and extended rays on the tail fin, *Stylephorus chordatus* would appear to be more closely related to the giganturids, but it is, in fact, related to the ribbonfishes. It was first described in 1791 by George Shaw, curator of the Zoological Collections at the British Museum, who

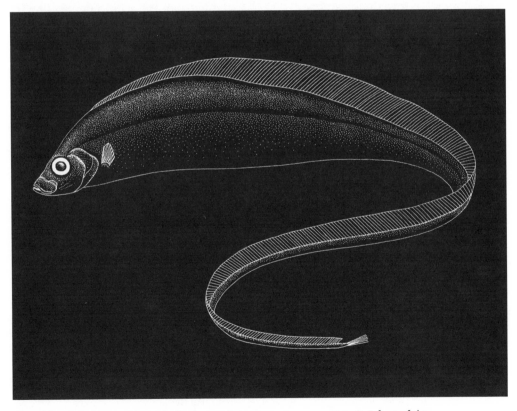

The ribbonfish (*Desmodema polystictum*) lives up to its name. It is 3.5 feet of thin, silvery fish, with bright red fins like those of the oarfish, to which it is related.

wrote, "Having lately had an opportunity of examining a very uncommon and curious fish, which, so far as I am able to judge, constitutes a new genus, I was induced to compose a short description of it. . . . Its true structure cannot be so easily described in words as conceived by the figure." He named it *Stylephorus,* which means "borne on pillars," and refers to what he called the "very singular figure and situation of the eyes," and *chordatus,* which means "thread-like," a reference to the "extraordinary thread-like process of the tail."* The ribbonlike *Stylephorus,* whose common names now include "tube-eye" and "thread-tail," reaches a foot in length and has two extremely elongated rays on its tail fin, which nearly triple its overall length. (The type specimen described by Shaw was 32 inches long, of which 22 inches was tail.) The dorsal fin lacks true spines, but the first two rays can be erected as a crest—like those of its larger relative, the oarfish.

Shaw noticed that there was something unusual about *Stylephorus's* head, and wrote, "The rostrum, or narrow part which is terminated in the mouth, is connected to the head by a flexible leathery duplicature, which permits it either to be extended in such a manner that the mouth points directly upwards, or to fall back so as to be received into a sort of case, formed by the upper part of the head.") This is indeed the strangest feature of this "very uncommon and curious fish": an expandable mouth cavity that permits it to feed in a manner that is unique. Hovering vertically, *Stylephorus* can expand its buccal (mouth) cavity to as much as thirty-eight times its original size, creating negative pressure and therefore a powerful suction that enables it to suck in small planktonic organisms through its elongate, tubular mouth, rather like drinking through a straw. The water rushes into the enlarged mouth cavity, the tubular mouth closes, and the water is forced backward out through the gills. The large, telescopic eyes, normally directed forward, are thrown upward when the fish flips its head back, and therefore, *Stylephorus* cannot see what it is eating. As Pietsch (1978) wrote, "Since no adjustments for movement of the prey can be made once the pouch begins to expand, *Stylephorus* must not only have accurate depth perception and be capable of extremely rapid expansion of the feeding mechanism, but must also be capable of rapid realignment of the eyes and jaws to be ready for the next feeding thrust."

Among the lesser-known fishes of the depths are the cetomimids, six-inch fishes with disproportionately large heads, tiny eyes (degenerate in some species), and very small teeth in very large mouths. The basic body plan—

---

* In his 1908 discussion of the systematic position of this species, C. Tate Regan of the British Museum (Natural History) managed to spell the generic and the trivial name wrong, calling the fish "*Stylophorus caudatus.*" You will remember that Regan, one of the foremost ichthyologists of his time, also misspelled the name of *Cryptopsaras,* the triplewart sea devil.

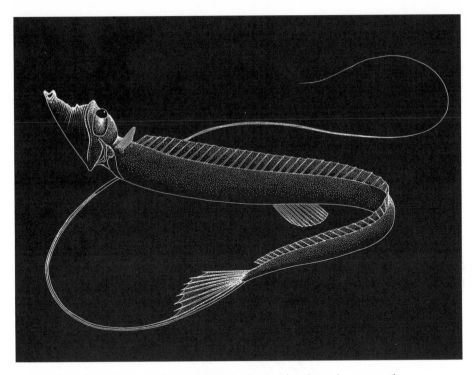

One of the oddest fishes in the world, *Stylephorus chordatus,* known as the "tube-eye" or "thread-tail," can expand its buccal cavity to as much as thirty-eight times its original size in order to suck in large amounts of water through its tubelike mouth—rather like drinking through a straw.

especially the comparatively huge mouth—seems to be responsible for the scientific name, which translates as "whale imitator" and has led to a common name that has nothing to do with size—they are known as "whale fishes" or "flabby whale fishes." *Cetomimus teevani,* a four-inch whale fish collected by the Bermuda Oceanographic Expeditions of 1929–30, was named for John Tee-Van, one of Beebe's associates at the New York Zoological Society. Unlike their namesakes, some whale fishes are colorful, with glowing orange and red patches of luminous tissue on the body. Although they lack a swim bladder, these fishes are able to maintain their position in the water without sinking because the lateral line system consists of a hollow tube with a series of large pores containing flotation devices.

The redmouth whale fish (*Rondeletia bicolor*) has a dark brown body and a reddish-orange mouth and jaws. Where the other whale fishes—and, in fact, most other fishes—have a lateral line that parallels the long axis, *Rondeletia* has a wide, papillate lateral line, composed of a series of vertical rows of pores.

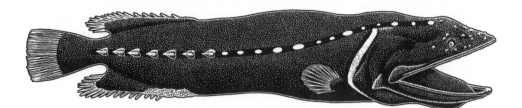

Whale fishes, such as *Cetomimus teevani,* are named for their huge heads and mouths, not for their size, which is about 15 inches.

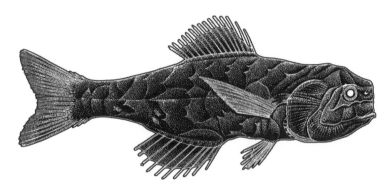

This six-inch fish is the bigscale *Scopelogadus beanii,* included in the order Xenoberyces, a motley collection of deep-sea fishes usually characterized by large, platelike scales, and including the gibberfishes and the pricklefishes.

The whale fishes are related to a motley group of deep-sea forms variously called gibberfishes, pricklefishes, and bigscales—lumped together by taxonomists into the order Xenoberyces. (*Xeno* is "strange" in Greek, and *beryx* is a perchlike fish.) In *Living Fishes of the World,* Earl Herald describes them as "small, obscure, deep-sea fishes, comprising six families and about thirty-five species . . . [with] large, cavernous heads with many mucous areas, and large, platelike, deciduous scales on their bodies."

PERCIFORMES

Perciformes ("perchlike fishes") are the most diversified of all fish orders, and in fact, they are the largest vertebrate order. Many of our most familiar marine and freshwater fishes are Perciformes, including gobies, blennies, basses, sunfishes, butterfly fishes, angelfishes, mullets, wrasses, parrot fishes, mackerels, tunas, and billfishes, among the almost eight thousand species identified by J. S. Nelson (1993). Curiously, very few species of Perciformes are found in the depths; among them are the swallowers (*Chiasmodon* and *Kali*) and several large predators that may descend to the depths to feed.

A fish that is often used to demonstrate the terrifying aspect of deep-sea piscivores is the black swallower (*Chiasmodon niger*); its portrait is employed in publications whenever a fearsomely fanged visage is required. (The portrait is always that of a preserved specimen; the fish has never been photographed alive.) In these photos, we see a fish with a terrifying gape, and armed with incredible teeth. As frightening as it may appear, however, *Chiasmodon* is threatening only to its prey, but its victims might not expect a fish so much smaller than themselves to attack; a six-inch *Chiasmodon* was found to have engulfed a fish twice as long as itself. (In *The Sea Fishes of Southern Africa*, J. L. B. Smith referred to *Chiasmodon* as "rather horrible small fishes [that] can swallow others as large as themselves.") The swallower can accomplish this extraordinary feat because its jaws are attached to the skull at the front, not at the rear, and swing from a device known as the "suspensorium," which can be unhinged to permit it to engulf prey objects much larger than its head.

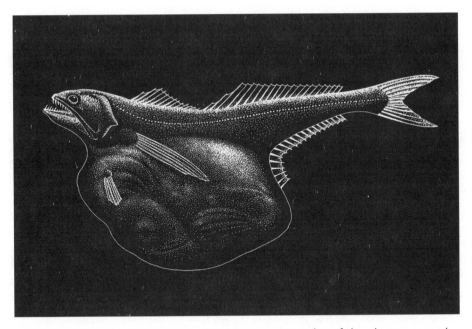

The black swallower (*Chiasmodon niger*) can capture and eat fishes that are considerably larger than it is. Its jaws are attached to the skull at the front, rather than the rear, allowing it to unhinge the jaws and engulf prey objects larger than its head.

Closely related to *Chiasmodon*—in fact, in the same family, the Chiasmodontidae—is another deepwater swallower with no common name but a dandy generic name: *Kali,* named for the Hindu goddess of destruction, usually depicted in mythology as a hideous hag smeared with blood, with bared teeth and protruding tongue. The fish *Kali* is not nearly as terrifying as its namesake, except perhaps to the small fishes upon which it feeds. (When A. E. Parr first described the species in 1926, he named it *Dolichodon,* which means "long-tooth," from the Greek *dolichos* for "long," but the name *Kali* had priority.) However terrifying its name or visage, *Kali*-of-the-long-teeth only reaches a length of six inches and weighs less than an ounce.

In a world of miniature predators like *Kali* and *Chiasmodon,* it is not a little surprising to find the snake mackerel, *Gempylus serpens,* a wicked-looking creature that is known to reach a length of five feet. It is easy enough to see where its common name comes from: its long, straplike body supplies the "snake" reference, and the little finlets at the base of the caudal fin are reminiscent of those of the mackerels—to which *Gempylus* is not related. The big eyes suggest a deepwater lifestyle, and the powerful jaws and teeth look not unlike those of a barracuda. (*Thyristes atun,* a related species from Australia and New Zealand, is known there as "barracouta.") Another closely related species is the oilfish, *Ruvettus pretiosus.*

Another perciform predator of the depths is *Alepisaurus ferox,* a seven-

The deep-sea swallower *Kali normani* is named for Kali, the Hindu goddess of destruction, usually depicted as a hideous hag smeared with blood, with bared teeth and protruding tongue. Not quite as terrifying as its namesake, the fish *Kali* is only six inches long and weighs less than an ounce.

foot-long, dagger-toothed fish with a sail-like dorsal fin, commonly known as the lancet fish. *Alepisaurus* means "scaleless and lizardlike," and *ferox* means "fierce," a description that more than adequately describes this ferocious-looking mesopelagic carnivore. (John Bardach refers to it as the "handsaw fish.") They are such voracious predators that entire studies have been done on their prey species, not so much to demonstrate what they eat—which seems to be anything that swims—but rather to examine some of the rare fishes taken from their stomachs, which would otherwise be uncollectable (see Haedrich and Nielsen 1966). *Alepisaurus* is iridescent black or blue in color, with black fins and tail, and large, emerald-green eyes. Even though they are believed to be inhabitants of the twilight zones of the deep ocean, lancet fishes are sometimes taken on longlines, and there are even records of specimens washing up on the beach.

In Madeira, there is a directed handline fishery for the fish they call *espada preta,* the black sword or black swordfish, *Aphanopus carbo.* Like the lancet fishes, the black sword (also known as the cutlass fish) is a formidable predator, and from the stomachs of captured specimens have come a wealth

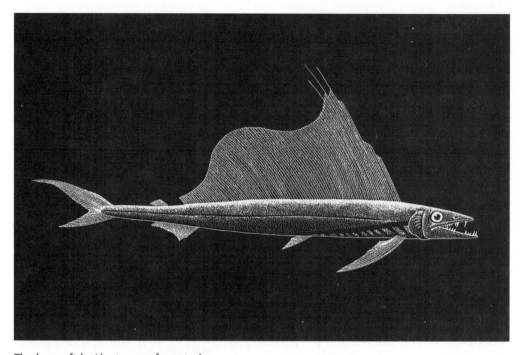

The lancet fish *Alepisaurus ferox* is the predator of predators. At a maximum length of seven feet, it roams the depths, feeding on anything it can catch—and it can catch almost anything. The only two juvenile giant squid ever examined were found in the stomachs of lancet fishes.

of rare and unusual prey items, providing a welcome source of information on other fishes that live at the depths where this predator hunts, between 400 and 1,200 meters deep.

Of all the large epipelagic teleosts, the deepest diver is the broadbill swordfish (*Xiphias gladius*), a creature that big-game fishermen know occasionally appears "finning" at the surface. From stomach contents and sightings from submersibles, we know that swordfishes can and do achieve depths in excess of 600 meters (almost 2,000 feet). The attack on *Alvin* (pp. 75–76) occurred at 610 meters, and in his 1967 discussion of this incident, Rudolf Zarudzki refers to captures of swordfish in halibut nets near the bottom at 400 meters, and also mentions R. L. Haedrich's observations of swordfish at 400 to 630 meters. A photograph in Zarudzki's article shows the stomach contents of a swordfish, and includes stomiatids and myctophids, deepwater species whose presence indicates that this particular fish was feeding at 300 meters or deeper. Even Jules Verne's fictional *Nautilus* was visited by swordfish. Submerged in the Indian Ocean, the passengers see "some swordfish, ten feet long, those prophetic heralds of the hurricane, whose formidable sword would now and then strike the glass of the saloon."

The slim, five-foot-long cutlass fish, or "black sword" (*Aphanopus carbo*), is a predator of the depths, using its powerful jaws and sharp teeth to capture smaller fishes.

The only two juvenile giant squid ever examined were found in the stomachs of lancet fishes, one from Madeira and the other from the eastern Pacific off Chile. What sort of a creature eats giant squid? The lancet fishes (there are two species, short-nosed and long-nosed) seem to be almost indiscriminate carnivores, eating almost anything within their range, with the curious exception of lantern fishes and stomiatids. Because the food is held in the stomach for later digestion in the intestine, prey items in the stomachs of captured specimens are often in remarkably good condition. Frank Lane quotes teuthologist Gilbert Voss as saying, "Stripping the stomachs of these fish is one of the approved methods of collecting deep-sea squid and octopods."

THE DEEPEST FISHES

In the oceans' greatest depths live various fishes that have neither lures nor spines. Some of the abyssal species look more "ordinary" than the bizarre anglers and stomiatids, but rows of lights or tripod fins are not prerequisites for life in the depths. The grenadiers (Macrouridae) are small fishes that rarely reach two feet in length, with a big head, very large eyes, and a long, tapering tail that accounts for their other common name, rattails. Like the cods (to which they are related), rattails have a blunt snout and a chin barbel, but the barbel has no lights or filaments and serves no purpose other than to feel around on the bottom as the fish searches for food. (Some species, however, have a bacterial light organ along the middle of the abdomen, with a reflecting

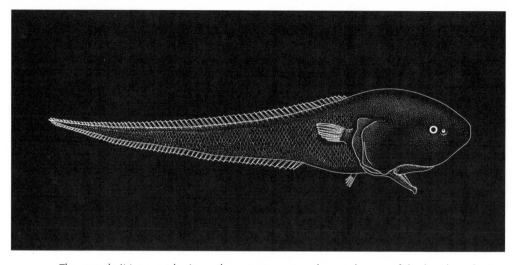

The rattails (Macrouridae) are the commonest and most diverse of the benthopelagic fishes. The inflated appearance of the large, rounded head of *Squalogadus modificatus* is due mainly to the very wide, mucus-filled lateralis canals, which enable the fish to respond to slight changes in pressure and movement in its normal habitat of water deeper than 3,000 meters.

cell layer to cast the light downward, producing a fascinating, although hypothetical, picture of a fish that lights up the bottom as it cruises along looking for food.) Furrows along the sea bottom are believed to be made by macrourids plowing through the sediment in search of buried food items. Fishes without auxiliary lights need some advantage for food-gathering, and the macrourids have extraordinarily sensitive eyes with a larger number of rods than any other animal on earth. (This distinction, however, applies only to species that live in shallower waters; according to N. B. Marshall and Tomio Iwamoto, "Upper slope–dwellers have large eyes; lower slope–dwellers medium-sized eyes; and deep-dwellers [about 2000m or more] small eyes.") Rattails also have well-developed swim bladders equipped with drumming muscles, which may be used to produce sounds that allow them to maintain aural contact with other members of the species. Marshall (1964) noted that since only the male rattails and brotulids have a drumming swim bladder, "the calls of the males might assemble the breeding stock and play a part in courtship and mating."

Just as the cyclothones and myctophids are numerically predominant in the bathypelagic zones, the macrourids are the most numerous fishes of the benthic regions, deeper than 3,000 meters. (In their examination of the photographs taken during the search for the lost submarine *Thresher* in 1963, Marshall and Bourne estimated that the density of abyssal fishes—mostly rattails—was approximately one fish for every 160 square meters.) There are more than 250 species of rattails, and Marshall (1980) wrote, "If overall oceanic diversity could be expressed in numbers of individuals and species, rat-tails would surely emerge as the most diverse family of benthopelagic fishes." The subfamily Squalogadus is characterized by a large, rounded head, containing wide, mucus-filled lateralis canals, which make it extremely sensitive to changes of pressure and movement in its deepwater habitat.

The brotulids—second only to the rattails in abyssal abundance—are also big-headed benthic fishes, which generally resemble the macrourids but lack their large eyes. The deeper the brotulids' habitat, the more degenerate the eyes; in the species *Tauredophidium* and *Leucicoris,* the eyes are so small that the fishes are functionally blind. Brotulids lack the chin barbel of the rattails, and probably do not root in the mud for food, but some species (such as *Typhlonus*) have a protrusible horseshoe-shaped mouth that may be used like a shovel to scoop up food items. They have a well-developed lateral line system (including a series of canals on the head) that can detect the faintest changes in current. While most brotulids are oviparous (egg-layers) some species give birth to live young. Before *Trieste*'s questionable record in 1960 (see footnote on p. 70), the depth records for fishes were held by brotulids: in 1897, Prince Albert of Monaco collected one at 19,800 feet south of the Cape Verde Islands and named it *Grimaldichthys profundissimus.* In 1913, Roule renamed it *Bassogigas profundissimus,* and in 1951, the *Galathea* nets hauled up

Typical of the grenadiers or rattails is *Coelorhynchus coelorhynchus,* characterized by the large eyes and chin barbel. Grenadiers have well-developed swim bladders equipped with drumming muscles, capable of producing sounds that may enable them to maintain contact with others of their deepwater species.

The sea snails (genus *Careproctus*) are flabby, almost gelatinous fishes of the great depths. They are equipped with a small suction disk on the underside of the head, which may help in keeping them on the bottom.

a *Bassogigas* from 23,386 feet in the Sunda Trench. *Galathea* also captured a fish of the family Liparididae at 6,660 meters, which beat Prince Albert's earlier record by some 2,000 feet.*

Commonly known as sea snails because of a small suction disk on the underside beneath the eyes, Liparid fishes of the genus *Careproctus* are semi-gelatinous, loose-skinned creatures that are less than a foot in length. They are characteristically creatures of great depths, resembling the brotulids in general form, with broad, massive heads on a relatively small body, and continuous dorsal and ventral fins.

The deepest living fish in the world is a brotulid, and it is a single species, found at abyssal or hadal depths all over the world. L. C. Staiger wrote of a specimen hauled up in 1970 from the Puerto Rico Trench, which was hailed as the record-holder. And indeed it was, since the depth from which it was taken was 27,453 feet. Only it was not *Bassogigas*. When Jørgen Nielsen examined "11 specimens from six different deep sea cruises covering all world oceans" and described the new species *Abyssobrotula galatheae*, he found that "Staiger's specimen . . . is not *B. profundissimus*, but instead should be re-

---

* On March 25, 1995, the Japanese unmanned submersible *Kaiko* descended to a depth of 35,798 feet in the Challenger Deep of the Mariana Trench. According to a report in *The New York Times*, the videotape taken at that depth showed fish living there, but as of the date of the newspaper report, the fish had not been identified. They were described as "small white fish, several centimeters long . . . resembling *medaka*, a Japanese fresh-water fish that looks something like a guppy."

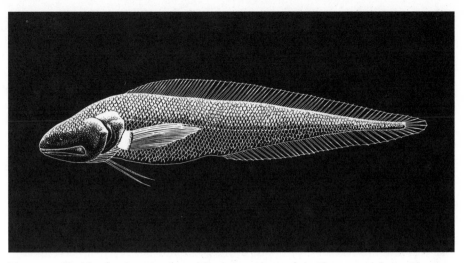

The record-holder for the title of world's deepest-living fish. The six-inch-long *Abysso-brotula galatheae* was dredged up from 27,453 feet in the Puerto Rico Trench in 1970.

ferred to as *A. galatheae*. . . ." As described by Nielsen in 1977, *Abyssobrotula* is a fish about six inches long, with "a short head, a slightly inferior mouth, and a swollen snout." Specimens were trawled up from the bottom in various locations, including the Kermadec Trench north of New Zealand, the South Atlantic off West Africa, and south of the Java Trench in the Indian Ocean, but the record-holder was caught on the very bottom of the Puerto Rico Trench—the deepest point in the entire Atlantic Ocean.*

---

* Of all the records for deepest recorded species, this is the only one from the deep Atlantic. According to Torben Wolff (1970), all known maximum depths for hadal invertebrates, such as polychaete worms, decapods, isopods, gastropods, bivalves, holothurians, and starfishes, were recorded from the various trenches of the Pacific.

Deep Atlantic Whales and Whaling

There are some seventy-seven species of whales, dolphins, and porpoises in the world's oceans, and many of these either live in or visit the Atlantic. Although much of the behavior and natural history of Atlantic whales and dolphins is duplicated by the cetaceans of other oceans—in many cases, the species are the same—we will address those histories and issues that are particular to the Atlantic, or to the depths in general. With some exceptions (such as the right and humpback whales which breed in protected bays close to shore), most whales are pelagic animals, and are therefore an important element in the fauna of the deep oceans. Moreover, some species are capable of dives to such depths that they are—at least until they have to surface to breathe—regular visitors to the mesopelagic zone, and thus legitimate candidates for our discussion of deepwater fauna.

For the most part, the history of the interaction of whales and men is told more poignantly for different localities: blue and fin whales in the Antarctic, humpbacks and right whales in Australia, and sperm whales around the world, all hunted mercilessly for their oil, meat, and baleen. The hunting has been greatly curtailed, partly because of the massive reduction in the whales' numbers, but also because of the almost universal sentiment that whale-killing for profit is an idea whose time has passed. The whales have managed to survive a thousand years of virtually uncontrolled predation, but only barely.

From 1870 to 1970, the Norwegians were the world leaders in whaling and whaling technology. In fact, the history of whales and whaling in the North Atlantic (and many other locations as well) has a decidedly Norwegian flavor. (The comprehensive *History of Modern Whaling*—not surprisingly—was written by two Norwegians, Johann Tønnessen and Arne Johnsen.) Early Norwegians had hunted various whale species in fjords, but they lusted after the gigantic blue and fin whales that they saw off their coasts but were unable to catch or kill. Then, in 1870, Svend Foyn, a sealing captain from Vestfold, invented the grenade harpoon, a device that changed the nature of whale-killing and made it possible to hunt the previously inaccessible rorquals: the blue, fin, sei, and minke whales.

Plying the waters of Norway and Iceland, Foyn and his compatriots slaughtered the rorquals until they were too scarce to make hunting economically viable, but then, in another turn of fate that again spelled disaster for the whales, the Antarctic populations were discovered. Led (as usual) by the Norwegians, the whalers headed to the south, where they encountered great whales in incredible profusion. And as whalers have always done, they killed as many of them as they could, with not much thought to the possibility that they might run out of whales—and by so doing, run themselves out of business. In the "whaling olympics" that took place in the early decades of the twentieth century, the Norwegians, British, Argentines, and South Africans led the way. (The Japanese and Soviets did not begin Antarctic whaling until the 1950s.) They killed every sort of whale, including rights, humpbacks, blues, fins, seis, and sperms. In the 1929–30 whaling season in the Antarctic, nearly 30,000 blue whales were killed. In the next season, the whalers could find only seven thousand blue whales, so they killed them, and then moved on to the next smaller species, the fin whale.

It occurred to some whalers that the resource was not inexhaustible, so the first faint stirrings of conservation were beginning to be heard. It took time before these small voices were acknowledged, however, and it was not until 1949 that the whalers convened in London to hammer out an international treaty that was designed to "protect the whales for the industry." It would have been unthinkable to see this organization as dedicated to anything but the slaughter of whales, and indeed, if one were to examine the records kept by the whalers, the hunt looked like nothing less than a worldwide effort to rid the world of whales, as if these benign creatures had somehow offended or threatened us.

From these first meetings, the International Whaling Commission (IWC) was born. For twenty-odd years, the whalers went about their business, killing and processing whales wherever they could find them. Innovations designed to make their jobs easier and more efficient were introduced: a slipway in the stern of the factory ships enabled them to process the whales at sea, freeing them from the restrictive umbilicus of the shore station. Diesel power made the catcher boats faster and more maneuverable, and by the middle of the twentieth century, more whales were being slaughtered every year than had been killed in the entire history of the Yankee sperm whale fishery. It was a vastly profitable business, limited only by the market price of whale oil, which was used for lubrication, and the manufacture of various foodstuffs and explosives, and every nation with a coastline wanted a piece of the action. By the 1960s, Japan and the Soviet Union had become the world's most powerful whalers, having driven the first whaling nations, like Norway, England, and the Netherlands, out of business. These government-subsidized whalers were killing more than twenty-five thousand sperm whales every year in the North Pacific.

The name "rorquals"—from the Norwegian *rorhval,* meaning "grooved whale"—is applied to several pleat-throated animals, one of which is the largest and heaviest creature ever to have lived on earth. Even the largest of the dinosaurs, with their long necks and tails, weighed considerably less than a full-grown blue whale, which can be as much as 100 feet of meat and muscle. Although it is obviously difficult to weigh such a leviathan, estimates of 150 tons have been accepted without question. The blue whale (*Balaenoptera musculus*) is found in both hemispheres and in all oceans. Because the same amount of effort is required to kill a large whale as a small one, Atlantic whalers focused on the blue whale until it became too scarce to hunt; then they turned to the next smallest, and the next, until they were hunting the diminutive* minke whale, a rorqual that reaches a maximum length of 30 feet. Protected worldwide since 1966, the blue whale has not made a comeback. Estimates on the current North Atlantic populations vary, but they have been seen in recent years in the Gulf of Saint Lawrence, where an ongoing study has been documenting individuals and behavior.

Where the blue whale is a mottled slate-blue, the fin whale (*Balaenoptera physalus*) has a complicated pattern of black, white, and gray elements. (The left side of the whale's lower jaw is black, and the right side is white, making it the only consistently asymmetrically colored animal in the world.) At a maximum length of 80 feet and a weight of 65 tons, a fin whale (also called "finback" or "razorback") was almost as much of a meat-and-oil bonanza as a blue whale, so the Norsemen established whaling stations all along their coasts (and in eastern Canada, too), to take advantage of the oily riches that were just waiting to be harvested. Of course, it couldn't last—no animal population could withstand such a concentrated assault on its numbers—and the population plummeted. (By then it didn't matter, because the whalers had found what they believed were the limitless stocks of the Antarctic.)

The sei whale gets its name from *seje* (pronounced "say"), the Norwegian name for the pollack or coalfish, which appears off the coasts in the spring. Sei whales wander in irregular migration patterns, perhaps related to their food

---

* The term "small" when applied to whales is relative at best. Compared to the gigantic blue whale, or the 80-foot finner, a 30-foot minke is small, but at a weight of 10 tons, it is still one of the largest animals on earth. In fact, the only creatures larger than the minke are other whales and two plankton-eating sharks, the whale shark and the basking shark. (The African elephant, the largest land animal, weighs a maximum of 6½ tons.)

supply, which consists primarily of copepods like *Calanus finmarchicus,* which they filter out with the finely matted bristles of their baleen plates. Smaller than the blue or fin whale, *Balaenoptera borealis* is still an impressive creature, reaching a length of 65 feet. In the summer of 1885, thousands of them appeared off the coast of northern Scandinavia, and 722 were taken by Norwegian whalers. Since that time, there has been no comparable invasion. Their black or slate-gray coloration, with no white on the jaws, distinguishes them from fin whales, but like their larger relatives, they were extensively hunted in the North Atlantic until the whalers forsook them for their more plentiful Southern Hemisphere relatives.

The next rorqual in size is Bryde's whale, which was named for yet another Norwegian, Johann Bryde, who was the consul to South Africa in 1913, when the first specimen was examined at a whaling station at Durban. (Although this discovery was christened *Balaenoptera brydei,* it was later recognized that it fit the description of *B. edeni,* which had been described in 1878 by John Anderson, from a skeleton found in Burma.) *B. edeni* is somewhat smaller than the sei whale, and is characterized by three ridges running from the blowhole to the tip of the rostrum. (All other rorquals have only a single median ridge.) Despite its Norwegian common name, Bryde's whale does not figure in our account of the whales of the Atlantic, since it is known primarily from the tropical and temperate Pacific (and the South Atlantic), with large concentrations having been recorded off West Africa, South Africa, the Seychelles, western Australia, Peru, Hawaii, and Japan.

The last and smallest of the rorquals is the minke whale, *Balaenoptera acutorostrata.* Named for another Norwegian, the minke used to be known as the "little piked whale" or the "lesser rorqual," but when one of Svend Foyn's whalers named Meincke mistook one for a baby blue whale, his shipmates named the whale for him, and the name stuck. (The story may be pure fiction, but it appears regularly in the literature, and even the Japanese now call the whale *minkukujira.*) Until the 1970s, whalers ignored the little minke (pronounced "minky") because it was simply not worth the effort. But with the larger species protected or so depleted that hunting has been halted, those who would continue to kill whales for profit have turned their harpoon cannons on the lowly minke. When the other, larger rorquals were extirpated, the minke populations increased in direct proportion to the decrease in other species. Therefore, with minke populations at an all-time high, the take of a couple of hundred probably wouldn't make that much difference—except perhaps to the whales. The notorious Japanese "research whaling" has been directed toward Antarctic minke whales, and when the Norwegians decided to flout the 1983 IWC regulations that had suspended all commercial whaling, they argued that their coastal fishermen needed to hunt minkes. And Iceland, which quit the IWC in 1991 in protest over quotas and restrictions, will undoubtedly be killing North Atlantic minke whales in the near future.

Whales were hunted by the Norwegians as early as the ninth or tenth centuries and by the Icelanders in the thirteenth century, but this seems to have been "catch-as-catch-can" whaling, where schools of whales—usually pilot whales, but occasionally sperm whales—were herded into fjords or bays and dispatched en masse. The first organized whaling—as contrasted with serendipitous encounters with whales at sea—was conducted in the Atlantic by the Basques, a people who lived along the coast of the Bay of Biscay, in what is now France and Spain. In his 1820 study of the whale fishery, William Scoresby wrote, "The Biscayans were the first who exercised their courage in waging a war of death with the whales," but he attributes their motivation to the protection of their fishing nets, which "would naturally suggest the necessity of driving these intruding monsters from their coasts." The Basques exhibited none of the ecological sensitivity required for the rational management of a resource, and within two centuries, after they had eliminated the right whale from European waters, they sailed across the Atlantic to Newfoundland in search of more.

The Basques may have crossed the Atlantic to fish for cod as early as the twelfth century, so there is a strong possibility that they may have encountered right whales, even if they did not actually hunt them. Using archival records and divers, Canadian archaeologist Selma Barkham found the remains of a Basque whaling ship and a longboat (*chalupa*) at Red Bay, believed to have sunk in a storm in 1565. On two of Red Bay's islands, the remains of tryworks were also found, evidence that the Basques processed the whales on shore (Tuck and Grenier 1981).

The northern right whale (*Eubalaena glacialis*) is an elongated, black teardrop of an animal that may reach a length of 60 feet and a weight of as many tons. Its face is decorated with horny "callosities" around the lips, chin, and blowhole, in a pattern that can be used to identify individual whales. The very long baleen plates of right whales are split into two "sides," with a large gap in the middle. The whales feed by swimming through rafts of copepods and other organisms with their mouths open, allowing a stream of water and food to enter their maw, with the tiny crustaceans becoming trapped in the fringes of the baleen. (The rorquals, whose baleen is much shorter, swim openmouthed through concentrations of food items, then close their mouths and force the water out through the sieve of baleen, which traps the food.) The first European settlers in Australia, New Zealand, and South Africa were looking for protected anchorages, and they often encountered right whales and calves, because it is the habit of these whales to give birth in protected bays and coves. One such protected anchorage was Cape Cod Bay.

The Pilgrims were headed for Jamestown, Virginia, in December 1620, but winter storms blew the *Mayflower* far off course, and she landed instead on Cape Cod. It is hard to imagine what might have led these intrepid emigrants to remain on this snowblown coast, but among the enticements—perhaps the only one—was a large population of right whales, "spewing up water into the air, like the smoke of a chimney, and making the sea about them white and hoary," according to Richard Mather. In any event, stay they did, and the men of the Plymouth Colony became the first European whalers based on North American soil. In the time-honored tradition of whalers, they killed as many of the oil-rich giants as they could, with hardly a passing thought to the future of the fishery and no concern whatsoever for the future of the whales.*

The first of the New England whalemen hunted right whales (and probably humpbacks), and it was only a fortuitous accident that spared the last of them. It is said (in what may be an apocryphal story) that around 1712, a Nantucket captain named Christopher Hussey was blown offshore while hunting right whales, and came upon a school of large, bluff-headed whales with forward-angled spouts. Hussey managed to harpoon one, and towed it back to Nantucket. It was examined by the curious populace, and seen to have peglike ivory teeth where the right whale had baleen plates, and a vast reservoir of clear amber oil in its nose. This event, whether it happened exactly this way or not, marks the beginning of the sperm whale fishery, and while the early phases were conducted offshore in the North Atlantic, the whalers soon realized that the sperm whales were to be found in greater numbers elsewhere. The stalwarts of Nantucket, New Bedford, Sag Harbor, Mystic, and numerous smaller ports outfitted their ships for three- or four-year voyages to the ends of the earth in the hunt for the great sperm whale, the animal that Herman Melville called "the largest inhabitant of the globe; the most formidable of all whales to encounter; the most majestic in aspect; and lastly, by far the most valuable in commerce. . . ."

The sperm whale—certainly well known as a resident of the Atlantic and a strander on its shores—is the quintessential deepwater cetacean. Generally considered the deep-diving champion of the mammalian kingdom (a title it shares with the bottlenose whale), the sperm whale qualifies for this discussion of the deep ocean on two counts: it hunts in the great depths, often chasing its prey two miles below the surface; and in order to dive to such prodigious depths (sometimes holding its breath for over an hour), it ob-

---

* It was long believed that the Basques—and the Yankees, who killed right whales by the hundreds in and around Cape Cod Bay—had also cleansed the waters of the western North Atlantic of right whales, but in recent years, *Eubalaena glacialis* seems to have made a comeback, and northern right whales are now seen regularly off New England and the Canadian Maritimes, as far north as the Bay of Fundy. They breed off the Atlantic coasts of Florida and Georgia.

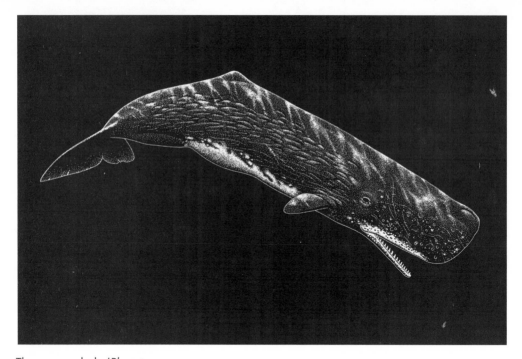

The sperm whale (*Physeter macrocephalus*) is one of the deep-diving champions of the mammalian world, capable of holding its breath for an hour and a half and descending to depths of two miles. Large bulls attain a length of 60 feet.

viously must inhabit deep waters.* *Physeter macrocephalus* ("big-headed blower") is primarily a teuthophage, but despite the hyperbolic tales of battles between the whale and the giant squid (*Architeuthis*), the sperm whale prefers smaller squids, preferably those that will serve as a meal rather than a mortal challenge. (It is likely that in all cases of sperm whale vs. giant squid—very few of which have actually been observed—it is the whale that is the aggressor.)

Since sperm whales have been hunted for the oil in their noses and in their blubber layer (carving the teeth into scrimshaw was only a by-product of the fishery; the whales were not hunted for their ivory) for hundreds of years, we have amassed a considerable body of information on the physiology of the *cachalot*. (As might be expected, until recently most of this information came from the whalers.) Males, which can grow a third again as large as females, can reach a length of 60 feet. Although it is difficult to weigh a 60-foot dead

---

* In recent experiments, depth-recorders and camcorders have been attached to elephant seals in the Pacific and have recorded dives of 5,000 feet and more. (See DeLong and Stewart 1991.) The 10,000-foot-deep dives of sperm whales have been only educated estimates, so until someone figures out how to attach a camcorder to a sperm whale, the elephant seals are the official record-holders.

whale (especially at sea), rough estimates assign it an approximate weight of a ton per foot. The sperm whale has a single S-shaped nostril at the end of its great nose through which it inhales and exhales. The exhalation (also known as the spout) is characteristically angled forward at approximately 45 degrees, a diagnostic feature at sea. The mechanisms that produce this spout—among other things—are wondrous to behold, and almost impossible to understand.

Inside its nose (the largest nose in history), *Physeter* has a series of tubes, one of which (the left) leads to the left nostril, while the right nostril seems to dead-end about halfway to the end. The oil—known as spermaceti, and responsible for the whale's common name—is found in a large organ known as the spermaceti organ (the "case" to the Yankee whalers), and a large male might have a thousand gallons. This oil in the whale's nose, which is technically a wax, is a clear amber liquid that solidifies when exposed to air. Unable to determine the purpose of this vast reservoir, early hunters thought it might be the whale's seminal fluid, hence the name "spermaceti," which means "seed of the whale." To this day, its function is unknown, but it is now believed to have something to do with sound production. (Spermaceti is an excellent conductor of sound, considerably better than water.) There is also a mysterious pair of "lips" inside and at the end of its nose. Known as the *museau du singe* ("monkey's muzzle"), these "lips" can be opened and closed at will, and are also believed to have something to do with sound generation. Recordings have been made of the whales' phonations, and they consist of clicks, "click trains" (a rapid sequence of clicks), pops, wheezes, bangs, snorts, and what William Watkins, the man who has spent more time recording and analyzing the sounds than any other, calls "codas": the specialized interaction between two whales. It is believed that the sounds are used for communication (although the nature of the communication is still an enigma), and also for echolocation. The whale broadcasts the sounds—perhaps originating in the *museau du singe* and reverberated through the oil—to identify itself and signal its location to others of its kind, and to bounce the sounds off objects in the water and read the returning echoes.

Because its prey inhabits the deep, dark levels of the ocean, the sperm whale must descend to these depths to hunt, and it must have a way of finding and capturing its prey. Like all cetaceans, the sperm whale is a mammal and it breathes air. This would appear to load the dice in favor of the squid, since cephalopods breathe water and should—in theory, anyway—be able to escape the cumbersome whale by swiftly disappearing into the darkness. (It is possible that the whale could locate the squid by their bioluminescence, but they can turn their lights off.) The whale, therefore, has had to develop a method of capturing the elusive squids while holding its breath in total darkness.

Nobody has ever observed a sperm whale hunting, so much of what follows is conjecture, based primarily on theories developed by Kenneth Norris. In 1970, at the last American whaling station (at Richmond, California), Norris examined a sperm whale that had been brought in. In his 1974 book, *The Porpoise Watcher,* he described the head:

> The head didn't look like the pictures I had seen. The bow was bluff, and to be sure, as one sees in old whalers' paintings, but from the front the upper part of the head was rounded, almost cylindrical, like the end of a boiler, and then just below it was narrow and indented, and a foot or so above the upper jaw it finally bulged again. The lower jaw was all but invisible under this peculiar snout, a long, thin rod of bone lined with teeth.

Norris dissected the head and examined the *museau* along with the spermaceti organ and the attendant air sacs and tubes. He thought he had resolved the problem of the whale's sound production, but, as he wrote, "inferences like these, made from anatomy without actual tests of true functions in life, are speculations. . . . While I thought I could see how this incredible system might work, I did not know that my speculations were right." He then did what any inquisitive cetologist would do: he built a testable model of a sperm whale. With engineer George Harvey he developed a model of the whale's resonating chamber, complete with a spermaceti-filled plastic tube, a sound generator, and an oscilloscope to display the results. Each of the clicks was composed of a packet of diminishing sounds, exactly like the recorded sounds of the whale. "I wondered," wrote Norris,

> why the sperm whale should make such peculiar sounds in the first place. What was different about the way a sperm whale lived that would require these particular bursts of sound? The only possibility that came to mind was that sperm whales feed in the deep sea, sometimes several thousand feet down, and eat mostly very large, swift prey—very large squid, some of which may be ten or even twenty feet in length. Probably the range at which the sperm whale locates its food is very long—a mile or more.

He suggested that the sound chamber in the whale's nose not only broadcasted the sounds but also amplified the returning echoes, enabling the whale to "hear tiny sounds that would otherwise be lost in the background noise of the deep sea."

While Norris's imaginative interpretation provided a possible explanation as to why and how the sperm whale's nose could produce "these particular bursts of sound," it did not answer the next question: Even if the whale managed to locate the squid in the black depths of the ocean, how did it manage to catch them? Squid are among the fastest-moving marine creatures; one source attributes burst speeds of up to 55 km per hour (34 mph) to them, and, as Norris notes, "the sperm whale is not a particularly fast or maneuverable odontocete." Nevertheless, the majority of sperm whale stomachs examined by whalers and cetologists are filled with squid, so they have to be able to catch them somehow. (One whale had the beaks of 14,000 squid in its stomach.) There was something most peculiar about the squid in the stomachs of whales: they rarely showed evidence of having been chewed or bitten. In his 1972 monograph, Soviet cetologist A. A. Berzin wrote, "Apart from the very rare exception, even on large food items found in sperm whale stomachs, no traces of teeth are visible." The teeth of sperm whales do not erupt from the gums until the animal is about ten years old—long after it has been weaned—and there are many cases of captured sperm whales with completely deformed lower jaws that nevertheless had full stomachs. The whales must obviously have developed a method of capturing the fast-moving squid that does not involve chasing them or snagging them with their teeth. Earlier theories had the whales attracting prey by dangling their white lower jaw in the water, or slurping the squid in by suction. "All these questions," wrote Norris (with Bertel Møhl, a Danish zoologist), "seem to be resolved if the sperm whale is able to immobilize its prey before engulfing it." In a paper published in 1983, Norris and Møhl wrote (emphasizing the speculative nature of their hypothesis), "The sperm whale may catch its swift squid prey leaving no evident tooth marks, and such prey may be alive in sperm whales' stomachs. The disparity between the speeds of sperm whale and squid and the costs of sperm whale acceleration are discussed [in the paper]. Sperm whales eat a very wide-sized range of prey, and small items will not repay the costs of the whale's locomotion. The forehead sound-beaming anatomy is postulated to allow prey debilitation."*

Understandably cautious, the authors included a section called "Problems for the Hypothesis," in which they noted that there have (to date) been no reports of high-intensity pulses from animals in nature. Also, "an indiscriminately used killing beam would certainly attract other predators to share in the prey," and "most intriguing of all are the questions about behavioral relations posed by having such a weapon available to all or nearly all members of a school." (Another theory about how sperm whales locate their food—presented without any documentation whatsoever in the National Geographic Society's 1995 *Whales, Dolphins and Porpoises*—suggests that the whales might

* Although Norris has published extensively on the sperm whale's ability to send out focused sound beams to immobilize its prey, the idea was not original to him, a situation he willingly acknowledges. In 1963, Soviet cetologists Bel'kovich and Yablakov published a little article entitled "The Whale—An Ultrasonic Projector," in which they wrote that the whale is able to focus a shock wave that can be "an effective instrument for stunning and immobilizing prey far away."

provide their own light. If the whales' sound bursts cause deepwater organisms to light up, their bioluminescence might provide enough light for the hunting whale to see—and therefore catch—its prey in what otherwise would be total darkness.) Until the moment comes when someone actually sees a sperm whale hunting, we can only speculate about the techniques it employs. Regardless of our hypotheses, however, *Physeter macrocephalus* continues its mysterious journey through life and time, its secrets effectively hidden by the impenetrable shield of the deep sea.

Unlike the sperm whale, whose habitat is Arctic to Antarctic and almost every other deepwater location in between, the bottlenose whale (*Hyperoodon ampullatus*) is—or was until recently—strictly an Atlantic resident.* (There is a Southern Hemisphere version known as *Hyperoodon planifrons*.) At a maximum length of 30 feet, it is one of the largest beaked whales (Ziphiidae), all of which are characterized by an extended rostrum, a small dorsal fin, and a broad tail that has no central notch. There are nineteen species of beaked whales, one of which (*Indopacetus pacificus*) is known only from two skeletons, and another, *Mesoplodon peruvianus,* was first described in 1991. Most of the other species are rare and poorly known, since they seem to be inhabitants of deep offshore waters and—unlike *Hyperoodon*—they tend to avoid boats. (Since most of our information has come from stranded specimens, it has been said that we know hardly anything about where they live; we only know where they die.) Most beaked whale species have unusual dental arrangements, in which the females have no teeth at all, and the males have two or four teeth in the lower jaw only. Most species live on a diet of squid.

The northern bottlenose whale is further distinguished in that the males and females are so different in appearance that they were originally believed to represent two different species. In an 1860 discussion of "the two British kinds of *Hyperoodon*," J. E. Gray, keeper of zoology at the British Museum, wrote, "The structure and form of the two skulls is so different, that it is much more likely that they should be referable to two very distinct genera than to species of the same genus." The male, which grows larger than the female, develops symmetrical bony crests on its skull as it matures, which gives the adult males a prominent, bulbous "forehead," a feature completely lacking in the females. (*Hyperoodon*—which is pronounced "hyper-ō-o-don"—means "over teeth," and refers to papillae on the palate, which were originally mistaken for

---

* Earlier discussions assigned this species only to the North Atlantic, but recent studies have described "*Hyperoodon* sp." from such un-Atlantic locations as the Gulf of California (Urban et al. 1994) and "the central and western Pacific" (Miyashita and Balcomb 1988.) In both cases, the animals were sighted from ships and not examined closely, so it is not clear if the *Hyperoodon* described in these studies is the same as the North Atlantic variety, or if it is *H. planifrons,* supposedly of the Southern Hemisphere. It might even be another species altogether; in their paper, Miyashita and Balcomb described it as "an unidentified beaked whale like *Hyperoodon*."

The northern bottlenose whale (*Hyperoodon ampullatus*) reaches a length of 30 feet and dives to great depths to hunt for squid. Males are lighter in color than females and have a bulbous forehead; females have a smoother profile.

teeth. *Ampullatus* means "flask-shaped," to describe the beak.) Males are born black or dark brown; they become progressively lighter as they grow older, passing through a brown or tan phase; and finally, the oldest males get to be yellowish-white with a white head and dorsal fin. Females are usually tan with white spots. Some older individuals also develop a white ring around the neck, which caused the Norwegian whalers to call them *ringfiskar,* i.e., "ringed fish."

Bottlenose whales are among the deepest-diving of all cetaceans, and they might even be the record-holders, although we have no way of measuring the exact depths of their dives. Whalers have recorded dives of one to two hours' duration (the record for a sperm whale is an hour and a half), and in a 1940 study of diving mammals, Swedish biologist Per Scholander wrote that "the bottlenose is probably the deepest and longest diver of all cetaceans." Examination of the stomach contents reveals that *Hyperoodon* eats squid, particularly the North Atlantic species *Gonatus fabricii,* which it dives to great depths to hunt. The exaggerated bony crests on the skull may serve as "acoustic baffles," enabling the bottlenose to direct bursts of sound that can stun or even kill the squid it eats. One bottlenose was examined with 10,000 squid beaks in its stomach. Whereas the nose of the sperm whale contains a great quantity of liquid oil (the spermaceti), the forehead of the bottlenose whale is equipped with a "solid lump of fat, similar in shape to, and twice the size of, a large water-melon" (Gray 1882). This may serve the same purpose as the spermaceti organ of the sperm whale—that is, to focus sound beams (assuming Norris and Møhl are correct), but then again, it may not. Whatever its function for the whale, however, this "lump of fat" provided oil that was almost identical to spermaceti—D. W. Thompson (1919) wrote that "the oil is of a fine quality, and hardly distinguishable from sperm"—and because bottlenoses were much easier to hunt than the large and dangerous sperm whales, "bottle-nosing" was assiduously pursued in the North Atlantic.

We know hardly anything about the hunting techniques *of* bottlenose whales, but because men have been hunting them for hundreds of years, we know quite a bit about hunting *for* bottlenose whales. They have been successfully sought by Norwegian, British, and Scots whalers in the cold waters of the Norwegian and Greenland seas, as far north as Spitsbergen and the edge of the polar pack ice. (Strays occasionally wander as far south as England, Rhode Island, and even the Cape Verdes.) The first bottlenose-hunters were probably early Norwegians, but with the introduction of harpoon cannons two decades before the turn of the twentieth century, the commercial fishery began in earnest.* Heading north from ports like Dundee and Peterhead (where two centuries earlier their forebears had departed on voyages to hunt the Greenland whale), Scots whalers killed bottlenose whales by the hundreds. According to R. W. Gray (the son of David Gray, who is said to have taught the Norwegians how to kill the bottlenose whales), "the *Chieftain,* of Kirkaldy, killed 28 bottlenose whales in the Davis Straits in 1850 . . . [but] their interest in it may be said to date from the year 1877, when the oil of ten killed near Iceland by the Peterhead whaler *Jan Mayen* found a ready market and realized a good price."

Capt. David Gray of Peterhead began his career as a bottlenoser in 1880, capturing 32 in his first season, and 39 the next. By 1882, he had hit his stride, and succeeded in dispatching 203. A big male yielded "two or three tons of oil, and two or three hundred-weights of spermaceti," wrote R. W. Gray, who accompanied his father in 1883 and watched as 157 bottlenoses were caught. Gray Jr. described the disposition of "flat-heads" or "johns" ("the latter term referring to their venerable appearance") when a ship approaches:

> When the sound of a ship's propeller reaches a herd, they very often hasten towards it, apparently bent on ascertaining the cause of the unusual

---

* The whalers were certainly aware that they were seeking mammals and not fish, yet in the early stages, they referred to their enterprise as a "fishery." This was probably because the techniques used in the early days of whaling resembled those used for catching fish—i.e., you caught one animal at a time and played it until it tired. With the advent of harpoon cannons and explosive grenades around 1880, the "fishery" became an industry.

disturbance, at the same time evincing their excitement by striking the water with their tails and even jumping out of it. . . . Their curiosity satisfied or their surplus energy exhausted, they either give up the diversion and disappear or they lie at the surface at no great distance from the ship as if it were a big friendly brother.

Bottlenose-whaling was neither difficult nor dangerous; rather, it was like shooting very large fish in a very large barrel. In his 1882 discussion of the "characters and habits" of the bottlenose whale, Capt. David Gray wrote,

> They are gregarious in their habits, going in herds of four to ten. . . . The herd never leaves a wounded comrade as long as it is alive; but they desert it immediately when dead; and if another can be harpooned before the previous struck one is killed, we often capture the whole herd, frequently taking ten, and on one occasion, fifteen. . . . They come from every point of the compass towards the struck one in a most mysterious manner.

To take advantage of the whales' fearlessness, the whalers armed their boats with cannons all around so they could shoot from any angle as the whales gathered around them. "The majority of the Norwegian bottlenose whalers are similar to the *Flora*," wrote R. W. Gray, "each carrying two guns in the bow, two in the stern, as well as the boats with a gun each. . . ."

Before Roy Chapman Andrews (1884–1960) went on to greater fame as a dinosaur hunter in the Gobi Desert, he compiled a collection of his observations and experiences with whales and whaling, which he entitled *Whale Hunting with Gun and Camera*. In this collection, published in 1916, Andrews went to Korea, where he found the supposedly "extinct" Pacific gray whale, participated in hunts for blue, fin, sperm, humpback, and killer whales, and discoursed at some length on the biology ("it seems certain that this whale can and does, remain under water longer than any other large cetacean") and hunting of the bottlenose—although he seems not to have signed on for a whaling voyage.

Andrews tells us that "these whales were never extensively hunted until 1882, when Capt. David Gray went north in the schooner *Eclipse* and returned with a profitable cargo of oil. (Gray evidently published his observations almost as soon as this voyage was over.) The next year, he got two hundred bottlenoses, and it was not long before the Norwegians began operations on a large scale. By 1891, seventy Norwegian ships took some three thousand bottlenoses, which were tried out for the high-grade oil and leather that was tanned from the skin. (By this time, the whales were being shot with cannons mounted on the decks, but as E. D. Mitchell reported in 1977, there was also "experimentation with chemical, explosive and other harpoon heads, bombs and grenades, lighter and stronger foregoers, spring systems to prevent breakage of lines when playing whales, motorised vessels, and many other innovations.")*

For the next thirty years, the Norwegians collected about fifty thousand bottlenoses, so it is not surprising to learn that by the 1920s, there were not enough whales left to make the commercial voyages profitable. The bottlenose fishery continued on a smaller scale, however, usually as an adjunct to the minke whale fisheries out of Norwegian fishing villages. In 1972, Benjaminsen wrote that more than five thousand bottlenoses had been caught by Norwegian whalers between 1938 and 1969, and in a 1976 International Whaling Commission report, Ivar Christensen wrote that "the direct [Norwegian] bottlenose fishery stopped in 1972 when only *Peder Huse* was catching bottlenoses. Only three bottlenoses were caught in 1973, and none in subsequent years." Soviet and Canadian whalers continued to catch small numbers of bottlenoses throughout the 1970s, but they too gave it up when the whales became too scarce. In 1976, the Red Data Book of the International Union for the Conservation of Nature (IUCN) listed the bottlenose whale as "vulnerable" and suggested "complete protection for the species at least until additional information is available to allow conclusions regarding present status of the species."

Other beaked whale species also frequent the Atlantic, but because they have never been fished commercially, we have considerably less information on their habits and biology than we do about *Hyperoodon*. Cuvier's beaked whale (*Ziphius cavirostris*) is an unusual creature, even for a beaked whale. It has a less pronounced beak than most of the other ziphiids, and because of the peculiar contour of the mouth, it is sometimes known as the "goose-beaked whale." Coloration ranges from dark gray to fawn-brown, and in older males, the back and head are often white. As with all other beaked whales, the skin is covered with linear scars, attributable to intraspecific fighting. It is indeed possible that these scars are caused by fighting, but as there are hardly any recorded observations of beaked whales in the wild, and none whatsoever of two of them fighting, the cause of the scars is still speculative. (The fighting— if it occurs at all—probably takes place underwater, making it that much more difficult to document.) Goose-beaked whales are found in practically all the world's oceans (except the high polar latitudes), but as far as we know, other species are more limited in their distribution.

* Not all of this whaling was a model of modern efficiency. According to Jonsgard's 1955 review of the Norwegian small whale industry, "The boats . . . were not built to withstand the strain caused by a gun. After a couple of shots the gun as a rule broke loose from the bollard, and in many cases it was then more dangerous to the gunner than to the whale which was to be harpooned . . . The lack of confidence whaling men had in their equipment is best shown by the fact that it was customary for them to make a trial shot by fastening a line to the trigger, standing behind the wheelhouse, and firing."

All other beaked whales belong to the genus *Mesoplodon*, which means "with a tooth in the middle of the jaw." Because they are hardly ever seen alive, most determinations are based on the examination of carcasses or skeletons, and the position of the teeth in the lower jaw is a diagnostic

Beaked whales are among the least known of all marine mammals. The Atlantic species known as Sowerby's beaked whale (*Mesoplodon bidens*) reaches a length of 20 feet and is known from strandings in Iceland, Norway, Sweden, and Scotland

feature. From those that occasionally wash ashore, we know that they are spindle-shaped animals with small heads and broad, un-notched tails. The blowhole is crescent-shaped, with the horns pointing forward, and the small dorsal fin is much closer to the tail than to the head. A typical example is True's beaked whale, properly known as *Mesoplodon mirus*. (*Mirus* means "wonderful" or "amazing" in Latin.) It reaches a known maximum length of about 18 feet, and is slate-black in color, sometimes lighter below. The species has been recorded from various North Atlantic locations, such as Nova Scotia and Florida in the west, and the Hebrides and Ireland in the eastern Atlantic, but to thoroughly confuse cetologists, there seems to be a small population off South Africa.*

* This anomaly is not unusual in the mesoplodonts. The scamperdown whale (*Mesoplodon grayi*) has been recorded almost exclusively from the Southern Hemisphere (New Zealand, Australia, and South Africa), except for the first specimen, which was washed ashore in the Netherlands. Another North Atlantic species, *Mesoplodon europaeus*, is known primarily from the east coast of the United States, from Florida to New Jersey, with a couple of records from Jamaica and Trinidad, but like *M. grayi*, the first specimen appeared somewhere else—in this case, floating in the English Channel.

Deep Atlantic Whales and Whaling   313

The whale known as Sowerby's beaked whale (*M. bidens*) is the north-ernmost species of the Atlantic and is sometimes called the "North Sea beaked whale." It reaches a known maximum length of 20 feet, and is known from strandings in Iceland, Norway, Sweden, and most other countries with coasts on the North Atlantic. From a specimen that stranded on Moray Firth in Scotland in 1800, it was the first beaked whale to be described. James Sowerby published a painting of the skull in his *British Miscellany* in 1804, and has therefore had his name affiliated with it since that date. (*Bidens* simply means "two teeth.") Sowerby's description (which evidently initiated the idea of a "beaked whale") reads as follows:

> We might have called it *Physter Rostratus,* with some propriety; but this might have created confusion. It is however a curious circumstance that such an appellation would suit better if it were described with the wrong side upwards; which would be easily observed, if the plate is reversed: and the jaws, in this case, very aptly resemble a bird's beak.

Then there is the Gulf Stream beaked whale, described by Paul Gervais from a single specimen found in the English Channel in 1848. (This species is sometimes known as Gervais's beaked whale, and indeed, it used to be named *Mesoplodon gervaisi.*) Since its appearance in the Channel, however, no other specimens have been found in Europe. So with the misleading name *Mesoplodon europaeus,* it has appeared on beaches in West Africa, the east coast of North America from New York to Florida, the Gulf of Mexico, Jamaica, Cuba, and Trinidad. It closely resembles True's beaked whale (*M. mirus*), and it has appeared at many of the same locations. (In a 1957 study of the two species, Moore and Wood identified several skeletal differences, and of their distribution wrote that "there is some segregation between the species, although there is considerable overlap.") The species can be differentiated by tooth position; the two teeth are about one-third of the way back from the tip of the lower jaw in the males of *M. europaeus,* and at the very tip in *M. mirus*. It is an indication of our profound ignorance of this enigmatic group of cetaceans that no one has even speculated as to how (or why) such similar animals might be able to share the same range and, presumably, the same squid supply.

Blainville's beaked whale, *Mesoplodon densirostris* (also called the "dense-beaked whale"), is one of the most widely distributed of all the beaked whales and has been recorded from such diverse locations as the Seychelles, Tasmania, Japan, Lord Howe Island, South Africa, Hawaii, and California; and in the Atlantic, from Nova Scotia, Massachusetts, Rhode Island, New Jersey, North Carolina, Florida, and the Bahamas. Adult males are quite possibly the most easily recognized of the beaked whales—although they are as rare as the other species—since they have a prominently arched lower jaw with the huge pair of teeth that Dale Rice (1977) said "protrude above the forehead somewhat like a pair of horns." (Females and juveniles, however, lack these teeth, and look very much like all other mesoplodonts.) Of the beaked whales, Peter Matthiessen wrote:

> Some species of small beaked whales, an ancient group which may be passing slowly from existence, appear rarely in North American waters. There are only a few scattered records, on the Atlantic coast, of the Sowerby and Gervais whales, and of the Stejneger's whale in the Pacific, and the habits of these mysterious creatures are virtually unknown.

Much is incorporated into the popular and scientific nomenclature of the humpback whale. Its hump does not exist (there is a minimal sort of two-step dorsal fin), but it does arch its back when it dives, which probably accounts for the common name. (Never deterred by a lack of firsthand observations, Herman Melville wrote that "he has a great pack on him like a peddler; or you might call him the Elephant and Castle Whale.") There is music, however, in the scientific name. *Megaptera* comes from the Greek for "big-wing," and refers to the elongated flippers that the humpback uses to steer with. *Novaeangliae* is a combination of *novae* ("new") and the Middle English *angliae,* which means "England." Thus, the entire name can be translated as "big-winged New Englander," a succinct appellation that includes its description as well as its address.

Humpbacks are the whales that sing. They perform on their warm-water breeding grounds (the Caribbean for North Atlantic populations; Hawaii for the whales of southeast Alaska), so the eerie, haunting music is not a part of the Atlantic whale experience. But off the Massachusetts coast they feed and gambol, making them the darlings of the whale-watchers. There are few records of Yankee humpbacking, but the appearance of these whales in the twentieth century, mostly off the coast of Massachusetts, suggests that they have been hanging around Stellwagen Bank for a long time. In 1975, when Capt. Alvin Avellar of Provincetown took the first whale-watchers aboard his fishing boat *Dolphin,* he had no idea that he was going to start an industry. Since that day, millions of people have joined Avellar and other charter captains to watch the whales only a couple of hours out of Boston or Provincetown. (There are even whale-watching cruises out of Montauk, Long Island, but they rarely see humpbacks because the whales are active too far to the north.)

Like the right whale—to which it is not related—the humpback comes into shallow, protected waters to breed. Its early history parallels that of the right whale as well, since settlers trying to find a place to live often spotted the blows of mother and calf humpbacks just offshore. In New England, eastern Australia, New Zealand, and South Africa, the humpbacks and the right whales usually fell to the harpoons of the settlers, even before professional whalers appeared to continue the job. Humpbacks were killed in great numbers during the early part of the twentieth century, off West Africa, South America, and in the Antarctic, but their current popularity depends on their vocal skills and their visibility. Along with the best-selling record by Roger and Katy Payne (*Songs of the Humpback Whale*) the sheer visibility of humpbacks has done more to elevate the whale to iconic status than anything else in recent history.

Once upon a time, there were gray whales that fed in the cold waters off Iceland and Greenland and came south—perhaps to the Bay of Biscay, or even to the English Channel—to breed. Morphologically, they were the same whales (now known as *Eschrichtius robustus*) as the California gray whales, which confine their migratory meanderings to the Pacific coast of North America, annually swimming south from the Bering Sea to Baja California and back again. (There also used to be a western Pacific population of gray whales, summering off Siberia and wintering in the breeding grounds off Korea and Japan, but during the twentieth century, this population was eliminated by Japanese and Korean whalers.) No living person has ever seen an Atlantic gray whale, but we do have conclusive paleontological and historical evidence to verify the existence of this version of the whale that the whalers used to call "devil-fish."

To date, the earliest mention of the Atlantic gray whale is in an Icelandic

The only known drawing of an Atlantic gray whale. It originally appeared in a seventeenth-century book about the mammals of Iceland, written by one Jon Gudmundsson, and was subsequently reproduced in Francis Fraser's 1970 article, "An Early 17th Century Record of the Californian Grey Whale in Icelandic Waters."

bestiary from about 1200 A.D. that describes some different kinds of whales, but not accurately enough for modern cetologists to identify them as to species. In the *Konungs skuggsjá* ("king's mirror"), a thirteenth-century document written in Norwegian, probably as a set of instructions for a king's son, there is a list of twenty-one sea creatures, some of which can be referred to living whales, dolphins, and pinnipeds, and some of which—mermaids and mermen, for example—are clearly mythological. Although it is not clearly identified, the gray whale is supposed to be one of the whales mentioned.

In a seventeenth-century work by an Icelander named Jon Gudmundsson (quoted in Hermannsson 1924), there is a list of the various whales that might be found in Icelandic waters, and one of these is *Sandloegja,* which has been translated as "sand-lier"—i.e., one that lies in the sand. The description of the *Sandloegja* is accompanied by a picture of a whale that is admittedly inconclusive, but since it is obviously not one of the verified Icelandic species, it is likely that this is an illustration of an Atlantic gray whale. The description—translated from the Icelandic—is as follows: "Sandloegja . . . Good eating. It has whiter baleen plates, which project from the upper jaw instead of teeth, as in all other baleen whales, which will be discussed later. It is very tenacious of life and can come to land to lie as a seal like to rest the whole day. But in sand it never breaks up." Many of these characteristics—for example, the "whiter baleen plates" and the sand-lying behavior that gave it its name—would appear to refer to the gray whale, which does indeed have short, whitish baleen, and a habit of coming into very shallow water, but other whales share some of these attributes, and none can be said to be absolutely diagnostic.

So far, the literature has produced nothing that can be positively identified as an Atlantic gray whale, but before the modern era, gray whales swam in the Atlantic Ocean. Fossil remains of a species similar to—if not identical with—the Pacific gray whale have been found in western Europe (Sweden, England, and the Netherlands) and on the east coast of North America from New Jersey to South Carolina. The Atlantic gray whale fed in cold northern waters (perhaps Iceland and Greenland) and then moved south (to Spain, France, or England?) to breed and calve. With the exception of the fossil evidence, the only clues to the identity of this whale are found in the work by Gudmundsson, and a debatable reference in a New England work of 1725, in which Paul Dudley describes the "scrag whale" as having characteristics that are not applicable to any other species except the gray whale. Dudley's entire citation, which appears in the *Philosophical Transactions of the Royal Society of London* for 1725, reads as follows: "The Scrag whale is near a-kin to the Finback, but instead of a Fin on his Back, the Ridge of the After part of his Back is scragged with a half Dozen Knobs or Knuckles; he is nearest the right Whale in Figure and for Quantity of Oil; his bone is white but won't split." (In his analysis of the whales of the *Konungs skuggsjá*, Ian Whitaker writes that "the gray whale was hunted in the Atlantic between 1100 and 1200, although it has not been found there since the 18th century." He is unable to correlate this species with any of the thirteenth-century Icelandic names, although he indicates that there are two "unallocated" names, which translate as "hog-whale" and "shield-whale."

In their 1984 study of the Atlantic gray whale, James Mead and Edward Mitchell recognize only Fraser's *Sandloegja;* the 1725 description of the "scrag whale" by Paul Dudley; and the 1611 instructions given by the directors of the Muscovy Company to Thomas Edge. Edge's instructions included descriptions of all sorts of whales that he might look for, including the "Otta sotta," which was described as being "the same colour as the Trumpa [sperm whale] having finnes in his mouth all white but not above a yard long, being thicker than the Trumpa but not so long. He yeeldes the best oyle but not above 30 hogs' heads."

The gray whale completely disappears from the Atlantic after the mention in 1725, but it has reentered the literature because of the recent discovery of subfossil remains in New Jersey and South Carolina on the western shore, and Sweden, England, and the Netherlands in the eastern Atlantic. Extrapolating from comparable Pacific data, we can assume that during the summer, the Atlantic gray whales fed in the deep, cold waters off Iceland and Greenland, and then, with the coming of autumn, they headed south, just as their Pacific cousins do. In protected bays (none of which have been identified), the cows would have delivered their calves and become impregnated, prior to the northward journey in the spring.

What happened to them? It is impossible to know for sure, but a certain portion of the responsibility is probably assignable to the Basques, who prowled the shores of the Bay of Biscay from approximately the year 1000 onward, and although they are best known for their decimation of the right whale, they probably would not have been averse to taking a gray whale if one wandered into harpoon range. In *Sea of Slaughter,* an impassioned condemnation of mankind's ecological excesses in the North Atlantic, Farley Mowat gives us a most dramatic version of the disappearance of the gray whales, which he calls *otta sotta.* Something or somebody eliminated the Atlantic gray whale, but Mowat's "evidence" is so flimsy that we are almost inclined to see the disappearance of the species as a natural evolutionary occurrence, and not the work of depraved whale-killers. (Although Mowat's book has a fairly extensive bibliography, he does not tell us the name of the work from which any particular information comes, so we cannot cross-check or verify any number or statement.) He says that the *otta sotta* was "the favorite prey of the Basque whalers until they exterminated it, relegated it to historical oblivion."

After vilifying the Basques for hunting the gray whale "to virtual extinction in European waters," Mowat turns his fire on the natives, who he says killed the "powdaree" along its southern migration route to the warm-water lagoons of Florida. There is hardly any reason at all to assume that the "powdawe" (or "powdare") was anything but the right whale, but it suits Mowat's argument to believe that it was the gray. He quotes the journal kept by Capt. George Waymouth on his 1605 voyage to America, included here to demonstrate that there is nothing whatsoever—except the length, which suggests that it was *not* a gray whale—to indicate what sort of whale it was:

> One especial thing is their method of killing the whale, which they call a *powdawe;* and will describe his form, how he bloweth up the water; and that he is twelve fathoms long; that they go in company of their king with a multitude of their boats; and strike him with a bone made in the fashion of a harping iron fastened to a rope, which they make great and strong from the bark of trees, which they veer out after him; then all their boats come about him as he riseth above the water; with their arrows they shoot him to death; when they have killed him and dragged him to the shore, they call all their chief lords together, and sing a song of joy; and those chief lords which they call sagamores, divide the spoil and give to every man a share, which pieces are so distributed, and they hang up about their houses for provisions; and when they boil them they blow off the fat and put to their pease, maize and other pulse which they eat.

Mowat bases much of his polemic on the use of the term "scrag whale," which is how Paul Dudley described a sort of whale that may have been a gray whale. Mowat claims to have looked at "old charts" and found "forty-seven Scrag Islands, Scrag Rocks, Scrag Ledges and Scrag Bays along the shores of Nova Scotia, the Gulf of Maine, and the American coastal states as far south as Georgia." But "Scrag Ledge" doesn't prove that there were gray—or any other—whales in the vicinity, for "scrag," according to the first definition in the Oxford English Dictionary, is "a lean person or animal," not necessarily a lean gray whale. (In the glossary of Clifford Ashley's *Yankee Whaler,* "scrag whale" is "a name formerly used to designate a Baleen Whale of poor quality—either a thin Right Whale or a Fin Whale.") The second set of definitions in the OED indicate that it was used to describe "the stump of a tree, or a rough projection," or "rough, rocky and barren ground," suggesting that "scrag" is a much more functional appellation for rocks and ledges than for whales. And finally, in Charles Melville Scammon's *Marine Mammals,* certainly the definitive early work on the *California* gray whale, the author lists all the known nicknames for the whale he introduced to the whalers, including "Hard-head," "Mussel-digger," "Devil-fish," "Grey-back," and "Rip-sack." Surely Scammon, whose 1874 book was based on years of firsthand experience as a captain in the fishery, would have heard the term "scrag whale" if any of his crew members or fellow captains had ever used it.

Into the Deep

In the preface to the 1961 edition of *The Sea Around Us,* first published in 1950, Rachel Carson wrote, "The sea has always challenged the minds and imaginations of men and even today it remains the last great frontier of Earth. It is a realm so vast and difficult to access that with all our efforts we have explored only a small fraction of its area. Not even the mighty technological developments of this, the Atomic Age, have greatly changed this situation." Now that another thirty-five years have passed, how much progress have we made in unlocking the sea's mysteries?

Since Rachel Carson's important book appeared (it won the prestigious National Book Award for nonfiction in 1951), the most momentous feat of exploration has been the moon landing by Neil Armstrong and Buzz Aldrin in July 1969. Man has always dreamed of breaking free of the earthly restrictions of his base planet, whether to scale the highest peaks or to plumb the greatest depths; the astronauts' accomplishment marked the first time that earthlings had set foot on another body in the solar system. Later that year, the *Apollo 12* mission brought back the first moon rocks. In 1976, the Viking spacecrafts successfully transmitted the first photographs of the surface of Mars, and subsequent space probes have given us astonishing pictures of Mercury, Venus, Saturn, Jupiter, and Uranus.

At the same time that NASA was sending men and cameras into space, men and women were also exploring the "vast and difficult realm" of the ocean. In 1960, the U.S. nuclear submarine *Triton* circumnavigated the globe underwater, and also in that year, Jacques Piccard and Lt. Don Walsh of the U.S. Navy landed the bathyscaph *Trieste* on the very bottom of the greatest depth in the ocean—35,800 feet in the Challenger Deep of the Mariana Trench. Once this record had been set, aquanauts who needed something else to prove and other horizons to conquer experimented with living underwater. Inventor and industrialist Edwin Link headed up the Man-in-Sea Project, of which he said (in a 1963 *National Geographic* article), "the ultimate aim is to enable men to live and work on the floor of the ocean at depths of 1,000 feet or possibly more for days, weeks, or even months." In the *Sea Diver*, a modified decompression chamber, Belgian diver Robert Sténuit remained underwater for twenty-four hours off Villefranche-sur-Mer on the French Riviera in 1962, breathing a mixture of helium and oxygen. Jacques Cousteau, who with Emile Gagnan invented the aqualung that enabled men to remain underwater longer than they had ever done before, developed the Continental Shelf Station (*Conshelf*), an environment that housed five divers on the bottom of the Mediterranean for a week. In 1963, the much more ambitious *Conshelf Two* descended to a depth of 40 feet in the Red Sea, and divers spent a month on the bottom in "Starfish House," while two men lived and worked for a week 50 feet farther down the slope in "Deep Cabin," an 11-foot-high rocket-shaped cylinder. The U.S. Navy, acknowledging the possibilities of undersea habitation, developed *Sealab I*, which was lowered to a depth of 193 feet off Bermuda in '64. More or less simultaneously, Link's Man-in-Sea program had Robert Sténuit and Jon Lindbergh (the son of the aviator) on the bottom of the Caribbean at 432 feet. By 1965, Cousteau's *Conshelf Three* kept six men alive and working for twenty-two days at 328 feet in the Mediterranean, and the U.S. Navy's *Sealab II*, a 57-foot-long cylinder, 12 feet in diameter, housed twenty-eight men in fifteen-day shifts, one of whom was Scott Carpenter, the first astronaut/aquanaut, 205 feet down in California waters. The U.S. Navy continued their experiments in underwater habitation; by 1969, a joint program of the Navy, the Department of the Interior, and NASA sent four men down in *Tektite I*. As the crew of *Apollo 11* was blasting off for the moon in 1969, the experimental submersible *Ben Franklin* was launched in Florida to cruise the Gulf Stream (underwater) for a month.

From the day she was launched in June 1964, the Woods Hole submersible *Alvin* has provided an unprecedented window into the depths. Scientists of every stripe have used the stubby little submarine to enhance and enrich our knowledge of the deep sea. But *Alvin*'s distinguished career (continuing as this is being written) consists not only of scientists looking at weird fishes, squid, and jellyfishes. Her first official mission, after her trials, was the search for and locating of a lost H-bomb off Spain. In 1974, along with the French submersibles *Archimède* and *Cyana* (the "diving saucer"), *Alvin* conducted extensive surveys of the Mid-Atlantic Ridge as part of Project FAMOUS (French-American Mid-Ocean Undersea Study), the first close-up look at the vast mountain range that splits the Atlantic Ocean floor. And just when we believed that we were beginning to understand the biology of the oceans, scientists in *Alvin* came across unbelievable life forms: giant tube worms, clams, and crabs that lived in superheated water on hydrothermal vents on the Galápagos Rift, subsisting on the synthesis of sulfur, not on the photosynthesis that sustains every other life form on the planet. Although the *Titanic* was not actually found by *Alvin,* the submersible was used by Robert Ballard to investigate and photograph the "unsinkable" White Star liner in 1986.

The scale of underwater exploration ranges from huge ships like the *Glomar Challenger,* a 400-foot-long drilling platform, to individuals in one-man (or one-woman, if the diver is Sylvia Earle) diving suits. *Glomar Challenger* was launched in 1968 and cruised around the world, drilling into the sediments of the ocean floor until 1983, providing a vast reservoir of information on such diverse subjects as sea-floor spreading, continental drift, and deep-sea mineral resources. In contrast, with only a pressurized diving suit as protection, 110-pound oceanographer Sylvia Earle descended to a record (for a woman in a diving suit) 1,250 feet in the Pacific. Now Graham Hawkes, the designer of various deep-sea vehicles, is working on a one-man submarine that he plans to take to the bottom of the sea—the Challenger Deep in the Marianas. (As of March 24, 1995, the Japanese unmanned submersible *Kaiko* duplicated the 1960 feat of Don Walsh and Jacques Piccard, and reached the bottom at 35,800 feet. Unlike *Trieste*'s pilots, however, *Kaiko* had a camera, and brought back a picture of the most inaccessible spot on earth.)

Man-made objects occasionally sink, and the need to find and retrieve them has provided another powerful impetus for the development of underwater exploration technology. When the submarine USS *Thresher* mysteriously sank in 1963 off Boston, the submersible *Trieste* (world's record-holder for deep-diving) was selected to conduct the search. The *Thresher* was located and photographed in 8,400 feet of water, but the decision was made not to try to salvage the doomed submarine and the bodies of her 129 crewmen. It was not a good idea to leave an unexploded hydrogen bomb lying on the sea floor off Palomares, Spain, so *Alvin*'s 1966 search-and-rescue mission was necessary. Even *Alvin* herself needed rescuing after she slipped a support cable and sank off her home port of Woods Hole. She lay on the bottom in 5,000 feet of water for eleven months before being located and hooked up by the submersible *Aluminaut* and hauled to the surface.

The prospects of underwater archaeology, however, provide even more of a stimulus for exploration of the deep-sea floor. Centuries of seafaring have engendered thousands of wrecks, and the lure of buried treasure or significant historical revelations have brought men to the bottom again. In 1953, Cousteau found a Greek merchant ship that sank in the Mediterranean around 230 B.C., and retrieved various artifacts, including statuary, pottery, and even a stove, that yielded important clues to the way of life of the ancient Greeks. The Swedish warship *Vasa* sank on her maiden voyage on August 10, 1628, and was raised in 1961, was carefully restored, and now sits proudly in her own museum in Stockholm, a monument to seventeenth-century shipbuilding—and underwater archaeology. Edwin Link led a 1959 underwater expedition to Port Royal, Jamaica, which was shattered by an earthquake in 1692, when, as the stunned survivors watched, two-thirds of the city (and two thousand people) tumbled into the Caribbean.

Willard Bascom, an oceanographic engineer (and manager of the ill-fated Mohole project), had patented devices for underwater archaeological investigation in 1962, but it was George Bass, a professor of archaeology at the University of Pennsylvania, who turned this esoteric subject into a full-scale discipline. (He went on to found the Institute for Nautical Archaeology [INA] at Texas A&M University.) His first find was a Bronze Age vessel that had sunk thirty-two centuries ago off Cape Gelidonya in Turkey, and under his inspiration, other divers located and excavated Greek, Etruscan, Egyptian, Phoenecian, and Roman vessels. In 1984, the INA launched a full-scale underwater dig at Ulu Burun on the coast of Turkey, where a Bronze Age trading vessel—perhaps from Cyprus—had sunk about thirty-three hundred years ago, carrying a cargo of glass, spices, tin, and about 20,000 pounds of copper ingots from Cyprus. (Tin and copper were combined to make bronze.) After nine years of diving, the INA had logged over five thousand hours of underwater time and collected more than four thousand artifacts.

In 1995, the U.S. Navy announced that it was going to use the nuclear-powered research submarine *NR-1* to search the Mediterranean for Roman wrecks, under the direction of Robert Ballard, who is severing his longtime association with the Woods Hole Oceanographic Institution and starting a center for undersea exploration at Mystic, Connecticut. The submarine, which is equipped with windows, wheels, and television cameras, and is manned by a crew of eleven, is scheduled to investigate the shipping lanes between Rome and Carthage.

One of the enduring myths connected to the Atlantic Ocean concerns the lost continent—or lost island, or lost city—of Atlantis. The origin of this tale, unlike many other legends, is clear. Atlantis is first mentioned by Plato in the dialogues *Timaeus* and *Critias*. He tells us that his predecessor Solon (639–559 B.C.) reported that the Egyptian priests of Saïs told him of an ancient papyrus that described a great island that lay in the Atlantic Ocean, just off the Pillars of Hercules.

Plato's dialogues contain the only reference to the disappearing island of

Atlantis in the whole of ancient literature, and no other mention is made of this story until other people begin quoting Plato, who died in 348 B.C. (Not even the Greek historian Herodotus mentions the story, and he is said to have spoken directly with the priests at Saïs, the very priests who passed the story to Solon.) There are people who take everything he said literally (even though they are unable to locate the missing island), and others who dismiss the whole story as "science fiction." Others categorize it as a fictional account that Plato introduced for his own reasons.

Another aspect of Plato's discussion of Atlantis is found in *Critias,* where he describes the nature of the island's civilization before its destruction. In this description we might find some indication of what Plato actually had in mind, for he describes a fanciful civilization, replete with boundless natural riches, "which then lay open to the sun, in marvelous beauty and inexhaustible profusion." The royalty of Atlantis were enormously wealthy ("they possessed wealth such as had never been amassed by any royal line before them"), perhaps because they were able to mine the mineral orichalch, which was higher in value than any other except gold. The forests and pastures were exceptionally bountiful, and "the soil bore all aromatic substances still to be found on earth, roots, stalks, canes, gums exuded by flowers and fruits," and there were two springs, a cold and a warm, and "the supply from both was copious and the natural flavor of their waters remarkable." Man-made structures included temples, gymnasiums, dockyards, all in excellent order. Since this description fits no known land, and since the plains, the forests, the waters, and the city are so sumptuous, it seems not unreasonable to conclude that Plato was describing a mythical utopia, and that to explain its disappearance, he invented a great natural catastrophe. Future Atlantologists would attempt to fit Plato's description into almost every political and geological system known, with varying degrees of success.

Later students of the Atlantis story have pointed out that it is curious that no other ancient historians made reference to Atlantis, except, of course, to quote Plato. In his 1978 essay on the historical perspective regarding Atlantis, J. Rufus Fears wrote, "In the absence of any evidence from the Egyptian sources, the silence of Thucydides, Herodotus, Isocrates, and Aelius Aristedes seems conclusive. Plato's story does not reflect a historical tradition derived from Egypt or Solon or from anywhere or anyone else. It is a poetic invention of Plato." Moreover, its hypothetical location has not always remained just outside the Straits of Gibraltar, but has wandered from the Canary Islands to the Sahara desert, Scandinavia, Germany, Nigeria, and Palestine, currently coming to rest on various Aegean islands, especially Thera and Crete.

Books have been written about the affiliation of Atlantis with the collapse of the Minoan civilization on Crete, and about the volcanic explosion of the island of Thera around 1500 B.C., which may have generated tsunamis of such size and power that they eliminated the Minoans and their palaces. (The much smaller explosion of the Indonesian volcano of Krakatau in 1883 drowned thirty-six thousand people in waves that were 135 feet high.) But during Plato's lifetime, an event occurred that may have had even more influence on the perpetuation of the story of Atlantis: in 373 B.C., on the southern shore of the Gulf of Corinth, the city of Helice (also spelled "Helike") slid into the sea as a result of an earthquake. (The event is documented by the contemporaneous Greek geographers Pausanias and Strabo.) Various archaeological adventurers—from a French team in 1950, to Harold "Doc" Edgerton in 1966 and Peter Throckmorton in 1971—have tried to find this lost Greek city, but with no success.

Of course, not all underwater searches are conducted for purely historical reasons. When Europeans—usually from Spain or Portugal—were plundering the riches of the Americas, they transported their booty in sailing ships, which were at the mercy of the unforgiving ocean. Thousands of treasure ships ran aground in storms or sank in bad weather, and while many of them still lie undisturbed on the sandy bottom, many others have been found by treasure hunters, who search the libraries of Castile and Lisbon for clues about the treasure fleets. Millions of dollars worth of gold, silver, and jewelry have been retrieved so far, and the search continues, enhanced and encouraged by the new technology.*

Surely the most celebrated shipwreck in history is the *Titanic,* which sank on April 15, 1912, after colliding with an iceberg some 360 miles off the Grand Banks of Newfoundland. For seventy-three years the shattered hulk lay in the black silence of the North Atlantic, until a joint French-American expedition located the ship. After quartering the area where they believed the great ship had gone down on that "night to remember," the French ship *Le Suroît* and the American research vessel *Knorr* deployed side-scan sonar and obtained images that they believed pinpointed the position of the ship. They then sent down a pair of robotic-camera vehicles (*Argo* and ANGUS) that returned television images, first of one of her gigantic boilers, and then of the 882-foot-long hull broken into two parts, lying on the bottom in a field of rubble. The finding and photographing of the *Titanic* was prob-

---

* Carrying two tons of gold slated for delivery to Germany's war machine, the Japanese submarine known as *I-52* was torpedoed by a U.S. Navy dive-bomber on June 23, 1944, and sank in water three miles deep in the North Atlantic west of the Cape Verde Islands. In the spring of 1995, using the most modern technology, researchers located the drowned submarine, and are planning to salvage the gold—worth perhaps $25 million—and maybe even the submarine itself.

ably the most important demonstration to date of what Ballard referred to as "telepresence": the use of robotically controlled video equipment to explore the depths with a degree of safety and economy previously unavailable to underwater explorers. Unmanned submersible vehicles will dominate underwater exploration in the future. They can be equipped with television and still cameras, magnetic sensors, robotic arms, and numerous other devices that will enable scientists at computer consoles to accomplish what earlier explorers tried to do while sealed in watertight little vessels floating in the darkness.

There are some for whom an electronically enhanced "telepresence" is far from sufficient. Cindy Van Dover, *Alvin*'s first woman pilot, wrote, "There is an undefinable advantage to seeing the ocean bed with one's own eyes. . . . As a colleague of mine once pointed out, no one who has a choice between watching a video of Paris or going there in person is going to opt for the arm-chair approach. The same holds true for the seafloor."

Space travel by humans is not now considered feasible or practicable, since it has been shown to be too expensive and too dangerous. But we do not have to travel hundreds of thousands of miles to find vast tracts of unexplored territory. The bottom of the sea—only seven miles away at its deepest point— still beckons. On August 14, 1995, *Time* magazine ran a cover story entitled "Mysteries of the Deep." (The cover's subtitle is "Scientists are set to conquer the last frontier: the ocean floor"; and the table of contents lists the article as "Voyage to the Bottom of the Sea.") The article covers manned and unmanned submersibles, the ocean floor, and hydrothermal vents, and includes a portfolio of photographs of "sea monsters": half a dozen of "the creatures that live in the harsh conditions far below the surface. . . ." The *Time* story could serve as a succinct introduction to this book, as the authors (Dorfman et al.) write, "Despite the budget cuts, despite the inhospitable environment, despite the pressing danger, there is little doubt that humans, one way or another, are headed back to the bottom of the sea. The rewards of exploring the coldest, darkest waters—scientific, economic, and psychological—are just too great to pass up." As with so many of her trenchant observations, Rachel Carson was right about the lure of the depths.

But despite our enthusiasm and technological advances, the deep sea will remain largely unexplored. We can send submersibles down to the bottom, and, if we are very lucky, direct searchlights toward some of the stranger creatures of the abyss and the powerful manifestations of the geology that shapes and affects our planet. But much of the sea's unfathomable volume is deep, black, and, by its very magnitude, unknowable. We may know something about the patch that we have chosen to explore, but beyond the range of our lights, just outside the swath dragged by our trawls, there are unquestion-ably creatures that we have never known. Consider *Architeuthis,* the giant squid. We know that these 60-foot-long monsters exist because we have seen their tattered carcasses washed up on shore, but no diver, no submersible, no robotic camera has ever captured an image of this elusive cephalopod. Do we know if one of these saucer-eyed creatures stared at the *Alvin* as she circled the encrusted, broken hull of the *Titanic?*

Bibliography

The deep Atlantic is one of the most complicated ecosystems in the world. Because of the intricate integration of subjects required for even a perfunctory discussion, this bibliography may appear overlong and, for some, overtechnical. The literature on oceanography, bioluminescence, oceanic geology, submersibles, hydrothermal vents, deep-sea fishes and invertebrates, and sharks and whales is enormous, and rather than load this book with an even more intimidating list of references, I have selected only those that I believe are necessary for specific documentation. With the exception of general works—such as Heezen and Hollister's *Face of the Deep,* Marshall's *Deep-Sea Biology,* or Idyll's *Abyss*—most of the studies listed below deal with one aspect of an often complicated subject, and subsequent investigations have been consulted to enhance the original discussion, to dispute it, or simply to provide more information.

ABE, T., AND M. FUNABASHI. 1992. A Record of an Adult Female of the Deep Sea Ceratioid Anglerfish *Cryptopsaras couesi* Gill with Four Parasitic Males from off Ibaraki Peninsula, Japan. *Uo* 41:1–3.

ADAMS, H. 1918. *The Education of Henry Adams.* Massachusetts Historical Society. Sentry edition, 1961.

ADLER, T. 1994. Bacteria Found Deep Below Ocean Floor. *Science News* 146(14):215.

AGASSIZ, A. 1888. *Three Cruises of the United States Coast and Geodetic Survey Steamer "Blake."* Sampson Low, Marston, Searle & Rivington.

ALLDREDGE, A. L. 1976. Appendicularians. *Scientific American* 235(1):95–102.

ALLEN, J. A. 1978. Evolution of the Deep Sea Protobranch Bivalves. *Phil. Trans. Royal Soc. London* 284:387–401.

———. 1979. The Adaptations and Radiation of Deep-Sea Bivalves. *Sarsia* 64:19–27.

———. 1983. The Ecology of the Deep-Sea Mollusca. In W. D. Russell-Hunter, ed., *The Mollusca,* pp. 29–75. Academic Press.

ALLEN, J. A., AND H. L. SANDERS. 1966. Adaptations to Abyssal Life as Shown by the Bivalve *Abra profundorum*. *Deep-Sea Research* 13:1175–84.

ALLEN, T. B. 1987. "William Beebe." In J. B. Tourtellot, ed., *Into the Unknown: The Story of Exploration,* pp. 297–301. National Geographic Society.

ANDERSON, D. L. 1984. Seismic Tomography. *Scientific American* 250(4):60–68.

ANDERSON, H. H. 1973. Edwin Link: The Triumphs and Tragedies in One Man's Quest to Launch Man-in-Sea. *Skin Diver* 2(11):40–43, 73.

ANDERSON, W. W., F. H. BERRY, J. E. BÖHLKE, J. W. GEHRINGER, R. H. GIBBS, W. A. GOSLINE, N. B. MARSHALL, G. W. MEAD, R. R. ROFEN, AND N. J. WILIMOVSKY. 1966. Order Iniomi, Order Lyomeri. Part 5, *Fishes of the Western North Atlantic.* Memoirs of the Sears Foundation for Marine Research. Yale University.

ANDREWS, R. C. 1914. Notice of a Rare Ziphioid Whale, *Mesoplodon densirostris,* on the New Jersey Coast. *Proc. Acad. Nat. Sci. Phila.* 66:437–40.

———. 1916. *Whale Hunting with Gun and Camera.* Appleton.

ANON. 1970. Five Miles of Fish. *Nature* 226:501–2.

ANTCIL, M. 1972. Stimulation of Bioluminescence in Lanternfishes (Myctophidae). Part 2. *Canadian Jour. Zool.* 50(2):233–37.

ANTCIL, M., AND C. G. GRUCHY. 1970. Stimulation and Photography of Bioluminescence in Lanternfishes (Myctophidae). *Jour. Fish. Res. Bd. Canada* 27(4):826–29.

ARATA, G. F. 1954. A Note on the Flying Behavior of Certain Squids. *Nautilus* 68(1):1–3.

ARRHENIUS, G. 1963. Pelagic Sediments. In M. N. Hill, ed., *The Sea, Vol. 3: The Earth Beneath the Sea,* pp. 655–727. Wiley Interscience.

ASHKENAZY, I. 1979. Benthic Currents: Unstable Highways in an Arcane World. *Oceans* 17(6):34–36.

AYLING, T. 1982. *Collins Guide to the Sea Fishes of New Zealand.* Collins.

BACKUS, R. H. 1966. A Large Shark in the Stomach of a Sperm Whale. *Jour. Mammal.* 47(1):142.

———. 1968. Solving the Mystery of "Alexander's Acres." *Oceanus* 14(3):15–20.

BACKUS, R. H., J. E. CRADDOCK, R. L. HAEDRICH, D. L. SHORES, J. M. TEAL, A. S. WING, G. W. MEAD, AND W. D. CLARKE. 1968. *Ceratoscopelus madrensis:* Peculiar Sound-Scattering Layer Identified with this Myctophid Fish. *Science* 160:991–93.

BAGLEY, P. M., A. SMITH, AND I. G. PRIEDE. 1994. Tracking Movements of Deep Demersal Fishes in the Porcupine Seabight, North-east Atlantic Ocean. *Jour. Mar. Biol. Assoc. U.K.* 74:473–80.

BAILEY, H. S. 1953. The Voyage of the Challenger. *Scientific American* 188(5):88–94.

BAIRD, R. C., D. F. WILSON, R. C. BECKETT, AND T. L. HOPKINS. 1974. *Diaphus taaningi* Norman, the Principal Component of a Shallow Sound-Scattering Layer in the Cariaco Trench, Venezuela. *Jour. Mar. Res.* 32:301–12.

BAKER, A. DE C. 1957. Underwater Photographs in the Study of Oceanic Squid. *Deep-Sea Research* 4:126–29.

———. 1960. Observations of Squid at the Surface in the N.E. Atlantic. *Deep-Sea Research* 6:206–10.

BAKER, R., ED. 1981. *The Mystery of Migration.* Viking Press.

BALLARD, R. D. 1975a. Project FAMOUS II: Dive into the Great Rift. *National Geographic* 147(5):604–15.

———. 1975b. Photography from a Submersible during Project FAMOUS. *Oceanus* 18:31–39.

———. 1976. The Cayman Trough: Window on Earth's Interior. *National Geographic* 150(2):228–49.

———. 1977. Notes on a Major Oceanographic Find. *Oceanus* 20(3):35–44.

———. 1983. Argo-Jason. *Oceans* 16(2):18–19.

———. 1984. The Exploits of Alvin and ANGUS: Exploring the East Pacific Rise. *Oceanus* 27(3):7–14.

———. 1985. How We Found *Titanic*. *National Geographic* 168(6):696–719.

———. 1986. A Long Last Look at the *Titanic*. *National Geographic* 170(6):698–727.

———. 1987a. Epilogue for the *Titanic*. *National Geographic* 172(4):454–63.

———. 1987b. *The Discovery of the Titanic*. Warner/Madison Press.

———. 1989. The *Bismarck* Found. *National Geographic* 176(5):622–37.

———. 1990. *The Discovery of the Bismarck*. Hodder & Stoughton.

———. 1994a. Deep-Sea Exploration: The Challenge Continues. *Woods Hole Currents* 3(1):4–5.

———. 1994b. Riddle of the *Lusitania*. *National Geographic* 185(4):68–85.

———. 1995. *Explorations: My Quest for Adventure and Discovery Under the Sea*. Hyperion.

BALLARD, R. D., AND J. F. GRASSLE. 1979. Return to Oases of the Deep. *National Geographic* 156(5):689–705.

BARDACH, J. 1968. *Harvest of the Sea*. Harper & Row.

BARHAM, E. G. 1966. Deep Scattering Layer Migration and Composition: Observations from a Diving Saucer. *Science* 151:1399–1403.

BARHAM, E. G., N. J. AYER, AND R. E. BOYCE. 1967. Macrobenthos of the San Diego Trough: Photographic Census and Observations from Bathyscaphe *Trieste*. *Deep-Sea Research* 14(6):773–84.

BARNARD, J. L. 1961. Gammaridean Amphipods from Depths of 400 to 6000 Meters. *Galathea Report* 5:23–128.

———. 1969. The Families and Genera of Marine Gammaridean Amphipoda. *Bull. U.S. Nat. Mus.* 271:1–535.

———. 1973. Deep-Sea Amphipoda of the Genus *Lepechinella*. *Smithsonian Contrib. Zool.* 133:1–30.

BARNEA, J. 1972. Geothermal Power. *Scientific American* 226(1):70–77.

BARNES, A. T., AND J. F. CASE. 1972. Bioluminescence in the Mesopelagic Copepod *Gaussia princeps* (T. Scott). *Jour. Exp. Mar. Biol. Ecol.* 8:53–71.

———. 1974. The Luminescence of Lanternfish (Myctophidae): Spontaneous Activity and Responses to Mechanical, Electrical, and Chemical Stimulation. *Jour. Exp. Mar. Biol. Ecol.* 15:203–21.

BARNES, A. T., L. B. QUETIN, J. J. CHILDRESS, AND D. L. PAWSON. 1976. Deep-Sea Macroplanktonic Sea Cucumbers: Suspended Sediment Feeders Captured from Deep Submergence Vehicle. *Science* 194:1083–85.

BAROSS, J. A., AND S. E. HOFFMAN. 1985. Submarine Hydrothermal Vents and Associated Gradient Environments as Sites for the Origin and Evolution of Life. *Orig. Life* 15(4):327–45.

BARTON, O. 1930. The Bathysphere. *Bull. N.Y. Zool. Soc.* 33(6):232–34.

———. 1953. *The World Beneath the Sea.* Crowell.

BASCOM, W. 1959. The Mohole. *Scientific American* 200(4):41–49.

———. 1961. *A Hole in the Bottom of the Sea.* Doubleday.

———. 1969. Technology and the Ocean. *Scientific American* 221(3):198–217.

———. 1971. Deep-Water Archeology. *Science* 174:261–69.

———. 1988. *The Crest of the Wave: Adventures in Oceanography.* Harper & Row.

BASS, A. J., J. D. D'AUBREY, AND N. KISTNASAMY. 1975. Sharks of the East Coast of Southern Africa. Part 5. The Families Hexanchidae, Chlamydoselachidae, Heterodontidae, Pristiophoridae and Squatinidae. *Oceanogr. Res. Inst. Invest. Rep.* 43:1–50.

———. 1976. Sharks of the East Coast of Southern Africa. Part 6. The Families Oxynotidae, Squalidae, Dalatiidae and Echinorhinidae. *Oceanogr. Res. Inst. Invest. Rep.* 45:1–103.

BASS, G. F. 1966. *Archaeology Under Water.* Praeger.

———, ED. 1972. *A History of Seafaring, based on Underwater Archaeology.* Thames and Hudson.

BEEBE, W. 1926. *The Arcturus Adventure.* Putnam.

———. 1929a. Fishing a Mile Down in the Hudson Gorge. *Bull. N.Y. Zool. Soc.* 32(2):69–77.

———. 1929b. Deep Sea Fish of the Hudson Gorge. *Zoologica* 12(1):1–19.

———. 1929c. *Halophryne hudsonius:* A New Species, Description and Osteology. *Zoologica* 12(1):21–36.

———. 1930a. The Bermuda Oceanographic Expedition. *Bull. N.Y. Zool. Soc.* 33(2):35–76.

———. 1930b. A Perfect Depth Recorder. *Bull. N.Y. Zool. Soc.* 33(6):244–47.

———. 1931. A Round Trip to Davy Jones's Locker. *National Geographic* 59(6):653–78.

———. 1932a. The Depths of the Sea. *National Geographic* 61(1):5–68.

———. 1932b. *Nonsuch: Land of Water.* Harcourt, Brace.

———. 1932c. Nineteen New Species and Four Post-Larval Deep-Sea Fish. *Zoologica* 13(4):47–107.

———. 1932d. A New Deep-Sea Fish. *Bull. N.Y. Zool. Soc.* 35(5):175–77.

———. 1933a. Deep-Sea Stomiatoid Fishes: One New Genus and Eight New Species. *Copeia* 4:160–75.

———. 1933b. Deep-Sea Isospondylous Fishes: Two New Genera and Four New Species. *Zoologica* 13(8):159–67.

———. 1933c. New Data on the Deep-Sea Fish *Stylophthalmus* and *Idiacanthus. Science* 78:390.

———. 1933d. Preliminary Account of Deep-Sea Dives in the Bathysphere with Especial Reference to One of 2200 Feet. *Proc. Nat. Acad. Sci.* 19(1):178–88.

———. 1934a. A Half Mile Down. *National Geographic* 66(6):661–704.

———. 1934b. *Half Mile Down.* Harcourt, Brace.

———. 1934c. Deep-Sea Fishes of the Bermuda Oceanographic Expedition—Family Idiacanthidae. *Zoologica* 16(4):149–241.

———. 1934d. Five Hundred Fathoms Down. *Bull. N.Y. Zool. Soc.* 37(6):157–70.

———. 1934e. Three New Deep-Sea Fish Seen from the Bathysphere. *Bull. N.Y. Zool. Soc.* 37(6):190–93.

———. 1938a. *Ceratias,* Siren of the Deep. *Bull. N.Y. Zool. Soc.* 41:50–53.

———. 1938b. Slaying Scientific Dragons. *Bull. N.Y. Zool. Soc.* 42(4):118–23.

BEEBE, W., AND J. CRANE. 1939. Deep-Sea Fishes of the Bermuda Oceanographic Expeditions. Family Melanostomiatidae. *Zoologica* 24(6):65–238.

BEEBE, W., AND G. HOLLISTER. 1930. Log of the Bathysphere. *Bull. N.Y. Zool. Soc.* 33(6):249–64.

BEHRMAN, D. 1969. *The New World of the Oceans: Men and Oceanography.* Little, Brown.

BEL'KOVICH, V. M., AND A. V. YABLAKOV. 1963. The Whale—An Ultrasonic Projector. *Yuchnyi Tekhnik* 3:76–77.

BELLO, G. 1991. Role of Cephalopods in the Diet of the Swordfish, *Xiphias gladias,* from the Eastern Mediterranean Sea. *Bull. Mar. Sci.* 49(1 & 2):312–24.

BELYAYEV, G. M. 1962. Rostra of Cephalopods in Oceanic Bottom Sediments. *Okeanologiya* 2(2):311–26.

BENDER, M. L., T. L. KU, AND W. S. BROEKER. 1966. Manganese Nodules: Their Evolution. *Science* 151:325–28.

BENJAMINSEN, T. 1972. On the Biology of the Bottlenose Whale *Hyperoodon ampullatus* (Forster). *Norw. Jour. Zool.* 20:233–41.

BENJAMINSEN, T., AND I. CHRISTENSEN. 1979. The Natural History of the Bottlenose Whale, *Hyperoodon ampullatus* (Forster). In H. E. Winn and B. L. Olla, eds., *Behavior of Marine Animals, Vol. 3: Cetaceans,* pp. 143–64. Plenum Press.

BENNETT, F. D. 1840. *Narrative of a Whaling Voyage Around the Globe from the Year 1833 to 1836.* Richard Bentley.

BERG, C. J. 1985. Reproductive Strategies of Molluscs from Abyssal Hydrothermal Vent Communities. *Bull. Biol. Soc. Wash.* 6:185–97.

BERG, C. J., AND C. L. VAN DOVER. 1987. Benthopelagic Macrozooplankton Communities at and near Deep-Sea Hydrothermal Vents in the Eastern Tropical Pacific Ocean and Gulf of California. *Deep-Sea Research* 34A:379–401.

BERGMAN, E. A. 1992. Mid-Ocean Ridge Seismicity. *Oceanus* 34(4):60–67.

BERGSTAD, O. A. 1990. Distribution, Population Structure, Growth and Reproduction of the Roundnose Grenadier *Coryphaenoides rupestris* (Pisces: Macrouridae) in the Deep Waters of the Skagerrak. *Marine Biology* 107:25–39.

BERGSTAD, O. A., AND B. ISAKSEN. 1987. Deep-water Resources of the Northeast Atlantic: Distribution, Abundance and Exploitation. *Fisken og Havet* 1987(3):1–56.

BERRA, T. M. 1977. *William Beebe: An Annotated Bibliography.* Archon Books.

BERTELSEN, E. 1943. Notes on the Deep-Sea Anglerfish *Ceratias holbölli* Kr. Based on Specimens in the Zoological Museum of Copenhagen. *Vidensk. Medd. fra Dansk Naturh. Foren.* 107:185–206.

———. 1951. The Ceratioid Fishes: Ontogeny, Taxonomy, Distribution and Biology. *Dana Report* 39:1–276.

———. 1958. A New Type of Light Organ in the Deep-Sea Fish *Opisthoproctus*. *Nature* 181:862–63.

———. 1973. A New Species of Deep-Sea Anglerfish, *Linophryne sexfilis*. *Steenstrupia* 3:65–69.

———. 1976. Records of Parasitic Males in Three Species of *Linophryne* (Pisces, Ceratioidei). *Steenstrupia* 4:7–18.

———. 1980. Notes on Linophrynidae, Part 6. A Revision of the Deepsea Anglerfishes (Ceratioidei) of the *Linophrnye arborifer* Group. *Steenstrupia* 6(6):29–70.

———. 1982. Notes on Linophrynidae, Part 8. A Review of the Genus *Linophryne,* with New Records and Descriptions of Two New Species. *Steenstrupia* 8(3):49–104.

BERTELSEN, E., AND J. GRØNTVED. 1949. The Light Organs of a Bathypelagic Fish *Argyropelecus olfersi* (Cuvier) Photographed by Its Own Light. *Vidensk. Medd. fra Dansk Naturh. Foren.* 111:163–67.

BERTELSEN, E., AND G. KREFFT. 1965. On a Rare Ceratioid Fish, *Linophryne lucifer* Collett, 1886. *Vidensk. Medd. fra Dansk Naturh. Foren.* 128:293–301.

BERTELSEN, E., AND O. MUNK. 1964. Rectal Light Organs of the Argentinoid Fishes *Opisthoproctus* and *Winteria*. *Dana Rep.* 63:1–17.

BERTELSEN, E., AND J. G. NIELSEN. 1987. The Deep-Sea Eel Family Monognathidae. *Steenstrupia* 13(4):141–98.

BERTELSEN, E., AND T. W. PIETSCH. 1983. The Ceratioid Anglerfishes of Australia. *Rec. Aust. Mus.* 35:77–99.

BERTELSEN, E., AND P. STRUHSAKER. 1977. The Ceratioid Fishes of the Genus *Thaumatichthys*: Osteology, Relationships, Distribution and Biology. *Galathea Report* 14:7–40.

BERTELSEN, E., J. G. NIELSEN, AND D. G. SMITH. 1989. Suborder Saccopharyngoidei. Families Saccopharyngidae, Eurypharyngidae, and Monognathidae. In Part 9, Vol. 1, *Fishes of the Western North Atlantic,* pp. 636–55. Memoirs of the Sears Foundation for Marine Research. Yale University.

BERTELSEN, E., T. W. PIETSCH, AND R. J. LAVENBERG. 1981. Ceratioid Anglerfishes of the Family Gigantactinidae: Morphology, Systematics, and Distribution. *Contrib. in Science, Natural History Museum of Los Angeles County* 332:1–74.

BERTIN, L. 1934. Les Poissons apodes appartenant au sous-ordre des Lyomères. *Dana Report* 3:3–55.

———. 1937. Les Poissons abyssaux du genre *Cyema* Günther. *Dana Report* 10:4–30.

———. 1938. Formes nouvelles et formes larvaires de poissons apodes appartenant au sous-ordre des Lyomères. *Dana Report* 15:1–25.

———. 1954. Les Larves leptocéphaliennes géantes et le problème du "serpent de mer." *La Nature* 3232:312–13.

———. 1956. *Eels: A Biological Study*. Cleaver-Hume.

BERZIN, A. A. 1972. *The Sperm Whale*. Izdatgel'stvo "Pischevaya Promyshlennost" Moskva 1971. Translated from the Russian by Israel Program for Scientific Translations, Jerusalem.

BIGELOW, H. B. 1931. *Oceanography: Its Scope, Problems, and Economic Importance*. Houghton Mifflin.

BIGELOW, H. B., AND T. BARBOUR. 1944. A New Giant Ceratioid Fish. *Proc. New Engl. Zool. Club* 23:9–15.

BIGELOW, H. B., AND W. C. SCHROEDER. 1948. Sharks. In Part 1, *Fishes of the Western North Atlantic*. Memoirs of the Sears Foundation for Marine Research. Yale University.

———. 1951. Fishes of the Gulf of Maine. *U.S. Fish and Wildlife Service Fisheries Bulletin* 53:1–577.

———. 1953. Sawfishes, Guitarfishes, Skates and Rays; Chimaeroids. In Part 2, *Fishes of the Western North Atlantic*. Memoirs of the Sears Foundation for Marine Research. Yale University.

———. 1954. Deep Water Elasmobranchs and Chimaeroids from the Northwestern Atlantic Slope. *Bull. Mus. Comp. Zool.* 112:37–87.

———. 1957. A Study of the Sharks of the Suborder Squaloidea. *Bull. Mus. Comp. Zool.* 117(1):1–150.

BIGELOW, H. B., W. C. SCHROEDER, AND S. SPRINGER. 1953. New and Little Known Sharks from the Atlantic and from the Gulf of Mexico. *Bull. Mus. Comp. Zool.* 109:213–76.

BIGELOW, H. B., M. G. BRADBURY, J. R. DYMOND, J. R. GREELEY, S. F. HILDEBRAND, G. W. MEAD, R. R. MILLER, L. R. RIVAS, W. C. SCHROEDER, R. D. SUTTKUS, AND V. D. VLADYKOV. 1963. Salmon, Trouts, Tarpon, Ladyfish, Bonefish, Charrs, Anchovies, Herrings, and Others. In Part 3, *Fishes of The Western North Atlantic*. Memoirs of the Sears Foundation for Marine Research. Yale University.

BIGELOW, H. B., D. M. COHEN, M. W. DICK, R. H. GIBBS, M. GREY, J. E. MORROW, L. P. SCHULTZ, AND V. WATERS. 1964. Soft-Rayed Bony Fishes: Order Isospondyli (Argentinoidea, Stomiatoidea, Escoidea, Bathylaconoidea), Order Giganturoidei. In Part 4, *Fishes of the Western North Atlantic*. Memoirs of the Sears Foundation for Marine Research. Yale University.

BILLETT, D. S. 1986. The Rise and Rise of the Sea Cucumber. *New Scientist* 109(1500):48–51.

BILLETT, D. S., AND B. HANSEN. 1982. Abyssal Aggregations of *Kolga hyalina* Danielsen and Koren (Echinodermata: Holothurioidea) in the Northeast Atlantic Ocean. *Deep-Sea Research* 29A:799–818.

BIRD, G. J., AND D. M. HOLDICH. 1985. A Remarkable Tubicolous Tanaid (Crustacea: Tanaidacea) from the Rockall Trough. *Jour. Mar. Biol. Assoc. U.K.* 65:563–72.

BLAXTER, J. H. S., AND R. I. CURRIE. 1967. The Effects of Artificial Lights on Acoustic Scattering Layers in the Ocean. *Symp. Zool. Soc. London* 19:1–14.

BODEN, B. P., AND E. M. KAMPA. 1957. Records of Bioluminescence in the Ocean. *Pacific Science* 11:229–35.

———. 1967. The Influence of Natural Light on the Vertical Migrations of an Animal Community in the Sea. *Symp. Zool. Soc. London* 19:15–26.

BOLIN, R. L. 1961. The Function of the Luminous Organs of Deep-Sea Fishes. *Proc. 9th Pacific Sci. Congress* 10:37–39.

BONATTI, E. 1990. Not So Hot "Hot Spots" in the Oceanic Mantle. *Science* 250:107–11.

———. 1994. The Earth's Mantle Below the Oceans. *Scientific American* 270(3):44–51.

BONATTI, E., AND K. CRANE. 1984. Oceanic Fracture Zones. *Scientific American* 250(5):40–51.

BONATTI, E., M. SEYLER, AND N. SUSHEVSKAYA. 1993. A Cold Suboceanic Mantle Belt at the Earth's Equator. *Science* 261:315–20.

BONE, Q., AND B. L. ROBERTS. 1969. The Density of Elasmobranchs. *Jour. Mar. Biol. Assoc. U.K.* 49:913–37.

BOSS, K. J., AND R. D. TURNER. 1980. The Giant White Clam from the Galápagos Rift, Calyptogena magnifica species novum. *Malacologia* 20:161–94.

BOULENGER, E. G. 1935. *A Natural History of the Seas.* Duckworth.

BOWEN, M. F. 1990. *Jason*'s Med Adventure. *Oceanus* 33(1):61–69.

BRADLEY, A., D. R. YOERGER, AND B. B. WALDEN. 1995. An AB(L)E Bodied Vehicle. *Oceanus* 38(1):18–20.

BRIGGS, P. 1968. *Men in the Sea.* Simon & Schuster.

———. 1971. 200,000,000 *Years Beneath the Sea.* Holt, Rinehart and Winston.

BRITTON, P. 1995. Undersea Explorers. *Popular Science* 246(5):39–42.

BROAD, W. J. 1993. Navy Listening System Opening World of Whales. *New York Times,* August 21, 1993: A12.

———. 1994a. Squid Emerge as Smart, Elusive Hunters of Mid-Sea. *New York Times,* August 30, 1994: C1, C8.

———. 1994b. Drillers Find Lost World of Ancient Microbes. *New York Times,* October 4, 1994: C1, C7.

———. 1995a. Secret Sub to Scan Sea Floor for Roman Wrecks. *New York Times,* February 7, 1995: C1, C10.

———. 1995b. The Core of the Earth May Be a Gigantic Crystal Made of Iron. *New York Times,* April 4, 1995: C1, C6.

———. 1995c. Lost Japanese Sub with 2 Tons of Axis Gold Found on Floor of Atlantic. *New York Times,* July 18, 1995: C1, C7.

———. 1996. Biologists Closing on Hidden Lair of Giant Squid. *New York Times,* February 13, 1996: C1, C9.

BROECKER, W. S. 1978. Benthic Oceanography. *Oceanus* 21(1):3–4.

BROOKS, J. M., M. C. KENNICUTT, C. R. FISHER, S. A. MACKO, K. COLE, J. J. CHILDRESS, R. R. BIDIGARE, AND R. D. VETTER. 1987. Deep-Sea Hydrocarbon Seep Communities: Evidence for Energy and Nutritional Carbon Sources. *Science* 238:1138–42.

BROWER, K. 1981. A Galaxy of Life Fills the Night. *National Geographic* 160(1):834–47.

BRUUN, A. F. 1937. Contribution to the Life Histories of the Deep Sea Eels: Synaphobranchidae. *Dana Report* 9:1–31.

———. 1943. The Biology of *Spirula spirula* (L.). *Dana Report* 24:1–44.

———. 1951. The Philippine Trench and Its Bottom Fauna. *Nature* 168:692–93.

———. 1956a. The Abyssal Fauna: Its Ecology, Distribution and Origin. *Nature* 177(4520):1105–8.

———. 1956b. Animal Life of the Deep-Sea Bottom. In A. F. Bruun, S. Greve, H. Mielche, and R. Spärck, eds., *The Galathea Deep Sea Expedition, 1950–1952,* pp. 149–95. Allen and Unwin.

———. 1957. Deep Sea and Abyssal Depths. *Mem. Geol. Soc. Amer.* 67(1):641–72.

BRYAN, W. B. 1992. From Pillow Lava to Sheet Flow: Evolution of Deep-Sea Volcanology. *Oceanus* 34(4):42–50.

BUCKLIN, A. 1988. Allozymic Variability of *Riftia pachyptila* Population from the Galápagos Rift and 21° N Hydrothermal Vents. *Deep-Sea Research* 35(10/11):1759–68.

BULLARD, E. C. 1969. The Origin of the Oceans. *Scientific American* 221(3):68–75.

BULLARD, E. C., J. E. EVERETT, AND A. G. SMITH. 1965. The Fit of the Continents Around the Atlantic. *Phil. Trans. Roy. Soc. London* 258:41–51.

BULLIS, H. R. 1967. Depth Segregations and Distribution of Sex-Maturity Groups in the Marbled Catshark, *Galeus arae.* In P. W. Gilbert, R. F. Mathewson, and D. P. Rall, eds., *Sharks, Skates, and Rays,* pp. 141–48. Johns Hopkins University Press.

BULLOCH, D. K. 1986. *Marine Gamefish of the Middle Atlantic.* American Littoral Society. Sandy Hook, New Jersey.

BURCKHARDT, R. 1900. On the Luminous Organs of Selachian Fishes. *Ann. Mag. Nat. Hist.* 7(6):558–68.

BURGESS, R. F. 1975. *Ships Beneath the Sea: A History of Subs and Submersibles.* McGraw-Hill.

BURKENROAD, M. D. 1943. A Possible Function of Bioluminescence. *Jour. Mar. Res.* 5:161–64.

BURTON, M. 1957. *Animal Legends.* Coward-McCann.

BUSCHBAUM, R., AND L. J. MILNE. 1966. *Living Invertebrates of the World.* Doubleday.

BUSCHBAUM, R., M. BUSCHBAUM, J. PEARSE, AND V. PEARSE. 1987. *Animals Without Backbones.* University of Chicago Press.

CANN, J. 1992. Onions and Leaks: Magma at Mid-Ocean Ridges. *Oceanus* 34(4):36–41.

CARALP, M.-H. 1987. Deep-sea Circulation in the Northeastern Atlantic over the Past 30,000 Years: The Benthic Foraminiferal Record. *Oceanologica Acta* 10:27–40.

CAREY, F. G. 1973. Fish with Warm Bodies. *Scientific American* 228(2):36–44.

CAREY, F. G., AND B. H. ROBISON. 1981. Daily Patterns in the Activity of Swordfish, *Xiphias gladias,* Observed by Acoustic Telemetry. *Fish. Bull.* 79:277–92.

CARRINGTON, R. 1960. *A Biography of the Sea.* Basic Books.

CARSON, R. 1951. *The Sea Around Us.* Oxford University Press.

———. 1955. *The Edge of the Sea.* Houghton Mifflin.

CARY, S. C., H. FELBECK, AND N. D. HOLLAND. 1989. Observations on the Reproductive Biology of the Hydrothermal Vent Tube Worm *Riftia pachyptila. Marine Ecology Progress Series* 52:89–94.

CASE, J. F., J. WARNER, A. T. BARNES, AND M. LOWENSTINE. 1977. Bioluminescence of Lanternfish (Myctophidae) in Response to Changes in Light Intensity. *Nature* 265:179–81.

CASTLE, P. J. H. 1959. A Large Leptocephalid (Teleostei, Apodes) from off South Westland, New Zealand. *Trans. Royal Soc. New Zealand Zool.* 87(1&2):179–84.

———. 1964a. Deep-Sea Eels: Family Synaphobranchidae. *Galathea Report* 7:29–42.

———. 1964b. Eels and Eel-Larvae of the *Tui* Oceanographic Cruise 1962 to the South Fiji Basin. *Trans. Royal Soc. New Zealand Zool.* 5(7):71–84.

———. 1967. Two Remarkable Eel-Larvae from off Southern Africa. *Spec. Pub. Dep. Ichthyol. Rhodes Univ. South Africa* 1:1–12.

CASTLE, P. J. H., AND N. S. RAJU. 1975. Some Rare Leptocephali from the Atlantic and Indo-Pacific Oceans. *Dana Report* 85:1–25.

CASTRO, J. I. 1983. *The Sharks of North American Waters.* Texas A&M University Press.

CAVANAUGH, C. M. 1983. Symbiotic Chemoautotrophic Bacteria in Marine Invertebrates from Sulphide-Rich Habitats. *Nature* 302:58–61.

CEDERLUND, B. A. 1938. A Subfossil Gray Whale Discovered in Sweden in 1859. *Zool. Bldr. Uppsala* 18:269–86.

CHANDLER, D. L. 1994. Depth Perception: Sub Prowls Sea's Deepest Recesses. *Boston Globe,* August 8, 1994: 25–27.

CHAPIN, H., AND F. G. WALTON SMITH. 1952. *The Ocean River: The Story of the Gulf Stream.* Scribner's.

CHILDRESS, J. J. 1988. Biology and Chemistry of a Deep-Sea Hydrothermal Vent on the Galápagos Rift; The Rose Garden in 1985. *Deep-Sea Research* 35(10/11A):1677–80.

CHILDRESS, J. J., AND R. P. MEEK. 1973. Observations on the Feeding Behavior of a Mesopelagic Fish (*Anoplogaster cornuta:* Beryciformes). *Copeia* 3:602–3.

CHILDRESS, J. J., AND T. J. MICKEL. 1982. Oxygen and Sulfide Consumption Rates of the Vent Clam Calyptogena pacifica. *Marine Biology Letters* 3:3–79.

———. 1985. Metabolic Rates of Animals from the Hydrothermal Vents and Other Deep-Sea Habitats. *Bull. Biol. Soc. Wash.* 6:249–60.

CHILDRESS, J. J., H. FELBECK, AND G. N. SOMERO. 1987. Symbiosis in the Deep Sea. *Scientific American* 256(5):115–20.

CHILDRESS, J. J., C. R. FISHER, J. M. BROOKS, M. C. KENNICUTT, R. R. BIDIGARE, AND A. E. ANDERSON. 1986. A Methanotrophic Marine Molluscan (Bivalvia: Mytilidae) Symbiosis: Mussels Fueled by Gas. *Science* 233:1306–8.

CHRISTENSEN, I. 1975. Preliminary Report on the Norwegian Fishery for Small Whales: Expansion of Norwegian Whaling to Arctic and Northwest Atlantic Waters, and Norwegian Investigations of the Biology of Small Whales. *Jour. Fish. Res. Bd. Canada.* 32(7):1083–94.

———. 1976. The History of Exploitation and the Initial Status of the Northeast Atlantic Bottlenose Whale (*Hyperoodon ampullatus*). *Intl. Whal. Commn.* SC/28/L23:1–52.

CHUN, C. 1900. *Aus den Tiefen des Weltmeeres.* Gustav Fisher.

———. 1913. Cephalopoda. *Rep. Sci. Res. "Michael Sars" N. Atlantic Deep-Sea Expedition 1910.* 3(1):3–21.

CHURCH, R. 1971. *Deepstar* Explores the Ocean Floor. *National Geographic* 139(1):110–29.

CLARK, D. L. 1979. Life in the Warm Depths off Galápagos. *Oceans* 12(6):42–45.

CLARK, E. 1959. Functional Hermaphroditism and Self-Fertilization in a Serranid Fish. *Science* 129:215–16.

———. 1965. Mating of Groupers. *Natural History* 74(6):22–25.

———. 1969. *The Lady and the Sharks.* Harper & Row.

CLARK, E., AND E. KRISTOF. 1990a. How Deep Do Sharks Go? Reflections on Deep-Sea Sharks. In S. L. Gruber, ed., *Discovering Sharks,* pp. 79–84. American Littoral Society.

———. 1990b. Deep-Sea Elasmobranchs Observed from Submersibles off Bermuda, Grand Cayman, and Freeport, Bahamas. In H. L. Pratt, S. L. Gruber, and T. Taniuchi, eds., *Elasmobranchs as Living Resources: Advances in the Biology, Ecology, Systematics and the Status of the Fisheries,* pp. 269–84. NOAA Technical Report 90.

CLARK, E., E. KRISTOF, AND D. LEE. 1986. New Eyes for the Dark Reveal the World of Sharks at 2,000 Feet. *National Geographic* 170(5):680–91.

CLARK, J. P. 1982. The Nodules Are Not Essential. *Oceanus* 25:18–21.

CLARKE, A. H. 1962a. On the Composition, Zoogeography, Origin and Age of the Deep-Sea Mollusk Fauna. *Deep-Sea Research* 9:291–306.

———. 1962b. Annotated List and Bibliography of the Abyssal Marine Molluscs of the World. *Bull. Nat. Mus. Canada* 181:1–114.

CLARKE, G. L., AND R. H. BACKUS. 1956. Measurement of Light Penetration in Relation to Vertical Migration and Records of Luminescence in Deep-Sea Animals. *Deep-Sea Research* 4:1–14.

———. 1964. Interrelations Between the Vertical Migration of Deep Scattering Layers, Bioluminescence, and Changes in Daylight in the Sea. *Bull. Inst. Ocean. Monaco* 64(1318):1–36.

CLARKE, G. L., AND G. K. WERTHEIM. 1956. Measurements of Illumination at Great Depths and at Night in the Atlantic Ocean by Means of a New Bathyphotometer. *Deep-Sea Research* 3:189–205.

CLARKE, G. L., R. J. CONOVER, C. N. DAVID, AND J. A. C. NICOL. 1962. Comparative Studies of Luminescence in Copepods and Other Pelagic Marine Animals. *Jour. Mar. Biol. Assoc. U.K.* 42:541–64.

CLARKE, M. R. 1962. Stomach Contents of a Sperm Whale Caught off Madeira in 1959. *Norsk Hvalfangst-tidende* 51(5):173–91.

———. 1966. A Review of the Systematics and Ecology of Oceanic Squids. *Advances in Marine Biology* 4:91–300.

———. 1970. The Function of the Spermaceti Organ of the Sperm Whale. *Nature* 28:873–74.

———. 1977. Observations on Sperm Whale Diving. *Jour. Mar. Biol. Assoc. U.K.* 56:809–10.

———. 1978. Physical Properties of Spermaceti Oil in the Sperm Whale. *Jour. Mar. Biol. Assoc. U.K.* 58:19–26.

———. 1979. The Head of the Sperm Whale. *Scientific American* 240(1):128–41.

———. 1983. Cephalopod Biomass—Estimation from Predation. *Mem. Nat. Mus. Victoria* 44:95–107.

———. 1986. *A Handbook for the Identification of Cephalopod Beaks.* Clarendon Press.

———. 1988. Squids. *Biologist.* 35(2):69–75.

CLARKE, R. 1950. The Bathypelagic Angler Fish *Ceratias holbölli* Kröyer. *Discovery Reports* 26:1–32.

———. 1955. A Giant Squid Swallowed by a Sperm Whale. *Norsk Hvalfangst-tidende* 44(1):589–93.

CLARKE, W. D. 1963. Function of Bioluminescence in Mesopelagic Organisms. *Nature* 198(4887):1244–46.

COE, R. S., M. PRÉVOT, AND P. CAMPS. 1995. New Evidence for Extraordinarily Rapid Change of the Geomagnetic Field During a Reversal. *Nature* 374(6524):687–92.

COHEN, D. M. 1964. Argentinoidea. In Part 4, *Fishes of the Western North Atlantic,* pp. 1–70. Memoirs of the Sears Foundation for Marine Research. Yale University.

———. 1970. How Many Recent Fishes Are There? *Proc. Cal. Acad. Sci.* 38(4):341–45.

COHEN, D. M., AND R. L. HAEDRICH. 1983. The Fish Fauna of the Galápagos Thermal Vent Region. *Deep-Sea Research* 30A:371–79.

COHEN, D. M., R. M. ROSENBLATT, AND H. G. MOSER. 1990. Biology and Description of a Bythitid Fish from Deep-Sea Thermal Vents in the Eastern Tropical Pacific. *Deep-Sea Research* 37A:267–83.

COHEN, D. M., A. W. EBELING, T. IWAMOTO, S. B. MCDOWELL, N. B. MARSHALL, D. E. ROSEN, P. SONODA, W. H. WEED, AND L. P. WOODS. 1973. Order Heteromi, Suborder Cyprinidontoidei, Orders Berycomorphi, Xenoberyces, and Anacanthini. In Part 6, *Fishes of the Western North Atlantic*. Memoirs of the Sears Foundation for Marine Research. Yale University.

COKER, R. E. 1962. *This Great and Wide Sea*. Harper Torchbooks.

COLBERT, E. H. 1973. *Wandering Lands and Animals*. Dutton.

COMPAGNO, L. J. V. 1981. Legend Versus Reality: The Jaws Image and Shark Diversity. *Oceanus* 24(4):3–16.

———. 1984a. *Sharks of the World. FAO Species Catalog, Vol. 4, Part 1: Hexanchiformes to Lamniformes.* UN Development Programme. Rome.

———. 1984b. *Sharks of the World. FAO Species Catalog, Vol. 4, Part 2: Carcharhiniformes.* UN Development Programme. Rome.

COMPTON-HALL, R. 1984. *Submarine Boats*. Arco.

CONE, J. 1991. *Fire Under the Sea*. Morrow.

CORLISS, J. B., AND R. D. BALLARD. 1977. Oases of Life in the Cold Abyss. *National Geographic* 152(4):441–53.

CORLISS, J. B., J. DYMOND, L. I. GORDON, J. M. EDMOND, R. P. VAN HERZEN, R. D. BALLARD, K. GREEN, D. WILLIAMS, A. BAINBRIDGE, K. CRANE, AND T. H. VAN ANDEL. 1979. Submarine Thermal Springs on the Galápagos Rift. *Science* 203:1073–83.

CORNER, E. D. S., E. J. DENTON, AND G. R. FORSTER. 1969. On the Buoyancy of Some Deep-Sea Sharks. *Proc. Roy. Soc. London* B171:415–27.

COUSTEAU, J.-Y. 1954. To the Depths of the Sea by Bathyscaphe. *National Geographic* 106(1):67–79.

———. 1955. Diving Through an Undersea Avalanche. *National Geographic* 107(4):538–42.

———. 1960. Diving Saucer Takes to the Deep. *National Geographic* 117(4):571–86.

———. 1964. At Home in the Sea. *National Geographic* 125(4):465–507.

———. 1966. Working for Weeks on the Sea Floor. *National Geographic* 129(4):498–537.

———. 1981. The Ocean: A Perspective. *National Geographic* 160(6):780–91.

COUSTEAU, J.-Y., AND J. DUGAN. 1963. *The Living Sea*. Harper & Bros.

COUSTEAU, J.-Y., AND Y. PICCALET. 1981. *A La Recherche de L'Atlantide*. Flammarion.

COWEN, R. C. 1960. *Frontiers of the Sea: The Story of Oceanographic Exploration.* Doubleday.

COX, A. G., R. R. DOELL, AND G. B. DALRYMPLE. 1964. Reversals of the Earth's Magnetic Field. *Science* 144:1537–43.

———. 1967. Reversals of the Earth's Magnetic Field. *Scientific American* 216(2):44–54.

COX, R. A. 1959. The Chemistry of Seawater. *New Scientist* 6(149):518–21.

CRANE, J. 1934. Deep-Sea Creatures of Six Net Hauls. *Bull. N.Y. Zool. Soc.* 37(6):174–81.

CRANE, J. M. 1965. Bioluminescent Courtship Display in the Teleost *Porichthys notatus*. *Copeia* 1965:239–41.

CRANE, K., AND R. D. BALLARD. 1980. The Galápagos Rift at 86° W 4. Structure and Morphology of Hydrothermal Fields and Their Relationship to the Volcanic and Tectonic Processes of the Rift Valley. *Jour. Geophys. Research* 85:1443–54.

CRAVEN, J. P. 1977. Submarine Craft. In N. C. Flemming, ed., *The Undersea,* pp. 262–81. Macmillan.

CROZIER, W. J. 1918. The Amount of Bottom Material Ingested by Holothurians (*Stichopus*). *Jour. Exp. Zool.* 26:379–89.

CUVIER, G. 1831. *A Discourse on the Revolutions of the Surface of the Globe and the Changes Thereby Produced in the Animal Kingdom.* Philadelphia.

CUYVERS, L. 1994. Into the Trenches: The Japanese Search for Deep-Sea Earthquake Clues. *Sea Frontiers* 40(5):42–45.

DAHLGREN, U. 1916. The Production of Light by Animals. Light Production in Cephalopods. *Jour. Franklin Inst.* 81:525–56.

———. 1917. The Production of Light by Animals. Luminosity in Fishes. *Jour. Franklin Inst.* 183(6):735–54.

———. 1928. The Bacterial Light of *Ceratias*. *Science* 68:65–66.

DALY, R. A. 1936. Origin of Submarine Canyons. *Amer. Jour. Sci.* 31:401–20.

DARLING, J. D., C. NICKLIN, K. S. NORRIS, H. WHITEHEAD, AND B. WÜRSIG. 1995. *Whales, Dolphins and Porpoises.* National Geographic Society.

DARWIN, C. 1855. *The Voyage of the Beagle.* Henry Colburn. (Doubleday Anchor edition, 1962).

DAUGHERTY, C. M. 1961. *Searchers of the Sea: Pioneers in Oceanography.* Viking.

DAVID, C. N., AND R. J. CONOVER. 1961. Preliminary Investigations on the Physiology and Ecology of Luminescence in the Copepod *Metrida lucens*. *Biol. Bull.* 121:92–107.

DAVIE, M. 1987. *Titanic: Life and Death of a Legend.* Knopf.

DAVIS, K. S., AND J. A. DAY. 1961. *Water, the Mirror of Science.* Doubleday Anchor.

DAVISON, C. 1929. The Atlantic Earthquake of November 18, 1929. *Nature* 124:859.

DEACON, G. E. R. 1958a. Deep Ocean Currents. *Discovery* 18(9):386–87.

———. 1958b. Ocean Waves. *Endeavor* 17(67):134–39.

———, ED. 1962. *Seas, Maps, and Men: An Atlas-History of Man's Exploration of the Oceans.* Doubleday.

DEELDER, C. L. 1960. The Atlantic Eel Problem. *Nature* 4713:589–92.

DEEVEY, G. B., AND A. L. BROOKS. 1977. Copepods of the Sargasso Sea off Bermuda: Species Composition, and Vertical and Seasonal Distribution Between the Surface and 2,000m. *Bull. Mar. Sci.* 27(2):256–91.

DE LATIL, P., AND J. RIVOIRE. 1956. *Man and the Underwater World.* Putnam.

DELONG, R. L., AND B. S. STEWART. 1991. Diving Patterns of Northern Elephant Seal Bulls. *Marine Mammal Science* 7(4):369–84.

DENTON, E. J. 1990a. Light and Vision at Depths Greater Than 200 Metres. In P. J. Herring, A. K. Campbell, M. Whitfield, and L. Maddock, eds., *Light and Life in the Sea,* pp. 127–48. Cambridge University Press.

———. 1990b. Bioluminescent Communication in the Sea. In P. J. Herring, A. K. Campbell, M. Whitfield, and L. Maddock, eds., *Light and Life in the Sea,* pp. 245–64. Cambridge University Press.

DENTON, E. J., AND T. I. SHAW. 1963. The Visual Pigments of Some Deep-Sea Elasmobranchs. *Jour. Biol. Assoc. U.K.* 43:65–70.

DE VISSER, J., AND R. W. M. VAN SOEST. 1987. *Salpa fusiformis* Populations of the North Atlantic. *Biological Oceanography* 4(2):193–209.

DIETZ, R. S. 1961. Continent and Ocean Basin Evolution by Spreading of the Sea Floor. *Nature* 190:854–57.

———. 1962. The Sea's Deep Scattering Layers. *Scientific American* 207(2):44–50.

———. 1969. Ocean Basins and Lunar Seas. *Oceans* 2(1):7–15.

DIETZ, R. S., AND J. HOLDEN. 1970a. The Breakup of Pangaea. *Scientific American* 223(4):30–41.

———. 1970b. Reconstruction of Pangaea: Breakup and Dispersion of Continents, Permian to Present. *Jour. Geophys. Res.* 75:4939–56.

DIOLE, P. 1954. *The Undersea Adventure.* Julian Messner.

DORFMAN, A., I. M. KUNLI, A. PARK., AND T. SKARI. 1995. The Last Frontier. *Time* 146(7):52–60.

DOUBILET, D., E. KRISTOF, AND E. CLARK. 1990. Suruga Bay: In the Shadow of Mount Fuji. *National Geographic* 178(4):2–39.

DOWNING, M. B. 1984. Willard Bascom: Explorer. *Oceanus* 27(2):63–67.

DUDLEY, P. 1725. An Essay upon the Natural History of Whales. *Phil. Trans. Roy. Soc. London* 33:256–69.

DUGAN, J. 1956. *Man Under the Sea.* Harper & Brothers.

———. 1967. *World Beneath the Sea.* National Geographic Society.

DU TOIT, A. L. 1927. A Geological Comparison of South America with South Africa. *Carnegie Inst. Wash. Publ.* 381:1–157.

———. 1937. *Our Wandering Continents: An Hypothesis of Continental Drifting.* Oliver & Boyd.

DYBAS, C. L. 1993. Beautiful Ethereal Larvaceans Play a Central Role in Ocean Ecology. *Oceanus* 36(2):84–86.

EARLE, S. A. 1991. Sharks, Squids, and Horseshoe Crabs—The Significance of Marine Biodiversity. *BioScience* 41(7):506–10.

EARLE, S. A., AND A. GIDDINGS. 1980. *Exploring the Deep Frontier.* National Geographic Society.

EATON, J. P., AND C. A. HAAS. 1987. *Titanic: Destination Disaster.* Norton.

———. 1994. *Titanic: Triumph and Tragedy.* Norton.

EBELING, A. W., AND W. H. WEED. 1973. *Xenoberyces* (Stephanoberyciformes). In Part 6, *Fishes of the Western North Atlantic,* pp. 397–478. Memoirs of the Sears Foundation for Marine Research. Yale University.

EDGERTON, H. E. 1955. Photographing the Sea's Dark Underworld. *National Geographic* 107(4):523–37.

EDMOND, J. M., AND VON DAMM, K. 1983. Hot Springs on the Ocean Floor. *Scientific American* 248(4):78–93.

EGE, V. 1934. The Genus *Stomias* Cuv., Taxonomy and Bio-Geography (Based on Adolescent and Adult Specimens). *Dana Report* 1(5):1–58.

———. 1948. *Chauliodus* Schn., Bathypelagic Genus of Fishes. *Dana Report* 5(31):1–148.

EISELEY, L. 1957. *The Immense Journey.* Vintage.

ELLIS, R. 1975. *The Book of Sharks.* Grosset & Dunlap.

———. 1977. Of Men, Whales and Captain Scammon. *National Parks and Conservation* 51(10):8–13.

———. 1980a. *The Book of Whales.* Knopf.

———. 1980b. Beaked Whales. *Sea Frontiers* 26(1):10–18.

———. 1981. Observations on a Captive Sperm Whale, *Physeter macrocephalus,* at Fire Island, New York. Abstract. *Fourth Biennial Conf. Biol. Marine Mammals.* San Francisco.

———. 1991. *Men and Whales.* Knopf.

———. 1994. *Monsters of the Sea.* Knopf.

ELLIS, S. L. 1988. Allyn Collins Vine: Man of Vision. *Oceanus* 31(4):61–66.

EMERSON, T., AND H. TAKAYAMA. 1993. Down to the Bottom. *Newsweek* 72(1):60–64.

EMERY, K. O. 1969. The Continental Shelves. *Scientific American* 221(3):106–22.

ENRIGHT, J. T., W. A. NEWMAN, R. R. HESSLER, AND J. A. MCGOWAN. 1981. Deep-ocean Hydrothermal Vent Communities. *Nature* 289:219–21.

ERICSON, D. B., M. EWING, AND B. C. HEEZEN. 1951. Deep-Sea Sands and Submarine Canyons. *Bull. Amer. Geol. Soc.* 62:961–65.

ESCHMEYER, W. N. 1963. A Deepwater Trawl Capture of Two Swordfish, *Xiphias gladius,* in the Gulf of Mexico. *Copeia* 1963(3):590.

———. 1990. *Catalog of Genera of Recent Fishes.* California Academy of Sciences.

EWING, M. 1948. Exploring the Mid-Atlantic Ridge. *National Geographic* 94(3):275–94.

———. 1949. New Discoveries on the Mid-Atlantic Ridge. *National Geographic* 96(5):611–40.

EWING, M., AND B. C. HEEZEN. 1956. Mid-Atlantic Ridge Seismic Belt. *Trans. Amer. Geophys. Union* 37:343.

FAGE, L. 1958. Les Campagnes scientifiques du bathyscaphe *F.N.R.S. III,* 1954–1957. *Ann. Inst. Oceanogr. Monaco* 35(4):232–36.

FEARS, J. R. 1978. Atlantis and the Minoan Thalassocracy: A Study in Modern Mythopoeism. In E. S. Ramage, ed., *Atlantis: Fact or Fiction?,* pp. 49–78. Indiana University Press.

FELBECK, H. 1983. Sulfide Oxidation and Carbon Fixation by the Gutless Clam *Solemya reidi:* An Animal-Bacteria Symbiosis. *Jour. Comp. Physiol.* 152:3–11.

———. 1985. CO_2 Fixation in the Hydrothermal Vent Tube Worm *Riftia pachyptila* (Jones). *Physiol. Zool.* 58:272–81.

FELBECK, H., J. J. CHILDRESS, AND G. N. SOMERO. 1981. Calvin-Benson Cycle and Sulphide Oxydation Enzymes in Animals from Sulphide-Rich Environments. *Nature* 93:291–93.

FENN, W. O. 1970. Life Under High Pressure. *Proc. Amer. Phil. Soc.* 114(3):191–97.

FISHER, C. R., J. J. CHILDRESS, A. J. ARP, J. M. BROOKS, D. DISTEL, J. A. FAVUZZI, S. A. MACKO, A. NEWTON, M. A. POWELL, G. N. SOMERO, AND T. SOTO. 1988. Physiology, Morphology, and Biochemical Composition of *Riftia pachyptila* at Rose Garden in 1985. *Deep-Sea Research* 35(10/11A):1745–58.

FISHER, C. R., J. J. CHILDRESS, A. J. ARP, J. M. BROOKS, D. DISTEL, J. A. FAVUZZI, H. FELBECK, R. HESSLER, K. S. JOHNSON, M. C. KENNICUTT, S. A. MACKO, A. NEWTON, M. A. POWELL, G. N. SOMERO, AND T. SOTO. 1988. Microhabitat Variation in the Hydrothermal Vent Mussel, *Bathymodiolus thermophilus,* at the Rose Garden Vent on the Galápagos Rift. *Deep-Sea Research* 35(10/11A):1769–91.

FISHER, C. R., J. J. CHILDRESS, A. J. ARP, J. M. BROOKS, D. DISTEL, J. A. DUGAN, H. FELBECK, L. W. FRITZ, R. R. HESSLER, K. S. JOHNSON, M. C. KENNICUTT, R. A. LUTZ, S. A. MACKO, A. NEWTON, M. A. POWELL, G. N. SOMERO, AND T. SOTO. 1988. Variation in the Hydrothermal Vent Clam, *Calyptogena magnifica,* at the Rose Garden Vent on the Galápagos Spreading Center. *Deep-Sea Research* 35(10/11A):1811–31.

FISHER, J. 1956. *Rockall.* Geoffrey Bles.

FITCH, J. E., AND R. J. LAVENBERG. 1968. *Deep-Water Fishes of California.* University of California Press.

FLORIDA ESCARPMENT CRUISE PARTICIPANTS. 1984. Florida Escarpment Cruise: The Seeps Find at the Florida Escarpment. *Oceanus* 27(3):32–33.

FOELL, E. J., AND D. L. PAWSON. 1989. Assessment of Abyssal Benthic Megafauna on a Ferromanganese Nodule Deposit Using Videotaped Television Survey Data. Paper Presented at the 21st Offshore Technology Conference, Houston, Texas, May 1–4, 1989: 313–20.

FOSTER, D. 1988. A Pilot's View: Some Dangers and Many Delights [*Alvin*]. *Oceanus* 31(4):17–21.

FOUQUET, Y., H. ONDREAS, J.-L. CHARLOU, J.-P. DONVAL, J. RADFORD-KNOERY, I. COSTA, N. LOURENÇO, AND M. K. TIVEY. 1995. Atlantic Lava Lakes and Hot Vents. *Nature* 377(6549):201.

FOX, P. J. 1992. Bruce C. Heezen: A Profile. *Oceanus* 34(4):100–7.

FRANKLIN, B. 1786. On the Gulf Stream. *Trans. Amer. Phil. Soc.* 2:314–17.

FRASER, F. C. 1970. An Early 17th Century Record of the California Gray Whale in Icelandic Waters. *Invest. on Cetacea* 2:13–20.

FRASER-BRUNNER, A. 1949. A Classification of the Fishes of the Family Myctophidae. *Proc. Zool. Soc. London* 4:1019–1106.

FREUCHEN, P. 1957. *Peter Freuchen's Book of the Seven Seas.* Julian Messner.

FRICKE, H., O. GIERE, K. SETTER, G. A. ALFREDSSON, J. K. KRISTJANSSON, P. STOFFERS, AND J. SVARVARSSON. 1989. Hydrothermal Vent Communities at the Shallow Subpolar Mid-Atlantic Ridge. *Mar. Biol.* 102(3):425–29.

FUJITA, T., AND S. OHTA. 1988. Photographic Observations of the Life Style of a Deep-Sea Ophiurid *Asteronyx loveni. Deep-Sea Research* 35A:2029–43.

FURTADO, A. 1887. Sur une nouvelle espèce de céphalopode appartenant au genre *Ommastrephes. Mems. R. Acad. Sci. Lisbon* 6:1–17.

FUSTEC, A., D. DESBRUYERES, AND S. K. JUNIPER. 1987. Deep-Sea Hydrothermal Vent Communities at 13° N on the East Pacific Rise: Microdistribution and Temporal Variations. *Biological Oceanography* 4(2):121–64.

GAGE, J. D. 1978. Animals in Deep-Sea Sediments. *Proc. Royal Soc. Edinburgh* 76B:77–93.

———. 1979. Macrobenthic Community Structure in the Rockall Trough. *Ambio Special Report* 6:43–46.

———. 1986. The Benthic Fauna of the Rockall Trough: Regional Distribution and Bathymetric Zonation. *Proc. Royal Soc. Edinburgh* 76B:77–93.

GAGE, J. D., AND P. A. TYLER. 1991. *Deep-Sea Biology: A Natural History of Organisms at the Deep-Sea Floor.* Cambridge University Press.

GALT, C. P. 1978. Bioluminescence: Dual Mechanism in a Planktonic Tunicate Produces Brilliant Surface Display. *Science* 200:70–71.

GAMBELL, R. 1967. Seasonal Movements of Sperm Whales. *Symp. Zool. Soc. London* 19:237–54.

GAMOW, G. 1941. *Biography of the Earth: Its Past, Present, and Future.* Viking Press.

GARRETT, W. E. 1979. Strange World Without Sun. *National Geographic* 156(5):680–82.

GASKELL, T. F. 1960. *Under the Deep Oceans: Twentieth Century Voyages of Discovery.* Eyre and Spottiswoode.

———. 1964. *The World Beneath the Oceans: The Story of Oceanography.* Natural History Press.

———. 1973. *The Gulf Stream.* John Day.

GEISTDOERFER, P. 1986. Nouvelles Captures et redescription d'un poisson Zoarcidae (Pisces, Perciformes, Zoarcoidei) des sites hydrothermaux de la ride du Pacifique Oriental. *Bull. Mus. Nat. Hist. Natur. Paris* 4:969–80.

GENTHE, H. 1979. Search for the Black Sword. *Oceans* 12(6):9–13.

GEORGE, D., AND J. GEORGE. 1979. *Marine Life.* John Wiley.

GEYER, R. A., ED. 1977. *Submersibles and Their Use in Oceanography and Ocean Engineering.* Elsevier.

GIBBS, R. H. 1964. Family Astronesthidae. In Part 4, *Fishes of the Western North Atlantic.* Memoirs of the Sears Foundation for Marine Research. Yale University.

GILCHRIST, J. D. F. 1921. The Reproduction of Deep-Sea Fishes. *Ann. Mag. Nat. Hist.,* Ser. 9, 7:173–77.

GILL, T. N. 1863a. Deep-Sea Fishing Fishes. *Field and Stream* November 8, 1863: 284.

———. 1863b. Descriptions of Some New Species of Pediculati and the Classification of the Group. *Proc. Acad. Nat. Sci. Phila.* 15:88–92.

———. 1879a. Synopsis of the Pediculate Fishes of the Eastern Coast of Extratropical North America. *Proc. U.S. Nat. Mus.* 1:215–22.

———. 1879b. Note on the Antennariidae. *Proc. U.S. Nat. Mus.* 1:221–22.

———. 1879c. Note on the Ceratiidae. *Proc. U.S. Nat. Mus.* 1:227–31.

———. 1909. Angler Fishes: Their Kinds and Ways. *Smithsonian Inst. Ann. Rep.* 1909:565–615.

GILL, T. N., AND J. A. RYDER. 1883. On the Anatomy and Relations of the Eurypharyngidae. *Proc. U.S. Nat. Mus.* 6(382):262–73.

———. 1884. On the Literature and Systematic Relations of the Saccopharyngoid Fishes. *Proc. U.S. Nat. Mus.* 7(408):48–64.

GILLETTE, D. D. 1994. *Seismosaurus: The Earth Shaker.* Columbia University Press.

GLASS, B., AND B. C. HEEZEN. 1967. Tektites and Geomagnetic Reversals. *Nature* 214:372.

GLASS, B., D. B. ERICSON, B. C. HEEZEN, N. D. OPDYKE, AND J. A. GLASS. 1967. Geomagnetic Reversals and Pleistocene Chronology. *Nature* 216:437–42.

GOLDEN, F. 1988. A Quarter-Century Under the Sea. *Oceanus* 31(4):2–9.

GOODE, G. B., AND T. H. BEAN. 1895. *Oceanic Ichthyology.* Washington.

GORDON, J. D. M. 1986. The Fish Population of the Rockall Trough. *Proc. Royal Soc. Edinburgh* 88B:191–204.

GORDON, J. D. M., AND J. A. R. DUNCAN. 1985. The Ecology of the Deep-Sea Benthic and Benthopelagic Fish on the Slopes of the Rockall Trough, Northeastern Atlantic. *Progress in Oceanography* 15:37–69.

———. 1987. Deep-Sea Bottom-Living Fishes at Two Repeat Stations at 2200m and 2900m in the Rockall Trough, Northeastern Atlantic Ocean. *Marine Biology* 96:309–25.

GORDON, M. 1935. Swordfish Lore. *Natural History* 36:319–26.

GOSNER, K. L. 1978. *A Field Guide to the Atlantic Seashore.* Houghton Mifflin.

GOSSE, P. H. 1846. *The Ocean.* Society for Promoting Christian Knowledge. London.

GRASSLE, J. F. 1978. Diversity and Population Dynamics of Benthic Organisms. *Oceanus* 21(1):42–49.

———. 1984. Animals in the Soft Sediments Near the Hydrothermal Vents. *Oceanus* 27(3):63–66.

———. 1985. Hydrothermal Vent Animals: Distribution and Biology. *Science* 229(4715):713–17.

———. 1986. The Ecology of Deep-Sea Hydrothermal Vent Communities. *Adv. Mar. Biol.* 23:301–62.

———. 1988. A Plethora of Unexpected Life. *Oceanus* 31(4):41–46.

———. 1991. Deep-Sea Benthic Biodiversity. *BioScience* 41(7):464–69.

GRASSLE, J. F., H. L. SANDERS, R. R. HEISLER, G. T. ROWE, AND T. MCLELLAN. 1975. Pattern and Zonation: A Study of the Bathyal Megafauna Using the Research Submersible *Alvin. Deep-Sea Research* 22:457–81.

GRAY, D. 1882. Notes on the Characters and Habits of the Bottle-nose Whale (*Hyperoodon rostratus*). *Proc. Zool. Soc. London* 1882:726–31.

GRAY, J. E. 1860. On the Genus *Hyperoodon:* The Two British Kinds and Their Food. *Proc. Zool. Soc. London* 28:422–26.

GRAY, R. W. 1935. Do Whales Descend to Great Depths? *Nature* 135:656–57.

———. 1941. The Bottlenose Whale. *Naturalist* 791:129–32.

GREENBERG, D. S. 1964. Mohole—The Project That Went Awry. *Science* 143:115–18, 223–27, 334–37.

———. 1965. Mohole: Drilling Site in Pacific Favored as Time Nears to Award Construction Contract for Vessel. *Science* 147:487–88.

———. 1966a. NSF Appropriation: Mutiny on the Mohole. *Science* 152:895–96.

———. 1966b. Mohole: Senate Is Asked to Restore Funds. *Science* 153:38–39.

———. 1966c. Mohole: Aground on Capitol Hill. *Science* 153:963.

GREENWOOD, P. H., AND D. E. ROSEN. 1971. Notes on the Structure and Relationships of the Alepocephalid Fishes. *Am. Mus. Novitates* 2473:1–41.

GREY, M. 1955. Notes on a Collection of Bermuda Deep-Sea Fishes. *Fieldiana; Zool.* 37:265–302.

———. 1956. The Distribution of Fishes Found Below a Depth of 2000 Meters. *Fieldiana; Zool.* 36(2):75–377.

———. 1958. Descriptions of Abyssal Benthic Fishes from the Gulf of Mexico. *Fieldiana; Zool.* 39(16):149–83.

———. 1959. Deep Sea Fishes from the Gulf of Mexico with the Description of a New Species. *Fieldiana; Zool.* 39(29):323–46.

GRICE, G. D. 1972. The Existence of Bottom-Living Calanoid Copepod Fauna in Deep Water with Descriptions of Five New Species. *Crustaceana* 23(3):219–42.

GRICE, G. D., AND K. HULSEMAN. 1965. Abundance, Vertical Distribution, and Taxonomy of Calanoid Copepods at Selected Stations in the Northeast Atlantic. *Jour. Zool.* 146:213–62.

GROVE, N. 1973. Volcano Overwhelms an Icelandic Village. *National Geographic* 144(1):40–67.

GRUBER, S. H., D. I. HAMASAKI, AND B. L. DAVIS. 1975. Window to the Epiphysis in Sharks. *Copeia* 2:378–80.

GUDGER, E. W. 1940. The Alleged Pugnacity of the Swordfish and the Spearfishes as Shown by their Attacks on Vessels. *Mem. Royal Soc. Bengal* 12(2):215–315.

GÜNTHER, A. 1880. *The Study of Fishes.* Adam and Charles Black.

———. 1887. Report on the Deep-Sea Fishes Collected by H.M.S. *Challenger* During the Years 1873–76. *Rep. Sci. Res. Voy. Challenger Zool.* 22.

HAEDRICH, R. L. 1969. Alepisaurus. *Oceanus* 15(1):8–9.

———. 1974. Pelagic Capture of the Epibenthic Rattail *Coryphaenoides rupestris. Deep-Sea Research* 21:977–79.

HAEDRICH, R. L., AND N. R. HENDERSON. 1974. Pelagic Food of *Coryphaenoides rupestris. Deep-Sea Research* 21:739–44.

HAEDRICH, R. L., AND N. R. MERRETT. 1988. Summary Atlas of Deep Living Demersal Fishes in the North Atlantic Basin. *Jour. Nat. Hist.* 22:1325–62.

HAEDRICH, R. L., AND J. G. NIELSEN. 1966. Fishes Eaten by *Alepisaurus* (Pisces, Iniomi) in the Southeastern Pacific Ocean. *Deep-Sea Research* 13:909–19.

HAEDRICH, R. L., AND G. T. ROWE. 1977. Megafaunal Biomass in the Deep Sea. *Nature* 269:141–42.

HAEDRICH, R. L., G. T. ROWE, AND P. POLLONI. 1975. Zonation and Faunal Composition of Epibenthic Populations on the Continental Slope South of New England. *Jour. Mar. Res.* 33:191–212.

———. 1980. The Megabenthic Fauna in the Deep Sea South of New England, USA. *Mar. Biol.* 57:165–79.

HALDANE, J. B. S. 1954. The Origins of Life. *New Biology* 6:16–27.

HALLAM, A. 1972. Continental Drift and the Fossil Record. *Scientific American* 227(11):56–66.

———. 1973. *A Revolution in the Earth Sciences: From Continental Drift to Plate Tectonics.* Oxford University Press.

HALSTEAD, B. W. 1959. *Dangerous Marine Animals.* Cornell Maritime Press.

HAMILTON-PATERSON, J. 1992. *The Great Deep.* Random House.

HANAUER, E. 1983. Innerspace Shuttle: The Peregrinations of *Alvin*, Workhorse of the Underwater World. *Oceans* 16(1):20–25.

HANEDA, Y. 1950. Luminous Organs of Fish Which Emit Light Indirectly. *Pacific Science* 4(3):214–27.

———. 1951. The Luminescence of Some Deep-Sea Fishes of the Families Gadidae and Macrouridae. *Pacific Science* 5(4):372–78.

———. 1968. Observations on the Luminescence of the Deep-Sea Luminous Anglerfish, *Himantolophus groenlandicus. Sci. Rep. Yokosuka City Mus.* 14:1–6.

HANSEN, B. 1956. Holothurioidea from Depth Exceeding 6000 Meters. *Galathea Report* 2:33–54.

———. 1967. The Taxonomy and Zoogeography of the Deep-Sea Holothurians in Their Evolutionary Aspects. *Studies in Tropical Oceanography* 5:480–501.

———. 1968. Brood Protection in the Deep-Sea Holothurian *Oneirophanta mutabilis. Nature* 217:1062–63.

———. 1972. Photographic Evidence of a Unique Type of Walking in Deep-Sea Holothurians. *Deep-Sea Research* 19:461–62.

———. 1975. Systematics and Biology of the Deep-Sea Holothurians. *Galathea Report* 13:1–262.

HANSEN, K. 1970. On the Luminous Organs in the Barbels of Some Stomiatoid Fishes. *Vidensk. Medd. fra Dansk Naturh. Foren.* 133:69–84.

HANSEN, K., AND P. J. HERRING. 1977. Dual Bioluminescent Systems in the Anglerfish Genus *Linophryne. Jour. Zool. London.* 182:103–24.

HANSEN, L. C., AND S. A. EARLE. 1987. Submersibles for Scientists. *Oceanus* 30:31–38.

HARBISON, G. R., L. P. MADIN, AND N. R. SWANBERG. 1978. On the Natural History and Distribution of Oceanic Ctenophores. *Deep-Sea Research* 25:233–56.

HARDY, A. C. 1956. *The Open Sea: Its Natural History—Fish and Fisheries.* Collins.

———. 1967. *Great Waters.* Harper & Row.

HARRINGTON, R. W. 1961. Oviparous Hermaphroditic Fish with Internal Self-Fertilization. *Science* 129:215–16.

HARRISON, C. M. H. 1966. On the First Halosaur Leptocephalus: from Madeira. *Bull. Brit. Mus. Nat. Hist. Zool.* 14(8):444–86.

HARRY, R. R. 1952. Deep-Sea Fishes of the Bermuda Oceanographic Expeditions. Families Cetomimidae and Rondeletiidae. *Zoologica* 37:55–71.

HARVEY, E. N. 1921. A Fish with a Luminous Organ Designed for the Growth of Luminous Bacteria. *Science* 53:314–15.

———. 1926. Bioluminescence and Fluorescence in the Living World. *Amer. Jour. Physiol.* 77:555–61.

———. 1931. Stimulation by Adrenalin of the Luminescence of Deep-Sea Fish. *Zoologica* 12(6):67–69.

———. 1952. *Bioluminescence.* Academic Press.

HARVEY, H. W. 1928. *Biological Chemistry and Physics of Sea Water.* Cambridge University Press.

HASS, H. 1951. *Diving to Adventure.* Doubleday.

———. 1972. *Challenging the Deep.* Morrow.

———. 1975. *Men Beneath the Sea: Man's Conquest of the Underwater World.* St. Martin's.

HASTINGS, J. W. 1971. Light to Hide By: Ventral Luminescence to Camouflage the Silhouette. *Science* 173:1016–17.

HAWKES, G. 1983. Deep Rover. *Oceans* 16(2):16–17.

HAYGOOD, M. G., AND D. L. DISTEL. 1993. Bioluminescent Symbionts of Flashlight Fishes and Deep-Sea Anglerfishes Form Unique Lineages Related to the Genus *Vibrio*. *Nature* 363(6425):154–56.

HEATH, G. R. 1978. Deep-Sea Manganese Nodules. *Oceanus* 21(1):60–68.

HECKER, B. 1985. Fauna from a Cold Sulfur-Seep in the Gulf of Mexico: Comparison with Hydrothermal Vent Communities and Evolutionary Implications. *Bull. Biol. Soc. Wash.* 6:465–73.

HEEZEN, B. C. 1956. The Origin of Submarine Canyons. *Scientific American* 195(8):36–41.

———. 1957. Whales Entangled in Deep-Sea Cables. *Deep-Sea Research* 4:105–15.

———. 1960. The Rift in the Ocean Floor. *Scientific American* 203(4):98–110.

———. 1963. Turbidity Currents. In M. N. Hill, ed., *The Sea, Vol. 3: The Earth Beneath the Sea*, pp. 742–75. Wiley Interscience.

HEEZEN, B. C., AND M. EWING. 1952. Turbidity Currents and Submarine Slumps, and the 1929 Grand Banks Earthquake. *Amer. Jour. Sci.* 250:849–73.

———. 1963. The Mid-Oceanic Ridge. In M. N. Hill, ed., *The Sea, Vol. 3: The Earth Beneath the Sea*, pp. 388–409. Wiley Interscience.

HEEZEN, B. C., AND C. D. HOLLISTER. 1971. *The Face of the Deep*. Oxford University Press.

HEEZEN, B. C., AND A. S. LAUGHTON. 1963. Abyssal Plains. In M. N. Hill, ed., *The Sea, Vol. 3: The Earth Beneath the Sea*, pp. 281–311. Wiley Interscience.

HEEZEN, B. C., AND H. W. MENARD. 1963. Topography of the Deep-Sea Floor. In M. N. Hill, ed., *The Sea, Vol. 3: The Earth Beneath the Sea*, pp. 233–80. Wiley Interscience.

HEEZEN, B. C., M. EWING, AND D. B. ERICSON. 1951. Submarine Topography in the North Atlantic. *Bull. Amer. Geol. Soc.* 62:1407–9.

———. 1954. Reconnaissance Survey of the Abyssal Plain South of Newfoundland. *Deep-Sea Research* 2:122–33.

HEEZEN, B. C., M. EWING, AND E. T. MILLER. 1953. Trans-Atlantic Profile of Total Magnetic Intensity and Topography, Dakar to Barbados. *Deep-Sea Research* 1:25–33.

HEEZEN, B. C., C. D. HOLLISTER, AND W. F. RUDDIMAN. 1966. Shaping of the Continental Rise by Deep Geostrophic Contour Currents. *Science* 152(3721):502–8.

HEEZEN, B. C., M. THARP, AND M. EWING. 1959. The Floors of the Oceans. *Geological Society of America* (Special Paper) 65:1–122.

HEEZEN, B. C., E. T. BUNCE, J. B. HERSEY, AND M. THARP. 1964. Chain and Romanche Fracture Zones. *Deep-Sea Research* 11:11–33.

HEIRTZLER, J. R. 1968. Sea-Floor Spreading. *Scientific American* 219(6):60–70.

———. 1975. Project FAMOUS—Man's First Voyage Down to the Mid-Atlantic Ridge: Where the Earth Turns Inside Out. *National Geographic* 147(5):587–615.

HEIRTZLER, J. R., AND W. B. BRYAN. 1975. The Floor of the Mid-Atlantic Rift. *Scientific American* 233(2):78–90.

HEIRTZLER, J. R., AND J. F. GRASSLE. 1976. Deep-Sea Research by Manned Submersibles. *Science* 194:294–99.

HEIRTZLER, J. R., X. LE PICHON, AND J. G. BARON. 1966. Magnetic Anomalies over the Reykjanes Ridge. *Deep-Sea Research* 13:427–33.

HEIRTZLER, J. R., G. O. DICKSON, E. M. HERRON, W. C. PITMAN, AND X. LE PINCHON. 1968. Marine Magnetic Anomalies, Geomagnetic Field Reversals, and Motions of the Ocean Floor and Continents. *Jour. Geophys. Res.* 73:2119–36.

HERALD, E. S. 1961. *Living Fishes of the World.* Doubleday.

HERDENDORF, C. E., AND T. M. BERRA. 1994. The Deepest and Most Southerly U.S. Record of a Greenland Shark *Somniosus microcephalus* from the Wreck of the S.S. *Central America. Fish. Bull.* In press.

HERDMAN, W. A. 1923. *Founders of Oceanography and Their Work.* Edward Arnold.

HERMANNSSON, H. 1924. Jon Gudmundsson and His Natural History of Iceland. *Islandica* 15, I–XXVIII, 1–40.

HERRING, P. J. 1974. New Observations on the Bioluminescence of Echinoderms. *Jour. Zool. London* 172:401–18.

———. 1977a. Bioluminescence in Marine Organisms. *Nature* 267:788–93.

———. 1977b. Luminescence in Cephalopods and Fish. In M. Nixon and J. B. Messenger, eds., *The Biology of Cephalopods,* pp. 127–60. Academic Press.

———. 1978. Bioluminescence in Invertebrates Other than Insects. In P. H. Herring, ed., *Bioluminescence in Action,* pp. 199–240. Academic Press.

———. 1983. The Spectral Characteristics of Luminous Marine Organisms. *Proc. Royal Soc.* 220:183–217.

———. 1986. How to Survive in the Dark: Bioluminescence in the Deep Sea. *Symp. Soc. Exp. Biol.* 39:323–50.

———. 1990. Bioluminescent Communication in the Sea. In P. J. Herring, A. K. Campbell, M. Whitfield, and L. Maddock, eds., *Light and Life in the Sea,* pp. 245–64. Cambridge University Press.

———. 1993. Light Genes Will Out. *Nature* 363(6425):110–11.

HERRING, P. J., AND M. R. CLARKE, EDS. 1971. *Deep Oceans.* Praeger.

HERRING, P. J., AND N. A. LOCKET. 1978. The Luminescence and Photophores of Euphausiid Crustaceans. *Jour. Zool.* 186:431–62.

HERRING, P. J., AND J. G. MORIN. 1978. Bioluminescence in Fishes. In P. H. Herring, ed., *Bioluminescence in Action,* pp. 273–329. Academic Press.

HERRING, P. J., AND O. MUNK. 1994. The Escal Light Gland of the Deep-Sea Angler-fish *Halophryne mollis* (Pisces: Ceratioidei) with Observations on Luminescence Control. *Jour. Mar. Biol. Assoc. U.K.* 74:747–63.

HERRMANN, P. 1954. *Conquest by Man.* Harper & Brothers.

HERSEY, J. B. 1962. The Puerto Rico Trench: A Geophysical Laboratory. *Oceanus* 8(3):14–21.

———. 1963. *Thresher Search. Oceanus* 10(1):2–3.

HERSEY, J. B., AND R. H. BACKUS. 1954. New Evidence That Migrating Gas Bubbles, Probably the Swimbladders of Fish, Are Largely Responsible for Scattering Layers on the Continental Rise South of New England. *Deep-Sea Research* 1:190–91.

350   *Bibliography*

HERSEY, J. B., H. R. JOHNSON, AND L. C. DAVIS. 1952. Recent Findings About the Deep-Scattering Layer. *Jour. Mar. Res.* 11:1–9.

HESS, H. H. 1962. History of Ocean Basins. In A. E. J. Engle, H. L. James, and B. F. Leonard, eds., *Petrologic Studies: A Volume in Honor of A. F. Buddington,* pp. 599–620. Geological Society of America.

HESSLER, R. R. 1981. Oasis Under the Sea—Where Sulfur Is the Staff of Life. *New Scientist* 92(1283):741–47.

HESSLER, R. R., AND H. L. SANDERS. 1967. Faunal Diversity in the Deep-Sea. *Deep-Sea Research* 14:65–78.

HESSLER, R. R., W. M. SMITHEY, M. A. BOUDRIAS, C. H. KELLER, R. A. LUTZ, AND J. J. CHILDRESS. 1988. Temporal Change in Megafauna at the Rose Garden Hydrothermal Vent (Galápagos Rift; Eastern Tropical Pacific). *Deep-Sea Research* 35(10/11A):1681–1709.

HEUVELMANS, B. 1968. *In the Wake of the Sea-Serpents.* Hill and Wang.

HOLLISTER, C. D., R. FLOOD, AND I. N. MCCAVE. 1978. Plastering and Decorating [Sediment Drifts] in the North Atlantic. *Oceanus* 21(1):5–13.

HOLLISTER, C. D., A. R. M. NOWELL, AND P. A. JUMARS. 1984. The Dynamic Abyss. *Scientific American* 250(3):42–53.

HOLLISTER, G. 1930a. Fish Magic. *Bull. N.Y. Zool. Soc.* 33(2):72–76.

———. 1930b. Telephoning to Davy Jones's Locker. *Bull. N.Y. Zool. Soc.* 33(6):240–44.

———. 1936. A Fish Which Grows by Shrinking. *Bull. N.Y. Zool. Soc.* 39(3):104–9.

HOLT, E. W. L., AND L. W. BYRNE. 1910. Preliminary Diagnosis of a New Stomiatid Fish from Southwest of Ireland. *Ann. Mag. Nat. Hist.* 6:294–97.

HORTON, E. 1974. *The Illustrated History of the Submarine.* Doubleday.

HOUOT, G. S. 1954. Two and a Half Miles Down. *National Geographic* 106(1):80–86.

———. 1958a. Les Campagnes scientifiques du bathyscaphe *F.N.R.S. III,* 1954–1957. *Ann. Inst. Oceanogr. Monaco* 35(4):237–42.

———. 1958b. Four Years of Diving to the Bottom of the Sea. *National Geographic* 113(5):715–31.

HOUOT, G. S., AND P. H. WILLM. 1955. 2000 *Fathoms Down.* Dutton.

HSU, K. J. 1983. *The Mediterranean Was a Desert: A Voyage of the Glomar Challenger.* Princeton University Press.

———. 1992. *Challenger at Sea: A Ship That Revolutionized Earth Science.* Princeton University Press.

HUBBS, C. L. 1935. Review of *Half Mile Down,* by William Beebe. *Copeia* 2:105.

HUBBS, C. L., T. IWAI, AND K. MATSUBARA. 1967. External and Internal Characters, Horizontal and Vertical Distribution, Luminescence, and Food of the Dwarf Pelagic Shark, *Euprotomicrus bispinatus. Bull. Scripps Inst. Oceanogr.* 10:1–64.

HUREAU, J.-C. 1979. A New Species of Deep-Sea Brotulid Fish, *Typhlonus delosommatus* from the Tropical Atlantic Ocean. *Bull. Mar. Sci.* 29(2):272–77.

HUREAU, J.-C., P. GEISTDOERFER, AND M. RANNOU. 1979. The Ecology of Deep-Sea Benthic Fishes. *Sarsia* 64(1&2):103–8.

HURLEY, P. M. 1968. The Confirmation of Continental Drift. *Scientific American* 218(4):52–64.

HUSSAKOF, L. 1909. A New Goblin Shark, *Scapanorhynchus jordani,* from Japan. *Bull. Am. Mus. Nat. Hist.* 26(19):257–62.

HUYGHE, P. 1986. Seafloor Mapping. *Oceans* 19(6):22–29.

HYMAN, L. H. 1955. *The Invertebrates. Vol. 4: Echinodermata.* McGraw-Hill.

IDYLL, C. P. 1964. *Abyss: The Deep Sea and the Creatures That Live in It.* Crowell.

———, ED. 1969. *Exploring the Ocean World: A History of Oceanography.* Crowell.

ISAACS, J. D. 1969. The Nature of Oceanic Life. *Scientific American* 221(3):147–62.

ISAACS, J. D., AND R. A. SCHWARTZLOSE. 1975a. Active Animals of the Deep-Sea Floor. *Scientific American* 233(4):85–91.

———. 1975b. Biological Applications of Underwater Photography. *Oceanus* 18(3):25–30.

ISAACS, J. D., S. A. TONT, AND G. L. WICK. 1974. Deep Scattering Layers: Vertical Migration as a Tactic for Finding Food. *Deep-Sea Research* 21:651–56.

ISELIN, C. O'D. 1963. The Loss of the *Thresher. Oceanus* 10(1):4–7.

IWAI, T. 1960. Luminous Organs of the Deep-Sea Squaloid Shark *Centroscyllium ritteri* Jordan & Fowler. *Pacific Science* 14:51–54.

JACKSON, G. 1978. *The British Whaling Trade.* A. & C. Black.

JAHN, W. 1971. Deepest Photographic Evidence of an Abyssal Cephalopod. *Nature* 232:487–88.

JANNASCH, H. W. 1978. Experiments in Deep-Sea Microbiology. *Oceanus* 21(1):50–57.

———. 1984. Chemosynthesis: The Nutritional Basis for Life at Deep-Sea Vents. *Oceanus* 27(3):73–78.

———. 1985. The Chemosynthetic Support of Life and the Microbial Diversity at Deep-Sea Vents. *Proc. Roy. Soc. London* 225(1240):277–97.

———. 1988. Serendipity in Deep-Sea Microbiology: Lessons from the *Alvin* Lunch. *Oceanus* 31(4):28–33.

———. 1995. Life at the Sea Floor. *Nature* 374(6524):676–77.

JANNASCH, H. W., AND M. J. MOTTL. 1985. Geomicrobiology of Deep-Sea Hydrothermal Vents. *Science* 229(4715):717–25.

JANSSEN, J., AND G. R. HARBISON. 1981. Fish in Salps: The Association of Squaretails (*Tetragonurus* Spp.) with Pelagic Tunicates. *Jour. Mar. Biol. Assoc. U.K.* 61:917–27.

JENKYNS, H. C. 1994. Early History of the Oceans. *Oceanus* 36(4):49–52.

JOHNSON, F. H., AND O. SHIMOMURA. 1975. Bacterial and Other "Luciferins." *BioScience* 25(11):718–22.

JOHNSON, H. P., AND V. TUNNICLIFFE. 1985. Time-Lapse Photography of a Hydrothermal System; A Successful One-Year Deployment. *Eos* 9:1025–26.

JOHNSON, H. R., R. H. BACKUS, J. B. HERSEY, AND D. M. OWEN. 1956. Suspended Echo Sounder and Camera Studies of Midwater Sound Scatterers. *Deep-Sea Research* 3:266–72.

JOHNSON, K. S., J. J. CHILDRESS, AND C. L. BEEHLER. 1988. Short-Term Temperature Variability in the Rose Garden Hydrothermal Vent Field: An Unstable Deep-Sea Environment. *Deep-Sea Research* 35(10/11A):1711–21.

JOHNSON, K. S., J. J. CHILDRESS, R. R. HESSLER, C. M. SAKAMOTO-ARNOLD, AND C. L. BEEHLER. 1988. Chemical and Biological Interactions at the Rose Garden Hydrothermal Vent Field, Galápagos Spreading Center. *Deep-Sea Research* 35(10/11A):1723–44.

JOHNSON, R. K., AND E. BERTELSEN. 1991. The Fishes of the Family Giganturidae: Systematics, Development, Distribution and Aspects of Biology. *Dana Report* 91:1–45.

JOLLIVET, D., FAUGERES, J.-C., R. GRIBOULARD, D. DESBRUYERES, AND G. BLANC. 1990. Composition and Spatial Organization of a Cold Seep Community on the Barbados Accretionary Prism: Tectonic, Geochemical and Sedimentary Context. *Progress in Oceanography* 24:25–45.

JONES, E. C. 1963. *Tremoctopus violaceus* Uses *Physalia* Tentacles as Weapons. *Science* 139:764.

———. 1971. *Isistius brasiliensis,* a Squaloid Shark, the Probable Cause of Crater Wounds in Fishes and Cetaceans. *Fish. Bull.* 69(4):791–98.

JONES, M. L. 1980. *Riftia pachyptila,* a New Genus, New Species, the Vestimentiferan Worm from the Galápagos Rift Geothermal Vents (Pogonophora). *Proc. Biol. Soc. Wash.* 93(4):1295–1313.

———. 1984. The Giant Tube Worms. *Oceanus* 27(3):47–52.

———. 1985. On the Vestimentifera, New Phylum: Six New Species and Other Taxa, from the Hydrothermal Vents and Elsewhere. *Bull. Bio. Soc. Wash.* 6:117–58.

JONSGARD, Å. 1955. Development of the Modern Norwegian Small Whale Industry. *Norsk Hvalfangst-tidende* 44(12):698–718.

JORDAN, D. S. 1898. Description of a Species of Fish (*Mitsukurina owstoni*) from Japan, the Type of a Distinct Family of Lamnoid Sharks. *Proc. Calif. Acad. Sci. (Zool.)* 1(6):199–202.

JOUBIN, L. 1937. Les Octopodes de la croisière du "Dana," 1921–22. *Dana Report* 11:1–49.

JUNGE, G. C. A. 1936. Bones of a Whale from the Wieringermeer, Zuider Zee. *Nature* 138:78.

KAHARL, V. A. 1988. A Famously Successful Expedition to the Boundary of Creation. *Oceanus* 31(4):34–40.

———. 1990. *Water Baby: The Story of Alvin.* Oxford University Press.

KALMIJN, A. J. 1966. Electro-perception in Sharks and Rays. *Nature* 212:1232–33.

———. 1971. The Electric Sense of Sharks and Rays. *Jour. Exp. Biol.* 55:371–83.

———. 1977. The Electric and Magnetic Sense of Sharks, Skates, and Rays. *Oceanus* 20(3):45–52.

KAMPA, E. M., AND B. P. BODEN. 1954. Submarine Illumination and the Twilight Movements of a Sonic Scattering Layer. *Nature* 174:869–71.

———. 1956. Light Generation in a Sonic Scattering Layer. *Deep-Sea Research* 4:73–92.

KARSON, J. A. 1992. Tectonics of Slow-Spreading Ridges. *Oceanus* 34(4):51–59.

KAY, F. G. 1954. *The Atlantic Ocean: Bridge Between Two Worlds.* Museum Press.

KEACH, D. L. 1964. Down to the *Thresher* by Bathyscaph. *National Geographic* 125(6):764–77.

KENK, V. C., AND B. R. WILSON. 1985. A New Mussel (Bivalvia, Mytilidae) from Hydrothermal Vents in the Galápagos Rift Zone. *Malacologia* 26:253–71.

KENNICUTT, M. C., J. M. BROOKS, R. R. FAY, T. L. WADE, AND J. T. MCDONALD. 1985. Vent-Type Taxa in a Hydrocarbon Seep Region on the Louisiana Slope. *Nature* 317:351–53.

KIPLING, R. 1893. "Deep Sea Cables." In Elsie Kipling Bainbridge, ed., *Rudyard Kipling: Complete Verse,* p. 173. Doubleday edition, 1939.

KNUDSEN, J. 1964. Scaphopoda and Gastropoda from Depths Exceeding 6000 Meters. *Galathea Report* 7:125–35.

KOEFOED, E. 1927. Fishes from the Sea-Bottom. *Rep. Sci. Res. "Michael Sars" N. Atlantic Deep-Sea Expedition 1910.* 4(1):1–47.

KOLLIKER, R. A. 1853. Bau von Leptocephalus und Helmichthys. *Zeitschr. Wissench. Zool.* 4:360–66.

KOPPER, P. 1987. Into the Deeps. In J. B. Tourtellot, ed. *Into the Unknown: The Story of Exploration,* pp. 285–95. National Geographic Society.

KRAMP, P. L. 1956. Pelagic Fauna. In A. F. Bruun, S. Greve, H. Mielche, and R. Sparck, eds., *The Galathea Deep Sea Expedition, 1950–1952,* pp. 65–86. Allen and Unwin.

KRÖYER, H. 1844. Ichthyologiske Bidrag 10. *Ceratias holbölli. Naturhist. Tidsskr.* 1:639–49.

KUENEN, P. H. 1952. Estimated Size of the Grand Banks Turbidity Current. *Amer. Jour. Sci.* 250:874–84.

KUNZIC, R. 1993. Between Home and the Abyss. *Discover* 14(12):66–75.

KURTEN, B. 1969. Continental Drift and Evolution. *Scientific American* 220(3):54–64.

KUWABARA, S. 1954. Occurrence of Luminescent Organs on the Tongue of Two Scopelid Fishes. *Jour. Shimonoseki College Fisheries* 3(3):283–87.

LAMPITT, R. S. 1985. Fast Living on the Ocean Floor. *New Scientist* 105(1445):37–40.

LAMPITT, R. S., AND M. P. BURNHAM. 1983. A Free-fall Time-Lapse Camera and Current Meter System "Bathysnap" with Notes on the Foraging Behavior of a Bathyal Decapod Shrimp. *Deep-Sea Research* 30A:1009–17.

LAND, M. F. 1990. Optics of the Eyes of Marine Animals. In P. J. Herring, A. K. Campbell, M. Whitfield, and L. Maddock, eds., *Light and Life in the Sea,* pp. 49–166. Cambridge University Press.

LANE, F. W. 1960. *Kingdom of the Octopus.* Sheridan House.

LAUBIER, L., AND D. DESBRUYERES. 1985. Oases at the Bottom of the Ocean. *Endeavour* 9(2):67–76.

LAUGHTON, A. S. 1957. Exploring the Deep Ocean Floor. *Jour. Roy. Soc. Arts* 106:39–56.

———. 1959a. The Sea Floor. *New Scientist* 6(144):237–40.

———. 1959b. Photography of the Ocean Floor. *Endeavour* 18:178–85.

———. 1971. South Labrador Sea and the Evolution of the North Atlantic. *Nature* 232:612–17.

LAWLESS, C. 1991. *The Submarine Book.* Thames and Hudson.

LAWRY, J. V. 1974. Lantern Fish Compare Downwelling Light and Bioluminescence. *Nature* 247:155–57.

LEATHERWOOD, S., D. K. CALDWELL, AND H. E. WINN. 1976. *Whales, Dolphins, and Porpoises of the Western North Atlantic: A Guide to Their Identification.* NOAA.

LEIP, H. 1957. *The Gulf Stream Story.* Jarrolds.

LEMCHE, H. 1957. A New Living Deep-Sea Mollusc of the Cambro-Devonian (Class Monoplacophora). *Nature* Feb. 23: 414–16.

LEMCHE, H., AND WINGSTRAND, K. G. 1959. The Anatomy of *Neopilina galatheae* Lemche 1957 (Mollusca, Tryblidiacea). *Galathea Report* 3:9–72.

LEMCHE, H., B. HANSEN, F. J. MADSEN, O. S. TENDAL, AND T. WOLFF. 1976. Hadal Life as Analysed from Photographs. *Vidensk. Medd. fra Dansk Naturh. Foren.* 139:263–336.

LEPICHON, X. 1968. Sea Floor Spreading and Continental Drift. *Jour. Geophys. Res.* 73:3661–97.

LESLIE, C., AND L. NGUYEN. 1995. The Treasure of the I-52. *Newsweek* 126(5):64.

LEVI, C. 1964. Spongiaires des zones bathyale, abyssale, et Hadale. *Galathea Report* 7:171–81.

LEY, W. 1987. *Exotic Zoology.* Bonanza Books.

LIN, J. 1992. The Segmented Mid-Atlantic Ridge. *Oceanus* 34(4):11–18.

LINK, E. A. 1963. Our Man-in-Sea Project. *National Geographic* 123(5):713–17.

————. 1964. Tomorrow on the Deep Frontier. *National Geographic* 125(6):778–801.

————. 1965. Outpost Under the Ocean. *National Geographic* 127(4):530–32.

LINNAEUS, C. 1758. *Systema Naturae per Regna Tria Naturae, Secundum Classes, Ordines, Genera, Species cum Characteribus, Differentilis, Synonymis, Locis.* 10th ed., revised. Vol. 1. Guilielmi Engelman, Holmiae.

LITTLER, M. M., D. S. LITTLER, S. M. BLAIR, AND J. N. NORRIS. 1985. Deepest Known Plant Life Discovered on an Uncharted Seamount. *Science* 227:57–59.

LONSDALE, P., AND C. SMALL. 1992. Ridges and Rises: A Global View. *Oceanus* 34(4):26–35.

LORD, W. 1955. *A Night to Remember.* Holt, Rinehart and Winston.

————. 1986. *The Night Lives On.* Morrow.

LU, C. C., AND M. R. CLARKE. 1975. Vertical Distribution of Cephalopods at 40° N, 53° N, and 60° N at 20° W in the North Atlantic. *J. Mar. Biol. Assoc. U.K.* 55(1):143–64.

LU, C. C., AND C. F. E. ROPER. 1979. Cephalopods from Deep-Water Dumpsite 106 (Western Atlantic): Vertical Distribution and Seasonal Abundance. *Smithsonian Contributions to Zoology* 288:1–36.

LUSKIN, B., B. C. HEEZEN, M. EWING, AND M. LANDISMAN. 1954. Precision Measurement of Ocean Depth. *Deep-Sea Research* 1:131–40.

LUTZ, R. A. 1991. The Biology of Deep-Sea Vents and Seeps. *Oceanus* 34(4):75–83.

LUTZ, R. A., AND R. M. HAYMON. 1994. Rebirth of a Deep-Sea Vent. *National Geographic* 186(5):114–26.

LUTZ, R. A., D. JABLONSKI, AND R. D. TURNER. 1984. Larval Development and Dispersal at Deep-Sea Hydrothermal Vents. *Science* 226:1451–54.

MACDONALD, A. G. 1975. *Physiological Aspects of Deep-Sea Biology.* Cambridge University Press.

MACDONALD, K. C. 1992. Mid-Ocean Ridges: The Quest for Order. *Oceanus* 34(4):9–11.

MACDONALD, K. C., AND P. J. FOX. 1990. The Mid-Ocean Ridge. *Scientific American* 262(6):72–79.

MACKINTOSH, N. A. 1956. 2000 Feet Down: Deep-Sea Photographs Teach Us More About the Little-Known Squid. *New Scientist* 1:60.

————. 1965. *The Stocks of Whales.* Fishing News (Books) Ltd.

MACLIESH, W. H. 1989. *The Gulf Stream: Encounters with the Blue God.* Houghton Mifflin.

MADDOCKS, M. 1978. *The Great Liners.* Time-Life Books.

MARINO, G. 1994. Back to the Jurassic in Space Age Subs: Deep Ocean Exploration for the Next Millennium. *Science News* 146(8):122–26.

MARKHAM, C. R. 1881. On the Whale Fisheries of the Basque Provinces of Spain. *Proc. Zool. Soc. London* 62:969–76.

MARKLE, D. F. 1980. A New Species and a Review of the Deep-Sea Fish Genus *Asquamiceps* (Salmoniformes: Alepocephalidae). *Bull. Mar. Sci.* 3(1):45–53.

MARKLE, D. F., AND W. R. MERRETT. 1980. The Abyssal Alepocephalid *Rinoctes nasutus* (Pisces: Salmoniformes): A Redescription and an Evaluation of its Systematic Position. *Jour. Zool. London* 190:225–39.

MARSHALL, N. B. 1951. Bathypelagic Fishes as Sound Scatterers in the Ocean. *Jour. Mar. Res.* 10(1):1–17.

———. 1954. *Aspects of Deep Sea Biology.* Hutchinson.

———. 1955. Alepisaurid Fishes. *Discovery Reports* 27:303–36.

———. 1962a. Observations on the Heteromi, an Order of Teleost Fishes. *Bull. Br. Mus. Nat. Hist. Zool.* 9(6):249–70.

———. 1962b. The Biology of Sound Producing Fishes. *Symp. Zool. Soc. London* 7:45–60.

———. 1964a. Deep Ocean Sonic Fishes. *Oceanus* 11(1):3–7.

———. 1964b. Bathypelagic Macrourid Fishes. *Copeia* 1:86–93.

———. 1965a. Systematic and Biological Studies of the Macrourid Fishes (Anacanthini; Teleostii). *Deep-Sea Research* 12:299–322.

———. 1965b. *The Life of Fishes.* Weidenfeld & Nicolson.

———. 1979. *Deep-Sea Biology: Developments and Perspectives.* Garland.

MARSHALL, N. B., AND D. W. BOURNE. 1964. A Photographic Survey of the Benthic Fishes in the Red Sea and the Gulf of Aden, with Observations on Their Population Density, Diversity, and Habits. *Bull. Mus. Comp. Zool.* 132(2):223–44.

MARSHALL, N. B., AND T. IWAMOTO. 1973. Family Macrouridae. In Part 6, *Fishes of the Western North Atlantic,* pp. 496–665. Memoirs of the Sears Foundation for Marine Research. Yale University.

MARSHALL, N. B., AND J. C. STAIGER. 1975. Aspects of the Structure, Relationships and Biology of the Deep-Sea Fish *Ipnops murrayi* (Family Bathypteroidae). *Bull. Mar. Sci.* 25(1):101–11.

MATTHEWS, S. W. 1961. Mohole Drillers Probe the Ocean Floor. *National Geographic* 120(5):686–97.

———. 1981. New World of the Ocean. *National Geographic* 160(1):792–833.

MAUL, G. E. 1959. On a Specimen of *Bathylaco nigricans* Goode and Bean Taken from the Stomach of *Aphanopus carbo. Bocagiana* 4:1–8.

———. 1961. The Ceratioid Fishes in the Collection of the Museu Municipal do Funchal. *Bol. Mus. Munic. Funchal* 14:87–159.

MAURO, A. 1977. Extra-Ocular Photoreceptors in Cephalopods. In M. Nixon and J. B. Messenger, eds., *The Biology of Cephalopods,* pp. 287–308. Academic Press.

MAURY, M. F. 1855. *The Physical Geography of the Sea and Its Meteorology.* Sampson Low.

MAXWELL, A. E. 1994. An Abridged History of Deep Ocean Drilling. *Oceanus* 36(4):8–12.

MAYASHITA, T., AND K. C. BALCOMB. 1988. Preliminary Report of an Unidentified Beaked Whale Like *Hyperoodon* sp. in the Central and Western Pacific. *International Whaling Commission* SC/40/SM9:1–16.

MAYER, L. A., A. N. SHOR, J. H. CLARKE, AND D. J. PIPER. 1988. Dense Biological Communities at 3,850m on the Laurentian Fan and Their Relationship to the Deposits of the 1929 Grand Banks Earthquake. *Deep-Sea Research* 35(8A):1235–46.

MCALLISTER, D. E. 1967. The Significance of Ventral Bioluminescence in Fishes. *Jour. Fish. Res. Bd. Canada* 24(3):537–54.

MCAULIFFE, K. 1995. Elephant Seals, the Champion Divers of the Deep. *Smithsonian* 26(6):45–56.

MCCAMIS, M. J. 1988. "Captain Hook's" Hunt for the H-Bomb. *Oceanus* 31(4):22–27.

MCCAPRA, F. 1990. The Chemistry of Bioluminescence: Origins and Mechanisms. In P. J. Herring, A. K. Campbell, M. Whitfield, and L. Maddock, eds., *Light and Life in the Sea,* pp. 265–78. Cambridge University Press.

MCCOSKER, J. E. 1979. In Utter Darkness. *Oceans* 12(6):22–29.

MCDOWELL, S. B. 1973a. Order Heteromi (Notacanthiformes), Suborder Halosauridae. In Part 6, *Fishes of the Western North Atlantic,* pp. 32–123. Memoirs of the Sears Foundation for Marine Research. Yale University.

———. 1973b. Suborder Notacanthoidei, Family Notacanthidae. In Part 6, *Fishes of the Western North Atlantic,* pp. 124–207. Memoirs of the Sears Foundation for Marine Research. Yale University.

———. 1973c. Suborder Notacanthoidei, Family Lipogenyidae. In Part 6, *Fishes of the Western North Atlantic,* pp. 208–27. Memoirs of the Sears Foundation for Marine Research. Yale University.

MCLELLAN, T. 1977. Feeding Strategies of the Macrourids. *Deep-Sea Research* 24:1019–36.

MCVAY, S. 1966. The Last of the Great Whales. *Scientific American* 215(2):13–21.

MEAD, G. W. 1958. Three New Species of Archibenthic Iniomous Fishes from the Western North Atlantic. *Jour. Wash. Acad. Sci.* 48(11):362–72.

———. 1960. Hermaphroditism in Archibenthic and Pelagic Fishes of the Order Iniomi. *Deep-Sea Research* 6(3):234–35.

———. 1965. The Larval Form of the Heteromi (Pisces). *Breviora Mus. Comp. Zool.* 226:1–5.

MEAD, G. W., AND S. A. EARLE. 1970. Notes on the Natural History of Snipe Eels. *Proc. Cal. Acad. Sci.* 38(5):99–103.

MEAD, G. W., E. BERTELSON, AND D. M. COHEN. 1964. Reproduction Among Deep-Sea Fishes. *Deep-Sea Research* 11:659–96.

MEAD, J. G., AND E. D. MITCHELL. 1984. Atlantic Gray Whales. In M. L. Jones, S. L. Swartz, and S. Leatherwood, eds., *The Gray Whale, Eschrichtius robustus,* pp. 33–53. Academic Press.

MEEK, A., AND T. R. GODDARD. 1926. On Two Specimens of Giant Squid Stranded on the Northumberland Coast. *Trans. Nat. Hist. Soc. Northumb.* 6:229–39.

MEEK, R. P., AND J. J. CHILDRESS. 1973. Respiration and the Effect of Pressure in the Mesopelagic Fish *Anoplogaster cornuta* (Beryciformes). *Deep-Sea Research* 20(12):1111–18.

MEINCKE, J. 1977. The Water Itself. In N. C. Flemming, ed., *The Undersea,* pp. 46–65. Macmillan.

MENARD, H. W. 1969. The Deep Ocean Floor. *Scientific American* 221(3):126–42.

MENZIES, R. J., AND R. Y. GEORGE. 1967. A Re-evaluation of the Concept of Hadal or Ultra-abyssal Fauna. *Deep-Sea Research* 14(6):703–723.

MERO, J. 1960. Minerals from the Ocean Floor. *Scientific American* 203(6):64–72.

———. 1965. *The Mineral Resources of the Sea.* Elsevier.

MERRETT, N. R., J. BADCOCK, AND P. J. HERRING. 1973. The Status of *Benthalbella infans* (Pisces: Myctophidae), Its Development, Bioluminescence, General Biology and Distribution in the Eastern North Atlantic. *Jour. Zool. London* 170:1–48.

MILLAM, G. 1984. Tripping the Light Fantastic: The Sensitive World of Bioluminescence. *Oceans* 17(4):3–8.

MILLER, J. E., AND D. L. PAWSON. 1989. *Hansenothuria benti*, New Genus, Species (Echinodermata: Holothuroidea) from the Tropical Western Atlantic: A Bathyal, Epibenthic Holothurian with Swimming Abilities. *Proc. Biol. Soc. Wash.* 102(4):977–86.

————. 1990. Swimming Sea Cucumbers (Echinodermata: Holothuroidea): A Survey, with Analysis of Swimming Behavior in Four Bathyal Species. *Smithsonian Contrib. Mar. Sci.* 35:1–18.

MILLER, R. 1983. *Continents in Collision*. Time-Life Books.

MILLER, R. C. 1966. *The Sea*. Thomas Nelson.

MILLER, S. L., AND J. L. BADA. 1988. Submarine Hot Springs and the Origin of Life. *Nature* 334:609–11.

MILLER, W. J. 1976. *The Annotated Jules Verne: Twenty Thousand Leagues Under the Sea*. Crowell.

MILLIMAN, J. D., AND F. T. MANHEIM. 1968. Observations in Deep-Scattering Layers off Cape Hatteras, U.S.A. *Deep-Sea Research* 15:505–7.

MILNE-EDWARDS, A. 1879. On a Gigantic Isopod from the Great Depths of the Sea. *Ann. Mag. Nat. Hist.* 3(5):241–43.

MINER, R. W. 1935. Marauders of the Sea. *National Geographic* 68(2):185–207.

MITCHELL, E. D. 1977. Evidence That the Northern Bottlenose Whale Is Depleted. *Rep. Intl. Whal. Commn.* 27:195–205.

MITCHELL, E. D., AND V. M. KOZICKI. 1975. Autumn Stranding of a Bottlenose Whale (*Hyperoodon ampullatus*) in the Bay of Fundy, Nova Scotia. *Jour. Fish. Res. Bd. Canada* 37(7):1019–40.

MIYASHITA, T., AND K. C. BALCOMB. 1988. Preliminary Report of an Unidentified Beaked Whale like *Hyperoodon* sp. in the Central and the Western Pacific. *Int. Whal. Comm Paper* SC/40/SM9:1–16.

MOISEEV, S. I. 1991. Observation of the Vertical Distribution and Behavior of Nektonic Squids Using Manned Submersibles. *Bull. Mar. Sci.* 49(1&2):446–56.

MONASTERSKY, R. 1994. Light at the Bottom of the Ocean. *Science News* 145(1):14.

————. 1995. Earth's Magnetic Field Follies Revealed. *Science News* 147(16):244.

MOORE, J. C., AND F. G. WOOD. 1957. Differences Between the Beaked Whales *Mesoplodon mirus* and *Mesoplodon gervaisi*. *Amer. Mus. Novitates* 1831:1–25.

MORGAN, W. J. 1968. Rises, Trenches, Great Faults and Crustal Blocks. *Jour. Geophys. Res.* 73:1959–82.

————. 1972. Deep Mantle Convection Plumes and Plate Motions. *Bull. Amer. Assoc. Petrol. Geol.* 56:203–13.

MORROW, J. E. 1961. Taxonomy of the Deep Sea Fishes of the Genus *Chauliodus*. *Bull. Mus. Comp. Zool.* 125(9):249–94.

————. 1964. Family Malacosteidae. In H. B. Bigelow, D. M. Cohen, M. W. Dick, R. H. Gibbs, M. Grey, J. E. Morrow, L. P. Schultz, and V. Waters, Part 4, *Fishes of the Western*

North Atlantic, pp. 523–48. Memoirs of the Sears Foundation for Marine Research. Yale University.

MORROW, J. E., AND R. H. GIBBS. 1964. Melanostomiatidae. In H. B. Bigelow, D. M. Cohen, M. W. Dick, R. H. Gibbs, M. Grey, J. E. Morrow, L. P. Schultz, and V. Waters, Part 4, *Fishes of the Western North Atlantic,* pp. 351–511. Memoirs of the Sears Foundation for Marine Research. Yale University.

MORTENSEN, T. 1927. *Handbook of the Echinoderms of the British Isles.* Oxford University Press.

MOSELEY, H. N. 1880. Deep-Sea Dredgings and Life in the Deep Sea. *Nature* 21:543–47, 569–72, 591–93.

MOSER, D. 1976. The Azores, Nine Islands in Search of a Future. *National Geographic* 149(2):261–88.

MOWAT, F. 1984. *Sea of Slaughter.* Atlantic Monthly Press.

MUNK, O. 1959. The Eyes of *Ipnops murrayi* Günther 1887. *Galathea Report* 3:79–87.

———. 1964. The Eyes of Three Fishes Caught at Great Depths. *Galathea Report* 7:137–49.

———. 1966. Ocular Degeneration in Deep-Sea Fishes. *Galathea Report* 8:21–31.

———. 1968. On the Eye and the So-Called Preorbital Light Organ of the Isospondylous Deep-Sea Fish *Bathylaco nigricans* Goode & Bean, 1896. *Galathea Report* 9:211–18.

MUNK, W. 1955. The Circulation of the Oceans. *Scientific American* 193(3):96–104.

MURIE, J. 1865. On Deformity of the Lower Jaw in the Cachalot. *Proc. Zool. Soc. London* 1865:390–96.

MURRAY, J. 1876. Preliminary Reports to Professor Wyville Thomson, F.R.S., Director of the Civilian Scientific Staff, on Work done on board the *Challenger. Proc. Royal Soc.* 27:471–531.

———. 1895. A Summary of the Scientific Results Obtained at the Sounding, Dredging and Trawling Stations of H.M.S. *Challenger. Report on the Scientific Results of the Voyage of H.M.S. Challenger During the Years 1873–76* 2:1–1608.

MURRAY, J., AND J. HJORT. 1912. *The Depths of the Ocean.* Macmillan. London. Reprinted 1965, Stechert & Hafner.

MYERS, G. S. 1940. A Note on *Monognathus. Copeia* 1940(2):141.

NAFPAKTITIS, B. G. 1968. Taxonomy and Distribution of the Lanternfishes, Genera *Lobianchia* and *Diaphus,* in the North Atlantic. *Dana Report* 73:1–131.

NAFPAKTITIS, B. G., AND M. NAFPAKTITIS. 1969. Lanternfishes (Family Myctophidae) Collected During Cruises 3 and 6 of the R/V *Anton Bruun* in the Indian Ocean. *Bull. L.A. Co. Mus. Nat. Hist. Sci.* 5:1–79.

NAFPAKTITIS, B. G., R. H. BACKUS, J. E. CRADDOCK, R. L. HAEDRICH, B. H. ROBISON, AND C. KARNELLA. 1977. Family Neoscopelidae, Family Myctophidae, Atlantic Mesopelagic Zoogeography. In Part 7, *Fishes of the Western North Atlantic.* Memoirs of the Sears Foundation for Marine Research. Yale University.

NANSEN, F. 1911. *In Northern Mists.* Heinemann.

NASU, K. 1958. Deformed Lower Jaw of Sperm Whale. *Sci. Rep. Whales Res. Inst.* 13:211–12.

NATIONAL GEOGRAPHIC SOCIETY. 1990. World Ocean Floors: Atlantic Ocean. Map. *National Geographic* 177(1):61A.

NAWOJCHIK, R. 1994. First Record of *Mesoplodon densirostris* (Cetacea: Ziphiidae) from Rhode Island. *Mar. Mam. Sci.* 10(4):477–80.

NELSON, D. R., AND R. H. JOHNSON. 1970. Diel Activity Rhythms in the Nocturnal, Bottom-Dwelling Sharks *Heterodontus francisci* and *Cephaloscyllium ventriosum. Copeia* 4:732–39.

NELSON, J. S. 1993. *Fishes of the World.* Wiley Interscience.

NELSON, S. B. 1991. Naval Oceanography: A Look Back. *Oceanus* 33(4):10–19.

NESIS, K. N. 1977. Vertical Distribution of Pelagic Cephalopods. *Jour. General Biol.* 38(4):547–57. 1979 translation from National Museums of Canada Translation Bureau.

———. 1982. *Cephalopods of the World.* Translated from the Russian by B. S. Levitov. T. F. H. Publications.

NEWMAN, W. A. 1985. The Abyssal Hydrothermal Vent Fauna: A Glimpse of Antiquity? *Bull. Biol. Soc. Wash.* 6:231–42.

NICOL, J. A. C. 1958. Observations on Luminescence in Pelagic Animals. *Jour. Mar. Biol. Assoc. U.K.* 37:705–22.

———. 1961. Luminescence in Marine Organisms. *Smithsonian Rep.* 1960:447–56.

———. 1964. Luminous Creatures of the Sea. *Sea Frontiers* 10(3):143–54.

———. 1967. The Luminescence of Fishes. *Symp. Zool. Soc. London* 19:27–56.

NIELSEN, J. G. 1964. Fishes from Depths Exceeding 6000 Meters. *Galathea Report* 7:113–24.

———. 1966a. On the Genera *Acanthonus* and *Typhlonus* (Pisces, Brotulidae.) *Galathea Report* 8:33–48.

———. 1966b. Synopsis of the Inopidae (Pisces, Iniomi) with Description of Two New Abyssal Species. *Galathea Report* 8:49–75.

———. 1977. The Deepest Living Fish *Abyssobrotula galatheae.* A New Genus and Species of Oviparous Ophidioids (Pisces, Brotulidae). *Galathea Report* 14:41–48.

NIELSEN, J. G., AND E. BERTELSEN. 1985. The Gulper-Eel Family Saccopharyngidae (Pisces, Anguilliformes). *Steenstrupia* 11(6):156–206.

NIELSEN, J. G., AND V. LARSEN. 1968. Synopsis of the Bathylaconidae (Pisces, Isospondyli). *Galathea Report* 9:221–38.

———. 1970. Remarks on the Identity of the Giant *Dana* Eel Larva. *Vidensk. Medd. fra Dansk Naturh. Foren.* 133:149–57.

NIELSEN, J. G., AND D. G. SMITH. 1978. The Eel Family Nemichthyidae. *Dana Report* 88:1–71.

NIELSEN, J. G., E. BERTELSEN, AND A. JESPERSEN. 1989. The Biology of *Eurypharynx pelecanoides* (Pisces, Eurypharyngidae). *Acta Zoologica* 70(3):187–97.

NIWA, H. 1983. A Minireview of the Pineal Organ of Elasmobranchs. *Rep. Japan. Grp. Elasmobranch Studies* 16:4–9.

NOLAN, R. S., AND R. H. ROSENBLATT. 1975. A Review of the Deep-Sea Anglerfish Genus *Lasiognathus* (Pisces: Thaumatichthyidae). *Copeia* 1975:60–66.

NORMAN, J. R., AND E. TREWAVAS. 1939. Notes on the Eels of the Family Synaphobranchidae. *Ann. Mag. Nat. Hist.* 11(3):352–59.

NORMARK, W. R., AND D. J. W. PIPER. 1994. Turbidite Sedimentation. *Oceanus* 36(4):107–10.

NORRIS, K. S. 1969. The Echolocation of Marine Mammals. In H. T. Andersen, ed., *The Biology of Marine Mammals,* pp. 291–423. Academic Press.

————. 1974. *The Porpoise Watcher.* Norton.

NORRIS, K. S., AND G. W. HARVEY. 1972. A Theory for the Function of the Spermaceti Organ in the Sperm Whale (*Physeter catodon* L.). In S. R. Galler, K. Schmidt-Koenig, G. J. Jacobs, and R. E. Belleville, eds., *Animal Orientation and Navigation,* pp. 397–419. NASA.

NORRIS, K. S., AND B. MØHL. 1983. Can Odontocetes Debilitate Prey with Sound? *American Naturalist* 122(1):85–104.

NORTHROP, J., AND B. C. HEEZEN. 1951. An Outcrop of Eocene Sediment on the Continental Slope. *Jour. Geol.* 59(4):396–99.

NUSBAUM-HILAROWICZ, J. 1915a. Sur quelques points interessants dans la structure des reins chez *Gastrostomus bairdi* (Gill et Ryder), *Argyropelecus hemigymnus* (Cocco) et *Chauliodus sloani. Bull. Inst. Oceanogr. Monaco* 307:1–5.

————. 1915b. Quelques remarques sur les organes genitaux femelles de *Gastrostomus bairdi* (Gill et Ryder). *Bull. Inst. Oceanogr. Monaco* 313:1–4.

NYBELIN, O. 1957. Deep-Sea Bottom Fishes. *Rep. Swedish Deep-Sea Expedition. Zoology* 2(20):250–345.

O'DAY, W. T. 1973. Luminescent Silhouetting in Stomiatoid Fishes. *Contributions in Science, Nat. Hist. Mus. Los Angeles County* 246:1–8.

————. 1974. Bacterial Luminescence on the Deep-Sea Anglerfish *Oneirodes acanthias* (Gilbert 1915). *Contributions in Science, Nat. Hist. Mus. Los Angeles County* 255:1–12.

O'DAY, W. T., AND H. R. FERNANDEZ. 1974. *Aristostomias scintillans* (Malacosteidae): A Deep-Sea Fish with Visual Pigments Apparently Adapted to Its Own Bioluminescence. *Vision Research* 14:545–50.

OHLIN, A. 1893. Some Remarks on the Bottlenose Whale (*Hyperoodon*). *Lunds. Univ. Arskr.* 29:1–14.

OLNEY, J. E., G. D. JOHNSON, AND C. C. BALDWIN. 1993. Phylogeny of Lampridiform Fishes. *Bull. Mar. Sci.* 52(1):137–69.

OROWAN, E. 1969. The Origin of the Oceanic Ridges. *Scientific American* 221(5):102–18.

OSBORN, F. 1962. William Beebe: 1877–1962. *Animal Kingdom* 65(4):121–23.

OUTHWAITE, L. 1957. *The Atlantic: A History of an Ocean.* Coward-McCann.

OWEN, D. M. 1958. Photography Underwater. *Oceanus* 6(1):22–38.

PALMER, G. 1961. The Dealfishes (Trachipteridae) of the Mediterranean and Northeast Atlantic. *Bull. Br. Mus. Nat. Hist. (Zool.)* 7:335–51.

PARIN, N. V. 1966. Data on the Biology and Distribution of the Pelagic Sharks *Euprotomicrus bispinatus* and *Isistius brasiliensis* (Squalidae: Pisces). *Trudy. Inst. Okeanologii* 73:163–84.

PARR, A. E. 1926. Deepsea Fishes from off the Western Coast of North and Central America. *Bull. Bingham Oceanogr. Coll.* 2(4):1–53.

————. 1927a. Ceratioidea. *Bull. Bingham Oceanogr. Coll.* 3(1):1–34.

————. 1927b. The Stomiatoid Fishes of the Suborder Gymnophotodermi. *Bull. Bingham Oceanogr. Coll.* 3(2):1–123.

————. 1928. Deepsea Fishes of the Order Iniomi from the Western Waters Around the Bahama and Bermuda Islands. *Bull. Bingham Oceanogr. Coll.* 3:1–193.

————. 1930a. On the Probable Identity, Life-History and Anatomy of the Free-living and Attached Males of the Ceratioid Fishes. *Copeia* 4:129–35.

————. 1930b. A Note on the Classification of the Stomiatoid Fishes. *Copeia* 4:136.

————. 1930c. Deep Sea Eels, Exclusive of Larval Forms. *Bull. Bingham Oceanogr. Coll.* 3(5):1–41.

————. 1932. On a Deep-Sea Devilfish from New England Waters and the Peculiar Life and Looks of Its Kind. *Bull. Boston Nat. Hist. Soc.* 63:3–16.

————. 1933a. Two New Records of Deep-Sea Fishes from New England with Description of a New Genus and Species. *Copeia* 1933(4):176–79.

————. 1933b. Deepsea Berycomorphi and Percomorphi from the Waters Around the Bahama and Bermuda Islands. *Bull. Bingham Oceanogr. Coll.* 3(6):3–51.

————. 1948. The Classification of the Fishes of the Genera *Bathylaco* and *Macromastax,* Possible Intermediates Between the Isospondyli and Iniomi. *Copeia* 1:48–54.

————. 1951. Preliminary Revision of the Alepocephalidae, with the Introduction of a New Family, Searsidae. *Am. Mus. Novitates* 1531:1–21.

————. 1952. Revision of the Species Currently Referred to as *Alepocephalus, Halisauriceps, Bathytroctes,* and *Bajacalifornia,* with Introduction of Two New Genera. *Bull. Mus. Comp. Zool.* 107:254–69.

————. 1954. Review of the Deep-Sea Fishes of the Genus *Asquamiceps* Zugmayer, with Descriptions of Two New Species. *Am. Mus. Novitates* 1655:1–8.

————. 1960. The Fishes of the Family Searsidae. *Dana Report* 51:1–102.

PAWSON, D. L. 1976. Some Aspects of the Biology of Deep-Sea Echinoderms. *Thalassia Jugoslavica* 12:287–93.

————. 1982. Deep-Sea Echinoderms in the Tongue of the Ocean, Bahama Islands: A Survey Using the Research Submersible *Alvin. Aust. Mus. Memoir* 16:129–45.

————. 1983. *Psychronaetes hanseni,* a New Genus and Species of Elasipodan Sea Cucumber (Echinodermata: Holothuroidea). *Proc. Biol. Soc. Wash.* 96(1):154–59.

————. 1985. *Psychropotes hyalinus,* a New Species, a Swimming Elasipod Sea Cucumber (Echinodermata: Holothuroidea) from the North Central Pacific Ocean. *Proc. Biol. Soc. Wash.* 98(1):523–25.

PAWSON, D. L., AND E. J. FOELL. 1986. *Peniagone leander,* New Species, an Abyssal Benthopelagic Sea Cucumber (Echinodermata, Holothuroidea) from the Eastern Central Pacific Ocean. *Bull. Mar. Sci.* 38(2):293–99.

PAYNE, R., AND S. MCVAY. 1971. Songs of the Humpback Whale. *Science* 173:585–97.

PEARCY, W. G., AND A. BEAL. 1973. Deep-Sea Cirromorphs (Cephalopoda) Photographed in the Arctic Ocean. *Deep-Sea Research* 20:107–8.

PEQUEGNAT, W. E. 1958. Whales, Plankton, and Man. *Scientific American* 198(1):84–90.

PERES, J. M. 1958. Remarques générales sur un ensemble de quinze plongées effectuées avec le bathyscaphe *F.N.R.S. III. Ann. Inst. Oceanogr. Monaco* 35(4):259–85.

————. 1965. Aperçu sur les résultants de deux plongées effectuées dans le ravin de Puerto Rico par le bathyscaphe *Archimède. Deep-Sea Research* 12:883–92.

PERKINS, P. J., M. P. FISH, AND W. H. MOWBRAY. 1966. Underwater Communication Sounds of the Sperm Whale. *Norsk Hvalfangst-tidende* 55(12):225–28.

PERRY, R. 1972. *The Unknown Ocean.* Taplinger.

PETERSON, M. N. A., AND N. T. EDGAR. 1969. Deep Ocean Drilling with *Glomar Challenger. Oceans* 1(5):17–32.

PETERSON, S. 1985. Early American Oceanography. *Oceans* 18(4):26–30.

PETTERSSON, H. 1953. The Swedish Deep-Sea Expedition, 1947–48. *Deep-Sea Research* 1:17–24.

———. 1954. *The Ocean Floor.* Yale University Press.

PETTIBONE, M. H. 1984. A New Scale Worm Commensal with Deep-Sea Mussels in the Galápagos Hydrothermal Vent (Polychaeta: Polynoidae). *Proc. Zool. Soc. Wash.* 97:226–39.

PICCARD, J. 1960. Man's Deepest Dive. *National Geographic* 118(2):225–39.

———. 1971. *The Sun Beneath the Sea.* Scribner's.

PICCARD, J., AND R. S. DIETZ. 1957. Oceanographic Observations by the Bathyscaph *Trieste* (1953–1956). *Deep-Sea Research* 4:221–29.

———. 1961. *Seven Miles Down: The Story of the Bathyscaph TRIESTE.* Putnam.

PICKFORD, G. E. 1940. The Vampyromorpha, Living-Fossil Cephalopods. *Trans. N.Y. Acad. Sci.* 2(2):169–81.

———. 1946. *Vampyroteuthis infernalis* Chun, Part 1. Natural History and Distribution. *Dana Report* 29:1–45.

———. 1949a. The Distribution of the Eggs of *Vampyroteuthis infernalis* Chun. *Sears Found. Jour. Mar. Res.* 8(1):73–83.

———. 1949b. *Vampyroteuthis infernalis* Chun, Part 2. II. External Anatomy. *Dana Report* 32:1–131.

———. 1950. The Vampyromorphs (Cephalopoda) of the Bermuda Oceanographic Expeditions. *Zoologica* 35:87–95.

———. 1952. The Vampyromorpha of the "Discovery" Expeditions. *Discovery Reports* 26:197–210.

PIETSCH, T. W. 1972a. A Review of the Monotypic Deep-Sea Anglerfish Family Centrophrynidae: Taxonomy, Distribution and Osteology. *Copeia* 1972:17–47.

———. 1972b. Second Specimen of the Deep-Sea Anglerfish *Phyllorhyinicthys micractis* (Family Oneirodidae), with a Histological Description of the Snout Flaps. *Copeia* 1972:335–40.

———. 1974. Osteology and Relationships of Ceratioid Anglerfishes of the Genus *Oneirodes* Lutken. *Nat. Hist. Mus. Los Angeles Co. Sci. Bull.* 18:1–113.

———. 1975a. Precocious Sexual Parasitism in the Deep Sea Ceratioid Anglerfish *Cryptopsaras couesi* Gill. *Nature* 256:38–40.

———. 1975b. Systematics and Distribution of Ceratioid Anglerfishes of the Genus *Chaenophryne* (Family Oneirodidae). *Bull. Mus. Comp. Zool.* 147(2):75–100.

———. 1976. Dimorphism, Parasitism and Sex: Reproductive Strategies among Deepsea Ceratioid Anglerfishes. *Copeia* 4:781–93.

———. 1978. The Feeding Mechanisms of *Stylephorus chordatus* (Teleostei: Lampridiformes); Functional and Ecological Implications. *Copeia* 2:255–62.

———. 1979. Systematics and Distribution of Ceratioid Anglerfishes of the Family Caulophrynidae with the Description of a New Genus and Species from the Banda Sea. *Contrib. Sci. Nat. Hist. Mus. Los Angeles Co.* 310:1–25.

———. 1986. Systematics and Distribution of Bathypelagic Anglerfishes of the Family Ceratiidae (Order: Lophiiformes). *Copeia* 2:479–93.

PIETSCH, T. W., AND D. B. GROBECKER. 1987. *Frogfishes of the World.* Stanford University Press.

PIETSCH, T. W., AND P. F. NAFPAKTITIS. 1971. A Male *Melanocetus johnsoni* Attached to a Female *Centrophryne spinulosa* (Pisces: Ceratioidea). *Copeia* 1971:322–24.

PITMAN, W. C., AND M. TALWANI. 1972. Sea Floor Spreading in the North Atlantic. *Bull. Geol. Soc. Amer.* 83:619–46.

POE, E. A. 1845. A Descent into the Maelstrom. In *The Complete Tales and Poems of Edgar Allan Poe,* pp. 380–411. Modern Library edition, 1938.

POLLACK, A. 1994. Japanese Vessel Fails to Set Ocean Depth Mark. *New York Times,* March 2, 1994: C12.

PONOMARENKO, V. P. 1959. Rare Deep-Sea Fish of the North Atlantic. *Priroda* 2:83–85.

POTTS, G. W. 1990. Crepuscular Behaviour of Marine Fishes. In P. J. Herring, A. K. Campbell, M. Whitfield, and L. Maddock, eds., *Light and Life in the Sea,* pp. 221–27. Cambridge University Press.

POWELL, M. A., AND G. N. SOMERO. 1983. Blood Components Prevent Sulfide Poisoning or Respiration of the Hydrothermal Vent Tube Worm *Riftia pachyptila. Science* 219:297–99.

PRATT, R. 1964. The Mid-Atlantic Ridge: Youthful Key to an Old Ocean. *Oceanus* 11(2):8–15.

PURDY, G. M. 1993. Marine Seismology. *Oceanus* 35(4):63–69.

PURDY, G. M., J.-C. SEMPERE, H. SCHOUTEN, D. L. DUBOIS, AND R. GOLDSMITH. 1990. Bathymetry of the Mid-Atlantic Ridge, 24°–31° N: A Map Series. *Mar. Geophys. Res.* 12:247–52.

RABINOWITZ, J. 1994. Mystic Aquarium to Hire Leading Oceanographer. *New York Times,* November 29, 1994: B6.

RAFF, A. D. 1961. The Magnetism of the Ocean Floor. *Scientific American* 205(4):146–56.

RAGUSO, J. N. 1993. The Abyss. *Sport Fishing* 8(6):46–53.

RAINNIE, W. O. 1966. Alvin . . . and the Bomb. *Oceanus* 12(4):17–21.

RAJU, S. N. 1974. Three New Species of the Genus *Monognathus* and the Leptocephali of the Order Saccopharyngiformes. *Fish. Bull.* 72:547–62.

RATHJEN, W. F. 1973. Northwest Atlantic Squids. *Mar. Fish. Rev.* 35(12):20–26.

RED DATA BOOK. 1976. Northern Bottlenose Whale, *Hyperoodon planifrons.* Code 11.93.5.1.V. IUCN, Morges, Switzerland.

REES, W. J. 1950. On a Giant Squid *Ommastrephes caroli* Furtado Stranded at Looe, Cornwall. *Bull. Brit. Mus. Nat. Hist.* 1:31–41.

REGAN, C. T. 1907. On the Anatomy, Classification, and Systematic Position of the Teleostean Fishes of the Suborder Allotriognathi. *Proc. Zool. Soc. London* 43:634–43.

———. 1908. The Systematic Position of *Stylephorus caudatus. Ann. Mag. Nat. Hist.* 2:447–49.

———. 1913. A Deep-Sea Angler-Fish *Melanocetus johnsoni. Proc. Zool. Soc. London* 1913:1096–97.

———. 1924. The Morphology of the Rare Oceanic Fish, *Stylephorus chordatus,* Shaw; Based on Specimens Collected in the Atlantic by the "Dana" Expeditions, 1920–1922. *Proc. Roy. Soc. London* 3(96):193–207.

———. 1925a. A Rare Anglerfish (*Ceratias holbölli*) from Iceland. *The Naturalist* February 1, 1925: 41–42.

———. 1925b. Dwarfed Males Parasitic on the Females in Oceanic Anglerfishes (Pediculati, Ceratioidea). *Proc. Roy. Soc.* B97:386–400.

———. 1925c. The Fishes of the Genus *Gigantura*, A. Brauer, Based on Specimens Collected in the Atlantic by the "Dana" Expeditions, 1920–22. *Ann. Mag. Nat. Hist.* 15(9):53–59.

———. 1930. A Ceratioid Fish (*Caulophryne polynema* sp. n.), Female with Male, from off Madeira. *Jour. Linn. Soc. London* 37:191–95.

REGAN, C. T., AND E. TREWAVAS. 1929. The Fishes of the Families Astronesthidae and Chauliodontidae. *Dana Oceanogr. Rep.* 5:1–39.

———. 1932. Deep-Sea Anglerfish Ceratioidea. *Dana Report* 2:1–113.

REINHARDT, J. C. 1837. Ichthyologiske bidrag til den Groenelandske fauna. *K. Dansk Vidensk. Selsk. Nat. og Math. Afh.* 4(7):83–196.

REVELLE, R. 1969a. The Ocean. *Scientific American* 221(3):55–65.

———. 1969b. The Age of Innocence and War in Oceanography. *Oceans* 1(3):5–16.

REYES, J. C., J. G. MEAD, AND K. VAN WAEREBEEK. 1991. A New Species of Beaked Whale *Mesoplodon peruvianus* sp. n. (Cetacea: Ziphiidae) from Peru. *Mar. Mamm. Sci.* 7(1):1–24.

REYNOLDS, J. N. 1932. *Mocha Dick, or, The White Whale of the Pacific.* Scribner's.

RICE, D. W. 1977. *A List of the Marine Mammals of the World.* NOAA Technical Report NMFS SSRF-711.

RICHARDSON, P. L. 1985. Average Transport and Velocity of the Gulf Stream near 55° W. *Jour. Mar. Res.* 43:83–111.

RICHARDSON, S. 1994. Warm Blood for Cold Water. *Discover* 15(1):42–43.

RIDGWAY, S. H. 1971. Buoyancy Regulation in Deep Diving Whales. *Nature* 232:133–34.

RIVAS, L. R. 1953. The Pineal Apparatus of Tunas and Related Scombrid Fishes as a Possible Light Receptor Controlling Phototactic Movements. *Bull. Mar. Sci. Gulf and Carib.* 3:168–80.

ROBERTS, D. G. 1977. The Ocean Floor. In N. C. Flemming, ed. *The Undersea,* pp. 22–45. Macmillan.

ROBINS, C. R., D. M. COHEN, AND C. H. ROBINS. 1979. The Eels *Anguilla* and *Histiobranchus* Photographed on the Floor of the Deep Atlantic in the Bahamas. *Bull. Mar. Sci.* 29(3):401–5.

ROBINS, R. C., AND W. R. COURTENAY. 1958. A Deep Sea Ceratioid Anglerfish of the Genus *Gigantactis* from Florida. *Bull. Mar. Sci. Gulf Carib.* 8(2):146–51.

ROBISON, B. H. 1993. New Technologies for Sanctuary Research. *Oceanus* 36(3):75–80.

———. 1995. Light in the Ocean's Midwater. *Scientific American* 273(1):60–64.

ROBISON, B. H., AND R. E. YOUNG. 1981. Bioluminescence in Pelagic Octopods. *Pacific Science* 35:39–44.

ROBSON, G. C. 1925. On a Specimen of the Rare Squid *Sthenoteuthis caroli* Stranded on the Yorkshire Coast. *Proc. Zool. Soc. London.* 291–301.

ROELEVELD, M. A. 1977. Cephalopoda from the Tropical Eastern Atlantic Ocean. *Galathea Report* 14:123–32.

ROELEVELD, M. A. C., C. J. AUGUSTYN, AND R. MELVILLE-SMITH. 1989. The Squid *Octopoteuthis* Photographed Live at 1,000m. *S. Afr. Jour. Mar. Sci.* 8:367–68.

ROFEN, R. R. 1959. The Whale-Fishes: Family Cetomimidae, Barbourisiidae, and Rondeletiidae (Order Cetunculi). *Galathea Report* 1:255–60.

ROLAND, A. 1978. *Underwater Warfare in the Age of Sail.* Indiana University Press.

RONA, P. A. 1973. Plate Tectonics and Mineral Resources. *Scientific American* 229(1):86–95.

———. 1985. Black Smokers on the Mid-Atlantic Ridge. *Eos* 66(40):682–83.

RONA, P. A., G. KLINKHAMMER, T. A. NELSEN, J. H. TREFRY, AND H. ELDERFIELD. 1986. Black Smokers, Massive Sulfides, and Vent Biota at the Mid-Atlantic Ridge. *Nature* 321:33–37.

ROPER, C. F. E., AND K. J. BOSS. 1982. The Giant Squid. *Scientific American* 246(4):96–105.

ROPER, C. F. E., AND W. L. BRUNDAGE. 1972. Cirrate Octopods with Associated Deep-Sea Organisms: New Biologiocal Data Based on Deep Benthic Photographs (Cephalopoda). *Smithsonian Contributions to Zoology* 121:1–46.

ROPER, C. F. E., AND R. E. YOUNG. 1972. First Records of Juvenile Giant Squid *Architeuthis* (Cephalopoda: Oegopsida). *Proc. Zool. Soc. Washington* 85(16):205–22.

———. 1975. Vertical Distribution of Pelagic Cephalopods. *Smithsonian Contrib. Zool.* 209:1–51.

ROPER, C. F. E., M. J. SWEENEY, AND C. E. NAUEN. 1984. *FAO Species Catalogue, Vol. 3: Cephalopods of the World. An Annotated Catalogue of Species of Interest to Fisheries.* Rome.

ROPER, C. F. E., R. E. YOUNG, AND G. L. VOSS. 1969. An Illustrated Key to the Families of the Order Teuthoidea (Cephalopoda). *Smithsonian Contrib. Zool.* 13:1–32.

ROSA, N. 1979. All About Ooze. *Oceans* 12(6):30–33.

ROSENBLATT, R. H., AND D. M. COHEN. 1986. Fishes Living in Deep-Sea Thermal Vents in the Tropical Eastern Pacific, with Descriptions of a New Genus and Two New Species of Eelpouts (Zoarcidae). *Trans. San Diego Soc. Nat. Hist.* 21:71–79.

ROULE, L. 1910. Notice préliminaire sur la description et l'identification d'une larve leptocéphalienne appartenant au type *Oxystomus* Raf. (*Tilurus* Köll.) *Bull. Inst. Oceanogr.* 171:1–9.

———. 1911. Sur quelques larves de poissons apodes. *Compt. Rend. Acad. Sci.* 153:732–35.

———. 1913. Etude sur les formes larvaires tiluriennes de poissons apodes recueillies par le "Thor." *Ann. Inst. Oceanogr.* 6(2):1–22.

———. 1914. Diagnoses préliminaires des larves de poissons apodes recueillies dans les croisières par S.A.S. le Prince de Monaco. *Bull. Inst. Oceanogr.* 292:1–12.

———. 1919. Poissons provenant des campagnes du yacht *Princesse-Alice* (1891–1903) et du yacht *Hirondelle II* (1914). *Res. Campagnes Sci. Albert I Monaco.* 52:1–191.

ROULE, L., AND L. BERTIN. 1929. Les Poissons appartenant au sous-ordre des Nemichthydiformes. *Danish "Dana" Expeditions, 1920–22* 4:1–113.

ROULE, L., AND R. DESPAX. 1911. Larves tiluriennes de poissons recueillies par le "Thor." *Bull. Mus. Nat. Hist. Paris* 6:403–7.

ROWE, G. T., AND M. SIBUET. 1983. Recent Advances in Instrumentation in Deep-Sea Biological Research. In G. T. Rowe, ed., *The Sea,* Vol. 8, pp. 81–95. Wiley Interscience.

RUBY, E. G., AND K. H. NEALSON. 1976. Symbiotic Association of *Photobacterium fisheri* with the Marine Luminous Fish *Monocentrus japonica:* A Model of Symbiosis Based on Bacterial Studies. *Biol. Bull.* 151(3):574–86.

RYALL, P. J. C., AND B. T. HARGRAVE. 1984. Attraction of the Atlantic Wreckfish (*Polyprion americanus*) to an Unbaited Camera on the Mid-Atlantic Ridge. *Deep-Sea Research* 31(1):79–83.

RYAN, P. R. 1985. The *Titanic:* Lost and Found. *Oceanus* 28(4):4–15.

———. 1986. The *Titanic* Revisited. *Oceanus* 29(3):2–15.

RYAN, P. R., AND A. RABUSHKA. 1985. The Discovery of the *Titanic* by the U.S. and French Expeditions. *Oceanus* 28(4):16–35.

RYAN, P. R., S. L. ELLIS, AND J. KOHL. 1989. The *Bismarck* Saga: 1941–1989. *Oceanus* 32(3):11–25.

RYTHER, J. H. 1956. The Sargasso Sea. *Scientific American* 194(1):98–104.

SACHS, P. L. 1963. A Visit to St. Peter and St. Paul Rocks. *Oceanus* 9(4):2–5.

SAEMUNDSSON, B. 1922. Zoologiske Meddelelser fra Island, Part 14. 11 Fiske, Nye for Island, og Suplerende om Andre, Tidligere Kendte. *Vidensk. Medd. fra Dansk Naturh. Foren.* 74:159–201.

SAIBIL, H. R. 1990. Photoreception in Squid. In P. J. Herring, A. K. Campbell, M. Whitfield, and L. Maddock, eds., *Light and Life in the Sea,* pp. 199–207. Cambridge University Press.

SANDERS, H. L. 1956. Oceanography of Long Island Sound, 1952–1954. The Biology of Marine Bottom Communities. *Bull. Bingham Ocean. Coll.* 15:345–414.

———. 1979. Evolutionary Ecology and Life History Patterns in the Deep Sea. *Sarsia* 64:1–7.

SANDERS, H. L., AND R. R. HESSLER. 1969. Ecology of the Deep-Sea Benthos. *Science* 163(3874):1419–24.

SANDERS, H. L., R. R. HESSLER, AND G. R. HAMPSON. 1965. An Introduction to the Study of the Deep Sea Benthic Faunal Assemblages Along the Gay Head–Bermuda Transect. *Deep-Sea Research* 12:845–67.

SCAMMON, C. M. 1874. *The Marine Mammals of the Northwestern Coast of North America; Together with an Account of the American Whale Fishery.* Carmany, and G. P. Putnam's.

SCHERMAN, K. 1976. *Daughter of Fire: A Portrait of Iceland.* Little, Brown.

SCHLEE, S. 1973. *The Edge of an Unfamiliar World: A History of Oceanography.* Dutton.

SCHLESINGER, M. E., AND N. RAMANKUTTY. 1994. An Oscillation in the Global Climate System of Period 65–70 Years. *Nature* 367:723–26.

SCHLIEPER, C. 1968. High Pressure Effects on Marine Invertebrates and Fishes. *Mar. Biol.* 2(1):5–12.

SCHMIDT, J. 1922. Live Specimens of *Spirula. Nature* 110:788–90.

SCHMITT, W. L. 1965. *Crustaceans.* David & Charles.

SCHOFIELD, M. 1971. *Alvin* Is Back Again. *Oceans* 4(3):72–73.

SCHOLANDER, P. F. 1940. Experimental Investigations on the Respiratory Function in Diving Mammals and Birds. *Hvalradets Skrifter* 22(1):1–131.

SCHUESSLER, R. 1973. When They Laid the Atlantic Cable. *Oceans* 6(2):64–73.

SCORESBY, W. 1820. *An Account of the Arctic Regions with a History and Discussion of the Northern Whale-Fishery.* Archibald Constable, Edinburgh. 1969 edition, David & Charles.

SEIGEL, J. A. 1978. Revision of the Dalatiid Shark Genus *Squaliolus:* Anatomy, Systematics, Ecology. *Copeia* 4:602–14.

SEIGEL, J. A., T. W. PIETSCH, AND B. H. ROBISON. 1977. *Squaliolus sarmenti* and *S. alii,* Synonyms of the Dwarf Deepsea Shark *Squaliolus laticaudus. Copeia* 4:788–91.

SHAW, G. 1791. Description of the *Stylephorus chordatus,* a New Fish. *Trans. Linn. Soc.* 1:90–92.

SHENTON, E. H. 1970. Where Have All the Submersibles Gone? *Oceans* 3(6):38–56.

———. 1972. *Diving for Science: The Story of the Deep Submersible.* Norton.

SHEPARD, F. P. 1934. Canyons off the New England Coast. *Amer. Jour. Sci.* 27:24–36.

———. 1959. *The Earth Beneath the Sea.* Johns Hopkins University Press.

———. 1961. Submarine Erosion: A Discussion of Recent Papers. *Bull. Geol. Soc. Amer.* 62:1413–17.

———. 1963. Submarine Canyons. In M. N. Hill, ed., *The Sea, Vol. 3: The Earth Beneath the Sea,* pp. 281–311. Wiley Interscience.

SHEPARD, F. P., AND R. F. DILL. 1966. *Submarine Canyons.* Rand McNally.

SHOEMAKER, H. H. 1958. A Female Ceratioid Angler, *Cryptopsaras couesi* Gill, from the Gulf of Mexico, Bearing Three Parasitic Males. *Copeia* 1958:143–45.

SISSON, R. F. 1976. Adrift on a Raft of Sargassum. *National Geographic* 149(2):188–99.

SMITH, C. L. 1964. Hermaphroditism in Bahama Groupers. *Natural History* 73(6):42–47.

SMITH, C. R., H. KUKERT, R. A. WHEATCROFT, P. A. JUMARS, AND J. W. DEMING. 1989. Vent Fauna on Whale Remains. *Nature* 341:27–28.

SMITH, D. G. 1970. Notacanthiform Leptocephali in the Western North Atlantic. *Copeia* 1970(1):1–9.

———. 1989a. Order Anguilliformes. Family Anguillidae (Freshwater Eels). In Part 9, Vol. 1, *Fishes of the Western North Atlantic,* pp. 25–47. Memoirs of the Sears Foundation for Marine Research. Yale University.

———. 1989b. Suborder Cyematoidei. Family Cyematidae. In Part 9, Vol. 1, *Fishes of the Western North Atlantic,* pp. 630–35. Memoirs of the Sears Foundation for Marine Research. Yale University.

———. 1989c. Introduction to Leptocephali. In Part 9, Vol. 2, *Fishes of the Western North Atlantic,* pp. 657–68. Memoirs of the Sears Foundation for Marine Research. Yale University.

SMITH, D. G., AND J. G. NIELSEN. 1989. Family Nemichthyidae (Snipe Eels). In Part 9, Vol. 1, *Fishes of the Western North Atlantic,* pp. 441–59. Memoirs of the Sears Foundation for Marine Research. Yale University.

SMITH, J. L. B. 1961. *The Sea Fishes of Southern Africa.* Central News Agency.

SMITH, M. M., AND P. C. HEEMSTRA. 1986. *Smiths' Sea Fishes.* Macmillan South Africa.

SOMERO, G. N. 1984. Physiology and Biochemistry of the Hydrothermal Vent Animals. *Oceanus* 27(3):67–72.

SOMERO, G. N., J. F. SIEBENALLER, AND P. W. HOCHACHKA. 1983. Biochemical and Physiological Adaptations of Deep-Sea Animals. In G. T. Rowe, ed., *The Sea,* Vol. 8, pp. 331–70. Wiley Interscience.

SOUTHWARD, A. J. 1989. Animal Communities Fueled by Chemosynthesis: Life at Hydrothermal Vents, Cold Seeps and in Reducing Sediments. *Jour. Zool. Soc. London* 217:705–9.

SOUTHWARD, E. C. 1985. Vent Communities in Atlantic Too. *Nature* 317:673.

SOUTHWARD, E. C., AND A. J. SOUTHWARD. 1967. The Distribution of Pogonophora in the Atlantic Ocean. *Symp. Zool. Soc. London* 19:145–58.

SOUTHWELL, T. 1883. On the Beaked Whale (*Hyperoodon rostratus*). *Trans. Norfolk Norwich Nat. Soc.* 3:476–81.

SOWERBY, J. 1804. *The British Miscellany; or, Coloured Figures of New, Rare, or Little Known Animal Subjects, Many Not Before Ascertained to Be Inhabitants of the British Isles.* London.

SPÄRCK, R. 1956. The Density of Animals on the Ocean Floor. In A. F. Bruun, S. Greve, H. Mielche, and R. Sparck, eds., *The Galathea Deep Sea Expedition, 1950–1952,* pp. 196–201. Allen and Unwin.

SPAUL, E. A. 1964. Deformity in the Lower Jaw of the Sperm Whale (*Physeter catadon*). *Proc. Zool. Soc. London* 142(3):391–95.

SPRINGER, S. 1967. Social Organization of Shark Populations. In P. W. Gilbert, R. F. Mathewson, and D. P. Rall, eds., *Sharks, Skates and Rays,* pp. 149–74. Johns Hopkins University Press.

———. 1979. A Revision of the Catsharks, Family Scyliorhinidae. *NOAA Tech. Rep. NMFS Circular* 422:1–152.

SPRY, W. J. J. 1877. *The Cruise of Her Majesty's Ship "Challenger."* Harper & Brothers.

STARBUCK, A. 1898. *History of the American Whale Fishery from Its Earliest Inception to the Year 1876.* Rep. Comm. U.S. Comm. Fish and Fisheries, 1875–76. 1964 edition, Argosy-Antiquarian. New York.

STEENSTRUP, J. J. 1849–1900. *The Cephalopod Papers of Japetus Steenstrup.* 1962 English translation by A. Vølsoe, J. Knudsen, and W. Rees. Danish Science Press.

STEINBACH, H. B. 1951. The Squid. *Scientific American* 184(4):64–69.

STEINBECK, J. 1961. High Drama of Bold Thrust Through Ocean Floor. *Life* 50(15):111–22.

STENDALL, J. A. S. 1936. Giant Cuttlefish, *Sthenoteuthis caroli* Furtado, Ashore in Co. Londonderry. *Irish Nat. Jour.* 6:23–24.

STEPHEN, A. C. 1937. Recent Invasion of the Squid *Todarodes sagittatus* (Lam.) on the East Coast of Scotland. *Scot. Nat.* 131–32.

———. 1938. Rare Squid in Orkney. *Scot. Nat.* 119.

———. 1944. The Cephalopoda of Scottish and Adjacent Waters. *Trans. Roy. Soc. Edinburgh* 61:247–70.

———. 1950. Giant Squid, *Architeuthis* in Shetland. *Scot. Nat.* 62(1):52–53.

———. 1962. The Species of *Architeuthis* Inhabiting the North Atlantic. *Proc. Royal Phys. Soc. Edinburgh* 68:147–61.

STEVENSON, J. A. 1928. A Large Squid (*Stenoteuthis caroli*) at Scarborough. *Naturalist Hull* 217.

———. 1935. The Cephalopods of the Yorkshire Coast. *Jour. Conch.* 20:102–16.

STEWART, R. W. 1969. The Atmosphere and the Ocean. *Scientific American* 221(3):76–102.

STEWART, W. K. 1991. High Resolution Optical and Acoustic Remote Sensing for Underwater Exploration. *Oceanus* 34(1):10–22.

STOLZENBERG, W. 1993. The Familiar Stranger [Octopus]. *Sea Frontiers* 39(4):14–15, 58.

STOVER, D. 1995. Creatures of the Thermal Vents. *Popular Science* 246(5):54–57.

STRASBURG, D. W. 1963. The Diet and Dentition of *Isistius brasiliensis*, with Remarks on Tooth Replacement in Other Sharks. *Copeia* 1:33–40.

STRAUS, K. 1977. Jumbo Squid, *Dosidicus gigas*. *Oceans* 10(2):10–15.

SULAK, K. J. 1974. Morphological and Ecological Observations on Atlantic Ipnopid Fishes of the Genus *Bathytyphlops*. *Copeia* 2:570–73.

———. 1977a. The Systematics and Biology of *Bathypterois* (Pisces, Chlorophthalmidae) with a Revised Classification of Benthic Myctophiform Fishes. *Galathea Report* 14:49–108.

———. 1977b. *Aldrovandia oleosa*, a New Species of the Halosauridae, with Observations on Several Other Species of the Family. *Copeia* 1:11–20.

SULLIVAN, W. 1974a. Three Craft to Dive Deep in Mid-Atlantic Valley. *New York Times*, May 21, 1974: C32.

———. 1974b. *Continents in Motion: The New Whole Earth Debate*. McGraw-Hill.

———. 1984. Sinking Slabs of Sea Floor May Cause Shifts in Earth's Crust. *New York Times*, November 27, 1984: C2.

———. 1986. Deep Seeing. *Oceans* 19(1):19–23.

SUMMERS, W. C. 1990. Natural History and Collection. In D. L. Gilbert, W. J. Adelman, and J. M. Arnold, eds., *Squid as Experimental Animals*, pp. 11–26. Plenum Press.

SWEENEY, J. B. 1970. *A Pictorial History of Oceanographic Submersibles*. Crown.

———. 1972. *A Pictorial History of Sea Monsters and Other Dangerous Marine Life*. Bonanza Books.

SWITZER, D. M. 1984. North Atlantic Tiptoeing Star. *Sea Frontiers*. 30(1):51–53.

TANING, Å. V. 1932. In J. Schmidt, ed., *Dana's Togt Omkring* Jorden 1928–1930. Copenhagen.

TARASEVICH, M. N. 1968. The Diet of Sperm Whales in the North Pacific Ocean. *Zoologicheskiy Zhurnal* 47(4):595–601. National Technical Information Service, 1974.

TAYLOR, L. R., L. J. V. COMPAGNO, AND P. J. STRUHSAKER. 1983. Megamouth—A New Species, Genus, and Family of Lamnoid Shark (*Megachasma pelagios*, Family Megachasmidae) from the Hawaiian Islands. *Proc. Cal. Acad. Sci.* 43(8):87–110.

TAYLOR, M. A. 1986. Stunning Whales and Deaf Squids. *Nature* 323:298–99.

TCHERNAVIN, V. V. 1947a. Six Specimens of Lyomeri in the British Museum (with Notes on the Skeleton of Lyomeri). *Jour. Linn. Soc. London* 41:287–350.

———. 1947b. Further Notes on Structure of the Bony Fishes of the Order *Lyomeri* (*Eurypharynx*). *Jour. Linn. Soc. London* 41:377–93.

———. 1953. The Feeding Mechanisms of a Deep Sea Fish *Chauliodus sloani* Schneider. British Museum.

TEAL, J., AND M. TEAL. 1975. *The Sargasso Sea*. Little, Brown.

TEE-VAN, J. 1930. How the Bathysphere Was Operated. *Bull. N.Y. Zool. Soc.* 33(6):234–40.

———. 1933. The Laboratory of the Department of Tropical Research. *Bull. N.Y. Zool. Soc.* 41:102–9.

———. 1934. The Bathysphere of 1934. *Bull. N.Y. Zool. Soc.* 37(6):171–73.

TEMPLEMAN, B. 1966. A Record of *Bathypterois dubius* Vaillant from the Western North Atlantic, and a Review of the Status of the Species. *Jour. Fish Res. Bd. Canada* 23(5):715–22.

TERRY, R. D. 1966. *The Deep Submersible.* Western Periodicals.

TETT, P. B., AND M. G. KELLY. 1973. Marine Bioluminescence. *Oceanogr. Mar. Biol.* 11:89–173.

THARP, M. 1982. Mapping the Ocean Floor—1947 to 1977. In R. A. Scruton and M. Talwani, eds., *The Ocean Floor*, pp. 19–31. John Wiley & Sons.

THARP, M., AND H. FRANKEL. 1986. Mappers of the Deep. *Natural History* October 1986: 49–62.

THEEL, H. 1882. Report on the Holothurioidea Dredged by H.M.S. *Challenger* During the Years 1873–1876, Part 1. *Challenger Scientific Results (Zoology)* 4(13):1–176.

———. 1886. Report on the Holothurioidea, Part 2. *Challenger Scientific Results (Zoology)* 4(39):1–290.

THIELE, J. 1921. Die Cephalopoden der deutsch sud-polar Expedition, 1901–1903. *Dt. Sudpol. Exped.* 16(8):433–65.

THISTLE, D. 1980. A Revision of the Ilyarachna (Crustacea, Isopoda) in the Atlantic with Four New Species. *Jour. Nat. Hist.* 14:111–43.

———. 1988. A Temporal Difference in Harpacticoid-Copepod Abundance at a Deep-sea Site: Caused by Benthic Storms? *Deep-Sea Research* 35(6A):1015–20.

THISTLE, D., AND G. D. F. WILSON. 1987. A Hydrodynamically Modified, Abyssal Isopod Fauna. *Deep-Sea Research* 34(1):73–87.

THOMAS, L. 1961. *Sir Hubert Wilkins: His Life of Adventure.* McGraw-Hill.

THOMAS, R. F. 1977. Systematics, Distribution, and Biology of Cephalopods of the Genus *Tremoctopus* (Octopoda: Tremoctopodidae). *Bull. Mar. Sci.* 27(3):353–92.

THOMPSON, D. W. 1919. On the Whales Landed at the Scottish Whaling Stations, Especially During the Years 1908–1914. *Scot. Nat.* 85:1–16.

THOMSON, C. W. 1873. *The Depths of the Sea.* Macmillan.

———. 1878. *The Atlantic: A Preliminary Account of the General Results of the Exploring Voyage of H.M.S. Challenger.* Macmillan.

THORNDIKE, J. J., ED. 1980. *Mysteries of the Deep.* American Heritage.

THRESH, P. 1992. *Titanic: The Truth Behind the Disaster.* Crescent.

THURSTON, H. 1989. Quest for the Kraken. *Equinox:* 46:50–55.

TIVEY, M. K. 1991. Hydrothermal Vent Systems. *Oceanus* 34(4):68–74.

TOLSTOY, I. 1951. Submarine Topography in the North Atlantic. *Bull. Amer. Geol. Soc.* 62:441–550.

TØNNESSEN, J. M., AND A. O. JOHNSEN. 1982. *The History of Modern Whaling.* Hurst.

TOWNSEND, C. H. 1935. The Distribution of Certain Whales as Shown by Logbook Records of American Whaleships. *Zoologica.* 18:1–50.

TOWNSEND, C. H., AND J. T. NICHOLS. 1925. Deep Sea Fishes of the "Albatross" Lower California Expedition. *Bull. Amer. Mus. Nat. Hist.* 52:1–20.

TRUE, F. W. 1910. An Account of the Beaked Whales of the Family Ziphiidae in the Collection of the U.S. National Museum, with Remarks on Some Specimens in Other Museums. *Bull. U.S. Natl. Mus.* 73:1–89.

———. 1913. Description of *Mesoplodon mirus,* a Beaked Whale Recently Discovered on the Coast of North Carolina. *Proc. U.S. Natl. Mus.* 45:651–57.

TUCK, A., AND R. GRENIER. 1981. A 16th Century Basque Whaling Station in Labrador. *Scientific American* 245(5):180–90.

———. 1985. 16th Century Basque Whalers in America. *National Geographic* 168(1):40–68.

TUCKER, D. W. 1954. Report on the Fishes Collected by S. Y. *Rosaura* in the North and Central Atlantic, 1937–38. Part 4: Families Carcharhinidae, Torpedinidae, Rosauridae (nov.), Salmonidae, Alepocephalidae, Searsidae, Clupeidae. *Bull. Brit. Mus. (Nat. Hist.)* 2(6):163–214.

TUNNICLIFFE, V. 1988. Biogeography and Evolution of Hydrothermal-Vent Fauna in the Eastern Pacific Ocean. *Proc. Roy. Soc. London* B233:347–66.

TUNNICLIFFE, V., AND R. G. JENSEN. 1987. Distribution and Behaviour of the Spider Crab *Macroregonia macrochira* Sakai (Brachyura) Around the Hydrothermal Vents of the Northeastern Pacific. *Canadian Jour. Zoology.* 65:2443–49.

TUNNICLIFFE, V., AND S. K. JUNIPER. 1994. Dynamic Character of the Hydrothermal Vent Habitat and the Nature of Sulphide Chimney Fauna. *Progress in Oceanography.* In press.

TUNNICLIFFE, V., J. F. GARRETT, AND H. P. JOHNSON. 1990. Physical and Biological Factors Affecting the Behaviour and Mortality of Hydrothermal Vent Tubeworms. *Deep-Sea Research* 37(1):103–25.

TUREKIAN, K. K., J. K. COCHRAN, AND D. J. DEMASTER. 1978. Bioturbation in Deep-Sea Deposits: Rates and Consequences. *Oceanus* 21(1):34–41.

TURNER, H. J. 1963. Giant Squid. *Oceanus* 9(4):22–24.

TURNER, R. D., AND R. A. LUTZ. 1984. Growth and Distribution of Mollusks at Deep-Sea Vents and Seeps. *Oceanus* 27(3):54–62.

URBAN, J. R., S. S. RAMIREZ, AND J. C. V. SALINAS. 1994. First Record of Bottlenose Whales, *Hyperoodon* sp., in the Gulf of California. *Mar. Mam. Sci.* 10(4):471–73.

UYENO, T., K. NAKAMURA, AND S. MIKAMI. 1976. On the Body Coloration and an Abnormal Specimen of the Goblin Shark, *Mitsukurina owstoni* Jordan. *Bull. Kanagawa Prefect. Mus. Nat. Sci.* 9:67–72.

VAN ANDEL, T. 1977. *Tales of an Old Ocean.* Norton.

VAN DEINSE, A. B., AND G. C. A. JUNGE. 1937. Recent and Older Finds of the California Gray Whale in the Atlantic. *Temminckia* 2:161–88.

VAN DOVER, C. L. 1993. Depths of Ignorance. *Discover* 14(9):37–39.

———. 1996. *An Octopus's Garden.* Addison-Wesley.

VAN DOVER, C. L., P. J. S. FRANKS, AND R. D. BALLARD. 1987. Prediction of Hydrothermal Vent Locations from Distribution of Brachyuran Crabs. *Limnology and Oceanography* 32:1006–10.

VAN DOVER, C. L., E. Z. SZUTS, B. C. CHAMBERLAIN, AND J. R. CANN. 1989. A Novel Eye in "Eyeless" Shrimp from Hydrothermal Vents of the Mid-Atlantic Ridge. *Nature* 337:458–60.

VECCHIONE, M. 1987. A Multispecies Aggregation of Cirrate Octopods Trawled from North of the Bahamas. *Bull. Mar. Sci.* 40(1):78–84.

VECCHIONE, M., AND C. F. E. ROPER. 1991. Cephalopods Observed from Submersibles in the Western North Atlantic. *Bull. Mar. Sci.* 49(1&2):433–55.

VERNE, J. 1864. *Voyage au centre de la terre.* Paris. (English translation: *Voyage to the Center of the Earth,* Signet, New York, 1986.)

————. 1870. *Vingt mille lieues sous les mers.* Paris. (English translation: *Twenty Thousand Leagues Under the Sea,* Bantam, New York, 1981.)

VERRILL, A. E. 1874a. Occurrence of Gigantic Cuttlefishes on the Coast of Newfoundland. *Amer. Jour. Sci.* 7:158–61.

————. 1874b. The Giant Cuttle-fishes of Newfoundland. *American Naturalist* 8:167–74.

————. 1875. The Colossal Cephalopods of the Western Atlantic. *American Naturalist* 9:21–78.

————. 1879. The Cephalopods of the North-eastern Coast of America. Part 1: The Gigantic Squids (*Architeuthis*) and Their Allies; with Observations on Similar Large Species from Foreign Localities. *Trans. Conn. Acad. Sci.* 5:177–258.

————. 1880. The Cephalopods of the North-eastern Coast of America. Part 2: The Smaller Cephalopods, Including the "Squids" and the Octopi, with Other Allied Forms. *Trans. Conn. Acad. Sci.* 5:259–446.

VILLANUEVA, R., AND A. GUERRA. 1991. Food and Prey Detection in Two Deep-Sea Cephalopods: *Opisthoteuthis agassizi* and *O. vossi* (Octopoda: Cirrata). *Bull. Mar. Sci.* 49(1&2):288–99.

VILLIERS, A. 1973. *Men, Ships, and the Sea.* National Geographic Society.

VINE, A. C. 1975. Early History of Underwater Photography. *Oceanus* 18(3):2–10.

————. 1988. The Birth of *Alvin. Oceanus* 31(4):10–16.

VINE, F. J. 1966. Spreading of the Ocean Floor: New Evidence. *Science* 154:1405–15.

VINE, F. J., AND D. H. MATTHEWS. 1963. Magnetic Anomalies over Ocean Ridges. *Nature* 199:947–49.

VINE, F. J., AND J. T. WILSON. 1965. Magnetic Anomalies over a Young Oceanic Ridge off Vancouver Island. *Science* 150:485–89.

VOSS, G. L. 1956a. A Checklist of the Cephalopoda of Florida. *Q. Jour. Fla. Acad. Sci.* 19:274–82.

————. 1956b. A Review of the Cephalopods of the Gulf of Mexico. *Bull. Mar. Sci. Gulf Carib.* 6:85–178.

————. 1959. Hunting Sea Monsters. *Sea Frontiers* 5(3):134–46.

————. 1967a. Squids: Jet Powered Torpedoes of the Deep. *National Geographic* 131(3):386–411.

————. 1967b. The Biology and Bathymetric Distribution of Deep-Sea Cephalopods. *Studies in Tropical Oceanography* 5:511–35.

————. 1977. A Classification of Recent Cephalopods. In M. Nixon and J. B. Messenger, eds., *The Biology of Cephalopods,* pp. 575–79. Academic Press.

VOSS, G. L., AND D. S. ERDMAN. 1959. *Thysanoteuthis rhombus.* Large Cephalopod New to the Western Atlantic. *Nautilus* 73:23–25.

VOSS, G. L., AND R. F. SISSON. 1971. Shy Monster: The Octopus. *National Geographic* 140(6):776–99.

VOSS, N. A. 1980. A Generic Review of the Family Cranchiidae. *Bull. Mar. Sci.* 30(2):365–412.

VOSS, N. A., AND G. L. VOSS. 1962. Two New Species of Squids of the Genus *Calliteuthis* from the Western Atlantic with a Redescription of *Calliteuthis reversa* Verrill. *Bull. Mar. Sci. Gulf Carib.* 12:169–200.

WAKELIN, J. H. 1964. *Thresher:* Lesson and Challenge. *National Geographic* 125(4):760–63.

WALKLET, T. H. 1979. Manganese Nodules: Still Just Out of Reach. *Oceans* 12(6):57–61.

WALLACE, J. 1987. *The Deep Sea.* Gallery Books.

WALLER, R. A., AND R. I. WICKLUND. 1968. Observations from a Research Submersible—Mating and Spawning of the Squid *Doryteuthis plei. BioScience* 18:110–11.

WALSH, D. 1979. Voyage to the Bottom of the Sea: Twenty Years After the *Trieste* Dive. *Oceans* 12(6):37–41.

WALTERS, V. 1961. A Contribution to the Biology of the Giganturidae with the Description of a New Genus and Species. *Bull. Mus. Comp. Zool.* 125(10):297–319.

———. 1964a. Giganturoidei. In Part 4, *Fishes of the Western North Atlantic,* pp. 566–76. Memoirs of the Sears Foundation for Marine Research. Yale University.

———. 1964b. Order Giganturoidei. *Memoirs of the Sears Foundation for Marine Research* 1(4):566–77.

WARD, R. 1974. *Into the Ocean World.* Knopf.

WATERMAN, T. H. 1939a. Studies on Deep-Sea Anglerfishes (Ceratioidea), Part 1. An Historical Survey of Our Present State of Knowledge. *Bull. Mus. Comp. Zool.* 85(3):65–81.

———. 1939b. Studies on Deep-Sea Anglerfishes (Ceratioidea), Part 2. Three New Species. *Bull. Mus. Comp. Zool.* 85(3):82–94.

———. 1948. Studies on Deep-Sea Anglerfishes (Ceratioidea), Part 3. The Comparative Anatomy of *Gigantactis longicirra. Jour. Morphol.* 82(2):81–147.

WATKINS, W. A. 1977. Acoustic Behavior of Sperm Whales. *Oceanus* 20(2):50–58.

WATKINS, W. A., AND W. E. SCHEVILL. 1975. Sperm Whales (*Physeter catadon*) React to Pingers. *Deep-Sea Research* 22:123–29.

———. 1977. Sperm Whale Codas. *Jour. Acoust. Soc. Amer.* 62(6):1485–90.

WEAVER, P. P. E., AND P. J. SCHULTHEISS. 1983. Vertical Open Burrows in Deep-Sea Sediments 2 m in Length. *Nature* 301:329–31.

WEBB, D. W. 1897. A Large Decapod. *Nautilus* 10:108.

WEGENER, A. 1929. *The Origin of Continents and Oceans.* Dover edition, 1966.

WELKER, R. H. 1975. *Natural Man: The Life of William Beebe.* Indiana University Press.

WELLS, H. G. 1905. "In the Abyss." In *Twenty-Eight Science Fiction Stories by H. G. Wells,* pp. 493–509. Scribner's. Dover edition, 1952.

WELLS, M. J., AND R. K. O'DOR. 1991. Jet Propulsion and the Evolution of Cephalopods. *Bull. Mar. Sci.* 49(1&2):419–32.

WENDT, H. 1959. *Out of Noah's Ark.* Houghton Mifflin.

WERTENBAKER, W. 1974. *The Floor of the Sea: Maurice Ewing and the Search to Understand the Earth.* Little, Brown.

———. 1980. Land Below, Sea Above. In J. J. Thorndike, ed., *Mysteries of the Deep,* pp. 294–341. American Heritage.

WHELAN, M. 1994. The Night the Sea Smashed Lord's Cove. *Canadian Geographic* 114(6):70–73.

WHITAKER, I. 1984. Whaling in Classical Iceland. *Polar Record* 22(134):249–61.

———. 1985. The King's Mirror (*Konungs skuggsjá*) and Northern Research. *Polar Record* 22(141):615–27.

———. 1986. North Atlantic Sea Creatures in the King's Mirror (*Konungs skuggsjá*). *Polar Record* 22(142):3–13.

WHITEHEAD, H. 1995. The Realm of the Elusive Sperm Whale. *National Geographic* 188(5):56–73.

WILLIAMS, A. B. 1980. A New Crab Family from the Vicinity of Submarine Thermal Vents on the Galápagos Rift (Crustacea: Decapoda: Brachyura). *Proc. Biol. Soc. Wash.* 93:443–72.

WILLIAMS, A. B., AND F. A. CHACE. 1982. A New Caridean Shrimp of the Family Bresliidae from Thermal Vents of the Galápagos Rift. *Jour. Crustacean Biol.* 2:136–47.

WILLIAMS, A. B., AND P. A. RONA. 1986. Two New Caridean Shrimps (Bresliidae) from Thermal Vents on the Mid-Atlantic Ridge. *Jour. Crustacean Biol.* 6:446–62.

WILLIAMS, A. B., AND C. L. VAN DOVER. 1983. A New Species of *Munidopsis* from Submarine Thermal Vents of the East Pacific Rise at 21° N (Anomura: Galatheidae). *Proc. Biol. Soc. Wash.* 96(3):481–88.

WILLIAMS, F. L. 1963. *Matthew Fontaine Maury, Scientist of the Sea.* Rutgers University Press.

WILLIAMS, W. 1951. Friend Octopus. *Natural History* 60:210–15.

WILSON, J. T. 1963. Continental Drift. *Scientific American* 208(4):86–100.

———. 1965. A New Class of Faults and Their Bearing on Continental Drift. *Nature* 207:343–47.

———. 1966. Did the Atlantic Close and Then Reopen? *Nature* 211:676–81.

WILSON, R. R., AND K. L. SMITH. 1985. Live Capture, Maintenance and Partial Decompression of a Deep-Sea Grenadier Fish (*Coryphaenoides acrolepis*) in a Hyperbaric Trap-Aquarium. *Deep-Sea Research* 32(12A):1571–82.

WISEMAN, J. D. H., AND C. D. OVEY. 1953. Definitions of Features on the Deep-Sea Floor. *Deep-Sea Research* 1:11–16.

WOLFF, T. 1960. The Hadal Community: An Introduction. *Deep-Sea Research* 6:95–124.

———. 1961a. Animal Life from a Single Abyssal Trawling. *Galathea Report* 5:129–62.

———. 1961b. The Deepest Recorded Fishes. *Nature* 190:283.

———. 1970. The Concept of the Hadal or Ultra-Abyssal Fauna. *Deep-Sea Research* 17:983–1003.

———. 1971. Archimède Dive 7 to 4160 Metres at Madeira: Observations and Collecting Results. *Vidensk. Medd. Dansk naturh. Foren.* 134:127–47.

———. 1977. Diversity and Faunal Composition of the Deep-Sea Benthos. *Nature* 267(5614):780–85.

WOOD, G. L. 1982. *The Guinness Book of Animal Facts and Feats.* Guinness Superlatives Ltd.

WOODS, L. P., AND P. M. SONODA. 1973. Suborder Anoplogasteroidei. In Part 6, *Fishes of the Western North Atlantic,* pp. 386–94. Memoirs of the Sears Foundation for Marine Research. Yale University.

WORTHINGTON, L. V. 1962. Evidence for a Two Gyre Circulation System in the North Atlantic. *Deep-Sea Research* 9:51–67.

WORTHINGTON, L. V., AND W. E. SCHEVILL. 1957. Underwater Sounds Heard from Sperm Whales. *Nature* 180:91.

WU, N. 1990. Fangtooth, Viperfish, and Black Swallower. *Sea Frontiers* 36(5):32–39.

WYSESSION, M. 1995. The Inner Workings of the Earth. *American Scientist* 83(2):134–47.

YOERGER, D. R. 1991. Robotic Undersea Technology. *Oceanus* 34(1):32–37.

YOUNG, J. Z. 1938a. The Giant Nerve Fibres and Epistellar Body of Cephalopods. *Q. Jour. Microsc. Sci.* 78:367–86.

———. 1938b. The Functioning of the Giant Nerve Fibres of the Squid. *J. Exp. Biol.* 15:170–85.

———. 1977. Brain, Behaviour and Evolution of Cephalopods. In M. Nixon and J. B. Messenger, eds., *The Biology of Cephalopods,* pp. 377–434. Academic Press.

———. 1991. *Ctenopteryx* the Comb-Fin Squid is Related to *Loligo. Bull. Mar. Sci.* 49(1&2):148–61.

YOUNG, R. E. 1964. A Note on Three Specimens of the Squid *Lampadioteuthis megaleia* Berry, 1916 (Cephalopoda: Oegopsida) from the Atlantic Ocean, with a Description of the Male. *Bull. Mar. Sci. Gulf Carib.* 14:443–52.

———. 1972. Brooding in a Bathypelagic Octopus. *Pacific Science* 26(4):400–4.

———. 1973. Information Feedback from Photophores and Ventral Countershading in Mid-Water Squid. *Pacific Science* 27:1–7.

———. 1977. Ventral Bioluminescent Countershading in Midwater Cephalopods. In M. Nixon and J. B. Messenger, eds., *The Biology of Cephalopods,* pp. 161–90. Academic Press.

———. 1983. Oceanic Bioluminescence: An Overview of General Functions. *Bull. Mar. Sci.* 33:829–45.

YOUNG, R. E., AND F. M. MENCHER. 1980. Bioluminescence in Mesopelagic Squid: Diel Color Change During Counterillumination. *Science* 208:1286–88.

YOUNG, R. E., AND C. F. E. ROPER. 1976. Bioluminescent Countershading in Mid-Water Animals: Evidence from Living Squid. *Science* 191(4231):1046–47.

———. 1977. Intensity Regulation of Bioluminescence During Countershading in Living Midwater Animals. *Fish. Bull.* 75:239–52.

YOUNG, R. E., C. F. E. ROPER, AND J. F. WALTERS. 1979. Eyes and Extraocular Photoreceptors in Mid-Water Cephalopods and Fishes: Their Role in Detecting Downwelling Light for Counterillumination. *Mar. Biol.* 51:371–80.

YOUNG, R. E., E. M. KAMPA, S. D. MAYNARD, F. M. MENCHER, AND C. F. E. ROPER. 1980. Counterillumination and the Upper Depth Limits of Midwater Animals. *Deep-Sea Research* 27(9A):671–91.

ZAHL, P. A. 1954. Fishing in the Whirlpool of Charybdis. *National Geographic* 104(5):579–618.

———. 1958. Hatchetfish, Torchbearers of the Deep. *National Geographic* 113(5):712–14.

ZARUDZKI, E. F. K. 1967. Swordfish Rams the *Alvin. Oceanus* 13(4):14–18.

ZIMMER, C. 1995. North Atlantic Cycle. *Discover* 16(1):77.

ZOBELL, C. E. 1954. The Occurrence of Bacteria in the Deep Sea and Their Significance for Animal Life. *Intl. Union Biol. Sci.* 16:20–26.

ZWINGLE, E. 1987. "Doc" Edgerton: The Man Who Made Time Stand Still. *National Geographic* 172(4):464–83.

Index

Italicized page numbers indicate photographs and illustrations.

sounds produced by, 305, 306, 315
sperm whales (*Physeter macrocephalus*), 188*n*, 303–8, 304
whale watching, 315
whaling industry, 3, 3*n*, 22, 298–300, 301–2, 303, 310–12, 310*n*, 312*n*, 316, 318–19
Whitaker, Ian, 318
Wick, Gerald, 263
Wild, J. J., 15
Wilkes, Lt. Charles, 6, 7
Wilkins, Sir George Hubert, 60*n*, 62*n*
Wilkins, John, 53
Willemoesia indica, 168
Willemoesia leptodactyla, 16
Willemoes-Suhm, Rudolf von, 15, 168
Williams, Austin, 165, 169
Willis, Bailey, 37
Willm, Henri, 192
Willm, Lt. Pierre, 70
Wilson, J. Tuzo, 43, 44
Wilson, Val, 75
Wiseman, John D. H., 38
Wolff, Torben, 70*n*, 146–7, 157, 297*n*
Wood, F. G., 314
Wood, Gerald, 232*n*, 283
Woods, Loren, 275

Woods Hole Oceanographic Institution, 23, 24, 73
World War I, 24, 62
World War II, 62
worms, *113,* 114–16, 117, 140
Worzel, Lamar, 48
wreckfishes (*Polyprion americanus*), 205*n*
Wyville Thomson, Charles, *see* Thomson, Charles Wyville
Wyville Thomson Ridge, 20, 35

Xenoberyces, 288, *288*

Yablakov, A. V., 307*n*
Yankee Whaler (Ashley), 319
Yoerger, Dana, 87
Young, Richard, 172, 173, 182, 183, 191, 209–11, 212*n*

Zahl, Paul, 237–8
Zarudzki, Rudolf, 75–6, 292
zones of ocean, 146–7
zooplankton, 139–42, 144–6, 160–1

Illustration Credits

All other illustrations were drawn by the author.

A NOTE ON THE TYPE

This book was set in Fairfield, the first typeface from the hand of the distinguished American artist and engraver Rudolph Ruzicka (1883–1978). In its structure Fairfield displays the sober and sane qualities of the master craftsman whose talent has long been dedicated to clarity. It is this trait that accounts for the trim grace and vigor, the spirited design and sensitive balance, of this original typeface.

Rudolph Ruzicka was born in Bohemia and came to America in 1894. He set up his own shop, devoted to wood engraving and printing, in New York in 1913 after a varied career working as a wood engraver, in photoengraving and banknote printing plants, and as an art director and freelance artist. He designed and illustrated many books, and was the creator of a considerable list of individual prints—wood engravings, line engravings on copper, and aquatints.

Composed by North Market Street Graphics,
Lancaster, Pennsylvania

Printed and bound by Quebecor Printing Martinsburg,
Martinsburg, West Virginia

Designed by Cassandra J. Pappas